SERVICE OPERATIONS MANAGEMENT

SERVICE OPERATIONS MANAGEMENT

Roger W. Schmenner

Indiana University
School of Business

Prentice Hall
Englewood Cliffs, New Jersey 07632

To the memory of my mother,
Gwendolyn Jackson Schmenner

Acquisitions Editor: Tom Tucker
Production Manager: Lynne Breitfeller
Production Editor: Katherine Evancie
Managing Editor: Joyce Turner
Cover Designer: Jayne Conte
Design Director: Pat Wosczyk
Buyer: Paul Smolenski
Production Assistant: Renee Pelletier
Cover design by DeLuca Design

 © 1995 by Prentice Hall, Inc.
A Simon & Schuster Company
Englewood Cliffs, New Jersey 07632

Printed in the United States of America

10 9 8 7 6 5 4 3 2

ISBN 0-02-406811-X

Library of Congress Cataloging-in-Publication Data

Schmenner, Roger W.
    Service operations management / Roger W. Schmenner.
        p.   cm.
    Includes index.
    ISBN 0-02-406811-X
    1. Service industries—Management.   I. Title.
HD9980.5.S34 1995
658—dc20   94-41290
                        CIP

PRENTICE-HALL INTERNATIONAL (UK) LIMITED, *London*
PRENTICE-HALL OF AUSTRALIA PTY. LIMITED, *Sydney*
PRENTICE-HALL CANADA INC, *Toronto*
PRENTICE-HALL HISPANOAMERICANA, S.A., *Mexico*
PRENTICE-HALL OF INDIA PRIVATE LIMITED, *New Delhi*
PRENTICE-HALL OF JAPAN, INC., *Tokyo*
SIMON & SCHUSTER ASIA PTE. LTD., *Singapore*
EDITORA PRENTICE-HALL DO BRASIL, LTDA., *Rio de Janeiro*

Contents

Preface

The march has been inexorable. Services have been taking over. More and more of us are employed by service operations and much of what transpires within manufacturing firms relates to service as well. The field of operations management, long called production or production management, has ceased to be the exclusive domain of the factory. Yet, historically, so much of our thinking about operations has been colored by what we know about good factory performance.

The challenge for us has been to isolate those aspects of service operations management that are distinctive, where the analogies to factory operations start to break down. This book is my attempt at meeting that challenge. It is an attempt that I have been making with my students for a dozen years now. I owe them much for they have forced me to examine the field with eyes as fresh as I could make them and to listen intently to their own explorations.

This book takes the organization I have applied to my course in service operations management and merges with it insights that I have gleaned from cases and readings on the subject and from my own fieldwork with different service companies. The framework is one that my students have found to be a useful one in trying to cope with the dilemmas faced by operating managers.

That organization recognizes the primacy of the service encounter and the three aspects of service that surround it: the service task, service standards, and the service delivery system itself. I have always been impressed at how important plans and controls are to service businesses and that importance is mirrored in the attention paid to them in this book. Any book on service operations needs to pay its respects to some time-honored issues that both services and manufacturing face. I have tried not to dwell on these topics, however, in favor of spending more time on topics that truly differentiate services from manufacturing operations. The first part of the book is strictly text. That text is followed by five Service Tours, then by five cases, and finally by some problems and exercises.

Although this book can stand alone, personally, I think it is best viewed as a supplement. It provides background on the operations elements of service management, and it presents both Service Tours of diverse service operations and some cases to analyze. As such, it fits well with more general sources of cases and readings on service such as those found in the masterful book by Christopher Lovelock (*Managing Services: Marketing, Operations, and Human Resources*, second edition, Prentice Hall).

Over the years, my thoughts on service operations have been stimulated by scholars such as Chris Lovelock, Dave Maister, Vince Mabert, Earl Sasser, Jim Heskett, and Dave Collier. My thanks to them and to my students over the years who have seen me struggle with the material. My thanks, as well, to Chris Irpino who wrote the Sulfadyne case and to Vince Mabert who wrote the Metropolitan Transit System case.

R.W.S.

SERVICE OPERATIONS MANAGEMENT

The Nature of Services

WHAT ARE SERVICES?

Doctor, architect, janitor, plumber, teacher, cook—we all are comfortable in labeling what people like these do as "service operations." Pick an occupation and we are quick to categorize it as agriculture, manufacturing, or service. Exactly what characterizes a service operation? On reflection, the answer is surprisingly ambiguous.

Service operations are perhaps best defined in residual terms: that is, what service operations are not rather than what they are. Formally, the U.S. government defines service employment as a residual, namely as nonfarming, non-manufacturing employment. (For some, this also means excluding government employment as well.) Typically, that leaves services such as hotels, restaurants, and repair shops; amusements such as movie theaters and amusement parks; health care facilities such as hospitals and doctors' offices; professional services such as engineering, legal, and accounting; education; finance, insurance, and real estate functions; wholesale and retail trade; and transportation of all kinds.

Nevertheless, there remain some real definitional problems. For example, public utilities, such as electric power companies and telecommunications companies, are classified as service operations. However, one could consider power generation more of a manufacturing operation than a service operation. After all, these companies "make" electricity and distribute it along utility lines that are very capital-intensive, even more capital-intensive than many manufacturing operations.

An even more troubling aspect of what service means comes when people try to define whether a company such as IBM is a manufacturing company or a service company. As the old story goes, it may well depend on which part of the elephant you are touching. Clearly, the company is both. Some of IBM is surely manufacturing in character and other aspects of IBM are clearly service in character, be it the field repair of IBM computers or the data and consulting services IBM also sells.

It is also clear that as technology advances, we can expect that more and more labor will be driven out of the actual manufacturing of products. There will be less direct labor attached to those products, and more indirect labor. It is not uncommon these days for some manufacturers, especially high-tech manufacturers, to have overhead rates that are 6 to 10 times (or more) the direct labor component of their products. The importance of this, of course, is that the traditional management focus on direct labor—the workforce that actually operates machinery and touches the product—is becoming much less relevant for the manufacturer. More and more relevant is the management of the indirect labor force—the product and process engineers, the production planners, the material handlers, and the quality inspectors. This is the kind of labor that in a manufacturing company is oriented to support activities—to services. Keeping these workers motivated and productive will have a greater impact on product costs than most initiatives one could concoct for the factory floor itself.

Hence, the impact of service operations management is widespread. It falls not only on "service firms" but also on "service" wherever it may be found. Over the decades, the line that separates manufacturing and service has become more and more blurred. In the future, we can only expect more blurring to occur.

The Size of the Service Sector

It is clear that in mature economies such as the United States, service jobs account for about 70 percent of total employment. The millions of U.S. workers in services are distributed among a wide array of service sector industries, as displayed in Table 1–1. As shown in that table, the agricultural and goods-producing sectors of the economy have been shrinking in relative importance as measured by employment, while services have been picking up the slack. This trend is expected to continue, as Table 1–2 displays. The economic forecast for 2005 moves the fraction of employment in services up by several more percentage points. The particularly fast-growing areas of service include computer and data processing, research and consulting, health care, and legal services. However, there is no major service industry category that is expected to decline in absolute terms, as agriculture, mining, and manufacturing are expected to.

The growth of service employment has been steady over the decades. Several types of services, though, have been particularly explosive in their growth: business and repair services (the support services for the business sector of the economy) and professional services, including health care. Take note, too, that although many rant against government, public administration employment constitutes a considerably smaller share of service sector employment today than it did in 1970. Total government employment (a larger category than public administration), as seen in Table 1–2, has grown at a slower rate from 1975 to 1990 than other services, and it is expected to lag other service sector employment growth.

TABLE 1–1 EMPLOYMENT TRENDS BY INDUSTRY

	Employment (millions)				1970 Percent of total employed	1970 Percent of service total	1992 Percent of total employed	1992 Percent of service total
	1970	1980	1990	1992				
Goods-Producing								
Agriculture	3463	3364	3186	3210	4.4		2.7	
Mining	516	979	730	664	0.7		0.6	
Construction	4818	6215	7696	7013	6.1		5.9	
Manufacturing	20,746	21,942	21,184	19,972	26.4		16.9	
Services								
Transportation and utilities	5320	6525	8136	8245		10.8		9.5
Wholesale trade	2672	3920	4651	4765		5.4		5.5
Retail trade	12,336	16,270	19,618	19,589		25.1		22.5
Finance, insurance, real estate	3945	5993	8021	7764		8.0		8.9
Business and repair services	1403	3848	7409	6553		2.9		7.5
Personal srvices	4276	3839	4667	4400		8.7		5.1
Entertainment and recreation	717	1047	1503	1957		1.5		2.2
Professional	12,904	19,853	25,335	27,677		26.3		31.8
Including health	4471	7381	9447	10,271		9.1		11.8
Public administration[a]	4476	5342	5608	5620		9.1		6.5
Total services employment[b]	49,135	66,803	85,118	87,099	62.5		73.8	
Total employed	78,678	99,303	117,914	117,958				

[a]Includes workers in uniquely governmental jobs, such as legislative and judicial.

[b]Figured as a residual. Includes some employment not listed separately above.

Source: 1993 Statistical Abstract of the United States.

TABLE 1–2   EMPLOYMENT FORECAST FOR 2005

	Projected 2005 employment (millions)	Percent of wage and salary	Percent growth rates	
			1975–1990	1990–2005
Total U.S.	147,190		2.3	1.2
Total wage and salary	132,647			
Goods-producing				
Agriculture	3080	2.3	−0.4	−0.4
Mining	668	0.5	−0.4	−0.4
Construction	6059	4.6	2.5	1.1
Manufacturing	18,514	14.0	0.3	−0.2
Services	107,405	81.0	3.0	1.6
Transportation and utilities	6689		1.7	0.9
Wholesale trade	7210		2.3	1.0
Retail trade	24,804		3.0	1.6
Finance, insurance, real estate	39,058		3.3	1.3
Other services	39,058		4.8	2.3
Health services	11,519		4.4	2.6
Government	21,515		1.5	1.1

Source: 1993 Statistical Abstract of the United States.

It is clear that services are growing as a percentage of employment, but their growth is less dramatic when one looks at their percentage of gross national product, as Table 1–3 relates. There, one sees that agriculture and manufacturing account for greater percentages of gross national product than they do percentages of employment. This is because the sales per person in agriculture (particularly if one measures physical output instead of dollar-valued output that is affected by volatile agricultural commodity prices) and in manufacturing are considerably greater than the sales per person in services.

Over the course of the 1980s, manufacturing held its own as a percent of GNP, even while dropping as a percentage of total employment. This is an important result that helps us understand the links between productivity and job creation.

Productivity, Service, and Some False Concerns

This observation about service's share of employment versus its share of the GNP is tied directly to the history of productivity gain in various sectors of the economy. As one sees in Table 1–4, the percentage growth rates in output per hour for manufacturing and agriculture (the difference between the all-industries business sector and non-farm business) are vastly higher than the percentage growth rate in output per hour for service businesses. In general, service productivity lags behind both agriculture and manufacturing.

TABLE 1-3 SERVICES AND THE GROSS NATIONAL PRODUCT

	Constant 1982 dollars (billions)		
	1980	1985	1989
Gross national product (GNP)	3187	3619	4118
GNP from domestic industries	3132	3582	4008
GNP from private industries	2743	3200	3711
Percentage of private industry GNP			
Agriculture	2.8	3.0	2.7
Mining	5.2	4.3	3.4
Construction	5.6	5.2	4.8
Manufacturing	24.6	24.3	25.0
Total services (as residual)	61.8	63.5	64.1
Transportation and utilities	10.7	10.3	10.8
Wholesale trade	7.3	8.3	8.2
Retail trade	10.3	11.1	11.1
Finance, insurance, real estate	17.1	16.5	16.3
Other services	16.4	16.8	17.6
Government	14.0	12.5	11.6

Source: 1993 Statistical Abstract of the United States.

TABLE 1-4 PRODUCTIVITY MEASURES

	Index of labor productivity, output per hour (1982 = 100)			
	1980	1985	1990	1992
Business sector (all industries)	98.6	106.1	109.7	113.3
Nonfarm business	99.0	105.4	108.2	111.7
Manufacturing	94.4	108.0	125.7	131.9

Source: 1993 Statistical Abstract of the United States.

Indeed, it is for precisely this reason that the growth in employment in services is so great. As was observed 30 years ago,[1] when there are differential rates of productivity growth in an economy, one will invariably see the faster growing productivity sector shed jobs that will then be picked up by the more slowly growing sector. This has occurred for decades and decades within economies. For example, agriculture has consistently been the most productive sector of our economy, and as agriculture's productivity has grown, the percent of the population found on the farm has diminished considerably; now, less than 3 percent of our workforce remains on the farm. Yet, that 3 percent, being so much more productive these days, can feed a growing total population with agricultural products of the highest quality. A similar story can be told of

[1]The classic article that first espoused this principle, by economists Willam Baumol and William Bowen, looked at productivity in the arts.

manufacturing. Manufacturing has slipped to less than 20 percent of the workforce, but that is precisely because its productivity growth is much greater than that of services. Thus, manufacturing jobs have been shed and those workers, in the main, have been re-employed by the service sector.

Indeed, it is the so-called industrialized countries, including Europe and Japan, where services are most widely developed. This is no coincidence. Countries that were successful historically in creating manufacturing jobs are now the ones that have the ability to create service jobs.

As long as total productivity in the economy continues to grow and as real incomes grow along with it, one need not fear that productivity growth in agriculture or manufacturing will necessarily leave greater percentages of the total population unemployed. There is a continual stream of newly invented services for people to buy, and, of course, existing services can be bought in greater quantities than in the past.

Some people are not only unduly concerned that productivity advances in agriculture and manufacturing will increase unemployment, but they also fear that all the high-wage jobs will be in those industries, leaving service industries with low-wage "hamburger flippers." Such worries are likewise unfounded. If we look at Table 1–5, we can see that the wage rates for the various sectors of the economy tend to be much the same. Although it is true that some services have low average wages, there are others that exceed the average wage in manufacturing, and by a considerable margin. As it happens, the market for labor is a

TABLE 1–5   WAGE RATE COMPARISONS, 1980 AND 1992 (DOLLARS PER HOUR)

	1980 Per hour pay	1980 Pay as a percent of average	1992 Per hour pay	1992 Pay as a percent of average
Total U.S.A., private sector	$6.66		$10.59	
Mining	9.17	138%	14.51	137%
Construction	9.94	149	14.11	133
Manufacturing	7.27	109	11.45	108
Transportation and utilities	8.87	133	13.49	127
Wholesale trade	6.95	104	11.40	108
Retail trade	4.88	73.3	7.14	67.4
Finance, insurance, real estate	5.79	86.9	10.82	102
Business services	4.26	64.0	9.96	94.1
Advertising	8.07	121	14.87	140
Computer services	7.16	108	15.78	149
Hotel and motel	4.45	66.8	7.42	70.1
Auto repair	6.10	91.6	10.06	95.0
Health services	5.68	85.6	11.38	107
Legal services	7.35	110	15.03	142
Engineering and management services	NA	—	14.65	138

Source: 1993 Statistical Abstract of the United States.

very open one, and in bidding for talent, industries in services need to bid as high as manufacturers in order to secure the services of talented people. It is no wonder that wages are relatively similar across sectors of the economy.

If we look at the trends, we see even more support for the fact that service wages have been catching up with manufacturing and construction wages in the recent past. Thus, fears that all service jobs are low-wage jobs are overblown.

More than this, if one thinks of hamburger flipping at fast-food restaurants such as McDonald's as the job that more and more people will have to settle for, one misses the fact that it is precisely in the fast-food industry, and similar ones, that there is great incentive to produce with fewer and fewer people rather than with more and more. Technological change in a company such as McDonald's is somewhat greater than the technological change at other service industries. Thus, by using the same reasoning as above, there will probably be fewer and fewer hamburger flippers and more and more other kinds of service workers for whom productivity improvements are more difficult to implement.[2] The service jobs that will proliferate will be the ones that are in demand and the ones for which capital-for-labor substitution and other means of productivity improvement are more difficult.

CHARACTERISTICS OF SERVICE

Despite some vast differences among services and definitional problems that will continue to plague us, there are still some characteristics that many services share, and it is worthwhile examining those characteristics:

1. *Intangibility.* Services are often something one cannot touch or feel. Services may be associated with something physical, such as an airplane, a table and chairs and eating utensils, a legal brief, or a hospital bed. What people are actually buying, however, involves something intangible. It is not the airplane that is valued as much as the travel. It is not the table, chairs, and eating utensils as much as it is the ambiance of the meal. It is the resolution of the problem, not the legal brief. It is good health, and not the hospital bed itself that is valued. When a service is excellent, it is typically because of the intangible nature of what has been provided, not the associated physical things.[3]

2. *Inability to inventory.* By either circumstance or design, the consumption of a service is often nearly simultaneous with its production. One typically cannot inventory a service. When the plane leaves the runway, its revenue miles are already generated; one cannot secure any more revenue from that plane. After the night passes, one cannot have another guest-night for the hotel; the ability to generate revenue slips away.

---

[2]That is, unless the demand for hamburgers explodes to the point where so much is required that even very productive hamburger flipping will have to be expanded.

[3]For this reason, some commentators refer to the physical goods associated with services as "facilitating goods."

Because one cannot inventory services, capacity choice becomes critical. The size, the layout, and the exact location of a service operation are tremendously important to its ability to generate revenue. If the service's capacity is not enough, it forgoes revenue it could have generated. If the service capacity is too great, it may have to cover capital expenses that are beyond its financial ability.

The inability to inventory services also implies that the management of the demand for services is crucial. One always wants to shift demand, if possible, from peak times to off-peak times. One can do this with prices, both of one's own service and of competing services, or one can do it with ancillary services that may be offered together with the major service being purchased. Thus, if tennis courts are crowded at a certain hour of the day in a resort, the resort may, through its pricing or through some ancillary activities, try to lure people to the beach, to the golf course, or to some other amenity. In this way, the resort can continue to generate revenue but with more customers involved—and with more of them completely satisfied—and with fewer customers grumbling about what they would like to be doing if it were not for the lack of capacity.

3. *Service production/consumption often physically together.* Often services are created and delivered on the spot. That is, the intangibility of the service results from a service process accomplished precisely where the customer is located: the trip to the doctor's office, the night out at a restaurant, the airplane flight, or the insurance binder for the new car.

There may also be a lot of customer interaction with service providers in the course of this production and consumption. The service process itself is often more on display in service operations than in manufacturing. Quality control thus becomes more critical. One cannot be saved by a quality control check at the end of the line as one can in manufacturing. One has to create a quality service straightaway. Training of employees and good employee relations are especially important to service quality.

The fact that the consumer is right there as the service is provided also indicates that the interface between marketing and production is much more porous in service operations than it is in manufacturing. The two functions have to work together or the service is likely to die, whereas in manufacturing, marketing and production are often antagonists. Such a waste of time and energy is not only inexcusable in a service operation, it can mean the death of the enterprise.

4. *Easy entry.* A high proportion of service operations, although by no means all, require very little in the way of capital investment, multiple locations, or proprietary technology. For many services, therefore, barriers to entry are low. Low barriers to entry in turn imply that service operations must be very sensitive to potential as well as actual competitive actions and reactions. Even more than in manufacturing, one cannot neglect the competition in services because, generally speaking, the competition can move very quickly and new players can enter an industry easily. Thus, in services, there is continual jockeying for position and a constant need to think strategically about what is happening.

   5. *Outside influences.* Services can be affected greatly by outside influences such as technological advance, governmental regulations, and energy price increases. These outside forces can change the services that are offered, how they are offered, and the size and structure of the service company. In the past 20 years, there has been considerable governmental deregulation of services that, together with technological advance, has revolutionized a variety of service companies. Airlines and trucking firms have been deregulated, and there have been some tremendous competitive changes in those industries. New airlines and trucking companies have emerged, and existing ones have often been merged or acquired by others. The nature of the services provided has also changed dramatically. The financial services sector is another example of vast deregulation. There have been many mergers, especially across states, and deregulation, together with the computer age, has made possible a host of new financial services.

THE OPERATIONS FUNCTION IN SERVICE FIRMS

Although somewhat invisible to the marketplace, the operations function in a typical company accounts for well over half the employment and well over half the physical assets. That, in itself, makes the operations function important. In a company's organization chart, operations often enjoys parity with the other major business functions: marketing, sales, engineering, finance, control (accounting), and human resources (personnel, labor relations). Sometimes, the operations function is organized as a single entity that stretches out across the entire company, but more often it is embedded in the distinct divisions into which most major companies are organized.

   In some service businesses, the operations function is more visible. Service businesses are frequently organized into many branches, often with geographic responsibilities, such as field offices, and retail outlets. In such tiers of the organization, operations are paramount.

   The operations function itself is often divided into two major groupings of tasks: line management and support services. Line management generally refers to managers directly concerned with the delivery of the service. They are the ones who are typically close enough to the service that they can touch it. Line management supervises the hourly workforce. In a service operation, what is considered line management can be very broad. Often, order-taking roles, in addition to order-filling roles, are supervised by service line managers. Support services are those that are typically out of the reach of the customer—the more invisible jobs within the service firm. Such support services could involve computer support, financial and accounting information, personnel services (hiring, benefits, career development, training), and research and new service development, among others.

TABLE 1-6   KEY CHOICES FOR SERVICE OPERATIONS

I. Technology and Facilities
   Type of facility and equipment (Used by customers themselves? How? How
      attractive do they have to be? How are they used during a peak versus a
      nonpeak situation? General-purpose versus special-purpose equipment?
   Anything proprietary about equipment or its use?)
   Layout (Job shop-like? Fixed position? Other?)
   Location (How critical to attracting customers?)
   Size of the facility
   Geographic spread of any multiple facilities
   Degree of labor intensity
   Attitude toward capacity utilization (Facility for the peak demand or not?)
II. Operating Policies
   A. Planning the operation
      Forecasting (Extent required? Type used?)
      Logistics and inventory system used for materials employed
      Workforce planning
      Schedule setting (Can service provision be "leveled" in any way?)
      Demand management for peak and off-peak times
   B. Controlling the operation
      Labor issues—hiring, training, skill levels required, job content, pay,
         advancement, unionization
      Accounting controls used
      Checklists developed
      Foolproofing designed into the layout and the equipment
      Quality control audits and policies
      What triggers provision of the service and the pace of the operation?
         (Customer? Forecast?)
      Production control (How does the information flow within the operation?
      What is on track? What is not? How can anything gone amiss be fixed?
         How can any changes be implemented?)
III. Operations Organization
   What is kept at the individual unit level and what is centralized?
   Where is talent held in the organization?

Service Operations Choices

In defining how services are delivered, service operations managers face a long
list of choices. Table 1–6 outlines some major ones.

As we discuss services, it is important to keep these choices in mind.

A SPECTRUM OF SERVICE PROCESSES

Much as we have thought of manufacturing enterprises in terms of different
kinds of production processes, we can also think of service operations in terms of
distinct processes. It is helpful to view these different service processes in terms
of a matrix that contrasts the labor intensity of the process on one hand with the
degree of interaction with and customization of the service for the consumer on

	Degree of Interaction and Customization		
		Low	High
Degree of Labor Intensity	Low	**Service Factory** • Airlines • Trucking • Hotels • Resorts and recreation	**Service Shop** • Hospitals • Auto repair • Other repair services
	High	**Mass Service** • Retailing • Wholesaling • Schools • Retail aspects of commercial banking	**Professional Service** • Doctors • Lawyers • Accountants • Architects

Figure 1–1 The Service Process Matrix.

the other.[4] This matrix is shown in Figure 1–1. The quadrants of the matrix roughly define four reasonably distinct service processes.

The service factory. Some service processes have relatively low labor intensity (and thus a greater fraction of service costs associated with the facility and its equipment) and also a low degree of customer interaction and customization. These can be characterized as *service factories.* Much of the transportation industry, hotels, and resorts, for example, are service factories, as are back-of-the-house operations for banking and financial services companies. The Burger King Restaurant in Noblesville, Indiana (Tour B) is an example of a service factory.

The service shop. As the degree of interaction with—or customization for—the consumer increases, the service factory gives way to the *service shop,* much as a line flow operation gives way to a job shop operation when customization is required in manufacturing. Hospitals and repair services of all types are prime examples of service shops. Tour C of the Ogle–Tucker Buick auto repair operation is an example of a service shop.

Mass service. Mass service processes have a high degree of labor intensity, but a rather low degree of interaction with or customization for the consumer. Retail operations, retail banking, schools, and wholesaling are examples of mass services. The Thalhimers department store at the Cloverleaf Mall, described in Tour D, is an example of mass service.

Professional service. If the degree of interaction increases or customization becomes the watchword, mass service gives way to *professional service,* as provided by doctors, lawyers, consultants, architects, and the like. Arthur Andersen & Co.'s audit services in Charlotte (Tour E) provide an example of professional service.

[4]See Roger W. Schmenner, "How Can Service Businesses Survive and Prosper," *Sloan Management Review,* Spring 1986: 21–32.

Challenges to Management

Let us look at the challenges to management that are implied by labor intensity and interaction/customization differences (Figure 1–2). The service operation that is more highly capital-intensive has to look carefully at (1) its capital decisions regarding land, facilities, and equipment; and (2) technological advances that may affect them. Capital-intensive processes often cannot easily augment capacity, so demand must be managed to smooth any demand peaks and to promote the off-peak times. The inflexibility of capacity also implies that scheduling service delivery is more important for these process types.

For process types with high labor intensity, managing and controlling the workforce become paramount. Hiring, training, methods development and control, employee welfare, scheduling the workforce, and controlling what may be far-flung locations are critical. If new units of operations are contemplated,

Challenges for Managers
(low labor intensity)

• Capital decisions
• Technological advances
• Managing demand to avoid peaks
and to promote off-peaks
• Scheduling service delivery

| **Challenges for Managers** (low interaction/ low customization)

• Marketing
• Making service "warm"
• Attention to physical surroundings
• Managing fairly rigid hierarchy with need for standard operating procedures | **Service Factory** (low labor intensity/ low interaction and customization) | **Service shop** (low labor intensity/ high interaction and customization) | **Challenges for Management** (high interaction/ high customization)

• Fighting cost increases
• Maintaining quality
• Reacting to consumer intervention in process
• Managing advancement of people delivering service
• Managing flat hierarchy with loose subordinate–superior relationships
• Gaining employee loyalty |
| | **Mass Service** (high labor intensity/ low interaction and customization) | **Professional Service** (high labor intensity/ high interaction and customization) | |

Challenges for Managers
(high labor intensity)

• hiring
• Training
• Methods development and control
• Employee welfare
• Scheduling workforces
• Control of far–flung geographical
locations
• Startup of new units
• Managing growth

Figure 1–2   Challenges for Service Managers.

their startup may become a problem; managing the group of such new units can be difficult.

What about the challenges to management implied by differences in the interaction with and customization for the consumer? Service processes that have a low degree of interaction and customization face a stiffer marketing challenge. They must try to make the service "warm" and exciting even though they may not give the personal attention a customer might want. Attention to the physical surroundings and the layout become more important. With a low degree of interaction and with little customization, standard operating procedures can safely be instituted. The hierarchy of the service organization itself tends to be the classic pyramid, with fairly rigid relationships between levels.

As the service takes on a higher degree of interaction and customization, management must deal with higher costs and more talented labor. Keeping costs down and yet maintaining quality becomes a challenge. Talented employees need to know how they can advance in the organization. The hierarchy of control tends to be flat, with much less rigid relationships between superiors and subordinates. Keeping workers bound to the firm rather than hopping from job to job becomes a challenge as well. Service firms with a high degree of consumer interaction also must react to frequent consumer intervention in the process.

Naturally, there are some gray areas as one passes from low to high on either dimension of this matrix, and this complicates the placement of selected services within the matrix. For example, although fast-food restaurants are probably best seen as service factories, the traditional restaurant is more problematic. Traditional restaurants offer a higher degree of interaction and customization for the consumer, and they are more labor-intensive than fast-food restaurants. They may be best characterized as service shops, but they are fairly low in that quadrant, with at least some gourmet restaurants arguably characterized as professional services.

The characterization of services as service factories, service shops, mass services, and professional services can be used for comparing service processes in much the same way that we compared processes across the manufacturing spectrum. This is accomplished in Table 1–7. The various features compared there are placed into various groups: service, process, customer-orientation, labor, and management. These features undergird the challenges for management that were introduced above.

The Industrial Engineering Mentality

Seeing the service delivery system as a distinct type of process also helps in that it stresses how service operations' managers can apply the mentality of industrial engineering to improve what they do. Service operations have traditionally not used many of these process-related tools, and thus they are a gold mine for the methods engineer. Tools such as process flows diagrams, information flow diagrams, task analysis, time study, and the analysis of the movement of materials and information can all be very useful in improving the service operation.

TABLE 1-7 A SERVICE COMPARISON

	Service factory (example: Burger King Restaurant)	Service shop (example: Ogle–Tucker Buick)	Mass service (example: Thalhimers— Cloverleaf)	Professional service (example: Arthur Andersen & Co.)
Service features				
Mix of services	Limited.	Diverse.	Limited.	Diverse.
Primary basis of competition	Price, speed, perceived warmth or excitement.	Wide choice, competence.	Price, choice, perceived warmth or excitement.	Competence, range of expertise.
New or unique services introduced or performed	Infrequent.	Routine.	Limited experimentation.	Routine.
Process features				
Capital intensity	High.	High.	Low.	Low.
Pattern of process	Rigid.	Adaptable.	Rigid.	Very loose.
Ties to equipment	Integral part of process, little choice applies.	Equipment important to process, but usually several options exist for its use.	Limited ties to equipment, more tied to plant and layout.	No close ties to plant or equipment.
Importance of balance of tasks and any equipment to smooth process functioning	Balance critical.	Balance often not critical.	Balance not critical.	Balance can be critical.
Tolerance for excess capacity	Excess capacity abhorred.	Excess capacity often not a problem.	Excess capacity implies workforce adjustment that is fairly easily made.	Excess capacity abhorred.
Ease of scheduling	Sometimes tough to schedule, peak demand can be difficult.	Scheduling more easily done.	Scheduling easily done.	Sometimes tough to schedule, peak demand can be difficult.
Economies of scale	Some.	Some—permits better equipment use and thus justification.	Few, if any, except those related to any inventories.	Few, if any, although some specialization can occur.
Notion of capacity	Fairly clear-cut, sometimes definable in physical terms.	Fuzzy, very dependent on mix of demands. Only definable in dollar terms.	Not as fuzzy as with service shop. Limits are often due to plant, not processing time.	Fuzzy.

TABLE 1-7　　A SERVICE COMPARISION (*Continued*)

	Service factory (example: Burger King Restaurant)	Service shop (example: Ogle–Tucker Buick)	Mass service (example: Thalhimers— Cloverleaf)	Professional service (example: Arthur Andersen & Co.)
Process features				
Layout	Line flow-like preferred.	Job shop or fixed position.	Typically fixed position, although layout may change frequently, customers move through layout.	Job shop frequently.
Additions to capacity	Can be in variable increments, requires balance of capital and labor.	Can be in variable increments, aspects of balance more murky.	Often takes big changes to plant to enact. Processing can sometimes be sped up by adding some labor.	Means adding primarily to labor in incremental fashion.
Bottlenecks	Occasionally movable, but often predictable.	Movable, frequent.	Typically well-known, predictable.	Can sometimes be forecast, but otherwise are uncertain.
Nature of process change	Sometimes routine (rebalance), sometimes radical (new equipment.	Occasionally radical (new equipment and procedures).	Process change seldom occurs, although it can be radical (such as big change to plant).	Mostly incremental.
Importance of material flow to service provision	Both inventories and flow are important.	Inventories important; flow not as important.	Inventories are often important and must be controlled.	Incidental to most services.
Customer-oriented features				
Importance of attractive physical surroundings to marketing of service	Can be critical.	Often insignificant.	Critical.	Often insignificant.
Interaction of customer with process	Little, brief.	Can be great.	Some.	Typically, very great.
Customization of service	Scant.	Significant.	Scant.	Significant.
Ease of managing demand for peaks and nonpeaks	Can be done through price.	Some promotion of off-peak times can be done, but often difficult.	Same as for service shop.	Often very difficult to manage demand, may not be responsive to price.

(*Continued*)

TABLE 1-7   A SERVICE COMPARISON (*Continued*)

	Service factory (example: Burger King Restaurant)	Service shop (example: Ogle–Tucker Buick)	Mass service (example: Thalhimers— Cloverleaf)	Professional service (example: Arthur Andersen & Co.)
Customer-oriented features				
Process quality control	Can be formal, amenable to standard methods (such as control charts).	Can be formal. Checkpoints can easily be established. Training can be critical to quality.	Mainly informal. Training critical to quality.	Mainly informal. Training critical to quality.
Labor-related features				
Pay	Typically hourly.	Varies, could include individual incentive or commission schemes.	Same as for service shop.	Salary, often with bonus of some type.
Skill levels	Generally lower skills.	High skills.	Variable, but most often lower skill.	Very high skills.
Job content	Small.	Large.	Often medium, but variable.	Very large.
Advancement	With more skills or seniority acquired, greater responsibility given. Seniority can lead to change in department or shift assignment.	Often, worker is an independent operator of sorts and can exert some control on what he or she gives and gets from job; limited hierarchical progression.	Often a hierarchy to progress upward through.	Often a pyramid, up or out. Top of pyramid exerts leverage over bottom of pyramid.
Management features				
Staff-line needs	Large staff for process redesign, methods, forecasting, capacity planning, and scheduling. Line supervision and troubleshooting still critical.	Limited staff, mostly line operation.	Some staff, often focused on personal issues.	Limited staff, many line managers wear multiple hats.
Means of control	Variable. Can be cost or profit.	Usually a profit center.	Usually a profit center.	Usually a profit center.

More on these tools follows in subsequent chapters of this book.

Given this introduction to the nature of services, the remainder of this book is devoted to an exploration of what managers can do to improve the provision of services, both existing services and ones planned or expanded. The next segment of this book deals with improving existing services—improving their quality, productivity, and the satisfaction that customers derive from them. The segment after that deals with new or expanding service operations and how they can be managed well.

Supporting the Service Encounter

THE SERVICE ENCOUNTER AND WHAT SURROUNDS IT

In the provision of services, it has been noted that there is often a "moment of truth"—a phrase usually associated with Jan Carlzon, former CEO of SAS, the Scandinavian airline—where the service process comes face-to-face with the customer and where the customer can easily confront his or her willingness to purchase the service or to continue an association with the company. This occurs during what is termed the *service encounter*, when the customer and the service meet and interact. Surrounding and supporting the service encounter, where this "moment of truth" flourishes, are three attributes of service management that need to be clearly defined and that make the service encounter a pleasant one for all concerned. (See Figure 2–1.)

1. Service task. The service task states why the service exists in the marketplace and what the customer truly values about the service. It is a statement that conveys the essence of what the service provides the customer, and thus provides both management and the workforce with a goal to achieve. In more fashionable terms, it is the "voice of the customer" in how the service is delivered. Note that the service task is always defined with reference to the customer; a service task that ignores the customer is almost invariably from a service business that is suffering or, at least, is on the verge of a downturn.

2. Service standards. Service standards define what is effective service provision to the customer. The standards are the controls, the guardians of quality and cost efficiency in the service firm. Standards are measurable. Thus, one should be able to go down a checklist of standards or audit the service to determine how well it is being delivered.

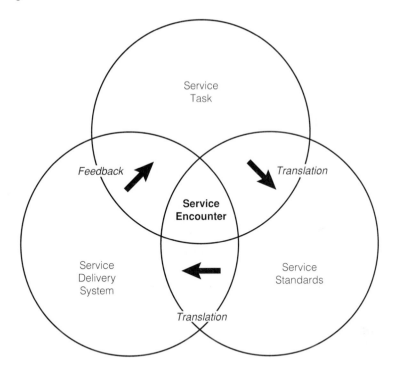

Figure 2–1 The Service Encounter.

3. The service delivery system. The service delivery system specifies how the service is produced, including how it is controlled for quality, cost, and customer satisfaction. The service delivery system needs to be synchronized with the service task and the service standards so that the service encounter remains a pleasurable one for all concerned.

As the previous chapter suggests, the service delivery system can be one of four different types (service factory, service shop, mass service, and professional service) and have an entire series of different choices made about it. Much of the content of this text deals with how services can improve their service delivery systems or make better choices about them.

To get a taste for how the service task, service standards, and the service delivery system interact to support the service encounter, consider two simple examples from the realm of retailing.

1. *Discounter.* Take discount retailing. Suppose the customer, in this instance, values the store because it provides brand names in its selected product categories at low margins. The store is easy to deal with, although it may not

provide very much personalized service or after-sale service. Its product range may not be as wide as some others, but it never runs out of what it chooses to sell. This, in broad outline, defines its service task. The service standards in this instance could concentrate on speed of service for the customer, inventory levels, maintaining vigilance in the marketplace to see that it is not underpriced, and offering no-hassle returns of merchandise. The service delivery system could be geared to sophisticated purchasing, distribution, and product tracking so that the store knows exactly what's selling and exercises as much leverage over its suppliers as possible.

2. *Boutique.* For the boutique retailer, suppose the customer values the store for its taste. In its product categories, the store always offers stylish, trend-setting merchandise presented in an atmosphere of refinement, so that the shopping experience is always pleasant and customers see clearly how the products offered for sale could be used, perhaps in combination with other products. Product choice, not price, is at issue. This is the service task. The service standards, in this example, could be geared to attracting customers into the shop and to the degree to which those customers are repeat ones. Revenue per customer over the year could be tracked. The service delivery system would concentrate on the development of unique, fashion-sensitive suppliers and the coordination of products within the shop. Tracking the tastes of customers and keeping them informed about new product acquisitions is another important activity.

Although both of these examples depict retailers, the discounter and the boutique are very different from one another. Their distinct service tasks necessitate different service standards and different service delivery systems.

Strengthening the Service Encounter

The service encounter is strengthened when the three attributes mentioned above—service task, service standards, and service delivery system—are mutually consistent. Service operations tend to lose out if these three compete with one another or if one or more of them is neglected.

Just as manufacturing choices work best when they are consistent with each other and with the competitive priorities implied by the business strategy, so do service operations choices. Service business competition can be as cutthroat as any, perhaps more so, because barriers to entry are frequently lower for service businesses. The service business with inconsistent operations choices is often quickly weeded out.

Service businesses can no more be all things to all customers than can manufacturers. The concept of *factory focus*—which argues that factories perform better when their goals are limited—has clear parallels in the service arena. A number of the criticisms leveled at various service companies reflect concern over too many different kinds of services offered or a failure to achieve the operational synergies touted when the merger or acquisition was first under-taken. One cannot assume that the formula that has been so successful in one service business will necessarily carry over to another service business, even if that business is merely a segmentation of the old one.

Think about the service companies with great reputations and strong financial performances. They are absolutely clear about why customers prefer them to the competition. They measure how they provide their services and what their levels of quality and cost are. Their service delivery systems are well-conceived and understood. This concern for clarity and consistency prompts the following proposition:

Proposition:
> If you can clearly state your service task in 50 words or less, you can make money. If you can clearly state it in 20 words or less, you can make a lot of money.

Defining the service task is tough. A lot of services have a wishy-washy, me-too type of character; they are services with not very well-defined service tasks. They lack a clear vision as to why a customer might choose them over somebody else. These wishy-washy, me-too services often earn returns below their potential; some do not last long at all in the marketplace. On the other hand, if the service task is well-defined, it can help to separate that service in the customer's eyes from the run-of-the- mill. Well-defined services thus stand a much better chance of making money. The resurgences of such firms as Sears have in large measure been stimulated by rethinking and restating their service tasks. The current malaise at other companies such as The Limited have been attributed, in part, to a lost appreciation for their customers and how they think. Stating the service task clearly, using 50 words or less, can help a company latch onto what it must do to keep its customers coming.

If the service task can be stated extremely clearly, say in 20 words or less, it is more likely that that service task can become ingrained in the workforce. Every worker knows what he or she has to do to fit into a grand scheme that the customer values. The service task becomes a part of the corporate culture, a motto, creed, or slogan that everyone respects and follows, almost instinctively. If that occurs, then you are much better off and stand a still better chance of making a lot of money. Thus, the simpler the statement of the service task, the easier it is for the workforce to provide the company with a real advantage.[1] McDonald's, for example, is famed for inculcating the virtues of Quality, Service, Cleanliness, and Value in its workforce, and this simple statement keeps its service task clear in every worker's mind.

---

[1] The clearer and more ingrained the service task, the less prone one is to the "heartbreak" of franchising. The more you get customers to identify with a particular company or particular service system, and not with individuals within the process, the better off you are. You are less vulnerable to a franchisee breaking off contact with the franchise and going it alone.

The goal of a good service task is to undergird a service that is so valued by customers that they keep coming back. There are some real advantages to such devotion, and they prompt another proposition.

Proposition:

The most profitable customer is the repeat customer.

Corollaries: 1. Always try to recover from screw-ups.
                          2. The service bookends are critical.

Studies indicate that the repeat customer is much more profitable than the initial customer. (See Figure 2–2.) Why? There are several reasons:

- The repeat customer buys more.
- The repeat customer buys a broader variety of services, including services with higher margins.
- The repeat customer is easier to service because he or she knows the system and places less of a burden on it.
- The repeat customer does not require elaborate advertising.
- The repeat customer provides the service firm with advertising because he or she is apt to discuss his or her satisfaction with others and thus refer business to the firm.

How can services induce people to become repeat customers? It can be done in any number of ways:

- Make it easy to reorder the service (e.g., automatic notices).
- Offer "freebies" if enough has been purchased in the past (e.g., airline frequent flyer programs, credit card premiums, a free car wash after the fifth time).
- Make it easy to give the repeat buyer more service (e.g., repairs, extra hours of operation, special payment procedures or terms).
- Offer special prices for long-term, repeat business.
- Offer special services (e.g., for children).
- Make it easy to enter the service encounter and somewhat harder to leave (e.g., book or record clubs that automatically send you something unless you inform them otherwise).

The importance of the repeat customer also means that companies should spend a lot of time trying to make sure that customers stay repeat customers, and this means trying to engage in *service recovery* when there are screw-ups in the process. The service recovery tries to make amends for a quality breakdown in the process. Perhaps additional services are offered (peace offerings) or perhaps price reductions are given on the service provided, or on future services— anything to keep customers from walking away from a potentially relationship-ending situation. Conventional wisdom has it that a satisfied customer is likely,

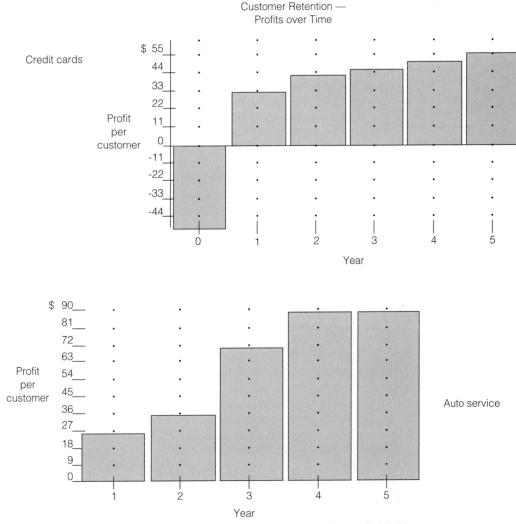

Figure 2–2 The Advantages of the Repeat Customer over Time. *(Source: Reichheld and Sasser, "Zero Defections: Quality Comes to Services," Harvard Business Review, Nov./Dec. 1990.)*

on average, to tell 5 or 6 others about the experience, whereas a dissatisfied customer is likely to tell 2 or 3 times as many people about a maddening or disappointing experience. Keeping such stories out of circulation is worth money to the typical service operation. It is also worth training the front-line service providers on techniques for cooling off a hot customer. Being empathetic is a very useful trait. Service recoveries can easily pay for themselves.

We are all likely to have experienced service recoveries. The airline has overbooked and someone must be bumped from the flight, so credit for a future flight is given. The restaurant is late with a meal or gets an order wrong, so dessert is on the house. The plumber, electrician, or painter has not been able to resolve a problem despite repeated attempts and it is clearly not the fault of the customer, so additional work is provided at no extra charge. The car dealership comes to your house to fetch your car for recall or warranty service. One could go on and on. The message is clear, however. By doing a little more now, the service business avoids the costs of attracting new business and also the harm to its reputation by having a disgruntled customer.

With this in mind, many companies have found it advantageous to make it easy for the disgruntled customer to complain. British Airways has special spots within airports where customers can lodge complaints. The ubiquitous "How Are We Doing?" cards found in hotels and elsewhere are another example. When complaining is easy, more of it will be done by unhappy customers, and perhaps less bad-mouthing of the firm will occur among the customer's friends and acquaintances. Moreover, it gives the service firm an early opportunity to initiate a service recovery.

The importance of repeat customers also means that the initial contact with the customer and the closing contact with the customer, the so-called "service bookends," are critical. One wants to make a favorable initial impression on the customer, and one also wants to make sure that the last memories of customer contact are good ones. This means that training the front-line service providers—those who routinely engage in service encounters—on how to greet the customer and begin the service process and on how to conclude the service process so that the customer walks away with a smile is absolutely critical. Salespeople, for example, are trained in detecting the body language of a customer so that their initial approach is most effective and the entire selling situation is brought to a satisfying conclusion. For example, do you let the customer browse, or do you immediately start suggesting merchandise? Is the customer ready to buy more, or would the customer be irked if additional sales suggestions were made? Attentive salespeople are aware of all of this and more.

Not every service encounter that needs a service recovery, however, is the fault of the service process. Sometimes customers are at fault. This prompts another proposition:

Proposition:
> The customer is *not* always right, but he or she expects to be right. Create a service delivery system that not only lets the unreasonable customer off gently, but that supports the front-line service providers.

Sometimes, customers make unreasonable and unrealistic demands on the service process, and literally abuse the front-line workers engaged in the service encounter in so doing. The service process cannot always cave in to such behavior, but it helps if there are firm and firmly established guidelines for the front-line providers to follow. If they have rehearsed scenes with unrealistic customers or if they have ready access to back-up resources, then they will not burn out and waste undo energy in coping with a situation that is clearly not their fault. Being able to handle problem cases off-line (say, by calling in a supervisor or a specialist) keeps the front-line providers fresh and gives the customer the illusion of accommodation, even when his or her unrealistic expectations are not fulfilled. Telephone customer service representatives, for example, are sometimes put in teams that face one another so that during a nasty call, the rep can seek emotional comfort from others around, if only through their understanding hand and facial gestures.

Both service recoveries and service bookends demonstrate how important the interaction of the service task and the service delivery system is. This prompts still another proposition:

Proposition:

Change one aspect of service, and look to change everything in the service delivery system.

Corollary: Some things don't fit.

A well-run service operation is an integral combination of the service task, service standards, and the service delivery system. The service delivery system itself is likely to be a well-developed, highly interactive creation that may be more fragile than one might expect. Thus, trying to use the service delivery system for something outside the original service task can lead to disappointment. Trying to add on to the service delivery system in a way to provide something extra not originally foreseen with the service task and the initial service standards may also trigger difficulties. Many services have suffered because management wanted to fiddle with what ordinarily would be a finely tuned system.

One must be prepared to accept the fact that some add-on services or some newly defined services might not fit an existing service delivery system. The shrewd and courageous service provider understands that some services will simply have to be forgone if the delivery system is not to be compromised and the service task, service standards, and the service encounter itself are to be optimized. Integrity can often be equated with profitability.

McDonald's, for example, has experimented with offering pizza in an effort to enhance late-evening sales. It is an experiment that has not spread widely or quickly, and it is not hard to see why. McDonald's service delivery system is geared to serving individual portions of items that can be cooked quickly and inventoried for short periods of time. The time between order-taking and order-filling is measured in a few minutes. Pizzas, on the other hand, are generally for more than one consumer (pan pizzas excluded, of course) and are bulky to handle. They cannot be shoved through drive-in windows easily and, furthermore, they need to be prepared and cooked for 20 minutes or so after an order is taken, so they would be ill-suited to drive-ins anyway. These elements of service task and service delivery system do not fit together very easily, and one can expect that if pizza were added to many McDonald's, the service times and the costs of provision (the company's service standards) would suffer.

Indeed, McDonald's stole a march on the competition years ago when it began offering breakfast service, largely because the competition was ill-prepared to copy the breakfast service. Their service delivery systems could not be readily altered without sacrificing their service tasks, service standards, and many of the choices they had made about their service delivery systems. Burger King, for example, cooks their burgers on a flame broiler, which is ill-suited for cooking eggs or pancakes. The McDonald's grills used for cooking their burgers, on the other hand, are perfect for preparing breakfast foods.

Not only do some things not fit, but some things may no longer be desirable to pursue. Such instances can have spectacular implications for the service encounter, the service delivery system—indeed all aspects of the service.

Further Corollary:

> The hand of government is never an invisible hand; government actions, regulations, and deregulations can create and destroy markets and raise or lower a company's competitiveness overnight. Service companies must be vigilant about new government initiatives and must calculate their effects so as to take advantage of them, if possible, and to avoid their worst implications, if they can.

The reference to an invisible hand, of course, is an allusion to Adam Smith's 1776 description of the workings of the marketplace in allocating resources throughout the economy. In uncomplicated situations, the workings of the marketplace, unimpeded, are often the best way to allocate resources to their best uses. There are a number of instances where the market fails (these are well-documented by economists) and it is here that governments can, and should, intervene. When they intervene, however, competition is always altered.

In the past several decades, there have been some significant government actions that have turned some service businesses upside down. Think, for example, of airline and trucking deregulations and of environmental regulations. Airline deregulation changed the way the airlines competed. Before deregulation, the prices of airline tickets and the city-pairs to be served were set. Airlines competed primarily on the convenience of their departures and the attentiveness of their service. After deregulation, neither prices nor city-pairs were set. Airlines could compete over broader areas and offer price discounts. It became advantageous to construct hub-and-spoke systems to tie many places together efficiently in a network that could "pulse" several times during a day. Departure time convenience was relinquished gladly by many travelers who enjoyed lower fares and the ability to connect to many places more easily than they could before. Hub-and-spoke systems are capital-intensive and they fostered more mergers among airlines. The face of airline competition changed dramatically.

The passing of various environmental laws and regulations has spawned new services in the waste-management sector. Think of the following cause and effects:

Cause:

The government has banned some types of hazardous waste from landfills.

Effects: 1. This prompts the construction and use of hazardous waste incinerators.

2. Companies that have invested in this technology lobby strenuously for its broad adoption and strict compliance so as to close out competitors that have not so invested. Such services could even strike up alliances with environmental groups.

3. Cement kilns and other facilities that could burn hazardous waste enter the marketplace, a marketplace that before never looked attractive.

4.. Incinerators and other competitors engage in disputes about who is in compliance with the regulations.

5. Companies that have seen the costs of getting rid of their hazardous waste increase look for ways to generate less hazardous waste in the first place.

One could go on. The point is that the strategic aspects of service are constantly changing (in part because of the government's actions) and that service companies must be on their guard to discern what can affect them and what they can do to thwart or to take advantage of it. Understanding the potential actions or reactions of customers is of prime importance. Often this means analyzing where the profit lies in any situation and how well that profit is protected by barriers to entry (such as patents, new technology, know-how, special training, large capital investments, and brand loyalty). Examining what can happen to supply and demand curves, especially demand and supply curves that describe what is happening in an industry, can frequently be very revealing.

Understanding the service encounter.   By concentrating on the service encounter and the three attributes that surround it, service firms can improve their performance and their strategic positions within the marketplace. The shrewd service provider is always asking questions about the service:

Are the three attributes surrounding the service encounter evident and are they understandable?

Are they well-defined, and acted upon by the workforce?

Are they mutually consistent?

How can they be affected by competitors or by outside (e.g., government) actions?

By asking such questions, the service manager can home in on what makes a service operation successful or unsuccessful. One of the first things to do in evaluating a service is to focus on the service encounter and to develop a statement for the service task, and then to list the service standards in place and the characteristics of the service delivery system. Weaknesses are often quickly revealed and strengths understood and appreciated. Understanding the service encounter is the bedrock of operations strategy for service firms.

IMPROVING THE SERVICE ENCOUNTER

Once the service encounter is well-understood, the firm can act to improve upon it. Often there is much that can be done. Consider the following proposition.

Proposition:

Service operations are more apt than manufacturing to delude themselves about their efficiency.

The service product is often less well-defined than the manufacturing product, so it is often tougher to discriminate between the effects of demand and supply. With service, it is so easy to say that performance is slipping because of faltering demand or tough competition or poor marketing, when in fact it may be slipping because operational issues are not being addressed as well as they should. This is often the opposite of the situation in manufacturing where, if the product does not sell, it is frequently blamed on manufacturing's inability to make it right or fast enough or cheap enough.

Many service operations think that they have good operations just because they have spent some time developing them, and they are not apparently in need of serious revision or continual improvement. If benchmarking is not performed, and performed well, this delusion about efficiency can be very harmful to a company's ability to maintain innovation and push back the threat of competition.

As in manufacturing firms, the search for continuous improvement is a never-ending one. Let us consider some of the means by which service companies have become more productive and competitive.

Service Productivity—Getting More With Less

Productivity has a classically simple definition:

$$\text{Productivity} = \text{output} \div \text{input}.$$

The idea is a simple and compelling one. We can improve productivity by getting more output for a given level of input, or we can get more productivity by getting the same output, but by using fewer inputs to do so.

So far so good. When we start to elaborate, however, the concept of productivity becomes fuzzier. What types of inputs are we talking about, for example? Are they labor inputs? Surely, but are there more inputs that we should be aware of, such as materials or the use of capital equipment? In services, more so than in manufacturing, labor inputs still tend to be the most important, but even for services, capital inputs and materials are not negligible and can contribute to a service business's productivity advance.

There are also a number of measurement issues that managers must face. How should output be measured: in dollars or in some physical unit? How should inputs be measured: in dollars, as well, or in some physical unit such as hours worked? Services have been notoriously difficult to measure, as those who keep our gross national product accounts can attest. Determining service outputs and measuring them correctly is a fiendishly difficult task, and too often services have suffered because there was no good output measure, and, as a result, much productivity was estimated from the input side only.

Be that as it may, these days we are much clearer about what it takes to improve productivity, even in services. Let us consider five major ways by which productivity can increase: substitution, waste removal, reducing variance and variety, managing demand, and reaping economies of scale and of density. Let us consider each of these in turn.

Substitution.   Substitution is the classic way to enhance productivity. Perhaps the most historically important means of improving productivity has been the substitution of capital for labor. Labor-saving machines have driven much of the productivity advance in manufacturing, transportation, communication, and other key sectors of the economy. The same is true for services, although capital-for-labor substitution generally works best in the back-office environment of service firms.

Another type of substitution is capital-for-capital substitution. This represents the replacement of obsolete or aging capital with modern, new, improved capital. Computerization, for example, is a key new capital-for-capital substitution, but one could also speak of new layouts for services, or for less costly replacements of equipment used to provide services.

Perhaps more important for services is the substitution of labor for labor. Many services have delegated tasks to less costly workers. For example, paramedics and paralegals are used so that the job of the expensive key service supplier, such as doctors and lawyers, is leveraged by the use of well-trained but less costly workers who do some of the job that the doctor or lawyer might ordinarily be expected to do. This kind of labor-for-labor substitution is widespread in many professional service firms and has spread to other types of services as well.

A slightly more subtle change—almost unique to services—is the substitution of customer labor for labor. This is where the customer, who is involved in the service project, ends up replacing some of the labor that one might ordinarily expect the service business to provide. This is the salad bar approach to productivity, and it occurs in all types of service businesses where there is an interested and willing customer to intervene in a service process, in a controlled manner, to customize the service or to provide desired interaction.

Of course, we can combine all of these types of substitutions. Automatic teller machines and their follow-ons combine much of it:

- Capital-for-labor substitution savings, where the teller labor is saved by the introduction of the machine,
- Customer labor-for-teller labor substitution savings.
- Capital-for-capital substitution, where old machines are replaced with new, fuller-featured machines.

Waste removal. This is another classic way to improve productivity, and one where manufacturing has pioneered. There are a number of subcategories worth exploring:

1. *Methods improvement.* This is the province of the traditional industrial engineering means of securing productivity gain. Time and motion studies and work sampling are the most evident. Services are newer territory for this than is manufacturing. Service businesses have resisted this kind of mentality in many instances, but there is still a vast improvement that can be made by this type of thinking. UPS, for example, is a famed user of industrial engineering for their methods, truck and rack design, and routings. (Consult the appendix to Chapter 6 for more on methods improvement.)

2. *Quality improvement.* Most managers these days would acknowledge that indeed quality and productivity are positively correlated. They are not substitutes for one another, as we may have believed years ago. Thus, all the means of improving quality should lead to productivity gain, perhaps not in the very short term, but in the medium to long term. (Consult the chapter on quality.) Fail-safing techniques are particularly inexpensive and thus very productive ways of improving quality.

3. *Time-based means.* One of the important recent contributions to productivity has focused on the importance of time for identifying waste in a process.[2] Many companies have examined their businesses and improved their productivity by outlining the processes that they engage in, such as order entry, product design, billing, service delivery, transportation, stock replenishment, or customer handling. Companies have recognized these processes and have flow-charted them in detailed fashion so that people really understand what is done and what isn't done in a particular process, where paperwork may be generated, where information may be dispersed, where routings are needed. They have worked at the time it takes for these processes to be accomplished and where the processes may bog down. It is in that bogging down where waste may well lurk, and these companies have investigated these slow areas to determine how the process might be changed in such a way to ensure better quality and more rapid delivery of the service. This type of thinking is at the heart of what has been termed *reengineering.*

4. *Modularity.* If work can be made more self-contained, often the productivity can be enhanced. This is because with more self-contained work, the feedback loops for quality and process modifications can be shortened and workers identify much more with what is being done. This is a common way of improving productivity in the back office. For example, a worker may handle all

---

[2]See George Stalk and Thomas Hout, *Competing Through Time,* Free Press, 1988; and Roger W. Schmenner, "The Merit of Making Things Fast," *Sloan Management Review,* 1988.

of a customer transaction rather than just a piece of it. When the changeover from task to task can be made simple, this type of arrangement can be much more productive than an arrangement where the worker does a smaller job all day long.

Reducing variance and variety.   As Chapter 4 will explain in more detail, variance in the demand placed upon a service operation, as well as variance in providing the service itself, can greatly affect the time customers have to wait. In essence, variance robs a process of capacity. Variety can also trim back a process's capacity. Thus, productivity can be enhanced to the degree to which variance and variety can be usefully reduced. There are two major ways by which this can be done in service businesses.

1. *Standardization.* For some, this means offering a more standard service where customization is trimmed back. Perhaps customization can be trimmed as far back as a no-frills approach to service, or perhaps it can be trimmed back only to the offering of a standard package of service characteristics. Either way, productivity is enhanced.

A slightly different means of standardization is a *triage system* to segregate the custom operations from the standard. Sometimes this can be done electronically. Many services have introduced *touchtone triage* in their communications with customers that segregates, for example, standard queries on bank accounts, or routine stock broker contacts, from the more difficult-to-handle queries or contacts. In some cases, the triage of customers is accomplished by the company's own workforce, and, sometimes, customers help to triage themselves to more effective service.

This kind of standardization has a corresponding concept in manufacturing: factory focus, which was mentioned earlier. In this approach, manufacturers enhance productivity by concentrating the production of particular product lines in their own factories or plants within the plant. With services, this type of thinking can readily apply where different types of services are concentrated in a few hands and other services are concentrated in other hands. This can speed worker learning and help improve the quality of service delivery.

Standardization is also vastly important as an aid to geographically dispersed operations. Many branch operations and franchise operations rely on standardization to frame service situations where there is greater control or less maintenance or less repair. Greater customer satisfaction can arise out of standardization of layouts, equipment, methods, customer handling, cash controls, and ordering.

2. *Less interaction.* To the extent that service processes can be designed so that customers cannot easily interact with the process, variance and variety can be reduced as a matter of course. Through education or through the design of the process itself, customers can be constrained from interruptions of the process that invariably increase variance and variety. If this is done skillfully, the customer may not suspect that the variety he or she would ordinarily want or the interaction he or she might be accustomed to is being manipulated so that productivity can be enhanced. In fact, if the customer is getting good value for money, he or she may welcome this kind of change.

Managing demand. Because of the lack of inventories in service businesses, managing demand can improve productivity. If demand can be shifted from peak periods to off-peak periods, queues can shrink and capacity can be better used. This shifting is often done by price incentives.

For some companies, demand has been managed by introducing additional services so that fixed assets can be used more intensively. The classic example here is the introduction of breakfast at fast-food restaurants. These issues are discussed in more detail in Chapter 7.

Economies of scale and of density. There may be economies of scale in some service businesses where bigger facilities are less costly to operate per dollar of sales. This may be particularly true of services that are capital-intensive, such as transportation and communication. More apropos, however, are economies of density. Economies of density occur when significant demand is bunched right on the spot. It is not just the scale of the operation that is important, it is whether demand is there to make full use of it. Economies of density can be important to retailing (by permitting specialized salespeople to operate) or to health care (by concentrating demand for facilities to make their use economically feasible).

What's not included. Productivity, for some people, means going after aggressive budgets and high capacity use. The thinking is conditioned by the way costs are built up in a company's product line. Research has not found these approaches to be very effective. Budgets are useful for controlling costs to make sure that one does not overshoot them, but budgets themselves, even aggressively managed budgets, do not point out where waste is and often do not lead the way to permanent process change.

This same thinking applies to the development of cost structures. Cost structures can keep score about the use of materials and labor and overhead in a product, but they are not good indications of where improvements can or should be made. One has to be much closer to the process to understand where productivity can be enhanced by quality improvements, waste removal, managing demand, or some other mechanism.

By the same token, high capacity use or great labor efficiency by themselves are not good indications of productivity improvement. Just because a machine is working does not mean that the services customers need are being provided. Similarly, just because a worker is working does not mean that the customer is being satisfied. One has to look at the whole process to make sure that workers and machines are adding true value.

Revisiting the Service Process Matrix: Changes to the Service Encounter

Chapter 1's classification of service businesses into four categories—service factory, service shop, mass service, and professional service—can be used to investigate what has happened strategically to service operations over time—specifically, what has been changing the nature of the service encounter. The most salient development in many service businesses has been vast segmentation and diversification. Services that were once clearly service shops or mass service firms are no longer so clearly labeled. Service firms are spreading themselves out across the service matrix. Some examples are instructive:

1. One of the classic changes has involved the development and evolution of fast food. The traditional restaurant could be positioned as a service shop with relatively high customization and interaction for the consumer and a middling labor intensity. The elegant gourmet restaurant may even be considered a professional service. On the other hand, with the advent of fast food, interaction and customization for the consumer has been dramatically lowered, as has the labor intensity. For the classic fast-food companies, the change has been from a service shop to a service factory. This has left the restaurant business with a wide diversity of operations types.

2. Another interesting innovation within the service shop quadrant has involved hospitals. The new kinds of hospitals developed by Humana, Hospital Corporation of America, and others are different from the traditional community hospital or university medical center. The traditional hospital (and especially the university medical center) is geared to treat any disease, and thus invests in all of the latest equipment and technology for diagnosis and treatment. This new breed of hospital customarily deals with the more routine kinds of medical treatment; often such care facilities do not include intensive care units and other high-expense units for very sick or dying patients. Such patients are referred to larger and better-equipped hospitals. The new type of hospital offers much lower cost service that is convenient for the consumer. The new hospital thus offers less customization but also a higher degree of labor intensity.

3. Another series of changes has occurred in some of the services characterized as mass service. Retailing offers some interesting examples. The expansion of catalog stores (such as Best's or Sharper Image), warehouse stores (such as Toys 'R' Us), mail-order sales (such as L. L. Bean), and brand name discounters (such as Wal-Mart) has broadened the traditional retailing operation toward a lower degree of labor intensity, largely by providing less service than department stores. On the other hand, the proliferation of boutiques and specialty operations within stores such as Bloomingdale's is evidence of a different kind of change, one in which interaction and customization are stressed, often with higher labor intensity (more than full-service). By being more professional (frequently with salespeople on commission), such stores hope to convert more browsers into buyers.

4. The deregulation of commercial banking and financial services has also created some intriguing strategic changes for operations within the mass service quadrant. Automation in commercial banking (automatic teller machines, electronic transfers, and other new technological advances) has pushed aspects of commercial banking to lower labor intensity. Indeed, credit card operations and check clearing are now placed in their own facilities, often at quite a distance from the commercial banks themselves, and they do essentially the kind of work one would expect in a service factory. This kind of change is evident in some other financial service companies. One of the justifications given for the acquisition of Lehman Brothers Kuhn Loeb by Shearson/American Express was the fact that the trading operations of Lehman Brothers could be easily absorbed by slack capacity in the back-room operations at Shearson.

However, even as technological advances have helped commercial banking become less labor-intensive, there is a move to customize some services even more. The unbundling of financial services brought on by such deregulation milestones as the removal of interest-rate ceilings on certificates of deposit, the cessation of fixed brokerage commissions, the demise of Regulation Q (which placed ceilings on interest payable by commercial banks), and the first steps toward interstate banking has promoted this development. Many of the services that have been acquired by the "financial supermarket" companies will give those companies greater interaction with and customization for consumers. The increasing menu of services from the traditional brokerage houses may cause the old-time broker, who tried to be all things to his or her client, to become an anachronism.

Moving Toward the Diagonal

Given the importance of focused operations and the quickening pace of segmentation and diversification of service businesses, understanding the dynamics of the service encounter and of service process change can be very helpful. There are several observations about these dynamics that bear attention. The first observation is that many of the segmentation moves that service businesses have made, as were just discussed, have been toward the diagonal that runs from the service factory to the professional service firm. Figure 2–3 illustrates this point. Why is this the case? What is it about the diagonal that is so attractive for existing services? The reason is likely to be related to control and to productivity improvement. Moves toward the diagonal are moves toward greater control over costs or the selling situation itself. They frequently involve some of the productivity-enhancing tactics that were discussed above. They have redefined the service encounter for some businesses.

Even though existing operations are being drawn toward the diagonal, we should not be alarmed that all service shops or mass service operations will become extinct. Many operations will be able to adhere to their traditional operations choices, and marketing pressures for increased customization and the

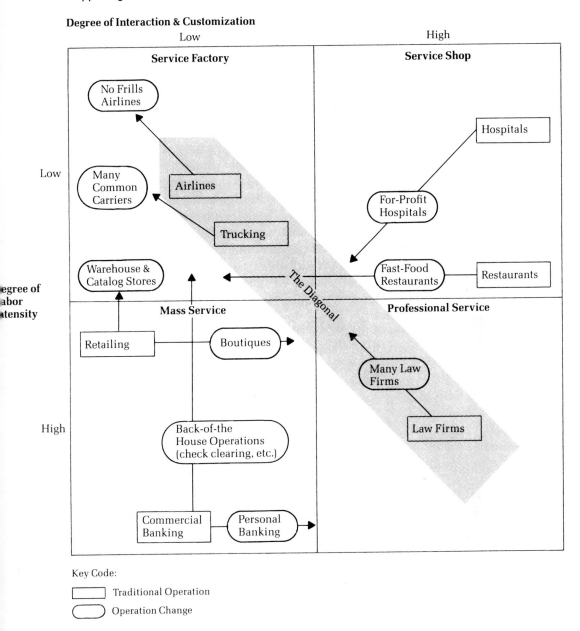

Figure 2–3 Strategic Operation Changes Within the Service Process Matrix.

generation of completely new services are likely to replenish the supply of service shops or mass service operations that are pressed to transform themselves. Witness, for example, the upsurge of luxury hotel accommodation and other specialized services. New services are being rendered to particular market niches. The recent change in how computers are sold, with more mass outlets as opposed to individual salespeople, is another example.

A second observation on the dynamics of service processes centers on some of the service businesses already located on the diagonal. The professional service firm and the service factory are not immune themselves from strategic changes. Of the services that have changed their positions within the service process matrix, most have moved up the diagonal. Consider the changes that have occurred within many law firms over the last decades. The growing staffs of paralegals and other lower-cost labor and the increasing specialization of what many law firms do have driven many firms within that professional service industry toward lower labor intensity and less customization (that is, less full service). Similarly, other professional service firms have invested in equipment, much of it for word processing or data processing.

In a similar vein, the deregulation of trucking and air travel has brought significant change to those service factories. Deregulation of trucking has forced many of the old-line common carriers to invest dramatically in breakbulks and additional freight terminals so as to do better with less-than-truckload shipments. These capital investments have meant increased barriers to entry by competitors to these trucking firms, but these firms can no longer afford to offer so customized a service for their clients. They are more specialized and offer fewer services. Their pricing structures have been changed to encourage the clients to ship in particular ways. This has meant movement up the diagonal for most of the common carriers.

A similar story can be told of the airlines. Deregulation, as mentioned earlier, encouraged their operations to shift to hub-and-spoke systems. As the major airlines have changed their operations in this way so that a number of "pushes" can be made from their major airport hubs during any day, the result has been both less customization in what they offer the consumer and lower labor intensity, because significant investments have been placed in the hubs.

Just as movement toward the diagonal does not necessarily mean that service shops and mass service firms will cease to exist, the move up the diagonal does not necessarily mean that professional service firms will all become small service factories. There will always be some firms that will be able to operate successfully with high labor intensity and high interaction and customization, and there will be new professional services rendered that, at least initially, will demand a combination of high labor intensity and high interaction and customization.

Flows, Bottlenecks, and Balance

The first tools of operations management to learn, and arguably the most important, are the process flow diagram, and its sister, the information flow diagram. They are the lightning rods for analysis and change of the process. They are stepping stones, as well, in identifying and remedying bottlenecks and in balancing capacities within processes. As a guide to this chapter, consider the following proposition:

Proposition:
Never underestimate the power of the process or the information flow diagram. Be clear where the customer fits in them.

Knowledge is power, and information and process flow diagrams are key ways to gain knowledge. They help the efficiency of the process by calling attention to—indeed, exposing—the process and its workings. They provide the bonus of revealing how marketing can be constrained by operations; that is, how the operation dictates what the company can and cannot sell.[1]

Process and information flow diagrams help to define the service delivery system, and they point out the places where controls and service standards may be needed in order to preserve the service task intact and thus to provide a pleasurable service encounter for the customer. The development of such diagrams can show where bottlenecks are, and thus where equipment or people need to be added, or how the process layout could be altered. Process and information flow diagrams can point out where procedures need to be standardized, or operations split off on their own. They can be very clear about where

---

[1]The aforementioned example of breakfast in the fast-food industry is a classic example, but there are many others. Quick-change oil shops are great for what they do, but they are ill-suited to tire rotations or any significant repairs to the engine; hydraulic lifts and much more equipment are required.

demands are placed on workers and what needs to be done in the peak times and the off-peak times.

It is very helpful to identify where within the process and information flows customers have a chance to interact, or perhaps interfere, with the process. Thus, one should indicate in a good process flow diagram when and where the customer places the order, where he or she walks away with the service, and how during the course of service provision he or she may be able to interact with the service process itself, and perhaps to modify what the service process provides.

PROCESS AND INFORMATION FLOW DIAGRAMS

A process flow diagram is a depiction of what the process does. It is a sequential depiction, noting which operations steps are accomplished before others and which can be done in parallel fashion. Different types of operations are typically designated with different symbols. Figure 3–1 depicts the process flow diagram from Tour C in the back of this book, the repair operations of Ogle–Tucker Buick.

Several points about the diagram ought to be noted:

1. Actual processing operations are usually distinguished from storage points or inspection steps in the process. In the diagram, different symbols take on different meanings.[2]

   Rectangle—a process step, an activity where something is accomplished

   Triangle—where an inventory exists or where the order or process comes to a halt and waits for something else to happen

   Circle—an inspection step

   Diamond—a decision point, usually with at least two paths (yes and no decisions) leading away from it

   Arrows—to show how the elements of the process flow fit together

2. Several operations could be bypassed and are indicated by two arrows emanating from one operation and pointing to others. For example, when a car fails the road test by management, it skips back to work by the technician.

   In addition, activities that can be done in parallel can be differentiated from activities that must be accomplished sequentially.

---

[2]Rectangles are used here because it is easier to fit the descriptions in them. However, typically in industrial engineering, circles are used to indicate processing operations and rectangles are used to indicate tests and inspections.

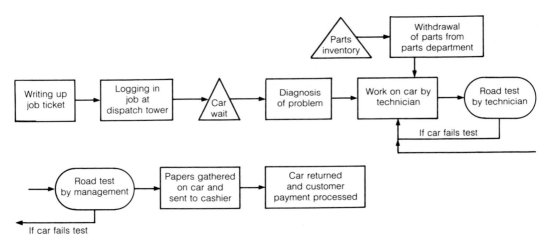

Figure 3–1   The Process Flow at Ogle–Tucker Buick.

3. The steps that are accomplished in the presence of the customer can be elevated in the diagram to a separate level so as to make it very clear when the customer can enter into the service process. (See Figure 3-3.) Thus, a service process flow diagram might include a lower half that tackles the back-of-the-house activities and an upper half that indicates when a customer has contact with the process.[3]

A production process is more than a series of operations performed on a collection of materials. What a process flow diagram can depict—the sequencing of process steps, the choice of equipment and technology, the capacity of process steps, the tasks required of the workforce—although critical, is only part of the story. Another part of the story involves the procedures that have been put in place to direct the process flow. We can usefully think of a companion to the process flow diagram—namely, an information flow diagram. Figure 3–2 provides an example of what might be placed in such a diagram, again for Ogle–Tucker Buick. Note how the actions of different layers of managers and workers are distinguished in the diagram and how information is fed back up the channels of communication.

The Importance of Process and Information
Flow Diagrams

Although simple in concept, process and information flow diagrams can be exceedingly helpful to companies. They can be used with vastly different levels

[3]This convention follows Lynn Shostack, who argues for this in what Shostack calls "blueprinting" a service operation. See, for example, G. Lynn Shostack, "Designing Services That Deliver," *Harvard Business Review*, January/February 1984: 133–139.

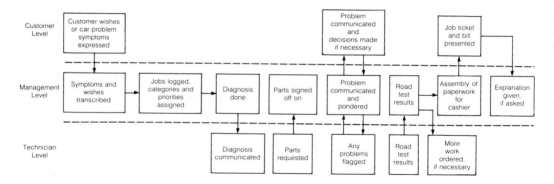

Figure 3–2 Information Flow at Ogle–Tucker Buick.

of detail. The flow charts above, for Ogle–Tucker Buick, are broad-brush representations of the process. If you wanted to examine the processes in detail, with the goal of redefining how workers actually did the job, then you would want to construct process and information flow charts in much finer detail. For example, the initial write-up of the auto repair order by the service writer, shown as a single box in the broad-brush flow chart above, could be broken down into such steps as:

1. Greet the customer.
2. Ascertain customer name.
3. Ascertain car registration number from examining windshield.
4. Enter car and take odometer reading.
5. Take this information to the service desk terminal for entry into the computer.
6. Enter data into the computer and wait for printout on the car that gives car's history and suggests maintenance items consistent with the car's odometer reading and the time since the last service.
7. Customer waits by the car during this sequence.
8. Service writer returns to the customer with printout.
9. Service writer quizzes customer on what the customer would like serviced and on what appears to be the problems/symptoms of the car.
10. Examine the car, if required.
11. Service writer makes initial decisions about the type of service that could or should be performed.
12. Communicate these decisions to the customer and make a joint determination about what is to be done to the car.
13. Suggestions are made for any additional service that would make sense to perform.

14. Final review with the customer on what is to be done with the car and the timing options for picking the car up.
15. Customer signs the work order.
16. Determine whether the customer has transportation from the dealership, and if not, whether the dealership can help.
17. End contact with the customer and say good-bye.
18. Enter car and place control number on car's rear-view mirror.
19. Return paperwork to the dispatch tower, thus initiating service on the car.

Most of these steps are front-office steps, in complete contact with the customer, but some, if only briefly, entail back-office work. See Figure 3–3.

Note that another symbol has been added: the diamond, the symbol classically associated with a decision point in the flow. In more fine-grained depictions of a process, a decision point is frequently encountered and can be depicted with this symbol, showing how the path of the process is altered when the decision goes one way or another.

In working with this finer grained detail, as well as with any flow chart, one can add a variety of useful statistics that help to define the process and its problems and capabilities:

- *Capacities.* One can categorize the capacities of each step along the way. Hence, one might want to check the capacities of the workforce performing these steps (the service writers in this case) and of the equipment, if any, that they work with (the computer and the printer).
- *Time taken.* How long does it take to perform certain tasks, on average? How great a variance is possible in performing them? How long does the customer wait? How long does it take to transport people, materials, or information? How long does the entire process take?
- *Workforce involved.* To perform these tasks, how many workers are involved? (An information flow diagram would indicate how the workforce is alerted to the tasks needed.)
- *Quality yields.* It may be the case that as the process proceeds, quality yields could be expected to drop. How severe is any fall-off in yields, usually measured for consistency as so-called first-pass yields?
- *Values or costs built up.* As the process progresses, costs (values) are built up. Such numbers, of course, reflect in part the workforce and quality yields involved, but other factors (equipment and materials costs) are also in play. By looking at this buildup, the company can see clearly where it is spending its money.

By tracking such statistics on the process or information flow chart itself, workers and management can easily examine things and begin questioning how things are done and how they might be improved. Typically, when companies engage in such flow-charting (sometimes termed *process mapping* or *blueprinting*),

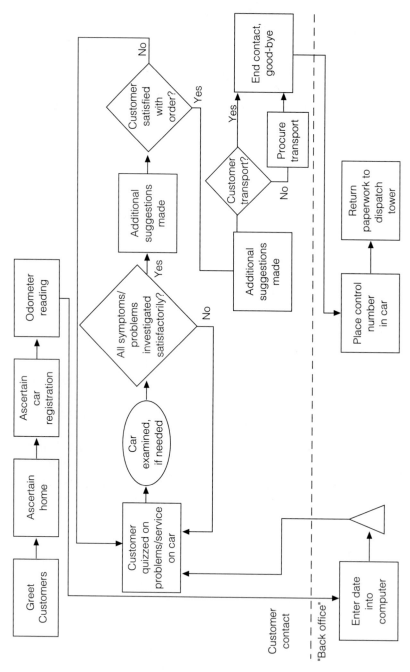

Figure 3–3 A More Detailed Process Flow Diagram for an Order Write-Up.

they begin with the charting of the as-is situation. This, in itself, is a useful task because different people (workforce vs. management, headquarters vs. the field) often have different concepts about how the process is accomplished. Getting agreement on exactly how things are currently done is frequently an important, eye-opening step in the improvement cycle.

With the as-is situation documented—and this is often done on big pieces of paper and hung on walls for people to examine easily—people can be free to question why some things are done as they are. Particularly useful in this regard is to question such steps as:

- Long waits, by customers especially, but also by workers in the system
- Long execution times
- Pass-offs of work or information from one worker to another, especially from one department to another or one location to another
- Generation of paperwork, particularly if multiple copies of that paperwork have to be routed to different people
- Generation of extraneous information that is not really needed by those who provide the service
- Steps where many different people get involved
- Steps where processing is held up for a decision, especially at a higher level
- Steps that involve lots of movement of people, customers, materials, or paperwork
- Steps that could be automated or computerized
- Steps that can be simplified, eliminated altogether, combined with other steps, rearranged, or standardized

By questioning such things and then by suggesting alternatives, usually alternatives that simplify the flow, reduce the number of people who handle the work, or call for lower levels to have more control over provision, the service delivery system can be improved.

Indeed, tools such as the process and information flow diagrams are essential to what is now termed *process re-engineering*. Countless companies have been awakened to the importance of regarding what they do as a series of processes of different types that can be flow-charted and questioned and then redone (re-engineered) for more efficient and effective service provision.

Some of the insights that can be generated from the use of flow charts is the topic of the next section on bottlenecks.

BOTTLENECKS

Bottlenecks are generally considered to be temporary blockades to increased output; they can be thrown up anywhere along the course of an operation. Some are easy to identify and to remedy, and others are devilish.

The bottleneck that is easy to cope with is stationary. Work or people pile up quickly behind it; clearly, little is getting through. Its cause is usually also clear—a machine has broken down or key workers are absent or demand has simply out-stripped the clear, rated capacity of the process—and the remedy follows easily. Such bottlenecks often occur in service operations, causing customer waits.

More subtle are bottlenecks that shift from one part of the process to another or that have no clear cause. Inventories of people or materials build up in different places and at different times. Such bottlenecks creep up on manage-ment and demand more thorough investigation. Perhaps they were detected as flaws in a service's quality caused inadvertently by one or more workers trying to keep pace with demands that should not have been placed on them. Or they may be caused by missing items. They may be caused by new procedures or by changes in the types of services provided. In such cases, the remedies are less clear-cut and some analysis is called for.

In analyzing bottlenecks, it is always helpful to trace the production process by using a process flow diagram and to assign capacity numbers to each stage of the process. Simply being systematic in this way and being as precise as possible with capacity measures can uncover primary and secondary bottlenecks imme-diately. Such an analysis is naturally easier with well-delineated processes and ones where capacity is unambiguous. The process flow diagram, in that case, becomes a planning aid for breaking significant, stationary bottlenecks. It also aids in the design of processes themselves, as it clearly shows how the capacities of process segments can be balanced against one another.

With this in mind, many services have structured their processes so that demand on the process can be segregated and dealt with individually. Consider the following proposition.

Proposition:
Small can be beautiful. Flows can be aided by chopping things up (triage).

Often, one's ability to react well at the peak is a function of the process's ability to keep things simple. Thus, the small operation that has been focused on a particular task can often do much better during the peak times than more complicated, large-scale operations. What is important to control is the flow of goods and information in the service process, and these flows are often enhanced by keeping them short and simple, and perhaps by designating certain types of services for certain types of processes. This is triage, where certain categories of demand are handled in ways different from other categories of demand.

Triage is more likely to be seen in service than in manufacturing. If one can identify the customer's particular needs early in the delivery process and assign that customer to a specific service path through the process, often customer satisfaction, time, and productivity are enhanced. Hospitals use triage in their emergency rooms. Often, triage is used when you phone in to find out informa-tion about your bank account or mutual fund, and furthermore, it is done in automated fashion to smooth out the delivery.

There is great potential in process flow-charting and its analysis. Traditionally, service operations' process and information flows have only seldom been analyzed systematically, and seemingly minor adjustments in the service delivery process can frequently yield significant improvements.

More than this, understanding bottlenecks in a service business is important because many service businesses make their money during peak times and not steadily through the nonpeak times, as many manufacturing enterprises do. Thus, knowing how to study and cope with bottlenecks is a key endeavor for services. Consider the following proposition:

Proposition:
> Peak for the peak. Efficiency really only counts then. Average measures usually don't tell the story.

For many service operations, real revenue gains and profitability occur during the peak operations, not during the off-peak. This makes it absolutely critical that the operation be as efficient as it can be. Usually there is little lost during off-peak operations if efficiency is down. But if efficiency is not at a high level when the peak comes, then opportunity costs are incurred left and right as potential sales walk away from a long waiting line or as quality declines with the volume that is being placed on the process. This, in turn, means that if one is going to evaluate a process, one needs to develop measures that evaluate it during the peak times. This often means that average measures that cover both peak and off-peak times are not very informative about the true capabilities of the process to earn money when the peak times come.

Where should excess capacity be kept?   The fact that peak-period sales are often crucial for a service business and cannot be anticipated with a buildup of inventory raises the important issue of whether some excess capacity ought to be kept, and if so, how much. We should realize that in certain circumstances, especially those that relate to peak periods, excess capacity is a very desirable thing. However, perfect balance—with no obvious bottlenecks— may well *not* be the most appropriate state for a service process.

There are several reasons for holding excess capacity in particular locations in the process:

1. Holding excess capacity in the early stages of the process:

   If quality yields drop off the further one goes in the process, having excess capacity early on is useful.

   If changes to the service are easy to make late in the process, excess capacity earlier may be desired.

2. Holding excess capacity in the late stages of the process:

   If changes to the service are hard to make late in the process, excess capacity later is desirable.

3. Other reasons for holding excess capacity anywhere in the process:

Often capacity additions entail large, fixed-increment ("lumpy") invest-ments. This can force you to hold excess capacity.

Sometimes capacity is cheap to build. If growth is expected, often it makes sense to hold excess capacity for what is cheap to build. This can work especially well if, over time, the bottleneck segment of the process can be broken by taking small, incremental steps.

THE CAUSES OF BOTTLENECKS

At this point, and for no matter what type of service operation, it makes sense to discuss why bottlenecks occur. Such a discussion helps put several concepts in perspective. Of course, we cannot hope to cover all the remedies to the problems that cause bottlenecks. Nevertheless, outlining the most common causes of bottlenecks helps build appreciation for some of the topics to follow.

Bottlenecks can be divided into two types: chronic, recurring ones and ones more episodic in character. Of course, individual bottleneck episodes can easily develop into chronic problems. Episodic bottlenecks call on the "fire fighting" skills of the workers and managers involved, whereas chronic bottlenecks demand more planning or design changes.

Episodic Bottlenecks

Episodic bottlenecks can be classed into three major categories: (1) machine breakdowns, (2) material shortages, and (3) labor shortages. Let us consider these bottlenecks in more detail

1. *Equipment breakdowns.* Perhaps the biggest of the fires to fight in a service operation are pieces of equipment that break down (be they computers or other more mundane but necessary machines for the provision of the service). When this happens, lots of scurrying around occurs to fix the broken equipment and to reroute, if possible, the order it was supposed to perform.

Some equipment breakdowns represent unavoidable accidents. On the other hand, many breakdowns can be prevented with some planning and preventive action. Preventive maintenance is a too-frequently neglected activity; there is never enough time for it when business is booming (so it is claimed), and it is a low priority item when business is faltering. Breakdown time often exceeds the planned downtime of preventive maintenance, and planned downtime is naturally easier to cope with and does not present the quality problems that surround breakdowns. Putting the operation's best maintenance tradespeople on the task of preventing breakdowns is increasingly being recognized as the most cost-effective policy.

2. *Material shortages.* If unplanned equipment downtime is the biggest of the fires fought, materials shortage is arguably the most common. The typical operation always seems to be short some item or material that is a facilitating good for the process. Sometimes it is traceable to a vendor; sometimes another department within the company is responsible.

3. *Labor shortages.* Unexpected absences, retirements, and terminations are all examples of how an operation can be temporarily short of workers. This tends to be more of a problem for some types of service operations, particularly those that rely on part-time workers anyway, but it has an impact for all.

Allied with this problem is the job bumping that is endemic to operations when there are many labor grades and when the most senior workers can bid for job openings in the next higher grade (these tend to be old, established service operations and ones that have historically been unionized). The cascade of job openings created by workers moving up to the next grade can be many times the number of jobs initially vacated. The residual problem is that lots of workers require training for their new positions and initially are not as productive as they will become. Significant job bumping has much the same effect as a labor shortage.

Chronic bottlenecks.   Chronic bottlenecks, much like episodic ones, can be categorized. Chronic bottlenecks can be thought of in terms of materials problems and process problems.

Materials Problems.

1. *Ordering the wrong materials or not enough materials.* This potentially recurring problem suggests deficiencies in planning or in purchasing. Not all vendor shortages are caused by the vendor; some can be traced to late or incorrect purchase orders, poor forecasting of needs, incorrect specifications, inappropriate inventory policies, myopic planning, unwillingness to release the funds, and the like.

2. *Constantly changing mix of things to do.* Even if the planning and purchasing people are on their toes, there could be bottlenecks simply because a constantly changing mix of things to do places irregular demands on the capacity of the process. That is, in aggregate the operation might have enough capacity, but the character of that capacity does not fit the mix of activities required of the process.

Process Problems.

1. *Insufficient capacity.* Often, it is not merely a problem of the mix of activities being inappropriate in the short term for the capacity in place. Rather, the demand, in the aggregate, may well exceed capacity. In this case, if the bottleneck is to be broken, capacity must be increased with more equipment, people, and perhaps new construction.

2. *Quality problems.* Quality problems may lead to episodes such as those associated with labor shortages or equipment breakdowns. If the fundamental causes of quality problems are not remedied, however, the problems become chronic.

3. *Poor layout.* One of the key aspects of a process is its layout. Poor layouts—those with crowded conditions, lengthy walks between people who need to interact with one another, convoluted routings of paperwork and information, difficult and costly materials handling, and the like—can be a terrible drain on an operation's productivity.

4. *Inflexible process.* Some bottlenecks turn out to be chronic because of the process design. In these cases, a bottleneck is designed into the process or is exposed by some shift in the pattern of demand. A classic reason for inflexibility is the purchase or development of a large, general-purpose piece of equipment or of a computerized system that is supposed to do a series of tasks. If the equipment or software delivers as expected, all is well. However, often such process designs run amok because the equipment or software does not deliver or is very temperamental. Because so much depends on it, when the equipment or system fails, the rest of the process becomes crippled. Better, in many people's eyes, to design a process of smaller scale that is less dependent on large-scale equipment or software.

REMEDYING BOTTLENECKS

Deciding how to remedy a bottleneck calls for an analysis of the costs associated with each of the options available. Specifically, the analysis involves comparing the *extra* costs incurred by each alternative because those were the only costs that differ between the options being considered. This is an important lesson. This type of analysis and the role of demand as well as supply considerations in confronting bottlenecks is pursued in the following example situation.

SITUATION 3–1

Citrus Airlines

Larry Klock had to confess that he hadn't thought of it, but his operations manager, Dave Dove, had proposed an intriguing, possible solution to Citrus Airlines' present shortage of seats. Larry was the president of Citrus Airlines, a small intrastate carrier serving Miami, Jacksonville, Orlando, Fort Lauderdale, Tampa, Tallahassee, and a host of smaller Florida cities. Recently, business had been booming, largely, Larry thought, because of an upturn in the economy. Citrus Airlines was using much of its equipment to the hilt and faced the prospect of having to purchase more in order to provide more seats. Larry was leery of this option because of the tenuousness of the current economic recovery and the comparatively recent financial good health of the airline. Dave Dove's proposal struck an imaginative middle ground.

Dove had proposed that Citrus eliminate first-class seating on all of the Boeing 727s Citrus owned. (The 727s operated primarily between the major Florida cities, averaging 91 flights each day.) Eliminating first class would create space for more seats. According to the cabin configuration of seats that Citrus had always maintained, 20 of the plane's total of 125 seats were provided for first-class passengers. If the first-class cabin were reconfigured to conform to the coach cabin, an additional eight seats could be provided. These seats could be added because coach sat five across in each row of the airplane (instead of four across, as in each first-class row) and because the distance between rows in coach was slightly less (less legroom) than in first class. Dove estimated that it would cost $15,000 to alter each of the fifteen 727s in Citrus' fleet.

Of course, eliminating first class meant eliminating first-class fares as well.

At present, the average first-class fare in the Citrus system was $71, as opposed to the average coach fare of $56. On the other hand, first class was a little more costly to serve, an average of $3.28 versus $1.77, because first-class food and beverage service was more elaborate.

Larry was concerned that the elimination of first-class service would adversely affect the patronage of Citrus' first-class travelers, even though Larry knew that the availability of more seats could mean substantially more revenue. To investigate these matters, Larry called upon Sarah Hammans, the airline's marketing manager. Hammans' report is shown in Figure 3–4.

Dave Dove's suggestion about eliminating first-class service would surely help cut down on the number of flights that leave standbys behind, but Larry Klock couldn't help but wonder whether that benefit would offset the costs of reconfiguring the first-class cabins and of losing loyal first-class passengers.

MEMORANDUM

To: Larry Klock
From: Sarah Hammans
Subject: Elimination of First-Class Seating on 727s

You asked for analysis of two points related to the elimination of our "sun-kissed" (first-class) service. Let me address them in turn.

1. Retention of "sun-kissed" travelers. Although our retention rates will vary by city-pair depending on our competition and the prevailing flight schedules, I think we would be hard-pressed to retain more than 60 percent if these travelers can go with another airline. If the loads continue high or if other airlines eliminate first class as well, we may retain them all. It's a tough call.

2. Current loads in first class and coach. Over the past two months (61 days) on our 727s, we have averaged a first-class load factor of 61.2 percent and a coach load factor of 82.9 percent.* The distribution of flights by load factor over the same period is shown in the table below:

			Incidence of Load Factors (percent of 727 flights)					
"Sun-kissed"	LESS THAN 50%	50– 60%	60– 70%	70– 80%	80– 90%	90– 100%	1–5 STANDBYS LEFT	MORE THAN 5 STANDBYS LEFT
Service	42.3%	11.6%	12.7%	13.8%	10.9%	7.7%	1.0%	—
Coach	16.4%	10.4%	10.7%	11.3%	20.9%	18.3%	7.4%	4.6%

NOTE: The load factor (the occupied seats as a percentage of all available seats) is a useful capacity measure, not only for airlines but for many other types of service businesses..

Figure 3–4 The Report on Eliminating First Class on Citrus Airlines' 727.

Discussion of Citrus Airlines

Citrus Airlines is experiencing a bottleneck. Given the heavy loads it has been carrying recently, an increasing number of standbys have been left at the airport. The heavy loads and the high number of completely booked flights have no doubt caused a number of customers to switch flight times or even airlines. If such a strong demand continues, Citrus may be well advised to add equipment and offer more flights.

As a way around the current bottleneck, Dave Dove has suggested that Citrus can fly eight more seats on every flight if first-class service is eliminated. This change has some real appeal. Not only does it solve the present oversubscription of some flights, but Citrus could conceivably make more money by flying an all-coach airplane.

How is this true? For every first-class passenger under the present scheme, the airline receives $71, on the average, and expends only $3.28 on services. The company thus stands to gain $67.72 for every first-class passenger. This is money it can use to pay back its debt on the planes and other facilities and the overhead it buys. This money is also the source of its profits. The figure ($67.72) is an important one; it is known as the contribution per first-class passenger.

Contribution and variable cost. Technically, *contribution* is the difference between a company's revenue and its so-called variable costs. Variable costs, as the name suggests, are the costs that vary directly with production activity. Drinks and dinners served on airlines are variable costs because they are only expenses to the airline when passengers are in their seats to drink and eat them.

These variable costs are easy to see, largely because they can be readily assigned to the units of output that people pay for, such as airplane tickets. The variability of other costs may not be quite so neat. For example, are flight attendants' salaries a variable cost? Salaries are certainly variable when it comes to devising the schedule of flights; more flights mean more flight crews. But once the flight schedule is set, the salaries paid flight attendants do not vary with the number of passengers. In terms of our situation at Citrus Airlines, the revamping of airplanes to eliminate the first-class cabin does not alter the flight schedule or the number of flight crews. Crew salaries, then, are fixed and only materials expenses are variable in this instance. This example serves to illustrate that one must be careful to determine which costs are fixed and which are variable with the particular production activity under consideration.

The $67.72 contribution per first-class passenger goes to pay crew salaries as well as to pay off airplane costs, ticketing, and a host of other costs that, for this decision, are fixed. Every additional passenger to first class who can be accommodated will contribute $67.72 to pay these fixed charges and to secure a profit for Citrus Airlines. Note that we can speak of contribution in a variety of forms. Total contribution is measured in dollars, as revenues minus all variable costs. Contribution per unit is total contribution per unit of output and is measured in dollars per unit. In using this notion of contribution, both total contribution and contribution per unit supply the same information, but it is sometimes easier to think in terms of one rather than the other. What is essential, however, is that the costs that are considered variable be consistent with the nature of the decision for which the contribution figures are being used.

Back to Citrus Airlines.   At present, the contribution per first-class passenger is $67.72. The similarly calculated contribution per coach passenger is $54.23 ($56 − $1.77). Given both an empty first-class seat and an empty coach one, Citrus Airlines would naturally prefer to have a first-class passenger. The issue, however, is not which type of passenger the airline prefers, but whether Citrus Airlines should eliminate its first-class seating.

At present, a full cabin of 20 "sun-kissed" travelers contributes $1354.40 (20 seats × $67.72 contribution per passenger). If these 20 seats were eliminated and replaced by 28 coach seats, the total contribution would be $1518.44 (28 seats × $54.23 contribution per passenger). Thus, if Citrus Airlines can be assured of filling its converted first-class cabin with coach travelers, the company will make more money than it currently does—$164.04 ($1518.44 − $1354.40) per flight more.

We can easily see that the $15,000 cost of cabin conversion can be paid off in just 92 flights. To wit:

$$\$15,000 \text{ cost} = \$164.04 \text{ contribution/flight} \times x \text{ flights}$$
$$x = 92 \text{ flights}.$$

If each Citrus Airline plane flies one completely booked flight every four days, the cabin conversion cost would be paid off in a year.

This analysis suggests that Dave Dove's recommendation to convert the first-class cabin should be followed. Yet, on closer examination, this entire analysis hinges on the assumption that the additional eight seats placed in the converted first-class cabin will be occupied. It is not enough to state that the average load factor for coach is higher than the average load factor for first class or that, if the plane were full, more contribution would ensue if all seats were coach. The decision rests with what Citrus Airlines can expect will actually happen with the additional seats in the former first-class cabin. This mode of thinking about decisions concentrates on the incremental (often called marginal) change involved; the use of such marginal analysis is absolutely fundamental to management decision-making.

Marginal analysis and sunk costs.   The concept of marginal (incremental) analysis for decision making is not fancy. It's just common sense that finds application in one business situation after another. In basic terms, marginal analysis states that the decision to do something should depend only on how that decision would change the situation and on nothing else. The question to ask is not whether a company will be profitable after some investment or policy change has been implemented, but whether the company will be more profitable for having made the choice than it would otherwise have been. Everything that has gone on before is irrelevant to the decision at hand.

This kind of situation is all too common: A project is almost finished when it is recognized as a turkey. Because the finish is so close, someone argues that "for just a little more money the project could be completed and the investment outlays to date will not be wasted." Marginal analysis says that what has gone before is irrelevant; the costs incurred are "sunk" and have no bearing on the decision. If the additional investment it takes to complete the project does not return additional revenues that are greater, the investment should be junked. As the old saying goes, "Don't throw good money after bad." The saying is absolutely right; the "bad" money represents sunk costs, and they have no bearing on the decision whether or not to continue with a project.

Back again to Citrus Airlines.   Can Citrus Airlines fill enough of the additional eight seats so that the total contribution of an all-coach plane exceeds that of the present airplane configuration? We have some information from the marketing report memorandum.

In the first place, we know about the standbys that have been left behind. Assuming an average of two left behind in the "1–5" category and six left behind in the "more than 5" category, we can calculate the number of passengers that we could have been sure to seat on the 91 daily flights over the past 61 days. To wit:

$$61 \text{ days} \times 91 \text{ flights} \times 1\% \times 2 \text{ standbys/flight} = 111.02$$
$$61 \text{ days} \times 91 \text{ flights} \times 7.4\% \times 2 \text{ standbys/flight} = 821.55$$
$$61 \text{ days} \times 91 \text{ flights} \times 4.6\% \times 6 \text{ standbys/flight} = 1532.08$$

$$111.02 + 821.55 + 1532.08 = 2464.65 \text{ people.}$$

At a contribution per coach passenger of $54.23, these stranded passengers could have provided a total contribution of $133,660 in those two months if the first-class cabin had been remodeled.

This is not the full story, of course, because the previous first-class passengers must be accounted for. At best, Citrus Airlines will forgo the increased contribution that the first-class passengers made on all of the 727 flights. This opportunity cost is every bit as real a cost as the $15,000-per-plane conversion change. The difference in contribution is $13.49 ($67.72 − $54.23) per first-class passenger. Over the past two months, the total added contribution forgone (the opportunity cost of remodeling the cabin) would have been $916,568 (61 days × 91 flights × 20 seats × 61.2% load factor × $13.49).

This figure is naturally much larger than the gain in contribution from seating standbys in the eight additional seats provided by remodeling. The vast contribution gained by having first-class passengers on the flights that are not completely booked far outweighs the opportunity costs represented by standbys who could not get on existing flights. This comparison is all the more unfavorable to remodeling the first-class cabin if customers begin deserting the airline.

Given these considerations, Dave Dove's ingenious plan for increasing capacity and breaking a bottleneck does not appear to be attractive enough to implement.

Lessons from Citrus Airlines. The Citrus Airlines situation brings together three of the basic concepts that guide good decision making at all levels of a company.

1. Opportunity cost (revenue forgone)
2. Contribution and its companion concept, variable cost
3. Marginal analysis and its companion concept, sunk cost

A useful analysis of Citrus Airlines' decision on "sun-kissed" service demands that these concepts be melded together.

Let us review how each concept fits into the analysis of Citrus Airlines' situation:

1. *Opportunity cost.* By eliminating first class, the airline was forgoing the difference in contribution between "sun-kissed" service and coach service. This loss would be every bit as much a cost to the airline as the cabin conversion expense of $15,000 per plane.

2. *Contribution.* For an already scheduled flight, the cost of adding more passengers is small because all the expenses of flying are fixed except for the drinks and food the airline serves. Thus, variable costs are very low, and the contribution each passenger makes to pay off the fixed investment in equipment and salaries is high. Contribution (revenue minus variable costs) is the key statistic used in deciding the issue in this situation.

3. *Marginal analysis.* The decision about eliminating first-class service rested on the use of the additional eight seats put into the first-class cabin. Could the change they represented, including the opportunity cost incurred, be expected to generate enough contribution to pay off the added expense of converting that cabin?

BALANCE IN SERVICE OPERATIONS

All service operations, no matter what they are, need to be balanced. Although there may be a good argument to hold excess capacity somewhere in the process, a service cannot expect to be significantly out of balance and hope to be very profitable. The quantities and combinations of labor, space, and equipment need to be carefully considered.

This observation should be clear for the service factory. There, much as one finds in manufacturing, idleness in the workforce or buildups of work-in-process (such as paperwork, orders, or people waiting for things to get done) can be fairly easily detected and steps can be taken to improve the balance.

Spotting problems of balance is tougher in the service shop and the mass service operation. There, the pace of demand may be very erratic, and thus, balance may depend greatly on the degree of wait time that customers experience. (More on this in the next chapter.)

In all of these services, the extent of management supervision for the process is likely to be well-understood, at least historically, within the company, and thus in reasonable balance as well.

Balance in the professional service firm is somewhat more elaborate, and, for that reason, worthy of some extended discussion.

Balance in the professional service firm: The pyramid. Many professional service firms, such as law firms, accounting firms, consulting firms, advertising agencies, and a host of other professional associations, are organized in a special way. They are not structured as corporations, but as partnerships, and the way in which they are managed is distinctly different. The partners, in essence the owners of the business, are compensated not simply with salaries but with shares of the firm's income, once other salaries and expenses have been paid. The partnership shares are not publicly traded as one would find in most service firms, but derive their value from the earnings of the partnership. Typically, the partners have worked their way up from the lower ranks of the firm. Because one finds the partners at the apex, this type of organization is frequently termed the pyramid.

Let us examine in general terms the nature of the professional pyramid (Figures 3–5 and 3–6) as it applies in all sorts of professional service firms. (This discussion follows David Maister, who has done much of the original work in studying professional service firms.[4])

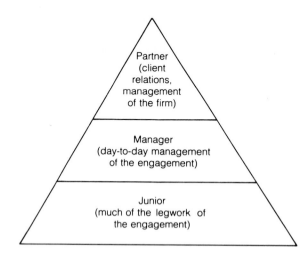

Figure 3–5 The Professional Service Pyramid.

Partner
(client relations, management of the firm)

Manager
(day-to-day management of the engagement)

Junior
(much of the legwork of the engagement)

[4]See Maister, David H., "Balancing the Professional Service Firm," *Sloan Management Review,* (Fall 1982): 15–29.

Source of the Firm's Competitive Advantage	Front-Room vs. Back-Room Operations		
		Back room	Front room
	Execution (Procedures)	**Pharmacy**	**Nursing**
	Experience (Grey Hair)		
	Expertise (Brainpower)	**Surgery**	**Psychiatry**

Maister's Professional Service Matrix. (*Source: Presentation by David Maister, Lausanne, Switzerland, 1987.*)

Maister studied different types of professional services whose characters and pyramids differ. He has devised a 2-by-2 matrix with some amusingly labeled quadrants. See the above figures.

Maister looks first at the common distinction of back room vs. front room. In the back room, the push is on technical skills and the content of the work, whereas in the front room, the stress is on interactive skills and the process of advising clients. The distinction, in part, is the distinction between consulting and consultation. Maister then also looks at a more subtle distinction, the source of the firm's competitive advantage. Here, he distinguishes among firms whose advantages are execution (procedure-driven), experience (grey hair-driven), and expertise (brainpower-driven).

Using these distinctions, Maister labels his quadrants with some intriguing and amusing medical terminology. The quadrant that stresses execution-experience in the back room resembles the pharmacy. The back-room operation that looks to both experience and expertise is more like surgery. The front-room operations are nursing and psychotherapy, one more attuned to execution-experience and the other more to experience-expertise.

Can we use these labels to distinguish among different professional service firms? Much of the audit attest services of accounting firms such as Arthur Andersen could be labeled as pharmacy work; juniors, properly supervised, can do much of the work. The other types of advising Arthur Andersen does, especially what the Andersen Consulting arm of the firm does, is surgery, depending more on insight and expertise than on following well-defined procedures.

Typical law firms and headhunter firms are more front-room in character, requiring both procedural execution and experience; they are nursing. A management consulting company such as McKinsey & Co. is more psycho-therapy, combining experience, expertise, and a good deal of interaction with the client.

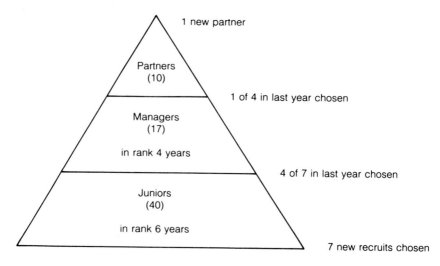

Figure 3–6 The pyramid and advancement.

For the sake of simplification, consider only three ranks of professionals: partner, manager, and junior. The partner is chiefly responsible for client relations and the running of the firm itself. The manager is the one responsible for the day-to-day activities of the project (sometimes called the engagement)—what there is to do, how it is to be done, and whether it is being done properly, on schedule, and within budget. The junior professional is assigned many of the tasks that constitute the legwork of the project. This dispersion of responsibility among partners, managers, and juniors has led some wags to label this hierarchy one of "finders, minders, and grinders."

Typically, the partners' income is high because they "leverage" their work with the work of the ranks below them in the pyramid. That is to say, the lower ranks create value that the upper ranks of the pyramid enjoy as increased income. That kind of carrot keeps many in the lower ranks eager to work their way up the ladder of the partnership. Naturally, if the pyramid is deep and broad, the partners at the top will enjoy larger incomes than if the pyramid is shallow and narrow.

What determines the shape of the pyramid—whether it is broad or narrow? The partners cannot simply will the shape of the pyramid. They are constrained by some important characteristics. In particular, there are two major determinants of the pyramid's shape:

• The composition of work on the projects undertaken.
• The utilization rates of the firm's professionals.

Let's explore these factors in greater detail. Assume, for example, that a typical project of 600 hours required certain time commitments from the firm's professionals and that the professionals were used on projects to the degree shown in the following table.

Professionals	Typical time commitment[a] (hours)	Utilization rate[a] (percent)
Partner	60	50
Manager	140	70
Junior	400	85
	600	

[a]These are meant to be illustrative and do not reflect figures for Arthur Andersen & Co., the subject of Tour E in the back of this book.

The utilization rates reflect the facts that other things take up professionals' time (training, recruiting, scheduling, counseling, soliciting new business) and that these other activities are relatively more demanding of the senior professionals in the firm. Given a planning figure of 2000 hours of work per person per year, one partner could sustain supervision of 16.67 average projects (calculated as 1000 hours of partner time available for projects divided by 60 hours of time per typical project, or 16.67 projects per year). A manager, on the other hand, could sustain direction of 10 projects (1400 hours available and 140 hours average for each project). Thus for the firm to be balanced, for every partner there have to be 1.67 managers. Similarly, a junior can work on 4.25 projects each year (1700 hours available and 400 hours for each project). In this way, the pyramid's shape is determined: Every partner supports 1.67 managers and 3.92 juniors.

The shape of the pyramid, in turn, largely determines the rate at which professionals can be advanced and how selective that advancement has to be. Assume, for example, that juniors are 6 years in rank and that managers are 4 years in rank. If there are 10 partners, the pyramid would look like Figure 3–6. Suppose that every year a partner has to be added, either to sustain the growth of the firm or to replace a partner who retires or otherwise leaves the firm. Every year, then, a manager has to be made a partner in order for the pyramid to be in balance. If, on average each year, 4 of the 17 managers are in the fourth year, the advancement rate has to be 1 in 4. Similarly, if during any year, four new managers are required and there are seven juniors in their final sixth year, then roughly half of the juniors can be promoted to manager status. In this way, the pyramid sustains itself. Of the 11 juniors and managers in their last year, 1 becomes a partner, 4 become managers, and 6 leave the firm. Of the 7 new recruits, only 1 can expect to make partner after 10 years.

When a professional service firm is growing at a rate consistent with the balance of its pyramid (in the above example, a new or replacement partner every year), then all is well. But suppose the firm wants to grow faster. More partners have to be created. This can be done by reducing the years that juniors and managers spend in their ranks, or it can be done by increasing the percentage of juniors and managers who are promoted. If the years in rank are reduced, the firm risks promoting people who have not learned all they should, perhaps, or have not experienced all the diversity in their jobs that they need to. If greater percentages are advanced, then the firm risks promoting people whose skills and talent may not be thoroughly up to the task.

Suppose, on the other hand, that the business does not expand as expected, or actually declines. How does the firm cope then? The firm typically extends the years in rank for juniors and managers and the percentages advanced start to shrink. Both of these measures, although understandable, can leave the juniors and managers increasingly disenchanted, and, perhaps, more willing to seek employment outside the firm.

Bottlenecks in Space and Time: Layouts and Variability

Chapter 4

The previous chapter addressed bottlenecks and balance in the process and introduced some tools for analyzing those concepts. There is more to discuss, however—two more concepts and some associated tools that have been ignored to date. These concepts relate to space (layouts) and time (variability). These topics round out the discussion of the important, interrelated topics of flows, bottlenecks, and balance.

LAYOUTS AND BOTTLENECKS

In the last chapter, we discussed the use of process and information flow diagrams as tools for identifying and analyzing bottlenecks. Those tools look essentially at process elements, their capacities, and the time involved. What those tools ignore, however, is the spatial aspect—how materials and people move from point to point in the operation. This geography is too important to ignore. As noted previously, bottlenecks can be created from poor layouts. Poor layouts can

Interrupt the physical flow of materials, including paperwork.

Add direct labor time to the service.

Introduce excessive handling of materials with the risk of damage and loss, or excessive "handling" of people.

Create excessive queues of customers or of work-in-process inventory (such as paperwork).

Keep workers and managers at a distance from one another when in fact they should be close.

Increase the time it takes to deliver the service.

Increase any time it may take to set up for one service after providing another.

Add to overhead.

Crowd departments into too little space.

Contribute to poor housekeeping.

Make any expansion more difficult to accomplish.

Otherwise add costs to the operation.

Some poor layouts are born, but most are made. That is, some poor layouts are bad designs from the beginning, but most poor layouts develop bit by bit over time as one change after another is made. New services are introduced and the space they need is hurriedly assigned. New equipment is purchased and a place is quickly found for it so that the rest of the process is not disturbed while it is debugged. The operation's layout is expanded, but to avoid disruption, it is not completely re-laid out; only a few areas are. In these ways, over time, bottlenecks are built into the process and its layout.

Types of Layouts

In manufacturing, materials handling is an important consideration. Layouts, therefore, are designed to facilitate the movement of materials and the routing of products through the factory. With this in mind, three main types of layouts have been concocted for manufacturing:

- *Job shop layouts.* A job shop is designed to produce anything, even in small quantities. To accomplish this, like equipment is grouped together and materials are routed from one department to another, anywhere at anytime.
- *Product-specific layouts.* These apply to most other manufacturing. Here, a particular product and the materials for it are routed along the same path. Different equipment is grouped together and the products are worked on sequentially by the equipment in place.
- *Fixed-position layouts.* Here, the products are usually so big or so delicate (airplanes, other defense and aerospace-related products) that they cannot be moved from workstation to workstation easily, so it makes sense to move the materials to the product, which stays put in a fixed position.

Only for the service factory—where back-office work dominates—do these layout types make a lot of sense. Only there is the movement of materials of real importance to the operation. For other types of service operations, the front-office work is of particular importance, and thus, the movement of people frequently dominates the movement of materials.

In the service shop, the fixed-position layout can be important, particularly if the service is a repair operation (hospitals, auto service). There, as in aerospace, the movement of the "product" being worked on (human being, car) is either impossible or difficult, so materials for the service are brought to the "product" being worked on.

In mass service operations, such as retailing, the presentation of materials is typically much more important than their movement. More consideration is given the customer and his or her environment than the cost of handling merchandise. Mass service operations are more concerned with the flow of people than with the flow of any facilitating goods or paperwork controls. (It is intriguing that only for the so-called warehouse stores is materials handling important; there, customers are willing to forgo some of the amenities usually associated with retailing in order to save money.)

Professional service firms are least affected by layouts. The layouts they offer tend to be general purpose in nature, and thus are most likely to resemble the manufacturing job shop. There may be different departments where workers doing a particular task are grouped together. In an advertising agency, for example, creative people are typically housed in a distinctive location apart from the research or media people. The same is true for a health clinic or an accounting firm (tax people are segregated from audit or consulting people).

Devising New Layouts

The industrial engineering of layout design is both art and science. It is beyond the scope of this book to explain in any depth the techniques used to develop new layouts or to improve existing ones. We will merely outline some key steps one can take in devising layouts for services:

1. *Examining the process flow.* Is there a dominant flow? What is it? What constraints to layout exist because of the process itself?
2. *Gauging the extent and importance of the flows.* How much material and information travels from one element of the process to another? Which flows are so important that close proximity is absolutely required?
3. *Determining area space needs.* How much space do particular operations or departments require? Are there special constraints to be aware of, such as with any existing structures?
4. *Arranging the layout.* What kinds of layouts satisfy the nature and extent of the flows within the process and do so within the space constraints specified? Which ones may be more flexible, or perhaps more streamlined, than others?
5. *Determining traffic flows.* What are the prevailing traffic patterns around and within the process? Do they intersect or otherwise threaten to cause congestion or compromise safety? Do the traffic patterns enhance sales opportunities?

There are computer models that use information on distance between operations, frequency of use, and special constraints to devise a trial layout.

These computer models try to minimize the distance traveled by those using the layout. Although interesting, these models are not widely used. Most layouts are devised through the application of common sense and trial and error.

VARIABILITY AND BOTTLENECKS: THE QUEUING PHENOMENON

So far we have not dealt with the impact of statistical uncertainty on bottlenecks. We have treated everything as if all were certain. Yet life tells us all the time that we live amid statistical uncertainty, and service processes are no exception. The remainder of this chapter is devoted to exploring what uncertainty does to services. The gist of this chapter can be encapsulated in the following proposition:

Proposition:

People don't like to wait, so know when the "big queue" is going to hit, and, if possible, keep excess capacity.

Corollary: If people have to wait, you can't give them enough hocus pocus.

Just like poor quality, a long wait for a service can destroy one's relationship with a customer, so it is absolutely essential for a service provider to know when peak times occur and how peak times are likely to affect customer waiting. It is very important to choose capacity in such a way that long waiting lines do not become routine, and thus a drag on the service process's ability to satisfy customers. This means in turn that if customers have to wait, you want to do all in your power to make the perceived wait as short as possible. There are many tricks one can employ to take people's minds off waiting, and these tricks need to be studied dutifully in cases where peak operations and long waiting lines are unavoidable.

There are a variety of ways by which statistical uncertainty or variability can intrude on a service process. However, we can usually divide such intrusions into those that affect the demand for the process—that is, the timing or the quantity of items for the process to work on—and those that affect the supply of the process—that is, the speed, capacity, quality, and capability of the process itself. Any of these variabilities can cause the process to lose some of its ability to produce products at a given level of quality or quantity.

Moreover, we know that the greater the variability involved with the demand or the supply side of the process, the greater the disruption to the process and the greater the likelihood that a significant bottleneck will occur. This unhappy state of affairs is an inevitable consequence of the phenomenon of queuing.

Perhaps the most important thing to understand about queuing phenomena is that as a process's capacity utilization nears 100 percent, waiting times grow at an increasing rate.[1] Figure 4–1 illustrates this truism, which has been observed in countless different situations where there is uncertainty about the

---

[1]Formally, the relationship in the figure is a hyperbola of the form $1/x$ where x is the difference between 100 percent utilization and the actual utilization.

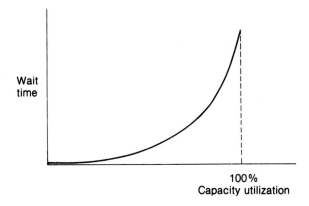

FIGURE 4–1 Wait Time Versus Capacity Utilization in Queuing Situations.

demand on the process or uncertainty about the capabilities of the process to do whatever it is supposed to do.

What is even more troubling, however, is that processes subject to particularly uncertain demand—such as some service shops and many professional services—will have waiting times increase at a faster rate than processes whose demands are more certain and less variable. The more demand-uncertain processes will have waiting times that look more like Curve *A* in Figure 4–2 than Curve *B*. They have a greater need for excess capacity than more demand-certain processes do.

Similarly, processes whose supply is more variable—whose capabilities are more erratic—will suffer the same fate: curves more like *A* than *B*. These service operations are likely to be ones that provide more opportunities for customization or interaction with customers (service shops and professional services) and those that have more labor-intensive processes. Thus, the service factory is apt to look more like Curve *B*, while the other quadrants of the service process matrix are likely to look more like Curve *A*.

Variability of all kinds saps capacity from a process and can cause shifting bottlenecks and buildups of inventory. Service providers can thus increase process capacities merely by figuring out ways to quell the variability in demand or supply (narrow the variance) that the process is subject to, without adding more equipment or labor. There are now a number of simulation programs on the market than can help discover the kinds of queue buildups and capacity breakdowns that uncertainty can bring and what can be done about them. Improvements in quality and process capabilities can lower variability as well.

Of course, excess capacity is an important consideration for many processes and all the more important when variability is great. Thus, some service processes *should* have lower capacity utilizations than other processes. Only then could the operation be expected to operate well enough to keep waiting times to satisfactory levels.[2]

[2]Ashton, J. E., and Cook, F. X., Jr., "Time to Reform Job Shop Manufacturing," *Harvard Business Review* 67, no. 2 (March–April 1989): pp. 106–11.

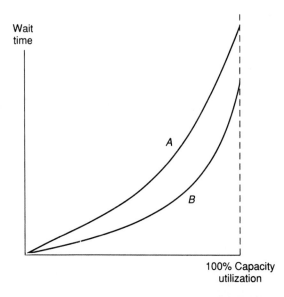

FIGURE 4–2 In Some Situations, Wait Time Goes Up Faster than in Other Situations.

The General Anatomy of Waiting Line Problems

There is a tremendous variety of waiting line problems that can afflict the service operation, due to the many combinations of the following types of characteristics they can exhibit:

1. The arrival (or input) process

   What kind of distribution do the arrivals follow? A popular, and useful, distribution to employ is the Poisson (discussed later), although others can be used.

   Do the arrivals come singly or do they sometimes also come in bulk? (Think of customers waiting to be seated at a restaurant in parties of one, two, three, four, and more.)

   Does the length of any line serve as a deterrent to arrivals, or will the arrivals all simply take their chances?

2. Queue discipline (the order in which arrivals are served)

   First come, first served? Last come, first served? Random?

   Are arrivals permitted to leave the waiting line? If so, what characterizes their leaving ("reneging")?

3. The service process

   What types of probability distribution describes how arrivals are served by the process? Is the rate of service a constant, or is it also a stochastic event, like the arrival rate? Clearly, in many types of service situations the amount of time a service employee must spend with a customer can vary markedly; we have all kicked ourselves for choosing the wrong line at the bank, ticket counter, or supermarket.

Is there more than one line? How many?

Must arrivals go from service person or station to service person or station, or can one handle all of an arrival's needs?

A mixed system includes more than one line (sometimes called a channel) and more than one person or station (sometimes called a phase). What kinds of paths through any mixed systems are there?

With so many possibilities for the arrival and service processes and the queue discipline, it is easy to appreciate that most queuing problems are tackled by either (1) simplifying the problem so that mathematically tractable means can be applied, or (2) using computer simulation techniques to mimic what we think the true behavior is and draw out its implications.

The Poisson Distribution and Some Useful Formulas

It has been discovered that many ordinarily occurring phenomena—radioactive decay, calls coming into a telephone switchboard, as well as people or trucks entering lines—come close to obeying a particular kind of probability distribution called the Poisson distribution, named for the French mathematician who first studied it in 1837.

According to the Poisson distribution, the probability that exactly k events (e.g., phone calls or people entering a line) will occur in a time period of length t is equal to

$$\frac{e^{-\lambda t}(\lambda t)^k}{k!}$$

where e is the base of the natural logarithms (e $\approx$ 2.71828) and $k!$ (k factorial) means $k(k-1)(k-2)\cdots1$. As it turns out, this distribution has a mean (arithmetic average) of (λt) and a variance of (λt) as well.[3] We can think of λ (the Greek lowercase letter lambda) as indicating the arrival rate, the number of events that occur per unit of time t. This arrival rate, λ, is a key component of the various waiting line formulas that can be applied.

---

[3]The variance of a distribution, $f(\ )$, of a random variable, x, is a measure of how dispersed the distribution is. It is obtained by squaring each deviation of x from the mean, $\bar{x}$, and weighting the squared deviations by their corresponding probabilities. Symbolically, for a discrete distribution of N values, the variance (var x) can be written as

$$\text{var } x = \sum_{i=1}^{N} P_i(x_i - \bar{x})^2,$$

where P_i is the probability that x_i occurs. Alternatively, it may be written as

$$\text{var } x = \sum_{i=1}^{N} P_i(x_i^2) - \bar{x}^2.$$

The standard deviation is another way to express the dispersion of a distribution. It is merely

$$\text{standard deviation } s_x = \sqrt{\text{var } x}.$$

The standard deviation has the advantage that it is measured in the same units as the random variable x itself.

The Poisson distribution anchors the simplest formulas for examining waiting lines and their performance. The performance of the simplest waiting line case, where there is one line (or channel) and one station (or phase), can be described by the formulas in Table 4–1. These formulas depend on λ (the arrival rate) and μ (the service rate, which is defined in exactly analogous fashion to λ). Naturally, μ must be greater than λ; otherwise, the service could never catch up with the arrival rate, and an ever-growing waiting line would result.

These formulas can help to explain the important results depicted in Figure 4–2. Take, for example, the formula for the mean time in the system, $1/(\mu-\lambda)$. If we substitute x for $(\mu-\lambda)$, the formula can be collapsed to

$$\text{mean time in system} = 1/x,$$

which is easily seen to be a hyperbola. That is precisely what curves A and B are—hyperbolas. Those curves are of the form

$$y = a/x,$$

where y is the waiting time, x is the difference between the service and the arrival rates, and a is an index of the variability of both the arrival and service processes.[4] The greater the value of a, the greater the variability of either the arrival rates or the service rates or both, and the further away Curve A is from Curve B, and thus the greater penalty paid in waiting time for not having excess capacity.

TABLE 4–1 FORMULAS DESCRIBING THE PERFORMANCE
OF A SINGLE-CHANNEL, SINGLE-PHASE WAITING LINE
WITH POISSON ARRIVAL AND SERVICE RATES

λ (the lowercase Greek letter lambda) = arrival rate (such as units entering the line per hour)

μ (the lowercase Greek letter mu) = service rate (such as units processed from the line per hour)

Average utilization = λ/μ

Mean number in the waiting line = $\lambda^2/(\mu(\mu-\lambda))$

Mean number in the entire system = $\lambda/(\mu-\lambda)$

Mean time in the waiting line = $\lambda/(\mu(\mu-\lambda))$

Mean time in the entire system = $1/(\mu-\lambda)$

---

[4]The simple formulas in Table 4–1 are based on Poisson arrival and service rates. With the Poisson distribution, however, the mean and the variance are the same. Hence, changing the variability (measured by the variance) for a Poisson process implies changing the mean as well; and thus the example of different variabilities in hyperbolas A and B in Figure 4–2 cannot be explained by a Poisson distribution. However, if we abandon the Poisson distribution, we can explain hyperbolas A and B, both with the same mean, but with different variabilities that imply different values for the numerator, a, and thus different positions for the hyperbolas.

Under a more general queuing formula, where the service rate is from a non-Poisson distribution, the formula for the waiting time in the queue is

$$\text{Waiting time in queue} = (1/\lambda) \cdot [\{(\lambda/\mu)^2 + \lambda^2\, V(t)\}/\{2(1-\lambda/\mu)\}],$$

where $V(t)$ is the variance. Thus, for a variance greater than that of the Poisson, the numerator takes a value greater than one; this creates a situation in which two hyperbolas have the same mean but different variabilities and thus different positions, as do curves A and B in Figure 4–2.

To see how these queuing formulas can help describe a process, consider the following example.

================================ **SITUATION 4-1** ================================

Department of Motor Vehicles

The local office of the state Department of Motor Vehicles was famed for long, boring waits to obtain either new license plates (for newly purchased cars) or new driver's licenses. There was a single line to the new plates counter and a single line to the new driver's license counter. People entering the office were assigned numbers and were free to sit anywhere. The workers at each counter called out which number was next in line, and people were then served in order.

An investigation for a morning in the latter half of the month revealed that people were being served at a rate of 20 an hour and that they were entering the line at a rate of 19 an hour.

What could be the expected waiting time and the expected number in the line itself at any one time?

From the formulas of Table 4-1, we find that the formula for waiting time is $\lambda/\mu(\mu-\lambda)$ and the formula for expected length of line is $\lambda^2/\mu(\mu-\lambda)$. From the data of the investigation, $\lambda = 19$ and $\mu = 20$. Thus,

Mean time in line $= 19/(20(20 - 19)) = 0.95$ hours.

The expected length of the line is

Mean length of line $= 19^2/(20(20 - 19)) = 18$.

Thus, for lack of excess capacity, a license plate process that takes only 5 minutes (20 per hour) ends up taking nearly an hour in line.

What would it take to reduce the wait to less than half an hour? Again, by using the formula for waiting time in line, $\lambda/\mu(\mu-\lambda)$, we see

0.5 hours $=$ Mean time in line $= 19/(x(x - 19))$,

which can be solved for $x = 20.8$. That is, if the workers can devise a way to squeeze out 1 more license plate an hour, then the wait can be cut to less than half an hour. An increase of capacity by 4 percent (20 to 20.8) results in a reduction of waiting by 47 percent (0.95 hours to 0.50 hours).

What would it take to reduce the wait to 15 minutes? A service rate of 22.4 licenses per hour. A productivity (or capacity) increase of another 7.7 percent results in a drop in waiting time of nearly 50 percent. Note, however, that in order to get another reduction in waiting of roughly the same magnitude, capacity had to be increased more than before, 7.7 percent versus 4 percent. This is one general result of queuing analysis, consistent with the hyperbolic curves of Figure 4-2.

Queuing analysis leads to several important insights:

1. Increases in capacity have the most impact on wait time reduction when capacity utilization is high. When capacity utilization is lower, capacity increases have less impact.

2. Going from a single-channel queuing system to a double-channel system can reduce waiting time disproportionately. This is the rationale for multiple cashiers at fast-food restaurants and multiple tellers at banks, for example.

3. Increasing the speed of service (having, in effect, a super-server) can do an even better job of getting people through the system. In contrast, with multiple service lines, people may be able to wait less time in line, although they will spend more time actually being served.

The queuing phenomenon reinforces the need to manage capacity effectively. In a service operation, not only is having some spare capacity essential to preventing lengthy waits, but that capacity must be available when needed. This typically means that labor must be scheduled to match peaks in demand and any equipment or supplies must be thoroughly prepared in advance.

There are, of course, more refined and complex formulas available for describing the performance of more complicated queuing problems. However, most of the queuing problems one finds in actual production and service operations quickly become more complicated than mathematical techniques can solve. One then confronts the choice of using mathematical techniques to approximate a solution or investing time and effort in simulating the waiting line and thereby discovering its properties. Frequently, a queuing problem that may be complex can be broken apart into smaller problems that resemble simpler queuing phenomena. A multichannel system, such as a drive-in bank with three lanes, might be approximated as three separate single-channel systems, each with a third of the demand of the full operation.[5] For many applications, however—especially if the waiting line problem is an important one to the operation—simulation is the best way to find a solution.

Simulation

The ever-increasing size and speed of computers have made simulation an attractive means of obtaining some acceptable solutions to large-scale and complex problems, such as many queuing problems. In many ways, simulation substitutes brute force (raw computer power) for the elegance (but lack of realism) of the mathematical model. Although often more realistic, simulation is often more art than science; mathematical models can often be characterized as right or wrong, whereas simu-

---

[5]Pooling multiple channels into the same system does have some advantages, so the pooled multichannel system is likely to have somewhat better performance than separate, single-channel systems. Thus, the bank with three drive-up lanes is likely to do somewhat better than three banks each with a single drive-up lane and one-third of the total demand.

lation models tend to be either good or bad. The typical simulation model is a kind of mathematical black box that takes some initial inputs, processes them, usually over a number of periods of time, and spits out some outputs.

The first step in constructing such a model is to identify the variables of interest. Variables are the values within the simulation that are permitted to vary over time. The choice of variables for a simulation takes judgment because only variables that are important to the result should be included and they should be defined in units of measure that are appropriate. A simulation of truck arrivals at a peanut processing plant, for example, would surely define arriving peanuts (measured in, say, tons per hour), truck wait (hours), and peanuts processed as variables. One might also include the moisture content of the peanuts as a variable as well, freeing the analysis from the assumption that all the arriving peanuts are uniformly soggy and thus need a full 36 hours in the dryer. On the other hand, the unloading time per truck may not matter much and thus not be worth including. Once identified, the variable should be set with some initial values (subject to change, of course) in different model runs.

Initial conditions apply not only to variables but also to some of the parameters of the simulation. Parameters, in contrast to variables, are simulation values that remain fixed during any single run of a simulation. Often, successive runs of a simulation will modify one or more parameters intentionally, but during any one run all parameter values remain fixed. For example, the mean rate of arrival of peanuts to the plant and the company's total drying capacity are likely parameters for a simulation of the operations.

A crucial stage in developing any simulation model is detailing the relationships among the variables and parameters and how they will vary, if at all, with the march of time. A number of these relationships will almost always be of an accounting nature, but many will serve to drive the model. The kinds of relationships that alter variable values in important and often systematic ways are frequently termed *decision rules*. They specify under which conditions variables of all kinds will be changed and how. In a simulation of a peanut processing situation, for example, one decision rule might check to see whether the drying capacity has been reached and then allocate arriving peanuts either to dryers or to the truck wait. Accounting relationships would then keep track of the peanuts dried and drying and the trucks waiting.

Simulation models can be either deterministic or probabilistic. That is, the simulation can be built to yield exactly the same outputs, given the same sets of initial conditions and parameters (a deterministic model); or some elements of chance can be introduced so that the same initial conditions and parameters would yield different, although probably similar, outputs (a probabilistic model). The most useful simulation of the peanut processing situation would be a probabilistic one (also called a Monte Carlo simulation, after the casino city in Monaco), which would draw at random a value for the arriving peanuts variable from a probability distribution such as the Poisson. The choice of probability distribution for such purposes is thus another important feature of building a simulation model.

Once a simulation model has been constructed—variables, parameters, initial conditions, accounting relationships, decision rules, and probability distributions—it is put through its paces. Usually, a lot of tinkering goes on—more or fewer periods are run, parameters changed, initial conditions revised, relationships altered, and variables added. All of this tinkering occurs to check on the simulation model's behavior. Are the results plausible? Do changes in parameters, initial conditions, or relationships yield the expected results?

After the model has been debugged and is functioning smoothly, its outputs can be used directly for decision making or (as is common for probabilistic models) can be accumulated in a data bank and investigated with statistical tools and hypothesis testing.

To understand more clearly how a simple simulation model might be developed, consider Situation 4–2.

SITUATION 4-2

Burger Queen—Steamer Inventory Decision

The Burger Queen restaurant in Gastonville operated much like a Burger King. It offered regular hamburgers and a large hamburger sandwich called The Big One. Burger patties were broiled at a high temperature on a continuous chain broiler; they had to be placed on the chain broiler no more often than one patty every 5 seconds. Meat patties of both sizes were completely cooked during their 30-second ride through the continuous chain broiler. After the broiler was a "burger board" where workers assembled regular burgers and Big Ones. A regular burger could be assembled, packaged, and placed in the finished goods chutes within 20 seconds; a Big One took 30 seconds.

Between the chain broiler and the burger board was a steamer that could keep cooked meat patties warm for 10 to 15 minutes without any deterioration in their taste and freshness. Burger Queen's management was interested in determining how many cooked meat patties of each type should be kept in the steamer at different times. The success of the inventory level for the steamer would be judged by whether a transaction time standard of 1 minute or less for any order could be maintained.

A typical stream of orders (a representative random sample) during a reasonably busy time of day was as follows:

ORDER NUMBER	ORDER
1	2 burgers
2	1 Big One
3	1 burger, 1 Big One
4	2 Big Ones
5	3 burgers
1 minute elapsed time	
6	2 burgers
7	3 Big Ones
8	1 burger
9	2 burgers, 1 Big One
10	1 Big One
11	4 burgers
2 minutes elapsed time	
12	2 burgers
13	1 burger
14	1 burger, 2 Big Ones
15	3 Big Ones
3 minutes elapsed time	
16	1 burger, 1 Big One
17	3 burgers
18	1 Big One
19	2 burgers, 2 Big Ones
20	1 burger
4 minutes elapsed time	

Discussion of Burger Queen steamer inventory decision.   Determining the level of cooked burger patty inventory that should be kept in the steamer is a problem ideally suited to simulation. Let us work through how such a problem could be simulated.

The parameters of this simulation—the values that stay unchanged during the simulation—include the ride time through the broiler (30 seconds), burger assembly time (20 seconds), Big One assembly time (30 seconds), waiting time interval between patties on the broiler (5 seconds), the number of patties that can be cooked per minute (12 patties), and the level of inventory in the steamer (maximum chosen for each run). Note that these service times are fixed; some simulations, of course, could have them vary, much as we assumed for the simple queuing model.

The key variable of interest is the transaction time—the time between the placement of the order and its presentation to the customer. The goal is to have that time be 1 minute or less. In this somewhat simplified situation, the transaction time for any order will equal the longest time to complete any burger or Big One in the order. We are assuming that on orders of more than one burger or Big One, assembly of the multiple items is simultaneous and that board capacity is great enough that sandwich assembly is not delayed for any sandwich. We are also assuming that all Big Ones in any order are worked on first because they have the longer assembly time. The variables that make up the computation of transaction time include the number of burgers in the order, the number of Big Ones in the order, the cooking time for each patty, and the extent of any wait in placing patties on the chain broiler.

To calculate the longest time to complete any burger or Big One in an order, one must compare the completion times for all the sandwiches in the order. A sandwich's completion time depends on whether the patty was drawn from the steamer or had to be broiled. If the former, the completion time equals the time it takes to assemble the sandwich. If the latter, the completion time is the sum of the assembly time and the cooking time (which is the ride time through the broiler plus any waiting because the broiler can take only one patty every 5 seconds). This wait can be calculated by multiplying 5 seconds times the number of patties preceding a particular one in an order through the broiler.

The simulation of transaction times is driven by the sequence of orders. One such sequence is given in the situation description, but others are possible and, indeed, desirable for computing an effective level of inventory for the steamer. Here we will use the stream of orders given above.

Table 4–2 displays the completion times for each sandwich in the order (Big Ones first) and the transaction times for that order, assuming that no inventory is kept in the steamer. These simulation results show that the transaction time standard is exceeded 6 times in the 20 orders simulated, or almost one-third of the time. This finding suggests that keeping an inventory of cooked meat patties in the steamer is indeed desirable. Hence, the next trial of the simulation model could attempt to keep one meat patty of each size in the steamer to see how transaction times are affected.

TABLE 4-2 COMPLETION TIMES AND TRANSACTION TIMES (ASSUMING NO INVENTORY IS KEPT IN THE STEAMER)

	Completion times (seconds)				Transaction times (seconds)
	Sandwiches				
Order number	No. 1	No. 2	No. 3	No. 4	
1	50	55			55
2	60				60
3	60	55			60
4	60	65			65
5	50	55	60		60
6	50	55			55
7	60	65	70		70
8	50				50
9	60	55	60		60
10	60				60
11	50	55	60	65	65
12	50[a]	55[a]			55
13	50				50
14	60	65	60		65
15	60	65	70		70
16	60	55			60
17	50	55	60		60
18	60				60
19	60	65	60	65	65
20	50				50

[a]Order no. 11 calls for the thirteenth and fourteenth meat patties in the previous minute's time. Thus if order no. 12 is called for within the first 10 seconds of its time period (between minutes 2 and 3), its transaction time will be later than 55 seconds because the broiler can cook only 12 patties in a minute. Its transaction time could be as high as 65 seconds. To be accurate, the simulation should keep track of capacity demands on the broiler.

How should the simulation keep track of the steamer inventory? This monitoring is clearly needed. The steamer inventory has to be constantly replenished, and it cannot be if more than 12 meat patties are ordered in a minute.

The appendix, in broad terms, describes the sophisticated simulation model the Burger King Corporation developed.

Managing the Queue

The raison d'être for both the mathematical and simulation techniques for analyzing queuing problems, of course, is to provide insights for management action on the queues themselves. Typically, queues can be managed in a host of ways: adding capacity or investing in statistical quality control or other measures to narrow service variances.

Earlier, in discussing the anatomy of waiting line problems, elements of the arrival process, queue discipline, and the service process were noted. Many of these elements can be affected by particular management actions. Indeed, in service industries, where customer happiness while waiting in line is crucial, significant management attention is focused on managing the queue properly and making the wait feel shorter.

David Maister has provided a thought-provoking list of propositions about wait time and how to manage it.[6] They point to a variety of things that service companies can do to improve the perceptions that people have about waiting.

> *Proposition 1: Unoccupied time feels longer than occupied time.* This suggests filling the wait time with something for the customers to do, preferably something beneficial.
>
> *Proposition 2: Pre-process waits feel longer than in-process waits.* Better to start customers through the process than to keep them waiting at the start.
>
> *Proposition 3: Anxiety makes waits seem longer.* Reassure the customers that they will be served and that they are not waiting in the wrong line.
>
> *Proposition 4: Uncertain waits are longer than known, finite waits.* If possible, give the customer information on how long the wait is likely to be. Reservation or appointment systems are good ways to alleviate uncertain waits, as long as they are kept by the service providers.
>
> *Proposition 5: Unexplained waits are longer than explained waits.* If you know why there is a wait, tell the customer.
>
> *Proposition 6: Unfair waits are longer than equitable waits.* Any departures from "first come, first served" systems may be seen by customers as unfair, and should thus be explained and justified.
>
> *Proposition 7: The more valuable the service, the longer the customer will wait.* For small-scale services, even short waits can displease customers.
>
> *Proposition 8: Solo waits feel longer than group waits.* In waiting, as elsewhere in life, misery loves company.

APPENDIX: The Burger King Restaurant Simulation Model

The Burger King Corporation's restaurant simulation model (actually, there were several models because each type of restaurant configuration required a different model) was one of the tools the corporation used in the 1980s to keep it a

---

[6]Maister, David H., "The Psychology of Waiting Lines," in John A. Czepiel, Michael R. Solomon, and Carol F. Surprenant, *The Service Encounter.* Lexington, MA: D. C. Heath and Company, 1985.

technological leader in the fast-food business. That a simulation model would be useful for helping to make many different decisions was not immediately apparent to Burger King management; the realization crept up on them gradually.

In the late 1970s, Burger King experimented with a number of innovations, the most prominent of which was the introduction of several specialty sandwiches. Market research had shown an encouraging consumer response to specialty sandwiches, but it was not known how they would affect service delivery at existing restaurants. As mentioned in the Tour B discussion of Burger King, a key measure of a restaurant's operation was its speed of service; the faster people can be served a high-quality product, the happier they will be and the more customers a restaurant will serve, particularly during peak periods. Burger King in the late 1970s had no easy way to assess the impact of specialty sandwiches or other innovations on a restaurant's speed of service. Before something like a new specialty sandwich could be rolled out to the thousands of Burger Kings worldwide, the company had to experiment in an actual restaurant to see what its effect on operations would be. Generally speaking, several restaurants were used for each experiment. Typically, 2 weeks' worth of data were collected so that there would be enough data for different days of high and low sales volumes. A typical experiment cost between $6000 and $8000 and required a good deal of time to analyze the results.

It occurred to some far-seeing Burger King managers that a mathematical description of a restaurant might be able to perform the same kind of service as a field experiment but at much lower cost. At first, a linear programming model was used to isolate particular bottlenecks in a restaurant's operations, but it was soon realized that a linear program could not adequately capture the dynamics of restaurant operations, where the most interesting problems occurred. Given this insight, it was decided to embark on building simulation models for Burger King restaurants.

THE STRUCTURE OF THE SIMULATION MODEL

As initially conceived, the simulation model, like an actual restaurant, consisted of three broad, interrelated areas: (1) customer arrivals and orders, (2) food preparation, and (3) the delivery of orders to customers. Within each of these areas, the simulation model had various modules that described particular aspects.

Customer Arrivals and Orders

Of course, Burger King has little or no influence on the arrival and order process. Thus, the simulation model simply attempted to mimic accurately what occurred in the typical restaurant on various days of the week and during various hours of the day. Particular modules isolated the behavior of in-store versus drive-thru arrivals as well as in-store versus drive-thru order generation.

These modules were based on observed facts. It had been observed, for example, that the arrival pattern of customers followed an exponential function (i.e., the plot of the cumulative percentage of arrivals versus the time between those arrivals traced out an exponential curve). It had also been observed that a relatively small number of order types account for most orders received at the restaurant (the five most common combinations of choices—such as burger, fries, and drink as opposed to specialty sandwich and shake—accounted for 45 percent of all the orders placed).

In sum, the customer arrival and order segment of the model was designed to reflect, on a day-by-day and an hour-by-hour basis, the specific orders that were typically placed at a Burger King.

Food Preparation

Of the three areas, Burger King had the most control over food preparation. The company had considerable discretion in changing equipment, procedures, layout, and staffing. The production system was thus modeled in considerable detail. Elements of this modeling included descriptions of all the operating procedures for making anything that could be requested of the kitchen. Thus, there were modules that detailed how regular Whoppers were made, how regular chicken sandwiches were made, how french fries were prepared, and how shakes were drawn. The model's descriptions of these activities, in turn, depended on (1) the labor times for each task (such as the time it took to dress a bun crown for the Whopper Sandwich), (2) the kitchen layout that determined the distances workers had to walk between tasks, and (3) the equipment configuration, because processing times depended in part on the choice of equipment for the kitchen. Other elements of the production system included the number of workers who worked at any time and their positions and responsibilities within the kitchen, and the inventory rules (e.g., 10-minute maximum hold time for all sandwiches). Typical simulation modules for the production system included such things as regular Whopper preparation, special Whopper preparation, regular burger preparation, shake preparation, broiler and steamer operation, and in-process and final inventory levels.

The Order Delivery System

This area of the simulation model dealt with how orders were taken, assembled, and presented to the customer. Tasks in this delivery system were divided between in-store and drive-thru tasks. The times for customers to state orders and for cashiers to punch them in, make change, and assemble orders were determined separately for different order configurations and staffing assignments of the cash registers. Representative simulation modules included in-store order assembly and delivery and drive-thru order assembly and delivery.

The Burger King simulation models are written with a special simulation computer language called GPSS. The GPSS simulation style is to simulate activities by orienting discrete events in time. A GPSS model begins its simulation at time period 0 and inquires about which activities are to begin then or are to be continuing at that time. When the model is stepped ahead to time period 1, it keeps track of the activities that are to be continued, those that will end in that period, and those that will start then. The simulation is analogous to constructing a movie by taking a series of snapshots at numerous points in time. In 1982, a typical Burger King simulation model application required 3000 lines of GPSS code and took about 1 minute of processing time on an IBM 3033 computer to execute.

The construction of the simulation model required an enormous amount of data. Time and motion studies specific to Burger King were used along with methods time measurement (MTM) data to develop time standards for the many operations performed by workers in the kitchen or at the counter. Information was also gathered from a sampling of 40 restaurants nationwide. These restaurants offered a variety of characteristics such as sales volumes, ownership (franchise versus company), and facilities (drive-thru versus non-drive-thru). The information gathered from these restaurants was incorporated into the model to ensure that its operation matched operations at typical Burger King restaurants.

Before the corporation was willing to use the simulation model to run low-cost experiments of proposed innovations, the model underwent a live test. The company took some space in a warehouse and set up an actual restaurant kitchen and service area. Actual orders from cash register tapes, representing both high and low sales volumes, were read to the service counter people. This live test ran an entire week, during which all aspects of the operation were measured and videotaped. The same streams of orders were fed into the simulation model, and its results were compared with those from the live test. The simulation model was adjusted until the differences between the two according to measures such as service times, lengths of queues, and locations of bottlenecks turned out to be very slight. This success convinced upper management of the worth of simulation for analyzing their type of operation.

The Burger King simulation model is modular in that any of the many restaurant configurations operating at any given staffing level can be represented relatively easily by joining the appropriate modules together. These individual models undergo constant revision because each innovation the company would like to test requires reprogramming at least certain aspects of the model.

USES OF THE SIMULATION MODEL

The Burger King simulation model has been used for a variety of purposes. Its first major use came in the development of the Burger King Productivity Improvement Program. For this program, manuals were developed that identified the potential service bottlenecks and their remedies for each level of restaurant sales. Thus, a franchisee could examine a manual to discover how to break those bottlenecks and so maintain service standards as restaurant sales grew. The manual also indicated the rates of return for expenditures on remedying any of the potential bottlenecks. These studies took between 6 and 8 months to complete, with about 300 runs of the model each month.

From this success, the corporation's industrial engineering and operations research department, responsible for the development and maintenance of the simulation model, moved on to develop labor staffing standards for each restaurant configuration. About a year was spent exploring the issue and developing the standards. Two key needs were addressed:

The minimum number of employees needed for any sales level and their duties so as to satisfy corporate speed-of-service goals.

A means for management to control the labor needs (a labor formula).

Through repeated use of the simulation model for different store configurations, given different levels of sales and different positioning of the workforce, a set of manning tables was derived. For example, before the use of the simulation model, it was not known definitely how best the tenth worker could be positioned as sales climbed. Was that worker best added to the burger board or added as a cashier? The output of the model showed that more customers could be served and the average speed of service could be kept within the 3-minute standard by shifting that worker to the cashier position. In fact, the model's results showed that five more customers per hour (150 versus 145) could be served in this way and that the average speed of service could be maintained at 176 seconds per customer as opposed to 188 seconds. Results of this type resulted in savings for each restaurant of 1 to 2 percent of sales.

To address the management control needs, equations were estimated by regression analysis to predict the aggregate level of labor needed, given an optimum schedule for that labor. The equations, defined for different restaurant configurations, used real weekly sales and the number of hours open as explanatory variables.

The simulation model was instrumental in the design of the BK87 restaurant configuration described in Tour B. The model permitted experiments that shifted equipment around the kitchen, seeing how these changes would affect service times and staffing levels. Burger King's use of a two-window drive-thru lane, rather than a multilane drive-thru as is often seen in drive-thru-banks, is another example of the use of the model. The simulation model predicted that this innovation would increase capacity by 15 percent during peak hours; this estimate has been borne out with actual increases of 14 percent.

In a drive-thru, what is the optimum stack size (number of car lengths) between the order board and the pick-up window? This was another question Burger King wanted addressed. If that distance was too short, a car would have to wait at the pick-up window because the food was not ready; if the distance was too long, the food would be cold by the time the car got there to pick it up.

Analyzing this question through the use of the simulation model was straightforward. The model's customer arrival and order system generated cars for the drive-thru lane. The model also specified the distance between the street and the order box and between the order box and the drive-thru window. Naturally, if the drive-thru lane between the order box and the window was filled, no other car could reach the order box to place an order.

A longer stack size was simulated simply by altering the capacity of the drive-thru lane between the order box and the window. By varying this parameter from one to 11 or 12 car lengths, the company was able to see which stack sizes were most conducive to reducing the transaction time at the drive-thru window and thus to increasing the number of cars served per hour. The graph in Figure 4–3 shows that a stack size of six to eight seemed optimal.

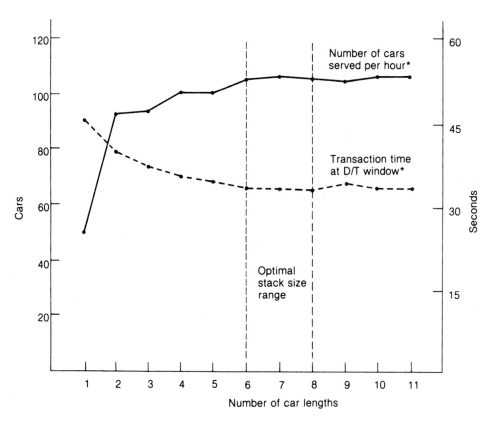

*Does not include car at window or at order box.
Based on (1) December 1979 Miami prices, (2) average company order configurations and product, (3) a capacity for 20 cars from pick-up window to drive-thru entrance, and (4) K-700 kitchen layout.

Figure 4–3 Stack Size Between Order Box and Pick-up Window (in car lengths).

A more challenging problem was whether to add small specialty sand-wiches to the Burger King menu to complement the large specialty sandwiches that were Burger King staples. It was known, for example, that if small specialty sandwiches were introduced, they would sometimes be ordered instead of large specialty sandwiches and sometimes instead of other Burger King menu items (particularly burgers). Specialty sandwiches take somewhat longer to prepare than burgers, and small specialty sandwich patties would have to be cooked separately from large ones because the frying times are different. At issue, then, was how the introduction of small specialty sandwiches would affect service times, given a different pattern of orders and some additional constraints on the kitchen.

Studying such a problem involved changes to five modules in the simulation model:

1. *Order generation.* To obtain data for changing this module, a marketing test on small specialty sandwiches was performed in Wilkes-Barre, Pennsylvania.

2. *Preparation of regular specialty sandwiches.* MTM analysis was used to obtain data for adapting the module on preparation of specialty sandwiches to the smaller sandwiches.

3. *Preparation of smaller specialty sandwiches.* Again, MTM analysis was used to study the changes in labor standards implied by the smaller sandwiches.

4. *Fry station operations.* This module had to be changed because the patties for these small specialty sandwiches would be cooked by the fry station operator. Moreover, at low volumes, the fry operator would also take on the responsibility of preparing the sandwich and not simply frying the patty.

5. *Stocking rules.* The introduction of small specialty sandwiches modified some of the stocking rules for work-in-process inventory and finished inventory in the chute. For example, the introduction of a small chicken sandwich might change the stocking rules for the large chicken sandwich, given some substitution away from the large chicken sandwich to the smaller one.

Table 4–3 reports the simulation results for small specialty sandwiches—what effect they can be expected to have on the use of equipment and labor and on customer service. As can be seen in the table, the introduction of small specialty sandwiches, even with the addition of an extra fryer, increased average transaction times by at least 10 seconds. This deterioration of service was even more pronounced at lower sales levels. There were two reasons for this deterioration:

Preparation times for the small specialty sandwiches remained longer than the preparation times for the burger and Whopper sandwiches that they sometimes replaced; thus they made the entire kitchen operation more labor-intensive.

TABLE 4-3   OPERATIONAL EFFECTS OF ADDING SMALL SPECIALTY SANDWICHES[a]

		Utilization with small specialty sandwich		
Effect type	Position/equipment/attribute	Before small specialty sandwich	Current fryer capacity	With extra fryer
Equipment	Fry operation (% of time busy)	52.8	54.2	57.4
and labor	Specialty board (% of time busy)	58.5	70.2	68.7
utilization	Multipot 1 (times down/hour)[b]	23	26	25
	Multipot 2 (times down/hour)[c]	—	—	3
Customer service	Average number of customers behind customer being served	1.14	0.95	0.93
	Average transaction time (seconds)	109	121	119

[a]The data are based on a product mix of 72 percent Whoppers and burgers, 19 percent specialty, and 9 percent small specialty.

[b]The frying vat that was used for cooking chicken.

[c]The frying vat that was added to break the potential bottleneck at multipot 1.

> The demand for small specialty sandwiches was rather low to begin with, and effective stocking was difficult, implying a high risk of waste. Consequently, an order for a small specialty sandwich was similar to an order for a special on any of the sandwiches, and these specials always took longer to prepare.

Based on these results and insights, Burger King withdrew its plans for the introduction of small specialty sandwiches.

Making Quality Happen

Everybody wants high quality. The worker or the executive who proclaims the need for low quality has yet to be found. More than this, managers consistently trumpet quality's role in their marketplace successes; quality is often acknowledged as a competitive prerequisite. Yet despite the acknowledged importance of quality, it is probably the most misunderstood concept about operations.

When one thinks about a high-quality service, one often equates it with high price and, perhaps, with lots of extras or with fawning attentiveness. That is not what quality professionals think. Quality means only one thing to such people: *conformance to the service's specifications as valued by customers.* Even a cut-rate service could be termed high quality if customers valued it and it conformed to all of its specifications. Such a service could even lead to *customer delight,* another term that is nearly synonymous with service quality.

By defining quality as conformance to specifications as valued by the customer, one removes the subjective elements about what quality may be and replaces them with objective and quantifiable ways of gauging it. Moreover, once one quantifies quality, one can think about attaching some costs to it.

The cost of quality (or, more precisely, the cost of off-quality) becomes the cost to the company of doing things wrong, of not conforming to the specifications. When viewed this way, the cost of quality takes on an importance that goes beyond many managers' thinking about service product costs. The cost of doing things wrong includes the cost of product failure to the company (often companies distinguish between external failure—failure found once the product has been sold—and internal failure—failure found while the service is still under the control of the service operation), the cost of trying to detect those failures before they are delivered, and the cost of preventing those failures in the first place. Table 5–1 lists key items in each of these cost areas. These costs frequently total 15 to 20 percent or more of a typical company's cost of sales.

TABLE 5-1 ELEMENTS IN THE COST OF QUALITY

Failure costs	Detection costs	Prevention costs
External failure costs	Process capability measurement	Design reviews
Consumer affairs (dealing	(e.g., control charts)	Engineering drawing checks
primarily with customer	Product acceptance	Engineering quality orientation
complains about quality)	Prototype inspection and tests	program
Field service (mostly repair of	Receiving inspection and tests	Engineering specifications
what should have worked)	Supplier surveillance	reviews
Product liability (insurance	Work-in-process and finished	Preventive maintenance
and settlements)	goods testing and inspection	Process capability studies
Product returns, recalls, and		Product qualification
corrective action costs		Quality audits
Warranty costs		Quality orientation programs
Internal failure costs		Supplier evaluations
Downtime due to defects		Supplier quality seminars
Engineering change orders		Tool and machines control
Purchasing change orders		Worker training and cross
Redesign		training
Retesting		
Rework in factory or service		
operations		
Scrap		

If a company is to avoid most of these costs of quality, it must deliver the service correctly the first time and every time. To do this, however, everybody in the organization must be convinced that things have to be done right the first time. It is a cop-out to say that quality is the strict province of the quality control department or that quality problems start with the front-line service providers. In fact, quality problems are more likely to start in places other than front-line service provision—in design, training, purchasing, customer order processing, accounting, or elsewhere. The late W. Edwards Deming, one of the early gurus of quality management and the man after whom Japan's Deming Prize for quality is named, insisted that management is responsible for 85 percent of a company's quality problems; workers are responsible for only 15 percent. Some estimate that product design (read service design) is itself responsible for 50 percent or more of a firm's quality problems.

As companies work diligently on quality, they often discover that not only do their total costs of quality decline but that the compositions of those costs of quality shift. Typically, the failure costs shrink in percentage importance while prevention costs expand.

IMPROVING QUALITY

Quality in an operation is improved only when everybody involved—those who deliver the service and those who do not—become aware that their tasks can affect quality and that they may need to redirect their procedures and habits toward preventing mistakes. The goal, of course, is to have no quality problems, to have every service encounter be perfect. The achievement of this goal, however, requires significant changes in management and worker attitudes and a relentless pursuit of all the small things that can ruin quality by causing work not to be done properly the first time.

A controversial step toward this goal of a perfect product is to discard traditional points of view about making mistakes. There is a big jump from making perfection a goal to making it a standard, but it is felt by many that such a change of attitude is essential to significant improvements in quality. According to this view, the standard is "zero defects" for everybody associated with the operation. A zero-defect standard does not say to all concerned merely that they are to do the best they can; rather, it says that everyone is expected to produce with zero defects or change the procedure so that they will produce zero defects. All the causes of errors or potential errors must be removed and the operation changed so that everything is done right the first time every time. This means that workers and managers must analyze mistakes to determine why particular defects were introduced into the service. Why were operations missed or put in the wrong sequence? Why did the service not perform as it was intended? Why was the customer not delighted? How can the provision of the service be made foolproof? Should it be designed differently?

One could go on and on about the sources of errors. What is critical, though, is that each error must be removed if the service is to be delivered with zero defects. This attitude change also affects the traditional roles of management and the workforce; no longer can workers be seen merely as executing the wishes of management or of those who have designed the service. Rather, management and designers have to be viewed as resources to be applied to the solution of quality problems that are, for the most part, known first to the front-line providers. The workforce can solve many quality problems itself, but should not have to find and remedy all of them. Thus, if the zero-defect standard is to be reached, management and designers must be brought in to help the workforce solve particular problems. Management and designers should serve the workforce, not the other way around.

The setting of the zero-defects standard and the importance of removing all causes of errors in the process have been debated. The debate centers on the various components of the cost of quality as noted above: failure costs, detection costs, and prevention costs. How are these costs of quality related to the number of defects in the service? As the number of defects changes, how do the total costs of quality (i.e., the sum of the costs of failure, detection, and prevention) change? Do they rise and fall? Figure 5–1 demonstrates the two opposing views on the issue. According to the traditional view (as represented in Figure 5–1a), the lowest cost is achieved at some nonzero level of defects. The other view (shown in Figure 5–1b) concludes that the zero defects standard is the lowest cost. The difference, of course, is that one side of the debate postulates that the

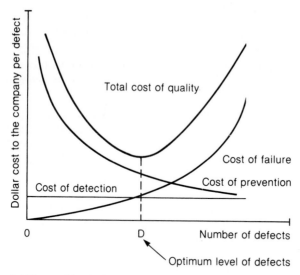

(a) The traditional view.

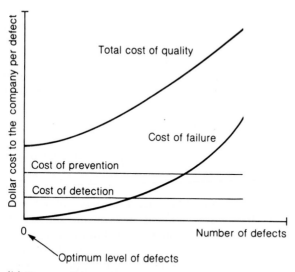

(b) The zero defects view.

Figure 5–1 The Debate on the Optimum Number of Defects.

costs of prevention and detection increase substantially as one gets closer and closer to zero defects. Supporters of this view reason that there have to be some diminishing returns from error removal as more and more errors are found and fewer errors persist. The last errors are thought to be the toughest to find and correct. The other school of thought states that the causes of defects are so simple, although numerous, that it takes no more expenditure to remove the last cause of error than to remove the first. It may take longer to determine what that last source of error is, but, so this school of thought goes, the steps to correct it are likely to be rather simple.

This debate on whether there is an optimal level of defects for a service is essentially an empirical debate, but as yet, no one has done a very good job of estimating what these curves look like. Are they more like Figure 5–1a or are they more like Figure 5–1b? In time, we will probably all have a better sense about whether the zero-defect standard is truly the lowest-cost way to deliver a service. Philip Crosby and his adherents believe that quality is "free" and that, in fact, the lowest-cost way is always to deliver the service right the first time.[1] According to Crosby, the cost of quality should not be higher than about 5 percent of sales, and given the fact that in many companies the cost of quality is 15 percent or more of sales, Crosby looks to quality improvement as the chief source of profit gain, and thus, it is "free." Others are not so sure that quality, at the level of zero defects, is, in fact, free.[2] What the Japanese and others have been teaching us, however, is that the optimal level of defects is far lower than anyone had previously dared to think.

For some, the service supplement to zero defects is *zero defections*. This suggests another measure of service quality, namely the number of repeat customers. Repeat customers, as mentioned earlier in this text, have some truly desirable characteristics that make them more profitable. (See Chapter 2.) All this comment leads to the following proposition:

Proposition:
> Service quality is free, and not just because customers stay happy and keep coming back.

In other words, this proposition says that doing things right the first time means lower costs for service provision and not simply satisfied customers. Many of the items in Crosby's cost-of-quality calculation apply to services as readily as they do to manufacturing.

Management Attitudes Toward Quality

There is much less debate about the attitudinal and organizational changes that have to be made to promote conformity to specifications. The importance of

[1]Crosby, Philip B., *Quality is Free.* New York: McGraw-Hill, 1979.

[2]Juran, Joseph M., and Frank M. Gryna, Jr., *Quality Planning and Analysis,* 2nd ed. New York: McGraw-Hill, 1980.

making quality everybody's business has already been discussed; a problem in one area of the company can easily overlap into problems elsewhere, with deleterious effects on the quality of the service delivered. Other attitudes about quality have to be rethought as well. In many non-quality-conscious companies, the identification of defects too often leads to blame and recrimination, with excuses abounding and managers and workers alike seeking to avoid being singled out for them.

In a quality-conscious company, defects are not an excuse for blaming others, merely an indication that everyone needs to work together to eliminate the causes of the defects. Moreover, the notion that quality should or must be sacrificed in order to promote delivery or cost goals is replaced by the notion that only by delivering a quality service can a company stay competitive and that, over time, costs will be lowered and delivery improved when the causes of quality problems are identified and remedied. In many quality-conscious companies, the cost of quality (failure costs, detection costs, and prevention costs) is known and reported consistently, typically as a percentage of sales or of the cost of sales. Hunches about the costs of quality are replaced by definitive statistics kept by the accounting function of the firm. Managers in the quality-conscious firm are evaluated on their quality.

Other changes are evident as well. Suppliers become important members of the quality team and are educated on what it takes to deliver quality services or services that meet the needs of the customer company; supplier ideas are even sought to assist design. The quality department is held in high regard by everyone; it is a leader in thinking about service delivery and changes to the service. It is a training and troubleshooting resource for the rest of the company. Quality control may not report to an operations manager but to a separate general manager, and thus is not subject to the schedule and cost measures applied to operations performance.

Convincing a skeptical workforce that quality is important, when for years management has not acted as if that were truly the case, can be a long, hard pull. Often senior management's hand has to be forced to demonstrate that quality prevails over the long-held goal of meeting orders or sales targets. When management is willing to halt service provision when there is a quality problem, and to take the heat from a customer about it, the workforce can begin to get excited about a new era at the company.

Management attitudes in many companies have been usefully altered by the adoption of formally recognized supplier–customer relationships within operations. In these progressive companies, managers and workers are imbued with an understanding that each of them is a supplier to someone else in the company and that each of them is also a customer of somebody else, even if it is only information that is passed. They are then evaluated in part by what their customer(s) say about them, just as they help evaluate those who supply them with materials or information. Such a reorientation of operations functions that may have long felt cut off from the rest of the company has usually had a very salutary effect on people. They come to realize readily that quality, up and down the organization, depends on them.

Changes in management organization and attitude can be achieved in many ways. A number of the quality "gurus" have proposed principles or plans for quality improvement. Perhaps the most famous of these plans is Deming's 14 Points. These are the points that Deming stressed in his many educational trips to Japan, beginning in 1950, which many credit for turning around Japan's thinking about quality and how it is achieved.

Deming's 14 points.   These points are at once philosophical and statistical in origin and reflect Deming's long years as both a statistician and a troubleshooter for industry.

1. Create constancy of purpose toward improvement of product and service. This means to take the long view, to spur innovation whenever possible, and to focus on the customer.
2. Adopt the new philosophy. Take on leadership for change.
3. Cease dependence on inspection to achieve quality. Eliminate the need for inspection by building quality into the product.
4. End the practice of awarding business to the lowest bidder. Move toward long-term relationships with single suppliers for any one item.
5. Improve the system of production and service constantly and forever. Quality, productivity, and cost reduction are linked.
6. Institute training on the job.
7. Institute leadership. The aim of supervision should be to help people and machines do a better job. This means removing barriers to doing the job right. It also means not treating every defect or problem as if it were a special case but to use the statistical tools available for management.
8. Drive out fear—do not let people go because they have helped to improve quality (and productivity and cost).
9. Break down barriers between departments. Promote teamwork.
10. Eliminate slogans, exhortations, and targets for the workforce asking for zero defects and new levels of productivity. Slogans do not help one to improve, and, because the vast majority of quality problems are due to the system and management, and not the workforce, slogans can lead to resentment in the workforce.
11. Eliminate quotas on the factory floor.
12. Remove barriers that rob people (workforce, management, engineering) of their rights to pride in workmanship. This means abolishing such things as piece-rates and other production incentives that depend on quantity and not quality. Avoid numerical goal-setting for managers (e.g., increase productivity by X percent this year or lower costs by Y percent).

13. Institute a vigorous program of education and self-improvement.
14. Put everybody in the company to work to accomplish the transformation. The transformation is everybody's job.

Deming's 14 Points is not the only method, of course. Other programs exist, typically associated with other leading figures in the crusade for better quality management, such as Philip Crosby, Joseph M. Juran, and Armand Feigenbaum. Although there is much that is common across the various programs available, there are some differences in emphasis and style. For example, Crosby is sometimes criticized for being too much of a "cheerleader" and not strong enough on the techniques of quality management. Deming's is sometimes viewed as too dogmatic an approach, and heavily statistical in nature, and this draws fire from some quarters. The Juran and Feigenbaum approaches are fairly eclectic in their treatment of the subject.

The logic of quality: The Malcolm Baldrige National Quality Award and the European Quality Award. These attitudes and principles on quality have been captured by some awards—the Malcolm Baldrige National Quality Award in the United States and the European Quality Award—that have quickly become prestigious and have driven considerable benchmarking among both manufacturing and service firms. These awards reflect our best interpretations of what quality is and how it can be achieved (the logic of quality); they have operationalized quality for firms of all stripes. For many, they define what Total Quality Management (TQM) really means. They are worth exploring.

The Malcolm Baldrige National Quality Award. In 1987, Congress instituted a new award for quality to honor a former Secretary of Commerce, Malcolm Baldrige, who had recently died in a rodeo accident. This award is analogous to the Deming Prizes in Japan, and since 1988 has been an increasingly visible and coveted award for American firms.[3] There are really three different awards that can be made in any year: a major manufacturing company award, a small company award, and a service business award. Up to two can win in any category, but there is no requirement that any award be given.

Seven categories are evaluated for the Baldrige award. They are each given point values that add up to 1000 points for a perfect score. Independent teams of examiners grade written applications from the applicant companies and make site visits to the most promising ones. The categories and point values for the 1994 award are as follows:

---

[3]Malcolm Baldridge Award winners have been heavily benchmarked by other firms. Indeed, as a condition of winning they must share their story and insights with other companies. Many companies use the Baldridge criteria to score themselves.

1. Leadership (100 points)—How the company's senior management create and sustain quality values in all areas of the company.
2. Information and Analysis (60 points)—The scope of data used (internal, customers, suppliers), its validity and timeliness, statistical analyses used, root cause determinations, countermeasures, etc. This measures the use of "management by fact" at the company.
3. Strategic Quality Planning (90 points)—How quality is integrated into the business planning of the company. The use of benchmarking against competitors and world-class companies of all types and how that benchmarking is used.
4. Human Resource Utilization (150 points)—The effectiveness of the company's efforts to involve and develop all its employees. Issues are full participation, employee empowerment, continuous improvement, and organizational growth (education, training, recognition, quality of work life).
5. Quality Assurance of Products and Services (150 points)—Use of total quality control in product design, testing, and supplier materials/parts/services. Issues here relate to standard setting, capability studies, designation of key process characteristics to control, design of experiments, quality audits, documentation, and quality assurance outside of manufacturing itself.
6. Quality Results (150 points)—What the actual results are from the adoption of quality programs based on both trends and independent assessments of customers and competitors.
7. Customer Satisfaction (300 points)—The company's knowledge of its customers and its performance in serving the customer well and quickly. This includes assessment of warranties, postsale service and contact, complaint handling, and customer feedback.

These categories are seen by many companies as a wonderful means of grading themselves and of seeking improvements to their processes, even if they do not apply for the award. The Baldrige award is certainly helping to focus management attention on quality and the mechanisms for achieving it. As of 1994, there have been three winners of the service quality award: Federal Express, the AT&T Universal Card, and the Ritz-Carlton Hotel in Atlanta.

The European Quality Award.   The European Quality Award (EQA) is the newest of the awards, having issued its first award in 1992. It is administered by the European Foundation for Quality Management, a group of more than 200 European companies, and is also sponsored by the European Commission and the European Organization for Quality, a federation of 25 national quality groups. Only one award is given in any year, although there are prizes (honorable mentions) given as well.

Where there are seven categories to the Baldrige Award, there are nine to the EQA. Although not radically different from Baldrige, the EQA does have some noteworthy distinctions.

One of these distinctions is an explicit recognition of cause and effect. That is, a world-class quality firm ought to be able to show linkages between the policies and actions it takes and the results it enjoys. These results are not only the quality results, but also the business results, including financial performance. The Baldrige Award is not as forceful about the link between quality policies and a firm's financial performance, although that link is, of course, the hope of every manager interested in quality. With this philosophy in mind, the first five EQA categories (50 percent of the award total) are labeled *enablers* and the next four categories (the other 50 percent) are termed *results.*

1. Leadership (10 percent)—This is much like Baldrige category 1. The emphasis is on what measurable things senior managers do: the values and plans they promulgate, the recognition they give their subordinates, the customers, and suppliers they personally see to discuss quality issues.

2. Policy and Strategy (8 percent)—This category, much like Baldrige category 3, is concerned with how Total Quality Management is reflected in the company's business policies and strategies. Is quality really a significant input to the company's business planning exercises?

3. People Management (9 percent)—This category overlaps Baldrige category 4, and is devoted to the company's own workforce. How does the company help to release its potential with recruitment, training, career paths, performance measures, and involvement?

4. Resources (9 percent)—This category has no ready counterpart in the Baldrige criteria. It refers to how well the company actually makes available its many resources for quality management. The resources measured include funding, information, material, and technology.

5. Processes (14 percent)—This category, like its counterpart in Baldrige, examines how the many different processes in a company (e.g., order entry, billing, service delivery of all types, new service creation) are identified, reviewed, and improved. Included in this category are the statistical weapons to TQM and how they are used.

6. Customer Satisfaction (20 percent)—The most important of the results categories is this one, which measures how well customers are satisfied. Here firms need to show how external customers perceive their company and its goods and services. Firm evidence is required.

7. People Satisfaction (9 percent)—This category examines what the firm's own people think about the firms vis-à-vis their own needs and expectations. Again, firm evidence is required.

8. Impact on Society (6 percent)—How is the company perceived by society at large, including its approach and contribution to the quality of life and the environment?

9. Business Results (15 percent)—This category expands on Baldrige category 6 to include not only the hard data trends on quality, both company-specific

and supplier quality, but also hard data trends on company financial performance.

ISO 9000.   A sometimes confusing aspect of quality is ISO 9000. ISO 9000 is a series of standards set by the International Standards Organization, in association with the many countries belonging to that organization. The standards set are requirements for company quality management systems. ISO certification (termed "registration") is increasingly required to land contracts in Europe and the United States, especially for government work.

The key notion behind the ISO 9000 standards is whether, after some catastrophe (e.g., the plague) has wiped out all of a company's personnel, one could enter the company and, using only what the company had documented, reconstruct the company's processes and begin to make high-quality products or to deliver high-quality services. Thus, much of ISO 9000 is devoted to documentation. Indeed, it is often criticized for encouraging wasteful documentation and not for leading companies to improve their quality as the various awards can do. Steps are being taken to broaden ISO 9000 to counter these criticisms, however.

One of the new standards set by ISO is ISO 9004, which relates solely to service firms. (ISO 9001, 9002, and 9003 pertain only to manufacturing.) To date, not much has been done on this score, but in the future, government and other contracts in Europe and elsewhere may require ISO certification before they are awarded. When this happens, service firms of all types will quickly learn more about the requirements of ISO and quality standards.

TECHNIQUES FOR MAKING QUALITY HAPPEN

Because services are so often produced and consumed on the spot, neither inspection of services to determine which ones meet specifications nor sorting good services from bad has ever been an important activity.[4] There is now, however, a concerted effort to improve both service design and the design and control of the processes delivering the service. This shift of emphasis is very much in tune with the theme of "making it right the first time."

One of the most basic concepts of quality management is *fitness for use*; this notion largely governs all the subsequent techniques used to manage quality. Fitness for use is simply the extent to which the service, as designed, serves the real purposes of the consumer. What is it about the service that has value for the consumer? Conversely, what about the service has low value for the consumer? By carefully analyzing a service's fitness for use, managers and engineers can be sure that a service is designed expressly for its intended purpose. A service can be underdesigned or overdesigned and thus inappropriate for the use to which the consumer puts it.

---

[4]Indeed, sorting techniques (such as acceptance sampling) have only a limited applicability to service operations, such as those that engage in wholesaling, retailing, or distribution.

This discussion of fitness for use may sound very familiar to the careful reader. In particular, the careful reader may be asking, "Didn't the discussion of the *service task* in Chapter 2 sound very much like fitness for use? The answer is Yes, they are, at root, the same concept. After all, how can you expect to provide a high-quality service without understanding why the customer may value your service over somebody else's? How can purpose be given the service encounter without an understanding of what quality really means?

Improving a process, bit-by-bit in continuous fashion, demands repeated, systematic change to that process, and this demands real understanding of fitness for use. The problem areas of the process have to be identified and investigated, and changes must be made. Process improvement thus requires a set procedure and a toolbox of skills (including statistical ones) for identifying and analyzing the process's problems.

Quality Improvement Programs

The adoption of Deming's 14 Points or the pursuit of any of the quality awards typically entails education in and application of a procedure for attacking quality problems of all types.

Florida Power and Light, the utility company serving most of south Florida and the first recipient of the international Deming Prize, has adopted a seven-step procedure for problem-solving that has aided it and many other companies, including other service companies. It is worth examining. The seven steps, adapted from some Japanese sources, are as follows (the tools, in bold italics, will be discussed later):

1. *Reason for improvement.* Identify the problem area and why it is worth solving.
2. *Current situation.* Select the specific problem to work on and set a target for the problem-solving effort. ***Pareto charts*** may apply here as well as graphs of various sorts.
3. *Analysis.* Identify and verify the root cause(s) of the problem. This step makes use of such tools as ***fishbone diagrams*** and Pareto charts. It requires the gathering and analysis of various types of data.
4. *Countermeasures.* These are the actions to take to counter the root causes. To many they would be known as solutions, but they may never really eliminate the problem for all time.
5. *Results.* This is the test of the countermeasures. It often requires ***experimentation.***
6. *Standardization.* This is the identification of the actions to take to prevent the problem and its root causes from recurring. This may entail ***process capability studies*** and the development of ***control charts.***
7. *Future plans.* Plan action for any remaining problems and evaluate the effectiveness of the problem-solving team itself.

These seven steps are a more elaborate version of what has come to be known as the Deming cycle of Plan, Do, Check, Act (PDCA). The Deming cycle, which Deming attributed to his mentor, Walter Shewhart, the inventor of the quality control chart, goes as follows:

1. *Plan.* Plan a test of available data on the problem, or plan a change to the process, an experiment.
2. *Do.* Carry out the test or change, preferably on a small scale.
3. *Check.* Observe the effects.
4. *Act.* Study the results and ask what was learned. New knowledge can then lead to more data gathering, more testing and change, and more results to mull over. The process improves continuously by this method.

There are a variety of quality improvement programs (QIP) like this one. No one has an absolute monopoly on what is best. Experience with a number of them has underscored a number of points about them, however:

- Putting in a quality improvement program (QIP) is a major redirection for a company and must be led from the top. Without wholehearted support from top management, the QIP will wither and die.
- QIPs require "champions" whose role is to proselytize and encourage.
- QIPs require constant attention. They need to be consistent with the company's strategy and they need constant feedback mechanisms.
- Line management must own the QIP, with the quality department seen as a resource for training and troubleshooting.
- An extraordinarily useful concept for many companies has been the adoption of a customer–supplier relationship within the firm. Everyone is seen as having a customer (whoever uses the outputs of their labors) and having suppliers (those who feed them with products or information). This notion forces people to talk to their customers and suppliers and to make every effort to satisfy their requirements. It gives immediacy to the QIP process.
- What gets measured is what gets managed. This is a truism that is especially relevant for quality programs.
- Middle management, caught as they always are in the middle, will likely resist a quality improvement program unless top management provides them with the wherewithal to understand and to be integral parts of the QIP effort.

Doubtless, other insights could be stressed here. Suffice it to say that a QIP can be an exceedingly effective management tool, but one that has to be believed in and worked through religiously if it is to give all the benefits it can to the company.

Some Peculiarities About Service Quality

Although differences in the definition of quality between manufacturing and service firms are more differences of degree than differences of kind, there are some peculiarities involved with services that are worth bringing out.

With service, perceptions take on enhanced stature. Several commentators have suggested a formula for service quality that roughly could be characterized as

$$\text{Service quality (and profitability)} = \text{Service satisfaction}$$
$$= \text{Delivery} - \text{Expectation}$$
$$= \text{Perception} - \text{Expectation}.$$

What this formula says is that value to the customer will be generated by *over-delivering* and *under-promising*. Let us explore the ramifications of this formula.

Delivering means both managing the provision of the service itself and managing the set of customers. In managing the service, one needs to think about the service delivery system:

- How does it operate to provide quality?
- How does it operate, especially during the peak period?
- What kind of capacity does it have?
- How does it need to be staffed then?
- What is the queuing penalty that may be incurred during those peak times?

All of the various decisions that affect the service delivery system from its technology to its standards and controls to its workforce are relevant in making sure that the service over-delivers.

On the other hand, one wants to manage customers well so that the service delivery process is not taxed too strenuously. Can customers be shifted from peak to off-peak times through pricing or alternative services? Not only is the volume of customers important, but the kind of customer is important, too.

Expectations also matter, however. Expectations can be higher when there are different service providers, and, indeed, different services. A quick-change oil franchise would not be expected to have the expertise of an auto dealer's repair shop. One's unhappiness about a wait in a doctor's office is typically not as great per minute as one's unhappiness standing in a fast-food restaurant line. A company's past track record for delivery and quality also colors expectations.

The best companies try to manage their customers' expectations through advertising or promotions, or communications during the service encounter itself. Sometimes those expectations can be very high, as when guarantees are made. Alternatively, companies can downplay what they may know they can surely deliver. Catalog companies such as L.L. Bean frequently quote very conservative delivery dates so that customers do not get their hopes up unnecessarily and are more apt to be pleasantly surprised when their orders are delivered "early."

The research team of Berry, Zeithaml, and Parasuraman has spent considerable time documenting the importance of perception and service quality. They stress that perception depends on five characteristics of service:[5]

- *Tangibles:* The appearance of physical facilities, equipment, personnel, and communication material
- *Reliability:* The ability to perform the promised service dependably and accurately
- *Responsiveness:* The willingness to help customers and to provide prompt service
- *Assurance:* The knowledge and courtesy of employees and their ability to convey trust and confidence
- *Empathy:* The provision of caring, individualized attention to customers

The service delivery system must attend to these characteristics if the service's quality is to be perceived as high.

Berry, Zeithaml, and Parasuraman have developed a survey instrument, dubbed SERVQUAL, that is one means of assessing customer perceptions about services. They have also done work to link quality and service standards for employees in meaningful ways that can help companies improve quality. (See the discussion on standards and controls in the next chapter.)

Determining What's Important to Correct: Run Charts and Pareto Charts

One of the most useful devices for figuring out what a quality improvement program ought to work on is Pareto analysis. Pareto analysis is simply the categorization of the various problems that have been identified and the development of frequency distributions for them. Pareto analysis tracks what percentage of all the problems is due to Problem 1, what percentage is due to Problem 2, etc., so that the problems that are the most frequently occurring are readily identified. Such frequency distributions can quickly reveal what kinds of problems seem to be the most prevalent and are thus worthy of extended effort to solve. Typically, data for a Pareto analysis are reasonably easy to collect, and collection is frequently done by front-line service providers over the course of several days or several weeks; the time frame, of course, is dependent on the frequency of problems and the output rate of the process. Pareto analysis is an extremely useful tool isolating the "vital few" problems from the "trivial many," to borrow a phrase from Juran.

Another useful tool for determining what is important is the chronological run chart, a graph of some measured characteristics plotted in the order of service provision. Having this plot in chronological order identifies trends in the

[5]Leonard L. Berry, Valerie A. Zeithaml, and A. Parasuraman, "Five Imperatives for Improving Service Quality," *Sloan Management Review,* vol. 29 (Summer 1990): 29–38.

data that might be missed if just a calculation of the mean or median or standard deviation is performed. Chronological run charts differ from control charts (discussed later) in that they cannot demonstrate conclusively that a process is under statistical control, but they can offer strong evidence that something about the process has changed. Consult Figure 5–2, a run chart of the percent defective. It displays two suspicious runs, the span between time units 10 and 18, and the span between time units 21 and 30. What makes these two places suspicious is that the percent defective stays on one side of the median for at least 8 units of time in a row. That is akin to flipping a coin and having it come up eight heads in a row. It is so unlikely that it suggests a specific cause; for the section consistently below the median, something very good was at work, while for the section consistently above the median something adverse was operating. These suspicious patches of time are persuasive indications that the process is not under control and that their specific causes ought to be researched.

Investigating and Correcting Causes of Quality Problems

The causes of process problems must be researched and corrective measures taken. This is where quality improvement programs kick into gear. Several additional points are important in this regard.

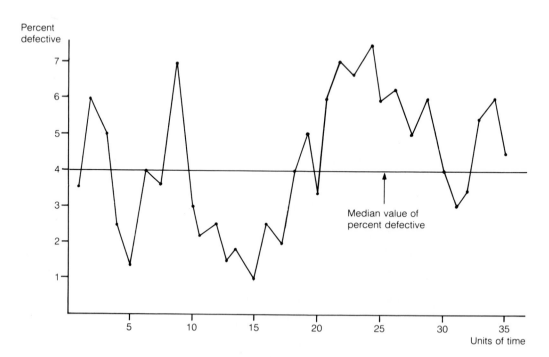

Figure 5–2 A Chronological Run Chart.

Data gathering. You are only as good as your data. There is nothing like good, meaningful data for tackling quality problems. Sometimes the data appropriate for investigating a problem are routinely collected. Other times the data of interest may not be readily available or may be subject to significant errors. If this is the case, the first step is to understand where the problem may be coming from (e.g., particular services provided, particular materials used, and particular segments of the process) and how important it is (vital or trivial). Once these things are understood, the kinds of data appropriate to the problem's study are usually apparent. Understanding this may take protracted talks with the customer to find out precisely what the customer wants and values. It may also take the determination of how quality may best be obtained: through service design, through the specification of materials or equipment used, or through the service delivery process itself. Once these things are understood, data can be collected and analyzed.

Collecting the appropriate data may require (1) measuring aspects of the process or the service, (2) keeping track of defects and their characteristics, (3) tracing particular defects to times or locations, and (4) noting any changes or conditions in the process and the materials, equipment, and labor used. The accumulation of these data may require a substantial investment in quality monitoring, and some experiments may have to be conducted.

Systematic investigation. One of the aids to quality problem investigation that has been particularly effective is the Ishikawa, or fishbone, diagram, which tries to pinpoint the causes and effects in the process (see Figure 5–3). The head

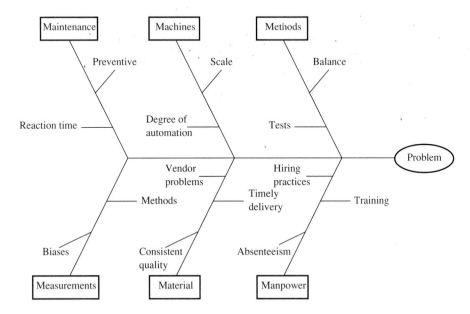

Figure 5–3 A "Fishbone," or Ishikawa, Diagram with Some Major Categories of Causes Indicated.

of the fish indicates the problem (the effect) whose causes are sought. The bones of the fish are the potential causes that are being brainstormed by this technique. The main bones are generally chosen to be some major categories of causes that one can readily examine. Often these six M's, or a subset of them, are investigated: methods, machines, manpower, material, measurements, and maintenance. Of course, other causes can be placed on the main bones of the fish. The smaller bones are more specific potential causes for the effect being investigated. They are generally decided upon by asking "why" repeatedly until one is satisfied that the root causes have been ferreted out.

Use of a fishbone diagram often leads to the collection of data or the design of an experiment so that causes can be checked out and effective solutions developed. Explicit diagrams of this type are reminiscent of the process flow and information flow diagrams considered earlier in this book. They, too, are means of making explicit what might otherwise be missed.

Getting and Keeping Control of Quality

There are two ways by which firms can get control of quality and keep it. Both have the property of foresight; they alert us to delivering good quality before the fact rather than providing us with mechanisms to sort bad from good quality after it is too late. One method is the use of statistical process controls (SPC) such as control charts, and the other is the use of foolproofing (sometimes called fail-safing or poka-yokes, after the Japanese). SPC is widespread in manufacturing, but is used seldom in services, primarily in services that can be readily measured. A discussion of SPC is included in the appendix to this chapter.

More prevalent, and always very cost-effective, is foolproofing. Foolproofing has been used in services for a long time, but only now are we conscious of its power and importance.[6]

Foolproofing.   Services can be foolproofed through the use of hardware, software, procedures, and gimmicks whose purpose is to make the quality way of delivering the service the only way the service gets delivered. Foolproofing can involve warnings automatically given before something goes awry, or they can involve automatic actions that stop the process before it creates something of inferior quality.

In manufacturing, foolproofing often comes from add-ons to machines (e.g., sensors of various types, fixtures) or from specific designs in the products (e.g., product asymmetry for easier assembly). In services, foolproofing is more apt to come from procedural and software means, with relatively little capital goods investment.

---

[6]The importance of foolproofing for services is perhaps best articulated by Richard B. Chase in his, "Failsafe Services" working paper, University of Southern California.

Chase has usefully distinguished between foolproofing devices that are server-based and those that are customer-based. There are some classic server-related foolproofing devices and schemes:

- The fast-food restaurants' french fry scoop for quick action and proper portion control
- Surgical trays with indentations or patterns for each instrument so that nothing gets misplaced, particularly not misplaced in the patient
- Color codes for proper installation, proper keying of data, and proper location for a piece of equipment
- Software prompts for the next piece of data, or software buzzes when the wrong piece of data has been entered
- Sequential numbering for those being served
- Rigid procedures for handling customers' money
- Rehearsed opening lines in a service encounter with the customer
- Layouts that compel people to move in the desired direction or that facilitate cleaning or maintenance

Other foolproof devices are related to the customer and are designed to affect his or her behavior:

- Reminder cards for appointments
- "Menu" boards to facilitate the information needed by the server when the customer's time comes
- Telephone touch-tone triage devices that route customer inquiries to the proper server
- Special uniforms or other cues so that customers know who, and who not, to ask for help
- Directions mailed ahead of time

These lists could go on and on. The genius of foolproofing is simply how low-cost it is as a way to improve quality for both the server and the process but also for the customer and how he or she interacts with the process.

Service Guarantees

When a service company's quality controls and foolproofing are well established, the company can begin to think seriously about offering service guarantees to its customers. Guarantees can be a powerful marketing tool that can increase sales substantially. They can even work to define particular service market niches and the "rules of the game" for those niches (e.g., Federal Express's guarantee of overnight delivery was instrumental in building up that industry). Guarantees are part of a product's service standards, the topic of the next chapter. Christopher Hart has studied service guarantees and offers a host of insights into what they are and why they work.[7]

Guarantees can take a variety of forms. Money back for substandard service provision, a free service for the next time, and other services performed to compensate for the substandard service initially provided are common ones. There are some well-known examples of service guarantees that have been etched into the minds of many consumers. Think of the Domino's Pizza guarantee of 30 minutes delivery or H&R Block's willingness to back up their tax work with representation if you are audited by the IRS, or the ability to return merchandise purchased at L.L Bean and other retailers, no questions asked, for replacement merchandise. Guarantees work best when they are:

- Unconditional—Without exception
- Easy to understand and communicate—Simple, specific
- Meaningful—Important to customers and financially significant without being over-generous
- Easy to invoke—No red tape or run-around to hurdle, no guilt involved
- Easy to collect—Quick and hassle-free

Guarantees work well for companies for a number of reasons:

- They force the service to focus on customers and their expectations, rather than the expectations of management.
- They stimulate feedback because they give customers an incentive to identify service that does not measure up.
- They force the service to understand why it may have failed because the expense of guarantees provokes remedial action from management, even if that action is better management of the customer and what he or she should do to get the most from the service
- As noted above, they can boost sales.

This boost to marketing is most pronounced under several conditions:

- The price of the service is high and thus a concern to the customer.
- The customer's ego is at risk if the service fails.
- The customer's knowledge of the service is low.
- The negative consequences of failure are high (high opportunity cost).
- The industry has a bad reputation that it needs to overcome.
- Repeat buyers are key to revenues.
- Word-of-mouth advertising is essential.

[7]Much of the analysis on service guarantees is due to Christopher W. L. Hart, "The Power of Unconditional Service Guarantees," *Harvard Business Review*, July–August 1988, pp. 54–62.

Naturally, a company risks something by guaranteeing its service. If substandard service is provided too frequently, the financial impact on a company can be severe. The company must be sure that the service is understood, foolproofed, and well under control.

APPENDIX: Statistical Process Control

CONTROL CHART BASICS

If the process is to produce quality products, its capabilities must be measured periodically so that management can be sure that it is performing as planned and is not drifting away from quality manufacture. In the last 50 years or so, a statistical means of assessing process capabilities has come to the fore—namely, the use of control charts to measure the adequacy of a particular process.

Control charts are used to separate random causes of variation in product quality from nonrandom, assignable causes of poor quality (operator error, faulty setup of a machine, poor materials). Assignable causes often demand a lot of work to remedy, but they can be remedied. Typically, such remedies may involve better training, more precise directions, improved methods, different materials, and the like. When these remedies are put in place, the process's capabilities are immediately improved; the assignable causes of poor quality have been removed. What remains is random variation in quality.

What gives the control chart power to discriminate between random causes of product nonquality and assignable causes is the fact that control charts depend on *samples* of products, not on individual units. Why does this afford power to the control chart? From statistics we know that no matter what the underlying distribution of the random causes of poor quality are, the means of samples taken from any distribution will tend to be distributed normally. This is the important *Central Limit Theorem.* Being able to use the normal distribution for the sample means taken permits us to say more about the process than we could by just using individual observations from the generally unknown underlying distribution of the process itself. We know a lot about a normal distribution and how it behaves.

Thus, using samples in control charts is a better, more powerful way to check on a process's capabilities than merely investigating single units as they are produced. Deming told of a famous example at the Nashua Corporation, a producer of carbon paper. Nashua produced carbon paper by spraying carbon black on tissue paper. The carbon black was sprayed on by a nozzle, the opening of which could be adjusted in size. Naturally, spraying too little carbon black yielded poor-quality carbon paper and spraying too much was wasteful and expensive. Before the use of control charts, the worker running the spraying equipment periodically measured the amount of carbon black on the finished product. If too little had been sprayed, he would open up the nozzle. If too much had been sprayed, he would close it off a bit. What was wrong with the way he was operating? We know that given a perfect process exhibiting only random variation, half of the carbon paper examined would be above the mean thickness of carbon black and half should be below the mean thickness. A perfect process would not have to be touched at all by the worker. Yet, according to this mode of operation, he would be adjusting the nozzle all the time, even if the process were perfect. In fact, he was introducing more variation to the process than the process had naturally. Better for the worker to collect data samples, take a mean of the sample, plot it on a control chart, and take action only when the control chart indicated. In that way, the worker would not be inadvertently adding variation to the process. The control chart would have taken into account the random nature of variation in the process and would have revealed any nonrandom, assignable causes of variation. Such is the advantage of using samples for the creation of control charts.

Control charts are of two general classes: variable control charts and attribute control charts. A variable control chart plots some specific measure along the y-axis (such as distances or times) and various sample numbers along the x-axis. The most common variables charts are $\overline{X}$ and R charts. The $\overline{X}$ chart plots the average of the measurements taken on each sample, and the R chart plots the range of measurement within each sample. Attribute control charts, on the other hand, typically deal with the "defects" of whatever kind in the samples taken. They can provide useful summary data about the process, but may have to be supplemented by the use of specific variables if particular explanations about the causes of the defects are to be tested. Indeed, these two classes of control charts can be used at the same time in cooperation with one another. Table 5–2 compares some of the basic variations.

Variable control charts can, in fact, be set up with an almost limitless number of quality characteristics measured on the y-axis. In developing control charts, it is thus important to distinguish the process characteristics that are most apt to be associated with defects (the vital few) and not to worry about other aspects of the process that, by all indications, appear under control (the trivial many). The characteristics chosen for study should logically be associated with remedies that can be taken. Often, Pareto analysis can be helpful in identifying the variables to plot.

Being in Statistical Control

A process that is operating in statistical control has no variation produced by specific, traceable, assignable causes. All its variation is at a minimum, given the process technology applied, and the variation represents merely random statistical variation—no variation that one can label as having a particular cause. If one wants to improve a process that is in statistical control (i.e., reduce the spread of the control limits), one has to change the process technology. One implication of this truism is sometimes startling to managers: If the process is out of control, yet tighter tolerances are desired, managers should not immediately go and buy new

TABLE 5-2 MAJOR TYPES OF CONTROL CHARTS

Type of chart	Statistical measure plotted on the y-axis	Comments
$\overline{X}$	Small sample averages of particular measurements	The most common control chart; indicates change in central tendency of process.
R	R = maximum–minimum values of small samples of measurements (R stands for range)	Frequently accompanies $\overline{X}$ chart; indicates when a significant loss (or gain) in uniformity has occurred.
X	Individual measurements, not averages	Less sensitive than the $\overline{X}$ chart; useful only when small samples cannot be taken conveniently and one observation per lot is all that is possible.
P	P = fraction defective	Most useful when go–no-go decision is needed; can help tell when to apply pressure for quality improvements; uses attributes data, not measurements data.
C	C = number of defects	Most useful when all samples are the same size and the number of defects possible is large but the likelihood of any single type of defect is small; avoids proliferating $\overline{X}$ or X charts in such situations; another attributes data control chart.

replacement equipment. Rather, managers should seek to uncover and remove the assignable causes of variation. Buying new equipment could be a very expensive way to tighten tolerances, and success in doing so is not ensured. Working to put the process under statistical control is the best measure before any creative, and perhaps costly, engineering and equipment revamping of the process.

Operationally, a process is in statistical control if it has no points outside the control limits, no suspicious-looking runs (portions where there are many points on one side of the mean line), and no definite trend that suggests that the process is drifting toward the control limits and thus out of control.

As process changes are made, a control chart can be updated. A new mean and new, tighter control limits can be calculated from the ever-increasing set of data on the process. By continual improvement, variation in the process can be reduced. At some point, the process may be in such good control that managers can forgo using a control chart for the particular variable of concern. Instead of regular samples being taken, periodic quality audits can confirm whether the process continues to produce high-quality items. Sometimes, only first-and-last-piece inspections of a batch of parts or products need to be performed.

The control chart is thus a way station on the road to quality—an important way station, but nevertheless just a way station. It is of little value when the process is known to be out of control, and it may be too time-consuming to keep up when the process is known to produce perfect pieces. The importance of the control chart lies in distinguishing random variation from variation caused by specific, traceable factors that can be remedied. As the process is worked on, the control chart is a record of the process's capability.

VARIABLE CONTROL CHARTS

Once it has been decided to develop a variable control chart, and the characteristics to be plotted have been picked, the next task is to construct the chart itself. Consider the $\overline{X}$ chart first (Figure 5–4). That chart's mean line is usually the average of past data. The mean line can be determined from a process capability study (more common in manufacturing companies) or from simply a history of data, typically at least 50 data points' worth. (Sometimes a design standard is initially used for the mean line, although actual data, of course, have the advantage.) The control limits for the $\overline{X}$ chart, for example, are generally set at 3 standard deviations (of the distribution of sample means) on either side of the mean line. Such limits ensure that random causes alone would indicate false alarms in only 0.3 percent of the cases because 99.7 percent of a normal distribution lies within 3 standard deviations of the mean. This is the way a control chart accounts for the random variation in the process and permits the nonrandom, assignable causes to be readily identified.

With today's calculators and computers, it is easy to calculate the standard deviation of a set of sample means, and such calculations should be used. Historically, however, that calculation was more time-consuming, and some formulas were developed to estimate the upper and lower control limits using the grand average (the average of the sample averages) and the average of the sample ranges. Those estimation procedures are still in use, and for the sake of completeness, they are presented here.

$$\overline{X} \text{ chart upper control limit} = \overline{\overline{x}} + 3\sigma_x \approx \overline{\overline{x}} + A_2 \overline{R}$$
$$\overline{X} \text{ chart lower control limit} = \overline{\overline{x}} - 3\sigma_x \approx \overline{\overline{x}} - A_2 \overline{R},$$

where $\overline{\overline{x}}$ (X double bar) = grand average (average of the sample averages), $\sigma_{\overline{x}}$ is the standard deviation of the sample means, $\overline{R}$ is the average of the sample ranges, and A_2 is the estimating factor, which varies with the size of the samples being taken. It is found in Table 5–3. Of course, the preferred means of computing the control limits now is not to use this shortcut estimation, but rather to calculate the standard deviation of the sample means straightaway.

The control limits can also be calculated from the computed process capability limits derived from a process capability study. The process capability study deals with single observations, x's. Control limits deal with samples. The mean of

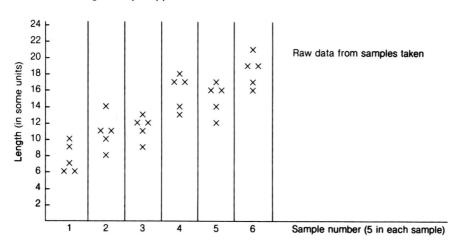

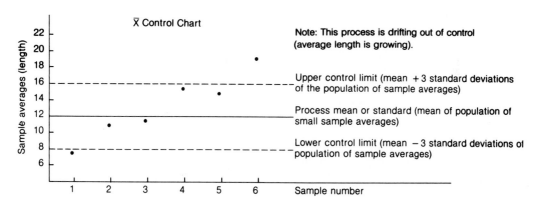

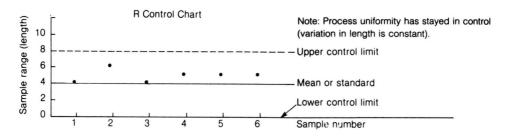

FIGURE 5–4 Sample $\overline{X}$ and R Control Charts.

TABLE 5-3 FACTORS FOR ESTIMATING CONTROL LIMITS IN $\overline{X}$ AND R CHARTS

Number of observations in samples taken	Factors for $\overline{X}$ chart for R, (A_2)	Factors for R chart	
		Lower limit D_3	Upper limit D_4
2	1.880	0	3.268
3	1.023	0	2.574
4	0.729	0	2.282
5	0.577	0	2.114
6	0.483	0	2.004
7	0.419	0.076	1.924
8	0.373	0.136	1.864
9	0.337	0.184	1.816
10	0.308	0.223	1.777

Source: J. M. Juran, ed., *Quality Control Handbook.* New York: McGraw-Hill, 1979, Table Y, Appendix II.

the process and the mean of the sample means taken are both unbiased estimates of the true process mean. However, the standard deviation of the sample means will always be smaller than the standard deviation of the individual observations. Knowing the number of observations per sample is all we need, however, to translate standard deviations of single observations into estimates of sample standard deviations. The two are related by the following formula:

$$\overline{\sigma}_x = \sigma_x / \sqrt{n},$$

where σ_x and $\overline{\sigma}_x$ are the standard deviations of the individual observations and of the samples, respectively, and n is the number of observations in each sample.

With the R chart, the mean line is precisely $\overline{R}$, the average of the sample ranges, and the control limits can be (1) calculated from the sets of samples taken, or (2) estimated from R itself.

$$\text{R chart upper control limit} = \overline{R} + 3\sigma_R \approx D_4 \overline{R}$$

$$\text{R chart lower control limit} = \overline{R} - 3\sigma_R \approx D_3 \overline{R},$$

where σ_R refers to the standard deviation of the sample ranges and D_3 and D_4 are estimating factors also found in Table 5-3. Again, the preferred technique these days is to calculate the standard deviation of the sample ranges straightaway.

ATTRIBUTE CONTROL CHARTS

So far, the discussion has centered on $\overline{X}$ and R charts, the major examples of variable control charts. Mentioned above was the other major class of control charts: attribute control charts. Attribute charts typically plot defects of one sort or another, and they are more common in service industries. These charts have to suffice when there is no clear measurement to make or where there are multitudes of defects possible, but with no single one of sufficient frequency on which to develop a variables chart. The two major types of attribute charts are the P chart, which tracks the percent defective in the samples taken, and the C chart, which tracks the number of defects in the samples taken. The samples taken for attribute charts are usually greater than those used for $\overline{X}$ and R charts by at least an order of magnitude.

Attribute charts make the assumption that defects are produced in much the same way that "heads" turn up when coins are flipped. That kind of a process is generally termed a Bernoulli process, and there are two similar statistical distributions that model Bernoulli processes: the binomial distribution and the Poisson distribution. These distributions make it easy to determine mean lines and control limits for attribute control charts.

The P chart assumes a binomial distribution of the percent defective created by the production process, where $\bar{p}$ is the mean percent defective and the standard deviation is

$$\sigma_p = \sqrt{\frac{\bar{p}(1-\bar{p})}{n}},$$

where n is the size of the sample taken. Thus the control limits are defined as

$$\text{P chart upper control limit} = \bar{p} + 3\sigma_p$$

$$= \bar{p} + 3\sqrt{\frac{\bar{p}(1-\bar{p})}{n}}$$

$$\text{P chart lower control limit} = \bar{p} - 3\sigma_p$$

$$= \bar{p} - 3\sqrt{\frac{\bar{p}(1-\bar{p})}{n}}.$$

The P chart has wide applicability and is particularly useful when you want to control a specific kind of defect that has been identified.

The C chart plots the number of defects in a sample and is applicable when the likelihood of any single type of defect is small but where there may be a large assortment of different types of defects possible. The C chart assumes that defects arrive at the process much as phone calls arrive at a telephone switchboard. The distribution that captures this phenomenon best is the Poisson, which is a particularly friendly distribution because its standard deviation is merely the square root of its mean. The mean line on a C chart is simply $\bar{c}$, the mean number of defects. The control limits are given by

$$\text{C chart upper control limit} = \bar{c} + 3\sigma_c = \bar{c} + 3\sqrt{\bar{c}}$$

$$\text{C chart lower control limit} = \bar{c} - 3\sigma_c = \bar{c} - 3\sqrt{\bar{c}}.$$

Attribute control charts, such as P and C charts, should be interpreted in the same way as variable control charts. If the process is operating in statistical control, as demonstrated by the control chart, all the variation is produced by random causes and not by assignable causes. If the percent defective is to be lowered, the process itself has to be changed.

Service Standards, Plans, Schedules, and Controls

Chapter 2 introduced the service encounter and the three aspects of service that support it. So far in this text, we have discussed the service task and at least some aspects of the service delivery system, and we have tied both of those concepts to quality. Now it is time to do the same for the third support for the service encounter, the service standards themselves. They were billed in Chapter 2 as the guardians of quality and cost efficiency. Now that we know more about what quality and cost mean for services, it is time to explore what service standards are and how plans and controls help make those standards meaningful.

STANDARDS

Standards can be very diverse. Some are clear-cut and easy to measure, natural measures to be used for certain situations. Time standards typically fit this category. In fast-food restaurants, for example, there are time standards for how long it should take for a customer to be served, both in the restaurant and via the drive-thru. Telephone customer sales representatives and information operators also typically have well-established standards on how long to take in handling a call. Even in professional service firms there are time standards for project work, used more for planning purposes than for evaluative purposes, but standards nevertheless.

Productivity-related standards can be natural ones as well. In service factories, there are often readily understood standards set on the items to be processed, be they policies or claims to handle or rooms to clean. In retailing, there are often commission pay schemes that effectively establish standards on sales.

Standards can also be natural and well-defined for cost control; often these have roots in manufacturing. Labor staffing, for example, is frequently accomplished with standards (often based on some model of how cost is built up in the process). Many services deal with materials that need to be inventoried, and the kinds of inventory controls that apply in manufacturing firms apply to service firms (see the tour of Burger King). Often service inventories are managed with non-time phased systems (see the next chapter). Service businesses often need safeguards on inventory: locked storerooms, sealed trucks, separate accounts kept for inventory items, checklists, and crosschecks on what has been handled, as is discussed in the Thalhimer's tour at the end of this book. Controls on cash are similar, and just as important.

Other standards, however, can be much more ambiguous and artificial. These are often standards of quality, particularly for those services not in service factories. What constitutes high-quality research for an ad agency or high-quality food service is harder to gauge with strictly objective measures. The controls become more subjective; firms have to resort to reviews and audits. Still, these standards are not so ambiguous that they cannot be used.

In all cases, these various types of standards detail the expectations that managers and designers of their respective service operations have toward what front-line service providers and their support personnel need to do in order to make quality outstanding and keep costs under control. This is the common thread and purpose to standard setting. (See Table 6–1.)

In their work on service quality, Berry, Zeithaml, and Parasuraman[1] have come upon what they see as a common failing of service firms, namely failing to define clearly what service providers are supposed to do. They call it *service role*

TABLE 6-1   A SAMPLING OF SERVICE STANDARDS AND THE CONTROLS ON THEM

Standard	Type of standard	Control mechanism
Time to serve customer	Time	Random stopwatch study
Time to process telephone order	Time	Automatically done with phone system
Policy claims handled per day	Productivity	End-of-day counts
Shoes sold	Productivity	Sales records, commission records
Weight of goods unloaded/loaded	Productivity	Shipping/movement records
Completeness of order filling	Quality	Random checks, complaints
Degree of customer satisfaction	Quality	Customer survey
Degree of rework demanded	Quality	Order records, complaints
Level of inventories held	Cost	Inventory records, locked storerooms, sealed shipments
Degree of overtime	Cost	Payroll records
Cash handled	Cost	Cash records, crosschecks
Customers per time period	Demand	Counts of customers, reliance on trends

[1] Leonard L. Berry, Valerie A. Zeithaml, and A. Parasuraman, "Five Imperatives for Improving Service Quality," *Sloan Management Review,* vol. 29 (Summer 1990): 29–38.

ambiguity. They have postulated some causes for this ambiguity, and they all relate to service standard setting. Such standards lose their impact in several ways.

- *No service standards set.* The lack of any standards communicates to the workforce that management is not serious about service quality (or cost).
- *Too many service standards.* This, as one might surmise, is confusing to the workforce. It makes determining priorities a chore.
- *General service standards.* Here the statement of the standards is too vague and unmeasureable to be of much use.
- *Poorly communicated service standards.* They may be there, but nobody really understands what they are.
- *Service standards unconnected to performance measurement, appraisal, and reward systems.* Being unconnected, the standards are toothless.

These insights provoke another proposition.

Proposition:

Control over costs and quality requires a clear definition of the service standards and the development of a clear system for checking on those standards.

Because service standards act as the guardians of cost and quality in the process, defining them clearly and objectively so that they can be used to measure the provision of service is very important. Standards can easily be muddled or ignored.

Standards can be set in a variety of ways:

- One can rely on experts to set standards. Their insight and experience thus determine what standards to set and how to set them. "Experts" can even be a firm's workforce; they can help set standards, especially for tasks that they know well, and their insights on how to measure performance against these standards are always useful.
- One can rely on industrial engineering techniques, such as[2]

  Motion study, where the actions of individual workers are broken down into their constituent parts, often through the use of process charts and videotaping, and those constituent parts studied to determine whether waste can be identified and removed and improvements made. The redesigned work can then be used as a standard.

  Time study, where stopwatches and videotaping are used to time elements of the job to determine where waste exists and how the job can be redefined.

  Work sampling, where an analyst observes what workers are doing at randomly determined moments of time, thus providing the analyst with insight into the percentages of time spent doing a variety of tasks. With this background, standards can be set, usually for jobs with high variety built into them.

[2]For more on these techniques, consult the appendix to this chapter.

> Work activity analysis, where workers list in chronological order the work performed, noting the type of task, the time spent on it, and the number of work items completed. This information, too, can be used to set a standard.
>
> Detailed flow-charting, where the nitty-gritty detail of a job can be diagrammed and scrutinized for improvement and standard setting.

- One can note where complaints start, and thus where customers may begin to feel uncomfortable with the service provision.
- One can be more proactive and use customer focus groups and customer surveys to help set the standards.
- One can benchmark the competition and establish a service standard that meets or betters the competition.

Setting standards for services is a lot like setting service levels for inventories. Typically, one has to go through a lot of trial and error. One has to probe how much people seem to tolerate poor levels of service provision. It means looking at the trade-off between having too much capacity and not having enough. It also means looking at how fastidious one can be about service provision and how costly that fastidiousness is.

Setting standards is tough work, and it is an Achilles heel to many service firms. Consider this proposition:

Proposition:

> Standard setting is often the neglected leg of the service task–service standard–service delivery system three-legged stool. Even companies with effective service delivery systems and clear service tasks can benefit from more attention to standard setting.

The place where many service businesses fall down is in the establishment of standards and controls. So many of their efforts are devoted to studying the market, developing a service task that makes sense, and building a service delivery system to fulfill that service task, that the controls on the process are neglected. This puts their continued success in jeopardy.

CONTROLS

Once the standards are set, of course, they must be checked on regularly to ensure that they are being maintained. This means not only that they must be measurable, but that a control system be put in place within the service delivery system. This frequently means setting up recordkeeping of some sort. Controls can be of many different types:

- One can have controls that affect customers, say by monitoring demand or tracking orders.
- One can have controls on the process and its capacities, its productivity, its scheduling, and its ability to deliver that track such items as productivity, service levels, overtime, and excess labor.

- There can be controls over inventories that track the level of inventory for particular products offered or that track how a product is handled through the system.
- Other controls can exist over quality. Statistical quality control is perhaps the most prominent, but one can have equally effective controls that affect the foolproofing of processes or that are simply checklists.
- Lastly, especially for services, one can use financial controls, especially cash controls, because for most services, cash represents another inventory that must be controlled.

Establishing effective controls is a particular concern for some types of service industries. Consider the following proposition.

Proposition:
Controlling service is tough, and all the tougher away from the service factory.

As one examines the service process matrix introduced above, one is struck by the fact that back-office operations are much more likely to exist in service factories. Those can be controlled in many of the same ways as one controls a manufacturing operation. In a service factory, one is not exposed to as much customer contact or interaction that can interrupt the flow of the process and introduce problems and unwanted variability. When flows and demands are regular, measures can be set up and monitored more easily and effectively. In the service factory, one can even hope to salvage quality with checks at the end of the service process. Costs, too, are likely to be much better controlled in an atmosphere that is back-office in character.

The more the service departs from the back office, however, the more difficult controlling service quality and cost becomes, especially if the service is far from the diagonal stretching from the service factory to the professional service firm. Many of the steps toward market segmentation that service businesses have taken have been toward that diagonal. What makes this diagonal so attractive? Better control, of all different types. Consider the following:

a. On one side of the diagonal, mass service controls often relate to labor costs and efficiency, for these services are trying constantly to get a grip on labor scheduling and productivity. Here, plant and equipment are rarely constraints. For example, in retailing, labor is a critical variable cost, and therefore, scheduling labor is an important activity. Point-of-sale terminals have permitted the tracking of sales of different items by 15-minute intervals (or finer) throughout the day. Such information, in combination with sales per salesperson per hour (a productivity measure), is tremendously useful for inventory control and workforce scheduling. Moves within the retail sector toward more customization (boutiques, personal selling) can also be understood as moves to increase control of the selling situation, to the end that sales, and commissions, are higher.

b. On the other side of the diagonal, the service shop frets about control of the service itself. With this kind of service, plant and equipment are constant constraints. Therefore, there are concerns for how frequently unpredictable jobs (e.g., auto repairs, patients) can be scheduled through expensive capital equipment. Control is also affected by the uncertainty over when and how people can tell when a service is rendered satisfactorily. Hospitals, for example, have a high proportion of fixed costs and thus worry a great deal about capacity utilization. Debates about who should dictate the utilization of hospital resources—administrative staffs or medical staffs—are, at root, debates about resource control. In this context, one can understand pressures to provide less customized or interactive service (e.g., fewer tests, more ambulatory care).

c. The service factory and, to a somewhat lesser extent, the professional service firm, suffer less from loss of control. Although control is still an issue for both kinds of services, for the professional service firm, control is more of an individual concern, relatively free from constraints of plant and equipment. The high degree of interaction and customization required of such firms is at least matched with a high degree of training and skill in the workforce.

d. The service factory can develop its production process to foster more control. The process that defines the service and the flow of information and materials is relatively smooth. In this regard, the service factory shares many of the benefits that manufacturing operations enjoy. The labor needed is well-known for given levels of demand, and scheduling of labor, plant, and equipment is fairly straightforward.

Can control become too unwieldy? Can you measure too much? The answer is yes, of course. One should always apply a Pareto principle, an 80–20 rule, to this. There are always a few controls that are going to be absolutely necessary, and many other potential ones that are much less important to the quality or cost of the service encounter. Typically, you want to know all that you can routinely know. You want to put enough controls in place to put teeth into the service task, so that the service delivery system itself does not deteriorate over time and thus compromise the firm's ability to keep its existing customers or to attract new ones.

Controls are arguably more important for services than they are for manufacturing:

- In services, because inventory cannot be accumulated and because demand can be erratic, queues often develop. Sometimes, these queues can be dramatic. Queues cry out for controls so that they can be spotted before they become too long and disruptive.

- Because service customization can be rampant, and because customers can actually intrude on the process itself, plans are frequently waylaid. This makes controls even more desirable.

- Often in services, one has fewer variables that can be measured for product quality. Thus, quality is often controlled by attributes control charts and not by variables control charts, and this means that you know less about what's going on in the process. The process itself becomes more variable. More of a premium has to be placed on fail-safing in order to ensure good quality for the customer, and on the development of good controls.

- The fact that cash is transferred in most services is another example of the highlighted need for controls in service businesses.

For these reasons, service processes need more controls, and often, more sophisticated controls, than those used in manufacturing companies.

PLANNING VS. CONTROL FOR SERVICES

It is helpful in a service operation to distinguish clearly between plans and controls. Plans are statements—intentions—that can be set in advance to serve as guides for decisions. Typical decisions that can be guided by plans include how much capacity there will be, or how much inventory there will be, or to what extent quality will be good. For example, a plan can be set in advance for the scheduling of a service workforce (the staffing plan). That staffing plan will, in turn, determine the extent of capacity that will be available for that service's customers. In like manner, one can plan for inventory levels to stock, for a given series of quality checks, or for a given delivery schedule served by trucks or planes.

Controls, on the other hand, are mechanisms that are established in conjunction with a service process to determine whether what is actually happening is or is not according to the plan. Controls then spur reactions from the process to make sure that what is desired can happen, given what is currently going on or what is currently expected.

Let's consider in more detail an example of a plan and a control mechanism that can be applied to that plan. Figure 6–1 displays a work schedule for the back-office operations of a bank, where checks come in by the pound and have to be processed.[3] This schedule is a plan, a plan for the workforce. Naturally, one hopes that the plan is a good one, that it will provide enough labor at the proper times to get the job done, and without too much waste (i.e., without an excessive amount of money paid out for workers who, in the end, were not needed).

Of course, one cannot tell if the plan was a good one without checking on how it does in reality. Are all the checks that come in processed on time? How far short does the plan fall, if, in fact, there is insufficient capacity? Part B of Figure 6–1 details this. As we can see there, when we look at actual volumes of work, the schedule leaves a lot of the work undone at the end of the shift, and in this particular case, such a hangover of work costs the bank a considerable

---

[3] This example is taken from a case by Vincent A. Mabert of Chemical Bank.

Part A: Schedule (A Plan)

Shift time	Number of workers scheduled
1–5 P.M.	13
4:00–9:30 P.M.	28
6–11 P.M.	81

Part B: Expected backlog of work yet to be done (a control)

Note: The work to be done is measured as Weight Arriving and is translated in Hours of Work Implied. The work as yet undone is the Ending Backlog, which is measured in hours. The figures here are considered to be representative by the bank.

Ending time	Weight arriving	Hours of work implied	Staff available	Hours of work available	Ending backlog (hrs.)
12:30	80.20	30.07	0.00	0.00	30.07
1:00	24.90	9.34	0.00	0.00	39.41
1:30	0.00	0.00	13.00	6.50	32.91
2:00	27.95	10.48	13.00	6.50	36.89
2:30	115.75	43.41	13.00	6.50	73.80
3:00	30.20	11.33	13.00	6.50	78.63
3:30	79.10	29.66	13.00	6.50	101.79
4:00	39.75	14.91	13.00	6.50	110.19
4:30	201.00	75.38	41.00	20.50	165.07
5:00	83.75	31.41	28.00	14.00	182.48
5:30	68.85	25.82	28.00	14.00	194.29
6:00	55.70	20.89	28.00	14.00	201.18
6:30	315.05	118.14	109.00	54.50	264.83
7:00	270.90	101.59	109.00	54.50	311.91
7:30	139.20	52.20	109.00	54.50	309.61
8:00	117.40	44.02	109.00	54.50	299.14
8:30	16.75	6.28	109.00	54.50	250.92
9:00	16.00	6.00	109.00	54.50	202.42
9:30	21.00	7.88	109.00	54.50	155.79
10:00	72.20	27.07	81.00	40.50	142.37
10:30	0.00	0.00	81.00	40.50	101.87
11:00	0.00	0.00	81.00	40.50	61.37

(Continued)

Figure 6–1 Plans and Controls: A Bank Example

amount of money. In fact, in this situation, it costs the bank so much that it rarely, if ever, wants to have any backlog at the end of the workday (11 P.M.).

A better schedule (plan) lies in Part C. For a slight increase in labor, all of the work is finished and the bank is more profitable as a result. Parts B and C of Figure 6–1 provide us with some controls (actual need vs. the plan) that we can use to devise better plans. (Part C's schedule is better than Part A's initial schedule.)

Part C: A different schedule (a new plan) and its impact on the work backlog

	Shift time			Number of workers scheduled	
	12 noon–5 P.M.			24	
	4:00–9:30 P.M.			26	
	6–11 P.M.			83	

Ending time	Weight arriving	Hours of work implied	Staff available	Hours of work available	Ending backlog (hrs.)
12:30	80.20	30.07	24.00	12.00	18.07
1:00	24.90	9.34	24.00	12.00	15.41
1:30	0.00	0.00	24.00	12.00	3.41
2:00	27.95	10.48	24.00	12.00	1.89
2:30	115.75	43.41	24.00	12.00	33.30
3:00	30.20	11.33	24.00	12.00	32.62
3:30	79.10	29.66	24.00	12.00	50.29
4:00	29.75	14.91	24.00	12.00	53.19
4:30	201.00	75.38	50.00	25.00	103.57
5:00	83.75	31.41	26.00	13.00	121.98
5:30	68.85	25.82	26.00	13.00	134.79
6:00	55.70	20.89	26.00	13.00	142.68
6:30	315.05	118.14	109.00	54.50	206.33
7:00	270.90	101.59	109.00	54.50	353.41
7:30	139.20	52.20	109.00	54.50	251.11
8:00	117.40	44.02	109.00	54.50	240.64
8:30	16.75	6.28	109.00	54.50	192.42
9:00	16.00	6.00	109.00	54.50	143.92
9:30	21.00	7.88	109.00	54.50	97.29
10:00	72.20	27.07	83.00	41.50	82.87
10:30	0.00	0.00	83.00	41.50	41.37
11:00	0.00	0.00	83.00	41.50	−0.13

Notes: 1) Hours of Work Implied: Each worker can process 2.67 lbs. of checks in an hour, on average.
2) Hours of Work Available: Given the half-hour time periods in the table.
3) Ending Backlog (hrs.) = Previous Ending Backlog + Hours of Work Implied − Hours of Work Available

Figure 6–1 Plans and Controls: A Bank Example (*Continued*)

Consider a different example, this time from a hotel.[4] In the hotel business, naturally, one wants to fill the hotel every night. In order to do that, one typically offers some rooms at a discount to corporations, conventions, tour groups, and others. Only a fraction of the rooms are typically offered at the full, "rack" rate. Nevertheless, one always prefers the customer who comes in at the last moment and pays the full rate. Offering all rooms at discounts leads to forgone revenues.

[4]This example is taken from a case by Penny Pittman Merliss and Christopher H. Lovelock titled "The Parker House: Sales and Reservations Planning," found in Lovelock's fine book, *Managing Services,* 2nd edition, Englewood Cliffs, NJ: Prentice-Hall, 1992.

This situation leads to the development of a plan that indicates how many rooms will be saved for the full, rack rate and how many will be offered at various levels of discount. Such a plan will usually differ by time of the year and by day of the week.

Along with the development of such a plan, one needs to develop some controls so that one can track the number of rooms already offered at different discounts and thus have an idea, when a customer calls, of exactly how many rooms are left in certain price categories. This may lead to actions such as accepting or rejecting a customer reservation, or to a rethinking of the plan to offer more rooms in a certain price category and fewer rooms in another. The controls that could be put in place could include a spreadsheet or database that is updated with every reservation made. Indeed, policy could insist that employees could not confirm reservations without first investigating the database to determine whether space was still available under the conditions sought.

From a management standpoint, one often needs to know whether significant resources should be attached more to controls than to plans. When do controls take over in importance from plans? Consider these points:

1. When the pattern of demand is very variable, planning becomes more difficult, and thus the value of controls increases.
2. When service stockouts — the times when service becomes unavailable — are costly for the service company, then a need for controls is highlighted. Even good planning may not be enough in such circumstances. Having controls to monitor how close one is to having a service stockout is important.
3. When service recoveries can be quick, and when one knows in advance how any recovery can or should be made, then control can take over in importance from planning. If, with control and recovery, one can keep customers happy, one may not need the expense of planning to as great a degree to achieve customer satisfaction.

LABOR SCHEDULING

In manufacturing, managers typically become concerned with scheduling jobs through the factory. Often that means they have to schedule the use of machines, as machines are frequently the scarce resource. Sometimes, they have to worry about scheduling the workforce, because workers can also be the scarce resource.[5] Fine minds have worked on how such scheduling can best be done. It is not easy, as one has to think about the due dates promised customers, the amount of work to be done for each order, or the congestion in the factory, particularly as it affects certain orders. In fact, what constitutes a good schedule is not so clear-cut. Certainly, meeting customer due dates is important (percent of

---

[5] Sometimes both machines and workers are jointly scarce, or intermittently scarce, and need to be considered together. This is known as the dual-constrained factory.

jobs tardy, for example), but one must also think of the total time spent working and the costs of production, including overtime.

While some service factory, back-office operations resemble factories in this regard and must address similar scheduling issues, labor scheduling is more peculiarly service-like in character. In essence, the issue is how best to schedule the workforce when demand is unknown and variable but front-line service providers must be there to cope with it. In the bank example above, the schedule was derived by a little trial and error with the use of a spreadsheet. Spreadsheets can be very helpful in simulating what certain labor schedules could be expected to achieve, but, with sufficient time and resources, one can do better than that. How such improvements can be made is worth a few words.

The typical labor-scheduling dilemma for a service firm has two major component questions:

1. How many workers should be on the job at any time? If demands are known with certainty and the productivity of the workforce is also a fixed, certain number, then this question is easy to resolve. But when uncertainty in either of those categories strikes, then some buffer should be set or else the firm may have too few workers to handle the demand, risking poor quality and customer backlash. Determining the extent of the buffer is not unlike determining the amount of safety stock inventory one should hold, an issue that is addressed in Chapter 8. (Answer: Hold more buffer if the cost of a unit of extra capacity (C_e) is small relative to the cost of being a unit short of capacity (C_s). The critical fractile approach of Chapter 8 has an exact analogy here, namely $C_e / (C_e + C_s)$.) Naturally, if too many workers are scheduled, the firm faces a wage bill that is higher than it should be.

2. What should the shifts of the workers look like? This is a trickier question because demands during a day can be very erratic, making the typical eight-hour shift with a lunch or dinner break in the middle a less than optimal choice. The firm might benefit more by creating some shifts with big breaks in the middle of them, by creating shifts for part-time workers, or by subcontracting some of the work.

Solving the first question is more straightforward than the second. The first question can usually be formulated as a linear program[6] where one tries to minimize the costs of the workers' wages for all workers over all the shifts worked plus any penalty costs associated with things like not getting the work done (opportunity costs) subject to some constraints. The constraints are typically ones that keep track of the work done (capacity has to be greater than or equal to the demand in any period) or of the machines that could be used.[7]

---

[6]Or, more properly, an integer or mixed integer program.

[7]See, for example, K. Baker, "Workforce Allocation in Cyclical Scheduling Problems: A Survey," *Operations Research Quarterly*, vol. 27, no. 1 (1974): 155–167, or V. A. Mabert, "A Case Study in Encoder Shift Scheduling Under Uncertainty," *Management Science*, vol. 25, no. 7 (July 1979): 623–631.

Solving the second problem involves intelligent picking of the many different kinds of shifts that service workers frequently can work, and then some simulation to see how costs are affected by the choices made.[8]

APPENDIX: Industrial Engineering Techniques for Setting Standards and Improving Methods

Methods improvement and engineering is too little appreciated in many companies, especially those in the service sector. As the service tours show, it is often detailed, nitty-gritty work but it can pay off. Methods improvement basically requires an open, inquisitive mind, an eye for detail, and a passion for keeping things simple. There are no pat solutions to apply in most instances; thus methods improvements usually involve a systematic study of the current methods, an appreciation of what the job really calls for, and a disdain for any explanation that is not thoroughly persuasive.

Over time, many do's and don'ts have evolved about good methods practice, especially regarding the actions of individual workers. Good methods practice is always concerned with what tasks can be *eliminated, simplified, combined* with other tasks, *changed* in sequence, or *automated*. These kinds of changes can often be accomplished with little or no investment in equipment or worker aids, but often methods study will lead to suggestions for capital investments of both large and small scale. Table 6–2 presents a list of suggestions for improving methods. This list provides a glimpse into the commonsense mind of the methods engineer.

STUDYING METHODS

As with most jobs, when one attacks a task systematically, one's productivity is likely to improve. Systematic methods improvement calls for systematic methods study. Formal study of work methods—including concern for raw materials, product design, process design, tooling, plant layout, and the workers' interaction with all of these features—is sometimes referred to as motion study. Although attention to methods has always existed, the formal study of work methods in operations is generally associated with Frank and Lillian Gilbreth, who in the late nineteenth and early twentieth centuries developed many of the charting techniques and early filming techniques that have done much to improve worker productivity. The Gilbreths had a passion for describing methods precisely through the isolation, identification, and subsequent improvement of the elements of a task.

---

[8]See, for example, W. B. Henderson and W. L. Berry, "Heuristic Methods for Telephone Operator Shift Scheduling: An Experimental Analysis," *Management Science*, vol. 22, no. 12 (August 1976): 1372–1380, and Vincent Mabert and Charles Watts, "A Simulation Analysis of Tour-Shift Construction Procedures," *Management Science*, vol. 28, no. 5 (May 1982).

TABLE 6-2 SOME BASIC PRINCIPLES OF METHODS IMPROVEMENT FOR WORKERS

A. Reduce total steps to a minimum.
B. Arrange in best order.
C. Combine steps where feasible.
D. Make each step as easy as possible.
E. Balance the work of the hands.
F. Avoid the use of the hands for holding.
G. The workplace should fit human dimensions:
  1. Can a suboperation be eliminated?
     a. As unnecessary?
     b. By a change in the order of work?
     c. By a change of tools or equipment?
     d. By a change of layout of the workplace?
     e. By combining tools?
     f. By a slight change of material?
     g. By a slight change in product?
     h. By a quick-acting clamp on jig, if jigs are used?
  2. Can a movement be eliminated?
     a. As unnecessary?
     b. By a change in the order of work?
     c. By combining tools?
     d. By a change of tools or equipment?
     e. By a drop disposal of finished material? (The less exact the release requirements, the faster the release.)
  3. Can a hold be eliminated? (Holding is extremely fatiguing.)
     a. As unnecessary?
     b. By a simple holding device or fixture?
  4. Can a delay be eliminated or shortened?
     a. As unnecessary?
     b. By a change in the work that each body member does?
     c. By balancing the work between the body members?
     d. By working simultaneously on two items? (Slightly less than double production is possible with the typical person.)
     e. By alternating the work, each hand doing the same job, but out of phase?
  5. Can a suboperation be made easier?
     a. By better tools? (Handles should allow maximum flesh contact without sharp corners for power; easy spin, small diameter for speed on light work.)
     b. By changing leverages?
     c. By changing positions of controls or tools?
     d. By better material containers? (Bins that permit a slide grasp of small parts are preferable to bins that must be dipped into.)
     e. By using inertia where possible?
     f. By lessening visual requirements?
     g. By better workplace heights? (Keep workplace height below the elbow.)
  6. Can a movement be made easier?
     a. By a change of layout, shortening distances? (Place tools and equipment as near place of use and as nearly in position of use as possible.)
     b. By changing direction of movements? (Optimum angle of workplace for light knobs, key switches, and handwheels is probably 30° and certainly between 0° to 45° to plane perpendicular to plane of front of operator's body.)
     c. By using different muscles? (Use the first muscle group in this list that is strong enough for the task.)
        (1) Finger? (Not desirable for steady load or highly repetitive motions.)
        (2) Wrist?
        (3) Forearm?
        (4) Upper arm?
        (5) Trunk? (For heavy loads, shift to large leg muscles.)
     d. By making movements continuous rather than jerky?
  7. Can a hold be made easier?
     a. By shortening its duration?
     b. By using stronger muscle groups, such as the legs, with foot-operated vises?

Source: Marvin E. Mundel, *Motion and Time Study: Improving Productivity,* 5th ed., Englewood Cliffs, NJ: Prentice-Hall, 1973, 230–31.

Today, motion study of repetitive tasks can involve a number of techniques, most involving charts of one variety or another. Methods engineers have found that by charting methods and the process, they can be more effective in thinking creatively and exhaustively about potential methods changes. Four forms of these charts are worth mentioning:

Process flowcharts for materials (e.g., paperwork) typically focus on what happens to products as they move through the process—where they get caught in bottle-necks, how materials are handled, and what has to come together before a product can proceed. A simplified form of these charts was introduced in Chapter 2, where it was called a process flow diagram. Vastly more detailed diagrams—involving maybe even floor plans—are often helpful in tracking materials movement and in documenting how long it takes to perform particular operations.

Process flow charts such as the one in Figure 6–2 are sometimes used to document what occurs with materials used by a particular worker. Charting such a task forces the methods engineer to break down the elements of the job thoroughly

Quantity Processed	Distance Involved	Task	Explanation
1	8 feet	○ □ ⇨ D ▽	Procure headlight from bin
1		○ □ ⇨ D ▽	Inspect headlight for damage
	8 feet	○ □ ⇨ D ▽	Move headlight to line
2		○ □ ⇨ D ▽	Procure two mounting screws from bin at line
		○ □ ⇨ D ▽	Wait for next car to reach work station
1		○ □ ⇨ D ▽	Mount headlight and tighten screws
1		○ □ ⇨ D ▽	Inspect positioning of headlight
1		○ □ ⇨ D ▽	Make any needed adjustments

○ Operation performed

□ Inspection made of quality or quantity

⇨ Movement of material

D Temporary storage or delay experienced by materials

▽ Controlled storage of materials (requisition required for withdrawal)

Figure 6–2 A Sample Detailed Process Flow for Materials: A Hypothetical Description of Headlight Mounting on an Assembly Line.

and to question which elements can be improved—as by adding a worker aid, laying out the workstation differently, resequencing the operations, eliminating needless movement of workers or materials, or perhaps redesigning the product or the materials going into it. The objective of such systematic study is to simplify the operation so that the worker can do it quickly and well.

Process flowcharts for workers focus solely on what the worker does. Whereas it is usually more advantageous for methods study to track materials and what happens to them, worker-oriented flowcharts can sometimes be more effective, particularly when the worker's job forces him or her to travel around the operation, interrupting contact with the service. A chart like that in Figure 6–2 can be used to detail such a worker's efforts, just as it can be used to detail the flow of materials and what workers do with them. In this case, however, movement would refer to the movement of the worker and not the materials, and temporary storage or delay would refer to the delay of the worker, not the materials.

Worker-machine charts are typically time-specific bar charts that track a worker together with his or her machine(s). This tracking can be in general terms or it can be as specific as the hand, feet, and body movements necessary to perform a given task. One popular analysis is to chart a machine's cycle time against the cycle time of the machine operator, so that any conflicts between the two can be isolated and resolved. Figure 6–3 is an example. In this analysis, the worker is seen as a "machine," with his or her own cycle time. Like the machine, the worker can be either functioning or idle. Such a worker-machine chart helps to coordinate the two so that their idle times are minimized and their outputs are maximized.

Worker-worker charts investigate the potential interference and room for coordination of one worker with others. Such charts are the simple extension of the worker-machine charts in Figure 6–3. They are particularly effective in service operations, which tend to be more labor-intensive than many manufacturing operations.

The data for these charts can come from several sources. The most widely used, quite naturally, is in-person observation of the task in question by the methods engineer. This is often the quickest, easiest, and least costly means of studying the job. Given some preliminary observation to determine what the important aspects of the job are, the methods engineer can then devise the most appropriate chart(s).

For tasks that are either very complex or of long duration, methods engineers have often found that filming or videotaping is useful. Films and videotapes have a number of advantages: (1) they catch everything in the field of view of the camera; they do not inadvertently miss seeing something; (2) they can be viewed over and over again; and (3) they are accurate. For these reasons, films and videotapes are especially helpful for methods study involving great detail or many workers. If the film is taken at unusually slow speeds, long or complex tasks can be reviewed quickly. (This is termed *memomotion analysis*.)

The analysis of great detail—generally for small-scale tasks—for which filming or videotaping is useful is termed micromotion analysis. This technique was pioneered by the Gilbreths, who divided movements into 17 distinct

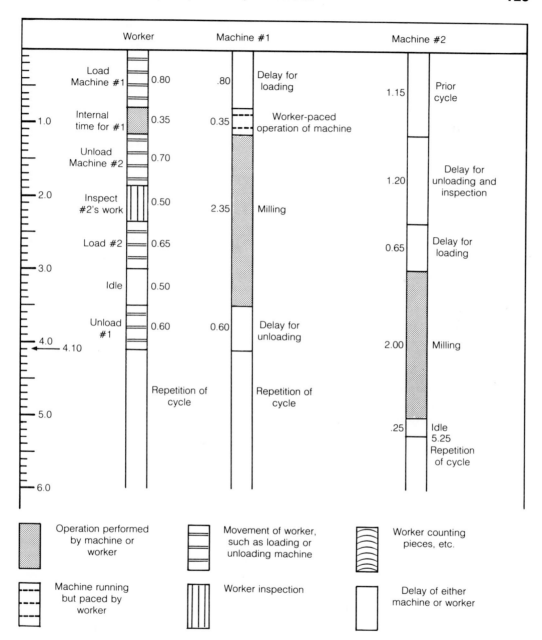

Figure 6–3 An Example of a Worker-Machine Chart.

categories, which they named "therbligs" (loosely, their name spelled back-wards). These therbligs (grasp, position, pre-position, use, assemble, disas-semble, release load, transport empty, transport loaded, search, select, hold, unavoidable delay, avoidable delay, rest, plan, and inspect) provide a convenient and clear framework for analyzing small-scale manual tasks and suggesting ways to improve or eliminate elements of them through the use of tools, fixtures, equipment, workplace layout, or just a different sequence of motions.

OTHER WAYS TO IMPROVE METHODS

The discussion so far has concentrated on the study of worker methods when repetitive motions in standard settings are the rule. Many jobs, particularly those in support roles or in the service sector, are not repetitive, however. Memomotion analysis can be of use in such situations. Frequently, two other techniques are employed: work activity analysis and work sampling.

Work activity analysis simply calls on the worker to list chronologically the work he or she performs, indicating the type of task, the time spent on it, and the number of actions completed (forms processed, memos written). Because work activity analysis can be time-consuming for the worker (especially when many short tasks are performed), this analysis is generally not extended over a long period. It is more appropriate for jobs with an irregular daily pattern of work but fairly stable day-to-day and week-to-week content. It can indicate the need for change in a job and point up aspects of the job that require further study.

Work sampling is the random observation of a worker and the ensuing calculation of the relative amounts of time spent performing specific tasks or tied up in avoidable or unavoidable delays (e.g., 10 percent of the time making phone calls, 20 percent of the time writing reports, 5 percent of the time waiting for materials). As such, it is a good means of analyzing jobs whose pattern of work is irregular over long periods of time. Although less disruptive than work activity analysis, work sampling can entail much travel throughout the operation by the analyst or supervisor involved and much time to gather enough observations. In its favor, work sampling enjoys some advantages over stopwatch or film/tape studies. For example, a single industrial engineer can study a number of tasks simultaneously; if the tasks involve a considerable amount of machine time, as opposed to operator time, work sampling can be more efficient. For nonstandard jobs, notably in support functions (such as engineering) or in service industries, work sampling is often the preferred means of studying the job and suggesting revisions to the responsibilities assigned or suggesting further study of particular aspects of the job.

The implementation of work sampling requires:

Categorizing what the studied worker does so that the relative frequencies of each task or type of delay as computed by the study can have real application to methods improvement.

Using an irregular pattern of observation of the worker; ideally, it should be random.

Making a suitable number of observations.

One approach to gauging how many observations are required is to make a certain number of observations and then calculate the relative frequency of each task or type of delay. Then another set of observations is made and added to the first set. The relative frequencies for specific tasks, as calculated for the first set of observations and the enlarged second set, are compared. If the computed relative frequencies are nearly identical, further sampling need not be done. However, if the relative frequencies differ by much, another set of observations should be taken and added to the other observations, relative frequencies should be computed, and comparisons should be made. When the calculated relative frequencies are judged to be stable, further sampling can cease.

Another approach to the determination of observation sample size is to use statistics. In this approach, the methods engineer states a preference for the probability that a given relative frequency is within X percent of the true relative frequency for the entire population (say a 95 percent probability that the relative frequency is within 10 percent of the true frequency). Assuming that the relative frequencies are distributed according to a binomial distribution, the sample size can be computed by the following formula:

$$N = (a \ / \ x)^2 \ [p(1 - p)],$$

where N is the number of observations required for the study, p is the relative frequency of interest (task or type of delay), a is the number of standard deviations associated with a given probability preference (such as 2 if the preference is a 95 percent chance), and x is the accuracy desired for the frequency (such as 0.10 for an accuracy within 10 percent of the true frequency).

As is clear from Table 6–3, the higher the level of confidence that the computed relative frequency is within tolerance, or the greater the accuracy

TABLE 6–3 REPRESENTATIVE OBSERVATION SAMPLE SIZES

Accuracy and relative frequencies	Probability preference level of confidence		
	90% (a = 1.645)	95% (a = 1.96)	99% (a = 2.576)
Accuracy of 10% (x = 0.10)			
p = 0.10	24	35	60
p = 0.25	51	72	124
Accuracy of 5% (x = 0.05)			
p = 0.10	97	138	239
p = 0.25	203	288	498

sought, the more observations must be made. The higher the relative frequency of the task or delay studied, the more observations are needed as well.

TIME STUDY AND TIME STANDARDS

Paralleling the motion study pioneering by the Gilbreths was the time study of individual worker tasks. The pioneer in this study was Frederick Taylor, who worked during the same period as the Gilbreths. Much of the work of Taylor and his followers had a similar intent to that of the Gilbreths—to improve productivity by looking closely at what workers did. However, rather than focus on the motions involved, Taylor broke down the job into elements and timed them. As in motion study, each element was studied to determine what should be kept and what should be discarded, but the stopwatch, rather than the movie camera or the process chart was the chief aid to the engineer.

Use of Time Standards

The time standards developed by Taylor have at least five broad applications:

1. They can be used for planning and budgeting. All different types of services have this need. Standards are critical for planning what to work on and for scheduling the workforce and any materials or machines.

2. They can be used to balance operations. In line flow operations, such as that found at Burger King and within many companies' back-office operations, it is essential to have an accurate appraisal of how long it takes to do the various jobs along the line. Line balance requires knowledge of precedence relationships, accurate time standards, and any constraints that could influence how the line is set up. Good line balance has as little idle time built into it as possible. Often that means concerted work on the limiting job along the line, the job with the longest time. After all, a line can only produce as fast and as much as its limiting, longest-time job permits it to.

3. They can be used to improve performance. Industrial engineering departments are charged with improving the operation of a plant's processing or assembly operations. These goals often require time studies to be done to evaluate technique and equipment changes. (See the Tour of Burger King later in this text.)

4. They can be used to evaluate individual workers and to serve as a basis for wage payments. In a variety of operations, time study is used as a basis for incentive wages. Time standards, once they are accepted as fair by the workers, can be used to evaluate worker performance: Workers who match or beat the standard can be rewarded, and workers who fail to reach the standard can be disciplined or even removed from the job.

5. They can be used to define a measure of labor productivity. The popular *efficiency measure* of labor productivity is conventionally defined as

$$\text{Efficiency} = \frac{\text{standard hours}}{\text{actual hours}} \times 100\%.$$

6. Thus efficiencies of more than 100 percent represent situations where the direct labor (i.e., workers for whom standards have been set) has beaten the standard. This efficiency measure is sometimes combined with a measure of utilization (the fraction of time the workplace was available to do work with all equipment "up" and all materials there) to yield an *effectiveness index*.

$$\text{Effectiveness} = \text{efficiency} \times \text{utilization}.$$

If utilization is less than 1 (and it always is), then effectiveness is always less than efficiency, in percentage terms.

Development of Time Standards

Time standards can be developed in a variety of ways.

History. The time standards some firms use in their planning are generally based on having worked on the same or similar parts or products before. Considering the diversity involved in a job shop, for example, using history is a very economical way by which to establish useful standards. Workers are not paid or evaluated according to these standards and thus great precision is not required. History provides enough rough but useful standards so that planning can be done effectively.

Time study. Time study typically involves dividing a job into distinct elements that have unambiguous starts and stops and recording the time spent performing each of those elements. Timing is frequently accomplished by an electronic stopwatch that automatically times different elements of the job. Alternative techniques include (1) the snap-back method (where three different stopwatches mounted on a special clipboard are started, stopped, and reset by a lever that is punched at the beginning of every job element), and (2) the continuous reading method (where a single stopwatch is used and elements are timed by reading off the running times).

Time study recognizes that the measured actual times of workers may not be appropriate for use as standards. Two major types of corrections are usually made: performance rating and allowances.

A worker, when timed, might purposely slow down so that the standard is set at an easily attainable level. To counter this possibility, methods engineers typically try to "rate" the worker's efficiency in doing the job. This performance rating serves to convert the measured actual time to so-called normal time, as follows:

Normal time = measured actual time × performance rating.

A performance rating less than 1 implies that the methods engineer thought the worker was underproducing. A rating greater than 1 implies that the methods engineer did not think an average worker could sustain the pace.

Performance ratings can be made of the entire job studied, but accuracy is enhanced if individual ratings are made of each element of the job. Normal times are then computed for each element. Establishing a performance rating is a tricky endeavor. Before a job can be rated, the methods engineer must appreciate the difficulty of the job and the conditions under which it is done. The engineer must then gauge what a normal pace would be under such circumstances and assess how the worker's efforts match up against the normal pace. Films or videotapes are often employed to give methods engineers a sense of what the normal pace should be; they also provide methods engineers with opportunities to practice rating workers.

Allowances, the other major correction to measured actual times, relate to delays in performing a job that are unavoidable for the worker or are irregular but that can nevertheless be expected as routine occurrences. Typically included as such delays are waits due to materials shortages, special instructions, machine adjustment or repair, quality problems, workplace housekeeping, and the like. Personal time taken to get a drink or to go to the bathroom are also generally counted as allowances. If fatigue was not taken into consideration in rating the job, it can be added as an allowance.

These allowances modify the normal time so that it can be used as a standard:

Standard time = normal time for the job × allowance factor for the job,

where

$$\text{Allowance factor} = 1 + \frac{\text{allowed minutes}}{\text{normal minutes}}.$$

The allowance factor is always greater than 1, often between 1.1 and 1.3. The methods engineer can arrive at the specific factor by studying the job to identify the delays inherent in it and the frequency of their occurrence. Such study can be made by continuous observation of the job for a reasonably long time (such as several hours) or by work sampling techniques.

Time study is a fairly accurate way to establish time standards for tasks for which the methods are well-known. In practice, however, time study has two drawbacks: (1) It cannot be used effectively for jobs that have not been well-defined and are only being contemplated, and (2) time study depends critically on the rating of the worker. The subjective determination of what the standard pace of the operation should be is often tricky and can become a bone of contention between industrial engineers and the workforce.

Predetermined motion-time systems. The two difficulties encountered with time study techniques are to some extent remedied by predetermined motion-time systems. These systems build on the notion that any task can be decomposed into a series of basic motions. The original task, then, can be seen as the sum of its basic motions. Extensive libraries of basic motion information indicate, for example, the time it takes to move one's hands various distances to perform tasks of varying complexity, with or without tools or materials of various weights. Using this information, an analyst can develop time estimates for tasks that are contemplated; such computations can be more objective than those computed by engineers rating actual operators. Standards set by good analysts are consistently shown to be accurate, although many companies periodically use direct time studies to check their use of predetermined motion-time systems.

The most widely known of these predetermined motion-time systems is MTM (method time measurement), developed by H. B. Maynard in the late 1940s. Several versions of the MTM system (MTM-1, MTM-2, MTM-3) have been developed. The original system, MTM-1, uses very short and well-defined movements to build up a particular task. Although MTM-1 can be used successfully for even short-cycle jobs (i.e., jobs that are accomplished within a short period of time) that are repeated over long periods, its application requires great skill. The industrial engineer must be very precise in breaking down a task into all its component motions and must carefully identify which of the multitude of choices from the MTM-1 database best characterizes each motion. Many of the problems encountered with MTM analysis are caused by engineer errors in its application rather than by inaccuracies in the time values.

Some of these applications problems are remedied in another predetermined motion-time system from the H. B. Maynard Company, which pioneered MTM. The MOST (Maynard Operation Sequence Technique) system was developed in the late 1960s and early 1970s. It was built on the observation that most worker tasks can be broken down into three basic sequences of motions:

A "general move" sequence for the movement of objects freely through the air. This sequence is represented by the series of letters ABGABPA where

A = action distance—the movement through space of one part of the body or the entire body

B = body motion—the up-and-down movement of the body or an action of the body to eliminate some obstruction to movement (e.g., opening a door)

G = gain control—typically, the manual dexterity needed to gain control over an object

P = place—the alignment of an object with one or more other objects before control is relinquished

A "controlled move" sequence for the movement of objects that remain in contact with a surface or attached to another object during the movement. This sequence is represented by the series of letters ABGMXIA where A, B, and G are defined as before and

M = move controlled—the manual control of the object through its path

X = process time—the work done by machine and not by the worker

I = align—worker actions needed to align objects after the controlled move itself or after the machine's work on the object

A "tool use" sequence for the use of common hand tools. This sequence is represented by the series of letters ABGABP ABPA, where the A, B, G, and P are defined as before and the blank space can be filled with an activity specific to the tool being used. Typical tool-related activities are fastening, loosening, cutting, treating an object's surface (painting or sanding), measuring, and recording.

Using the MOST system, the analyst follows these steps:

1. Determine the appropriate sequence from the task under study.
2. Index the movements that make up the sequence. (Each sequence has its own index definitions. Table 6–4 presents those for the general move sequence.)
3. Add these index numbers together.
4. Multiply by 10 to compute the time standard in time measurement units (TMUs), each of which is equal to 0.00001 hour (0.036 second).

Figure 6–4 illustrates, in general terms, the MOST system for a routine task such as might occur at a fast-food restaurant. (Recall that the Burger King

TABLE 6–4 GENERAL MOVE SEQUENCE WITH INDEX NUMBERS

	A	B	G	P
Index	Action distance	Body motion	Gain control	Place
0	< 2 inches			Hold or toss
1	Within reach		Move light object, or move light objects using simultaneous motions	Lay aside or loosely fit
3	1–2 steps	Bend and arise, 50% occurrence	Use nonsimultaneous motions; move heavy or bulky objects; move where vision is obstructed or not possible; disengage, interlock, or collect objects together	Make adjustments, use light pressure, or make two placements
6	3–4 steps	Bend and arise		Use care or precision; use heavy pressure; move where vision is obstructed or not possible, or make intermediate moves
10	5–7 steps	Sit or stand		
16	8–10 steps	Through door, climb on or off		

Movement   Fetching a bin of sliced tomatoes from under a counter and placing the bin into its slot

General move sequence ABGABPA		Appropriate Index from Table 6-4
1. Walking a step or two	Action distance	3
2. Bending down	Body motion	6
3. Picking the bin up	Gain control	3
4. Walking back a step or two	Action distance	3
5. Dropping the bin into its slot	Body motion, Place	0,1
6. Staying in the same place to resume other work	Action distance	0

Indexed sequence $A_3B_6G_3A_3B_0P_1A_0$

Time measurement units $(3 + 6 + 3 + 3 + 0 + 1 + 0) \times 10 = 160$ TMUs, or 5.76 seconds

Figure 6–4   Using MOST to Compute the Standard Time for a Sample Movement.

simulation model used MTM analysis to develop data on the making of Whoppers, drawing of drinks, and other tasks.)

By investigating sequences of motions rather than the motions themselves, the MOST system reaps some statistical benefits that help ensure the accuracy of its computed times if long enough sequences of movements are analyzed. Thus, the MOST system can be both accurate and intuitive as well as easier and faster. For many applications the MOST system is now preferred. It can operate manually or, as with other predetermined systems, in a series of computer programs, which can expedite the updating of time standards and process descriptions.

Standard data systems.   The MOST system represents an aggregation of the small movements that made up the original MTM system. Similarly, standard data systems can be viewed as aggregations of smaller, more specialized tasks for use by plants that have a number of routine jobs. Standard data systems are generally based on a wealth of data derived from many time studies of similar jobs. To apply them to a new or redefined job requires the breakdown of the contemplated job into not only the elements that have direct counterparts in the standard data base but also the elements that may not have precise counterparts but are related to tasks previously done and for which there are considerable data. By judiciously combining both types of elements, standards can be derived easily and with reasonable accuracy.

Choosing Among Systems

As we have seen, each of the methods for establishing time standards has advantages and disadvantages. Some (such as time study and MTM-1) are costly; some are detailed; and some are useful for particular purposes. Although the choices are not clear-cut, direct time study and very detailed MTM analysis are generally preferred when very accurate standards are required for relatively short-cycle jobs that may be repeated often and for which worker evaluation is important. Intensive time study may also be required in processes that pay incentive wages. For tasks that may not be repeated exactly over long periods of time, more aggregated predetermined motion time systems (such as the MOST system) are useful for developing standards; such systems are suitable when there is considerable worker discretion involved in each task. Standard data systems are particularly attractive for routine work that has a rich history of time study data. Purely historical data provide a very low-cost way to establish standards if great accuracy is not required and if the tasks studied are not routine.

Matching Demand and Supply

The ability to build up inventories in anticipation of demand makes life so much easier for manufacturers, despite all the troubles that inventory management gives them. It is a luxury that many service firms envy. Here is where the service firm is truly disadvantaged, and it is here that the service manager must be clever. The service firm often has to guess what demand will be and then define its capacity, within fairly narrow limits, to meet that demand. If demand falls below projections, the firm suffers the pain of having to pay off an excessive investment in capacity (e.g., facilities, equipment, or inventory). If demand exceeds the projections, then the firm incurs what could be significant opportunity costs (i.e., lost revenue). It can be a tricky business.

The previous chapter introduced the distinction between plans and controls and underscored the importance of establishing both good plans (good scheduling practices) and the mechanisms for monitoring them (effective controls). But there are other arrows in the service manager's quiver, and they relate to the management of both demand and supply. See Figure 7–1.

Let us consider supply management issues first, and then move to demand management.

SUPPLY MANAGEMENT

The chief considerations for the management of supply at service firms relate to making sure that there is enough capacity at the peak and to squeezing more capacity out of the process, if possible.

Preparation for the Peak

For many businesses, the peak period is a critical one for the financial health of the company. Retailers at Christmas are not the only ones for whom the results

133

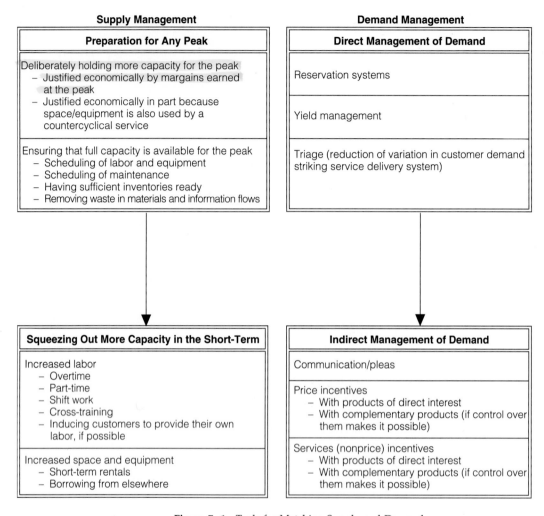

Figure 7–1 Tools for Matching Supply and Demand.

of the peak times toll either joy or gloom. Accountants experience a busy season in the spring. Florists have six holidays that are critical for them. Other businesses face their busy times on selected days of the week (Fridays at banks) or at selected hours of the day (lunch breaks or after 5 P.M.). In these cases it is mandatory to prepare well for the peak, however it occurs.

One way to prepare for the peak is to decide ahead of time to construct enough capacity to tide one over for that peak. This implies deliberately building up more capacity (space, equipment, materials, or labor) than is necessary for the rest of the time. Of concern, naturally, is paying for it. There are two ways to justify such excess:

1. *Margins earned at the peak.* It may be so lucrative for the firm at the peak, or the costs of building up excess capacity may be so cheap, that it pays for the service to exist with excess capacity for most of the time. Amusements are classic examples of this: large theaters, concert halls, amusement parks, golf courses, indoor tennis courts, etc.

2. *Countercyclical service.* Some service facilities have multiple uses, so that proceeds from an off-peak time can be significant enough to fund an excess of capacity to deal with a peak time. Ski resorts that double as summer resorts are examples of this; their size is dictated by the ski peak, but funded in part with substantially lower summer resort revenues.

The economic justifications behind these two scenarios are tricky. It is far from an easy calculation to make. The extent of the peak, the prices that can be charged, the costs of maintaining the facility, the costs of operating it, and the off-peak demand and its prices must all be factored into the calculation.

The other major way of preparing for the peak involves being sure that, whatever the capacity chosen, it is being used to the fullest. Here is where the scheduling plans introduced in the last chapter come to the fore. They exist to make sure that the service operation does not leave any money on the table. Several varieties of plans are important here.

Some deal with the scheduling of labor (How many people are needed when and for how long?)

Some deal with the scheduling of equipment (Which machines, when, and for how long?)

Some deal with the scheduling of inventories (How much should be held of which products used by the service? Reordered when? In what quantities?)

Some deal with maintenance (What is to be maintained when?)

Identifying and removing waste from an operation is another means by which money is not left on the table. This is the re-engineering that is so often discussed these days. It is very important that a service study its processes at the peak, so that they are efficient. Much as in a factory, where it is the bottleneck machine that dictates how much the factory can produce, the service operation depends on how much it can produce during the peak time. During nonpeak times, workers do not need to be so efficient in what they do; they typically will not constrain the service from earning revenues. During peak times, however, drops in efficiency translate directly into lost earnings. For this reason, firms are well advised to use process and information flow diagrams for analysis and to engage in good industrial engineering and quality management practices. For this reason, as well, fast-food restaurants schedule their best crews for their peak hours each week, and repair services schedule their best workers to particular bottleneck jobs during their peaks. Remember the proposition introduced earlier, in Chapter 3.

Proposition:

> Peak for the peak. Efficiency really counts only then. Average measures usually don't tell the story.

Squeezing Out More Short-Term Capacity

In many services, the most expensive controllable cost is labor. Thus, often there can be more service provided if labor is added to the process. Adding labor may not add tremendous amounts of capacity, but certainly enough so that the firm is willing to explore a variety of mechanisms to do so. Several different mechanisms are frequently used:

- Overtime work
- Part-time workers
- Extra work shifts (say, for the peak season)
- Cross-training, so that particular bottleneck tasks can be handled by the existing workforce, by rebalancing the process somewhat

Another mechanism that can add labor to the process during peak times is inducing customers to do things for themselves. Thus, restaurants, during their peaks, may schedule a buffet service. In so doing they relinquish control over the portions provided people, but they can save substantially on the wait staff and even kitchen help that they would otherwise require. Sometimes, special prices have to be resorted to to induce the desired behavior from customers, but the price breaks are usually much less than the costs that would have been incurred were customers not to provide their own labor.

There are also some services that are constrained at their peaks not by labor but by space or by equipment. Here is where short-term rentals or borrowing can take place. For example, airlines during peaks have been known to rent additional planes. The same is true for trucking firms or for warehousing operations, particularly if the peak is not expected to last very long.

With these insights behind us, let us now turn to the management of demand, a task that service companies engage in to a much greater degree than manufacturing companies.

DEMAND MANAGEMENT

The key notion behind the management of demand is shifting the timing of demand so that the peak is "shaved" and the off-peak times, with their excess capacities, are fed more. Sometimes this can be done directly, and other times it has to be done indirectly.

Direct Management of Demand

Reservations.   For a number of services, especially those that have a high intrinsic value for the customer, demand can be managed by introducing a reservation system. There are reservations for travel on airplanes, and sometimes trains, particularly when supply is likely to be constrained. There are reservations for doctors and other health care services, for traditional restaurants, for most professional services, for many services found in service shops, and for many other services.

Sometimes reservations do more than simply ensure full utilization of the service. They can also be used to segment demand and thus squeeze more revenue out of the customer who wants a better seat (at a game or a concert or on a plane) or a better room (at a hotel or in a hospital) or otherwise better or quicker service.

Reservations also act to regulate the arrival of demand and to reduce its variability. As was discussed in Chapter 4, a reduction in variability results in added effective capacity. Reduced variability in demand acts just like a "brick and mortar" addition to capacity.

Reservation systems cost money to install and operate but they are effective and usually regarded by consumers as fair and justified, particularly if the queue is managed by a first come, first served rule or by a rationing scheme whereby those who pay more are served first. Reservation systems do, however, require early, nonspontaneous action by consumers, and thus they are not well-suited to all kinds of services. One would be hard put to install a reservation system for retail operations,[1] unless what is being sold is of very high value (e.g., houses or works of art).

Often, of course, reservation systems exist side-by-side with first come, first served nonreservation systems (e.g., hotels, transportation, restaurants). This nearly always occurs with services that often have enough excess capacity that they do not want to turn away walk-in business. Consumers here, too, recognize that those who have planned ahead should be rewarded more than those acting on impulse, if capacity suddenly becomes constrained.

Yield management.   Closely allied to reservation systems is yield management. Airlines have done much to perfect this technique. The goal of yield management is to maximize the revenue that a service can realistically expect by offering "chunks" of the service, with differing restrictions on them, at a variety of price points. As reservations roll in, one can adjust the size of the chunks of service offered at each price with the goal of full utilization and maximum revenue.

Think of airlines. Airlines offer a variety of prices for seats with different restrictions. The lowest fares are limited in number and require the passenger to book significantly in advance, to stay a minimum amount of time at the destination, and to forfeit a considerable sum of money if any schedule change is desired. Higher fares carry fewer restrictions and offer the most flexibility.

---

[1]Or, for other mass service operations or for many service factory operations.

Hotels can play the same game, offering some rooms at cut rates to groups who book in advance and guarantee a certain number of rooms. Corporations that are regular users might get a somewhat higher rate. The "rack rate" is paid by the transient, and the hotel tries to keep at least some rooms available for such people because they provide the highest per room contributions.

Trying to maximize revenue in such situations, given the uncertainty of demand and the absolutely fixed capacity of the service, is an interesting dynamic problem. It is amenable to mathematical programming solutions, given the usual restrictive assumptions that constrain such techniques. Economic solutions that equate the expected marginal revenues across the fare classes have also been studied. In practice, most airlines and hotels, for example, create a "threshold curve" based on historical demand patterns over time. If demand runs significantly higher than past history, then one or more low fare classes are closed and demand is forced into the higher fare classes. If demand runs significantly behind past history, then the lower fare classes are left open or expanded.

Yield management, of course, requires an absolutely accurate and timely control system so that sales people have the best, most current data about the status of demand and knowledge about which fare classes are still open and which are either full or closed. It is no wonder that yield management is essentially a product of the computer age.

Triage.   Another mechanism that directly manages demand is triage. *Triage,* from the French word for "sorting," is originally a medical concept, usually applied to the battlefield, where the severity of patient medical needs is assessed and priorities for treatment are decided. Thus, some cases are taken on immediately, others wait, and still others are treated in a partial way.

In services, triage mechanisms can serve to segment demands of different kinds and route them to different service processes. This reduces the variation striking any one service process and permits some customers to be served more rapidly than they otherwise would. Triage mechanisms are widespread these days, especially "touchtone triage," where we are asked to press "1" for one need, and "2" if our needs are something else.

Triage mechanisms in combination with reservation systems permit airlines, for example, to handle first-class and business-class travelers more expeditiously than coach or tourist class travelers who have paid considerably lower fares.

Indirect Management of Demand

The indirect management of demand tries to induce customers who might ordinarily want service during peak times to shift their demand to nonpeak times when the service process's capacity can handle them better. The indirect management of demand focuses on the pricing and service policies that companies can use as inducements to customers.

Pricing policies. Customers understand price. As long as demand curves slope downward, lowering price is a great incentive for getting customers to buy more of what you have to offer, and raising price will choke off demand. If you want to shave peaks off of demand, raising prices for peak times and lowering prices for nonpeak times can work wonders for smoothing out the demand on the service process. Electric utilities offer electricity for lower prices if the peak days and hours of generation are avoided. Telephone companies offer cut rates in the evening and night hours. Movies have matinee specials. Hotels' lowest rates are offered during week-ends. The list goes on and on.

Non-price service policies. Less straightforward, and often not quite as effective as pricing policies, are nonprice service policies to shift demand. They are frequently used in conjunction with pricing policies. For example, not only does the hotel on the weekend offer rooms at reduced rates, but they may throw in a free breakfast or a round of golf or champagne in the room. The resort trying to shave off the late afternoon peak at the tennis courts may offer golf lessons at the same time, or some attraction on the beach. The early-bird user may get some extra service provided. Here is where the service manager has to be clever.

APPENDIX A: Forecasting Demand

As one might expect, there are different kinds of forecasting techniques that can be used to satisfy different forecasting needs. (See Table 7–1 for a breakdown

TABLE 7 – 1 FORECASTING REQUIREMENTS FOR DIFFERENT TIME PERIODS

	Short Term (≤ 6 months)	Medium term (6–18 months)	Long term (≥ 18 months)
Uses	Production schedules Staffing plans	Aggregate production plans Levels of employment and inventory	Capacity or process changes
Needs	High accuracy Detailed, disaggregated by product, model, style Forecast often by week or even day	Reasonable accuracy Some detail, some aggregation of products Forecast often by month	Ballpark accuracy Not detailed, high aggregation into product lines Forecast often by either month or quarter
	Turning points less important	Turning points of modest interest	Turning points important
	Low cost, quickly done Used by lower-level management	Modest cost and speed Used by middle-level management	High cost, takes time Used by top-level management

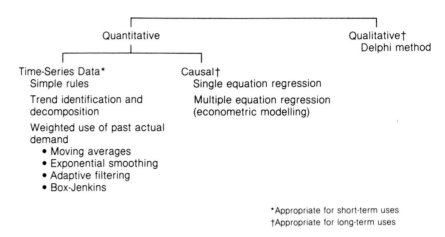

Figure 7–2   A Classification of Forecasting Techniques.

of needs.) Figure 7–2 divides the various forecasting techniques available into broad categories and distinguishes those that are appropriate for long-term forecasting from those that are appropriate for short-term forecasting. The next sections briefly describe each of the forecasting techniques introduced in Figure 7–2.

QUANTITATIVE TECHNIQUES USING TIME SERIES DATA

The simplest quantitative techniques use only the past history of the demand itself. These techniques try to isolate patterns that could be expected to repeat in the future. Their strength lies in identifying these patterns easily and translating them into predictions.

Simple rules are the least sophisticated quantitative forecasts. They involve rules such as "this period's demand equals last period's demand," or "this period's demand equals last period's demand plus 5 percent." Although simple, such rules do not yield consistently reliable predictions.

Trend identification and decomposition techniques are more sophisticated than simple rules because they break down the history into variations that may be cyclical or seasonal or that show a specific linear trend. These techniques, in a sense, massage the data (1) to remove seasonality or business cycle fluctuations and expose what may be general trends and (2) to isolate the extent to which variations and past demands have been random. The usefulness of this data decomposition and trend identification is evident from Situation 7–1.

The Young Forever Boutique

The Young Forever Boutique was started five years ago in space in an old, renovated factory in suburban Chicago. Kathy Wilkerson, its owner, had been a buyer with a department store chain in the area, but had always had an itch to run her own store. The boutique concentrated on casual and sports clothes for baby-boom generation women, although both younger and older women felt comfortable shopping there as well.

Kathy had been pleased with the store's progress. Sales each year had grown, and the store had been turning a nice profit. In late July of the boutique's third year, Kathy had been able to relocate the store to a modern mall, not too far from the renovated factory. The rent was more expensive, but Kathy saw the opportunity to attract more customers in the mall environment.

Recently, Kathy had sensed that sales were more erratic than they had been, and she was concerned that her sales forecasts were increasingly inadequate. She also wondered about how much of a boost to sales the move to the mall had been. Kathy hoped that more sophisticated forecasting techniques would help. Monthly sales since the shop's startup are found in Table 7-2.

Discussion of the Young Forever Boutique

Kathy Wilkerson's situation at the Young Forever Boutique presents a fine opportunity for contrasting some of the more important techniques of forecasting using time series data. One simple forecasting rule that Kathy could have used rests on the premise that next year's sales will follow the same growth and

TABLE 7-2   YOUNG FOREVER BOUTIQUE SALES VOLUMES BY MONTH

	Year 1	Year 2	Year 3	Year 4	Year 5
January	—	$ 6,381.07	$ 11,016.55	$ 11,965.68	$10,580.74
February	—	4,405.83	8,264.14	12,761.98	13,420.87
March	$ 4,566.40	9,126.95	6,843.95	18,126.70	34,476.27
April	6,941.89	10,970.45	20,109.68	19,092.90	19,108.79
May	7,047.23	10,189.28	11,148.64	15,384.01	18,109.54
June	6,784.37	7,043.85	8,365.40	12,237.00	13,743.60
July	5,814.23	6,717.37	9,469.08	13,252.53	18,339.25
August	6,906.38	9,139.72	10,221.00	13,819.77	—
September	8,075.13	11,315.19	15,161.41	21,755.64	—
October	7,913.56	10,838.40	17,713.08	24,838.10	—
November	9,054.18	11,150.94	17,508.99	15,955.60	—
December	14,114.58	17,592.20	27,566.89	19,370.70	—
Annual totals	$77,217.95 for 10 months	$114,871.25	$163,388.81	$198,560.61	$127,779.06 for 7 months

pattern as this year's sales. The implications of such a rule are left as exercises at the end of the book.

Although simple rules can often generate perfectly acceptable forecasts, they can, just as often, be wildly incorrect. Two of the most popular alternatives to the use of simple rules are the moving average and exponential smoothing. Both of these forecasting methods rely exclusively on the historical pattern of demand, under the assumption that the future will look like the past. In contrast to the simple rule, however, moving average and exponential smoothing estimates can be designed to adapt very quickly to abrupt changes in the historical pattern.

Let us consider the *moving average* first. It is simply an average of past data; each period, the data used in the average are updated to reflect, at least in part, what the most recent actual demand was. Moving averages can be simple in construction, with each period's value evenly weighted, or they can be more complex, with different weights applied to different time periods. When weights are used, they are typically defined so that they always sum to 1. In Kathy Wilkerson's case, for example, we could base the forecast on the past three months, but give the most weight (0.5) to the most recent month, less weight to the next to the last month (0.3), and the least weight to the month furthest back (0.2). This weighted moving average can be represented mathematically as

$$F_t = 0.5D_{t-1} + 0.3D_{t-2} + 0.2D_{t-3}$$

where F_t is the forecast for this time period (month), D_{t-1} is the actual demand last period, and D_{t-2} and D_{t-3} the actual demand two and three periods ago, respectively. Table 7–3 displays the forecast for year 3 for the Young Forever Boutique using this weighting scheme.

We could, of course, introduce more past data into the moving average calculation, or vary the weights applied, or specify particular time periods for use or exclusion (e.g., forecast first quarter data using only values from first quarters in the past, or exclude period $t-1$ from the calculation). The more weight applied to recent history, the more responsive the forecast is to changes in the pattern of demand. The less weight applied to recent history—perhaps by the inclusion of many past actual demands—the more stable the forecast and the less apt it is to be swayed by aberrations in the data. The choice of weights and data points to use should reflect the forecaster's desires for stability versus responsiveness in the forecast.

Exponential smoothing is allied to the moving average. It represents a special weighting scheme that has the advantage of being particularly easy to compute, requiring only the most recent forecast and the most recent actual value. The forecast for period t takes the following form:

$$F_t = F_{t-1} + \alpha(A_{t-1} - F_{t-1}),$$

which is built on the very logical assumption that the next period's forecast (F_{t-1}) equals the last period's forecast (F_{t-1}) plus the error in that forecast ($A_{t-1} - F_{t-1}$) adjusted by a correction factor (α).

TABLE 7-3 YOUNG FOREVER
BOUTIQUE MOVING AVERAGE ESTIMATES [a]

	Forecast year 3	Actual year 3
January	$ 14,309.06	$ 11,016.55
February	13,016.12	8,264.14
March	10,955.48	6,843.95
April	8,104.53	20,109.68
May	13,760.85	11,148.64
June	12,976.01	8,365.40
July	11,549.23	9,469.08
August	9,473.89	10,221.00
September	9,624.30	15,161.41
October	12,540.82	17,713.08
November	15,449.16	17,508.99
December	17,100.70	27,566.80
	$148,860.15	$163,388.72

[a] *Observations:*

Because the sales in year 3 are a dramatic increase over those for year 2, the moving average estimates lag behind the year's actual sales.

The weighting scheme ensures that the forecast does not dip as low or reach as high as actual sales do.

Algebraic manipulation of this equation yields the following alternative formulation, which is often preferred for doing computations:

$$F_t = A_{t-1} + (1 - \alpha) F_{t-1},$$

where F_t is the forecast value for the time t, A_{t-1} is the actual value for the last period, and F_{t-1} is the forecasted value for the last period. The factor α can vary between 0 and 1, although in practice it is frequently limited to less than 0.5. The higher α is, the quicker the forecast follows past actual demand. If high values of α work well (i.e., lower errors than others), there is a good case that a significant trend exists in the data. That is why values greater than 0.5 are not frequently used for α.

This smoothing technique is termed exponential because by substitution with past values, the weights of prior periods decline exponentially from the most recent period on back in time as shown:

$$F_t = \alpha A_{t-1} + (1 - \alpha)\alpha A_{t-2} + (1 - \alpha)^2 \alpha A_{t-3}$$
$$+ (1 - \alpha)^3 \alpha A_{t-4} + \ldots$$
$$+ (1 - \alpha)^{t-2} \alpha A_1 + (1 - \alpha)^{t-1} F_1$$

The forecast for the Young Forever Boutique's year 3 using exponential smoothing (= 0.3) is found in Table 7–4.

TABLE 7-4 YOUNG FOREVER
BOUTIQUE EXPONENTIAL SMOOTHING
WITH $\alpha = 0.3$ [a]

	Forecast year 3	Actual year 3
January	$ 17,592.20	$ 11,016.55
February	15,619.51	8,264.14
March	13,412.90	6,843.95
April	11,442.21	20,109.68
May	14,642.45	11,148.64
June	13,174.31	8,365.40
July	11,731.64	9,469.08
August	11,052.87	10,221.00
September	10,803.31	15,161.41
October	12,110.74	17,713.08
November	13,791.44	17,508.99
December	14,906.71	27,566.80
	$160,280.29	$163,388.72

[a] *Observations:*

The exponential smoothing technique, in this instance, yields forecasts that sum more nearly to the actual sales in year 3.

The sales estimates are really "smoothed" in the sense that they do not vary dramatically from one month to another. They are much smoother than the moving average estimates.

Evaluating Forecasts

A forecast's performance can be judged after the fact by its errors. Errors, however, can be assessed in various ways. Three commonly used errors are displayed in Table 7–5: the simple difference between actual and forecast needs or sales (sometimes called *bias*), the mean absolute deviation (i.e., the mean of the absolute values of the differences between actual and forecast), and the mean squared error (using the square of the differences). Table 7–5 compares the year three forecasts and actuals for the moving average and exponential smoothing techniques. The table reveals how the three different measures of error react in this situation. The results indicate that while the exponential smoothing estimates offer less bias than the moving average estimates, they differ more wildly on a month-to-month basis from the actuals, having a higher mean absolute deviation and a higher mean squared error.

Note that when the mean difference (or bias) is computed, errors that are positive and negative cancel one another out to some degree. This is eliminated by taking the absolute values of the errors in calculating the mean absolute deviation. Squared errors penalize forecasts that are far off much more heavily than forecasts that are only a little off; mean squared errors are much more sensitive to outlying observations than are mean absolute errors.

TABLE 7-5   YOUNG FOREVER BOUTIQUE ERROR ANALYSIS

A. Moving average estimates

	Forecast year 3	Actual year 3	Difference (bias)	Absolute deviation	Squared error (millions)
January	$ 14,309.06	$ 11,016.55	$-3,292.51	$ 3,292.51	$ 10.84
February	13,016.12	8,264.14	-4,751.98	4,751.98	22.58
March	10,955.48	6,843.95	-4,111.53	4,111.53	16.90
April	8,104.53	20,109.68	12,005.15	12,005.15	114.12
May	13,760.85	11,148.64	-2,612.21	2,612.21	6.82
June	12,976.01	8,365.40	-4,610.61	4,610.61	21.26
July	11,549.23	9,469.08	-2,080.15	2,080.15	4.33
August	9,473.89	10,221.00	747.11	747.11	0.56
September	9,624.30	15,161.41	5,537.11	5,537.11	30.66
October	12,540.82	17,713.08	5,172.26	5,172.26	26.75
November	15,449.16	17,508.99	2,059.83	2,059.83	4.24
December	17,100.70	27,566.80	10,466.10	10,466.10	109.54
	$148,860.15	$163,388.72			
Sum of errors			$14,528.57	$57,466.55	$398.90
Mean difference (bias)			$ 1,210.71		
Mean absolute deviation (MAD)				$ 4,787.21	
Mean squared error (in millions)					$ 33.24

B. Exponential smoothing with α = 0.3

	Forecast year 3	Actual year 3	Difference (bias)	Absolute deviation	Squared error (millions)
January	$ 17,592.20	$ 11,016.55	$-6,575.65	$ 6,575.65	$ 43.24
February	15,619.51	8,264.14	-7,355.37	7,355.37	54.10
March	13,412.90	6,843.95	-6,568.95	6,568.95	43.15
April	11,442.21	20,109.68	8,667.47	8,667.47	75.13
May	14,642.45	11,148.64	-3,493.81	3,493.81	12.21
June	13,174.31	8,365.40	-4,808.91	4,808.91	23.13
July	11,731.64	9,469.08	-2,262.56	2,262.56	5.12
August	11,052.87	10,221.00	-831.87	831.87	0.69
September	10,803.31	15,161.41	4,358.10	4,358.10	18.99
October	12,110.74	17,713.08	5,602.35	5,602.35	31.39
November	13,791.44	17,508.99	3,717.55	3,717.55	13.82
December	14,906.71	27,566.80	12,660.09	12,660.09	160.28
	$160,280.29	$163,388.72			
Sum of errors			$ 3,108.43	$66,902.68	$481.25
Mean difference (bias)			$ 259.04		
Mean absolute deviation (MAD)				$ 5,575.22	
Mean squared error (in millions)					$ 40.10

The *mean absolute deviation* (MAD) can be a handy number, for it can be used to approximate the standard deviation of a sample of observations. If a sample is drawn from a normally distributed population, then the standard deviation (σ) is related to the MAD as follows:

$$\sigma \approx 1.25 \text{ MAD}.$$

This relationship is sometimes employed in calculating safety stocks or in calculating control limits for quality control charts, topics discussed more in other chapters.

Dealing with Seasonality

The previous forecasts that use moving averages and exponential smoothing are flawed because they do not deal with the obvious seasonality of sales at the Young Forever Boutique. If adequate forecasts are to be made, this seasonality must be accounted for. There are several ways to deal with seasonality. Already mentioned is the technique of basing, say, a quarterly forecast on past data from similar quarters. In Kathy Wilkerson's case, however, when monthly forecasts are needed and only a few years of history are available, another technique is probably preferable.

This technique employs the observation that demand can be broken down into several components: a trend term, a seasonality term, and a randomness term.[2] Thus

Demand = trend × seasonality factor × randomness component.

If moving averages, exponential smoothing, or some other technique is to work well, then the data should be purged of their seasonality so that the trend can be identified and exploited for making the forecast. To purge seasonality, we can develop some seasonal indices (monthly, in this case) that can be used to deflate actual sales, leaving only the trend and the randomness components. These seasonal indices are typically ratios: average demand for the season (or month) divided by an average of demand for the twelve months surrounding it (or some time period not susceptible to the seasonality you are trying to control).

There are several steps to follow to deseasonalize data in this way. Consider them for the Young Forever case.

1. Calculate a twelve-month moving average of demand (where there is no seasonality, by definition) where that demand is centered on the month in question. For proper centering, we need an odd number of observations, so developing centered moving average of demand for 12 months is itself a three-step procedure:

    a. Calculate a twelve-month mean, using months 1–12. This will be centered on month 6-1/2.

---

[2]One could also include a cyclicality term to account for business cycle fluctuations. This discussion omits consideration of cyclicality, in part because cyclicality could have been expected to play a little or no role in explaining the Young Forever Boutique's steady growth. More complete discussion of forecasting demonstrates how cyclicality can be removed from an identified underlying trend.

b. Advance the calculation by a month and calculate the new 12-month mean that is centered on month 7-1/2. This calculation uses months 2–13.

c. Average the two twelve-month means to get a value centered on month 7.

Table 7–6 displays uncentered moving averages and then centered moving averages for the Young Forever data. Note that the first six months of data and the last six months are "lost" in the calculations.

2. Develop seasonal indices (or, in this case, monthly indices) by dividing the sales figures of Table 7–2 by the centered moving averages of Table 7–6 (see Table 7–7).
3. Average these seasonal indices over the years for which they were developed. That is, average all the January indices, average all the February indices, and so on (Table 7–7, panel B, column 1).

TABLE 7-6 MOVING AVERAGES FOR TWELVE MONTHS' DEMAND, CENTERED AND NOT CENTERED

	YEAR 1	YEAR 2	YEAR 3	YEAR 4	YEAR 5
Moving averages (not centered, value placed into month 7)					
January	—	$ 8,332.96	$11,041.85	$15,600.72	$18,202.68
February	—	8,408.22	11,271.16	15,916.01	18,626.57
March	—	8,594.33	11,361.26	16,215.90	
April	—	8,864.34	11,681.78	16,765.42	
May	—	9,108.07	12,254.67	17,359.18	
June	—	9,282.80	12,784.51	17,229.73	
July	—	9,572.60	13,615.73	16,546.72	
August	—	9,958.89	13,694.82	16,431.31	
September	$7,333.74	10,280.42	14,069.64	16,486.21	
October	7,713.78	10,090.17	15,009.87	17,848.68	
November	8,049.50	10,851.77	14,925.14	17,850.00	
December	8,311.33	10,931.72	15,278.09	18,077.13	
Moving averages (centered)					
January	—	$ 8,370.59	$11,156.51	$15,758.37	$18,414.63
February	—	8,501.28	11,316.21	16,065.96	
March	—	8,729.34	11,521.52	16,490.66	
April	—	8,986.21	11,968.23	17,062.30	
May	—	9,195.44	12,519.59	17,294.46	
June	—	9,427.70	13,200.12	16,888.23	
July	—	9,765.75	13,655.28	16,489.02	
August	—	10,119.66	13,882.23	16,458.76	
September	$7,523.76	10,185.30	14,539.76	17,167.45	
October	7,881.64	10,470.97	14,967.51	17,849.34	
November	8,180.42	10,891.75	15,101.62	17,963.57	
December	8,322.15	10,986.79	15,439.41	18,139.91	

TABLE 7-7 SEASONAL INDICES FOR THE YOUNG FOREVER BOUTIQUE

A. Data transformed to seasonal indices (raw sales divided by centered moving averages)

	YEAR 1	YEAR 2	YEAR 3	YEAR 4	YEAR 5
January	—	76.96	98.75	75.93	57.46
February	—	51.23	73.03	79.43	
March	—	104.55	59.40	109.92	
April	—	122.08	168.03	111.90	
May	—	110.81	89.05	88.95	
June	—	74.71	63.37	72.46	
July	—	68.78	69.34	80.37	
August	—	90.32	73.63	83.97	
September	107.33	111.09	104.28	126.73	
October	100.40	103.51	118.34	139.15	
November	110.68	102.38	115.94	88.82	
December	169.60	160.12	178.55	106.78	
		1,184.41	1,211.71	1,164.41	

B. Average of seasonal indices

	Uncorrected	Corrected
January	77.09	78.37
February	68.10	69.23
March	91.29	92.81
April	134.00	136.23
May	96.27	97.87
June	70.18	71.35
July	72.83	74.04
August	82.64	84.02
September	112.36	114.23
October	115.35	117.27
November	104.46	106.20
December	155.76	158.36
	1,180.33	

4. Sum these average indices and scale them up or down appropriately. In this case, the sum of the monthly indices is 1180.33. If sales were the same in every month, however, the monthly indices would total exactly 1200. Thus the indices as originally calculated can be scaled up by 1.0167 (1200/1180.33) (Table 7–7, panel B, column 2).

5. Divide the monthly sales figures of Table 7–2 by the seasonal (monthly) indices to purge the seasonality from those raw sales figures. Table 7–8 displays the deseasonalized sales figures.

Identifying Trends

Once the data have been purged of seasonality, what remains are the trend and randomness factors. Normally, we choose to think about the trend as a linear function of time (sales change by $ × each time period), although, just as easily, we could think of the trend as exponential, logarithmic, or something else. For

TABLE 7-8 DESEASONALIZED SALES FOR THE YOUNG FOREVER BOUTIQUE

	YEAR 1	YEAR 2	YEAR 3	YEAR 4	YEAR 5
January	—	$ 8,142.34	$14,057.10	$15,268.19	$13,501.01
February	—	6,364.05	11,937.22	18,434.18	19,385.92
March	$4,920.16	9,834.02	7,374.15	19,530.98	37,147.15
April	5,095.71	8,052.89	14,761.57	14,015.19	14,026.86
May	7,200.60	10,411.04	11,391.27	15,718.82	18,503.67
June	9,508.58	9,872.25	11,724.46	17,150.67	19,262.23
July	7,852.82	9,072.62	12,789.14	17,899.15	24,769.38
August	8,219.92	10,878.03	12,164.96	16,448.19	
September	7,069.18	9,905.62	13,272.70	19,045.47	
October	6,748.15	9,242.26	15,104.93	21,180.27	
November	8,525.59	10,499.94	15,486.81	15,024.11	
December	8,912.97	11,108.99	17,407.68	12,232.07	

TABLE 7-9 TREND IDENTIFICATION REGRESSION RESULTS FOR THE YOUNG FOREVER BOUTIQUE

Results for before-move data
Estimates of   a: $6,007.23
                 b: $223.59 per month $R^2 = 0.62$

Results for after-move data
Estimates of   a: $13,783.32
                 b: $307.27 per month $R^2 = 0.18$

the sake of simplicity, let us think of the trend as linear. Thus, mathematically, we view the sales data as exhibiting the following form:

$$(7-1) \qquad\qquad D_t = a + bP_t,$$

where D_t is the actual sales for period t, P_t is the time period applicable, a is a constant, and b describes the trend.

The constant term a and the trend coefficient b can be estimated statistically through a technique called *linear regression*. The deseasonalized sales of Table 7–8 can easily be used in a regression analysis of the suitable trend. Regression can also be used to determine whether the trend changed when Kathy Wilkerson moved the boutique from the renovated factory to the mall. This can be done by segmenting the data into before- and after-the-move groups and estimating equation 7–1 separately for each group. Table 7–9 shows the results of just such segmentation and estimation.

The results suggest that Young Forever's sales trend did increase after the move (i.e., b increased from $223.59 per month to $307.27 per month). Such a shift in the trend is called a turning point. The differences in R^2 statistics also suggest that Kathy was right to sense that sales were more erratic in the mall; the trend

TABLE 7-10 PREDICTING SALES FOR THE NEXT FIVE
PERIODS FOR THE YOUNG FOREVER BOUTIQUE

	Deseasonalized on trend	Seasonal adjustment made
August	$21,465.07	$18,034.95
September	21,772.34	24,870.54
October	22,079.61	25,892.76
November	22,386.88	23,774.87
December	22,694.15	35,938.46

explains less of the variation for the after-move data than it does for the before-move data.[3]

By using the estimated trend to predict a deseasonalized forecast and then by applying the relevant seasonal (monthly) index, we can make forecasts of the Young Forever Boutique's sales. Five months of forecasts are shown in Table 7–10.

There are other, more sophisticated techniques for forecasting. They are too elaborate for full explanation in a text on service operations management, but some brief comments on them are in order:

Adaptive filtering. This technique often gives better results than exponential smoothing or moving averages. It uses weighted averages of past actual demands but allows the weights to vary from period to period in such a way that the forecast error is substantially lowered. Each weight in the adaptive filtering scheme is adjusted by an equation that uses the error in the previous forecast period.

Box–Jenkins. Even more sophisticated than the adaptive filtering technique is the technique devised by George Box and Gwilym Jenkins. The Box–Jenkins method is particularly appropriate for complex time periods in which one suspects that a variety of patterns exists in the data. The technique is too complex to describe briefly, and it can be expensive to run, requiring considerable past histories of observations.

CAUSAL MODELS

The other major type of quantitative forecasting model uses not only time series data on the demand itself but also time series data on other variables that could be expected to influence demand in a cause-and-effect way. A model that can accurately capture the cause-and-effect relationship among the other variables and the demand can be very useful, especially in picking turning points in the demand pattern. However, these models tend to be expensive to run and the analysis required to define them properly takes more time; thus they are much more appropriate for long-term forecasting than for short-term forecasting. The two major classes of causal models are single-equation regression models and multiple-equation regression analysis, sometimes termed econometric modeling.

[3]There are also tests to determine whether the two regressions could reasonably be expected to be truly different from one another. Refer to statistical or econometrics texts for an explanation.

In single-equation regression analysis, the item forecast, or dependent variable, is postulated to vary systematically with one or more independent variables. These independent variables can be constructed in a variety of ways, including the use of time series data (GNP, industrial production), past values of the dependent variable, and dummy variables (e.g., 1 if the month is May and 0 otherwise). Regression analysis fits the specified independent variables to the dependent variable by using historical data; this is called estimating the coefficients of the model's specified independent variables. Predictions can then be made by assigning expected future values to the independent variables and solving the estimated equation for the dependent variable's value. Econometric modeling is a step up from simple regression analysis in that it looks at collections of regression equations where some of the dependent variables in one equation turn up as independent variables in the other equations. Econometric modeling, in particular, can be very expensive and time-consuming because the data demands are voracious and the estimation tricky.

QUALITATIVE TECHNIQUES

The techniques previously explored make use of quantitative data developed from history. However, if one thinks that the future is not likely to depend much on history—because of vast disruptions in the economy or the industry, or simply because what is to be forecast is new and uncharted—one may then want to rely on the expertise of specific people. Qualitative forecasting is often applied to new technology, trying to forecast the kinds of changes to expect. The Delphi Method is perhaps the most common qualitative approach. This method uses a panel of experts who are asked particular questions. Their answers are collected and summarized (with means, ranges, standard deviations, etc.), and this information is passed out to the panel. The panel then deliberates for another round of forecasting using the information provided. Their responses are again collected, summarized, and disseminated. Numerous rounds of prediction and summary can occur. In some cases, consensus is reached after several rounds; this is particularly true if outlying responses are not held with much conviction. On the other hand, consensus is not guaranteed if outliers are stubborn about their views.

Choosing a Forecasting Technique

As was mentioned at the start of this section, particular forecasting techniques are associated, in the main, with different forecasting needs. The simple time series techniques are easy to use and are generally applied to very short-term forecasts of individual product models and variations. In those cases, history is likely to be a good guide to the immediate future. The more sophisticated of the time series techniques are more useful when the historical pattern appears to be more confused and when varied trends in the data are likely to exist. The causal and qualitative techniques are more satisfactory for longer-term needs, with the qualitative techniques being at an advantage only when history is deemed to be of little significance for prediction.

Managing Inventories: Time-Independent Systems

Although it is true that one typically cannot inventory services themselves, it is often true that the facilitating goods that accompany some services are inventoried. Wholesale and retail trading is perhaps the most prominent service where inventory control plays a significant role, but there are others that need to pay attention to the inventories they carry. Most services use inventories in erratic fashion because their use is often triggered directly by customer demand. One cannot anticipate their use precisely, so these services are compelled to manage what is termed *time-independent inventories*.

It is not too far off the mark to visualize the problem of managing such inventories (think raw materials inventory or finished goods inventory) as a problem of managing piles of "stuff" that either the process itself or consumers in the marketplace draw down. The objective of good inventory management in this case is to offer good service to either the process or the market at reasonably low cost. This objective, in turn, means deciding how many items should be in each pile, when orders to replenish the piles ought to be placed, and how much each of those orders should contain. Managing such inventory stocks (as opposed to managing work-in-process) essentially means deciding these three questions of pile size, order time, and order size.

Because the timing of independent demands is often so uncertain, the techniques typically used for managing inventories of such demands are themselves independent of time. These techniques are sometimes also called non-time-phased inventory systems, meaning simply that they do not attempt to be so precise about timing orders to expected use. Their purpose is the same, however: to replenish a pile of items in timely fashion and at reasonably low cost. Again, think retailing and distribution activities where consumer demands are often variable and uncertain.

The two major non-time-phased techniques have these differing philosophies:

1.   Replenish the pile on a regular basis (daily, weekly, monthly) and bring it back up to the size you want (we will talk shortly about the desired size of the pile). The amount by which you replenish the pile may vary from one time to another, but you always replenish the pile. This basic strategy is often called a *periodic reorder system.*

2.   Keep a constant watch over the pile. When its size dips to a predetermined level (we will talk shortly about this level), replenish the pile enough to bring it back up to the size you desire. Under this philosophy, the amount by which you replenish the pile stays the same, but the time spans between replenishments may vary. This basic strategy is frequently termed a *reorder point system,* the reorder point being the predetermined level that, once reached, triggers the replenishment of the pile by the same amount.

More will be said about periodic reorder and reorder point systems and their application to independent demand inventories. These same systems can also be applied to dependent demands inventories as well, although frankly, with much less success. Let us examine them in greater detail.

THE WORKINGS OF NON-TIME-PHASED INVENTORY SYSTEMS

Relevant Costs and Concepts

The decisions that have to be reached in non-time-phased inventory systems—those of pile size, when to replenish the pile, and how much should be in a replenishment—involve balancing a variety of costs. Several kinds of costs are relevant, as described here.

Costs of holding the inventory.   Inventory is not costless to stock. There are a number of costs to consider, the major one being opportunity cost of capital. This is the cost incurred by having the company's capital devoted to financing the inventory rather than invested in some other, income-producing endeavor (machines, personnel, a bank account). Often the company's cost of capital is used to estimate the magnitude of this opportunity cost.

Other, lesser costs of holding inventory include the following:

1. *Storage and handling.* The costs of warehousing, handling, counting, and keeping track of the inventory.
2. *Insurance and taxes.* Standard, out-of-pocket costs mandated for inventories of all types.
3. *Obsolescence and shrinkage.* Costs that should be imputed to inventories because, typically, not all of the items placed into inventory can be pulled back out and used when needed. Some items become obsolete because of engineering changes. Other items deteriorate, break, or in some other way become unusable. This represents a cost of holding inventory.

Costs of securing more inventory.   Several kinds of costs are incurred in securing one more replenishment for a pile of inventory. Moreover, it is important to recognize that these costs ought to be marginal (incremental) costs and not average costs. For example, consider preparing a purchase order for an outside vendor. The average costs of that order might include the time of the buyer and clerk involved, as well as the cost of the paperwork and phone calls to place and keep track of the order itself. If, as is nearly always the case, the buyer and the clerk would be employed anyway, then their costs are not relevant to the calculation of the cost of the order and thus should be excluded.

The kinds of costs incurred to secure more inventory can include the following:

1. *Order costs.* Costs associated with placing orders for materials from outside vendors. The marginal costs of ordering are generally very low, consisting for the most part of some telephone charges and paperwork.

2. *Production changeover costs.* If the inventory to be secured is from within the operation, then the replenishment will probably impose some costs over and above the costs of the inventory units themselves. A new setup takes time, imposing an opportunity cost on the operation because that setup time might have been spent producing output. Sometimes the opportunity cost is zero (that is, no output would be forgone by using the time for setup), but it is a point well worth considering. The setup itself may involve costs—fresh tooling, cleaning, new materials, generated scrap. The replenishment may also cause the operation to increase capacity through overtime, new hires, subcontracting, or the like, and these means of enhancing capacity can be costly in incremental terms.

3. *Tracking costs.* Costs involved in determining when an order or production changeover should happen. Stashes of inventory have to be monitored, which takes people, systems, and paperwork. Frequently, inventory levels cannot be accurately determined easily, so real economies exist in tracking inventory items in bunches and in placing purchase or production orders in groups, rather than one at a time.

This is particularly true for items for which perpetual inventory records (records of the current quantities for each item, updated constantly through transactions of receipt and disbursement of the item from the stockroom) are not kept, or, at least, not kept very accurately.

4. *Volume discounts.* The considerable savings that often can be enjoyed by buying (or manufacturing) items in quantity. Many vendors publish price lists with discounts given for bulk purchases.

Costs of not having enough inventory.   When a company cannot meet demand out of finished goods inventory, it can incur several (sometimes significant) costs. If the customer is willing to wait for the item—the item is then said to be backordered—there are likely to be additional costs for tracking the order: expediting it, shipping it specially, and invoicing. If the customer is not willing to wait for the item and presumably goes elsewhere to purchase it or its substitute, the company forgoes a sale and, thereby, the contribution to fixed costs and profits that sale could have made. Indeed, by stocking out, the company may forgo all future sales by that consumer, thus losing the contribution possible from future purchases. Backorders are cheap compared to this kind of loss. However, determining the cost of a stockout, or even of a backorder, is fraught with problems because so many different assumptions can be made about the consumer's present and future actions. Sometimes a backorder is regarded as appropriate, whereas other times the penalty is stiffer: no future sales. A typical cost assigned to a stockout is the one-time loss of contribution from the item, but such an estimate could be high or low without the company knowing for sure.

Also relevant to inventory management are lead time for the item (the time it takes to receive an ordered shipment) and safety stocks held. Safety stock levels will be discussed later; for the present we will simply acknowledge their usefulness. Lead times are important to calculations of the expected demand for the item between ordering a supply of it and receiving the order.

Exactly how the costs of inventory interact among themselves and interact with lead times and safety stocks—to determine inventory levels, timing, and replenishment quantities—depends upon which approach is taken. The periodic reorder technique balances these costs differently from the reorder point technique. In general, though, the higher the costs of holding inventory, the less inventory we want to have on hand at any time, the more frequently we want it to be replenished, and the smaller we want any replenishment quantity to be. The higher the costs of securing more inventory or of not having enough, the more inventory we are willing to have on hand, the less frequent the replenishment, and the larger the replenishment quantity. These costs thus pull in opposing directions and must be balanced against one another. The next sections examine how those balances are made.

The Periodic Reorder System

The periodic reorder system is governed by the simple decision rule of "order enough each period (day, week, month, or whatever) to bring the pile of items inventoried back up to a targeted size." This is similar to filling the car's gasoline tank every Friday. The workings of the system can be clarified by reference to Figure 8–1. The solid line traces the actual level of inventory held. The replenishments arrive at equally spaced times (1, 2, 3, 4), but their amounts differ each time. The replenishments are also ordered at equally spaced intervals (A, B, C, D), separated from the arrival times by a consistent delivery lead time. The amount ordered each time is the difference between the targeted level and the actual amount on hand at the time the order is placed. Thus, it equals the actual demand during the previous period. Note that during time period 2, the actual inventory dips into the safety stock because of unforeseen demand.

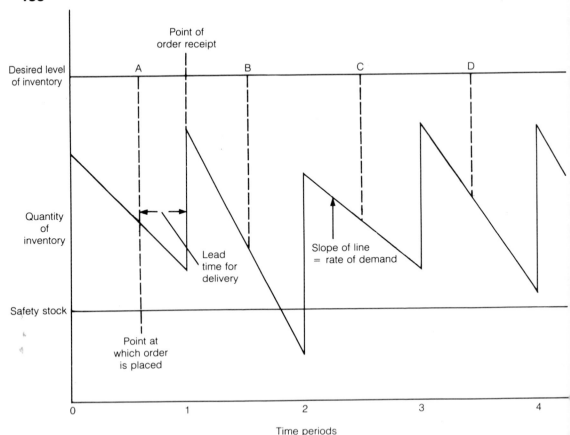

Figure 8–1   The Periodic Reorder System.

   In the workings of the periodic reorder system, a key question is what the targeted level of inventory is. If we know in advance exactly how much will be needed during any period, the answer is easy: Order the amount that will be used and no more. So, as the truck pulls in with the supply for next period, the last unit of this period's supply is being drawn off. This technique is similar to the basic philosophy of material requirements planning—to order just what is needed. In this case of certainty of demand, Figure 8–1's targeted level of inventory would change each period, along with the amounts anticipated (always correctly) to be consumed that period.
   Unfortunately, a company rarely knows in advance how much of a given item will be needed. Thus the targeted level of inventory cannot be determined so readily. Mere estimates of likely demand will have to be relied on, and some safety stock level will have to be set. (Safety stocks will be discussed later.)

The Reorder Point System

The reorder point inventory system follows the decision rule of "watch withdrawals from the pile of inventory until the designated reorder point is struck and then order the fixed amount needed to build the pile back up to its targeted size." This is similar to filling the gasoline tank whenever the gauge reads 1/4 full. But, again, the question is, What is the targeted size? Consult Figure 8–2.

The targeted size in this case is not determined, as in the periodic reorder system, by the expected usage over the period because there is no regular period following which inventory needs are checked. The pile is monitored continually, not every so often. Instead, the size of the pile depends fundamentally on a quantity called the *economic order quantity* (EOQ).

The choice of reorder point depends on how soon a shipment of the EOQ can arrive. If the shipment can, once ordered, arrive instantaneously, we are safe to run the stock to zero before reordering and the reorder point is zero. If the shipment takes a while to arrive, the choice of reorder point depends on an estimate of the expected pace of demand. The order point normally should leave enough so that a stockout does not occur before delivery of the EOQ. Computing this reorder point is much like computing a safety stock for uncertain demand in a periodic reorder system. If there were no uncertainty, the reorder point would simply be the average expected rate of withdrawal from inventory per time period (x parts per day) times the number of time periods it will take to receive

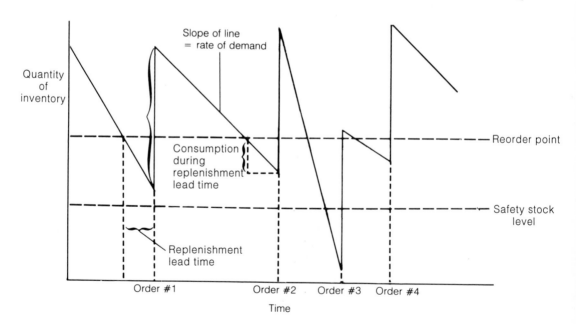

Figure 8–2 The Reorder Point System.

the order of EOQ. Given uncertainty, however, the reorder point has to be larger by the amount of a buffer or safety stock (calculating the size of the buffer stock is addressed later). No matter what the reorder point, however, the decision rule stays the same: When the reorder point is struck, order the EOQ.

How does the company determine how much the EOQ should be? The key to this order quantity and the reason it can be claimed as economic is the process by which it is found. The EOQ is chosen as the order quantity that minimizes the "total variable costs associated with changing order quantities." Every word of this phrase is meaningful. There are a variety of EOQ formulas, but what is important is the process by which the EOQ is found, not any formula that might seem to apply.

Let us consider a very simple, conventional, but suggestive case where we can discover a minimum for the total variable costs. In this case, there are only two variable costs that are in any way associated with any changing of order quantities.

1.   *Inventory carrying costs.* These carrying costs vary directly with the order quantity because the larger the order quantity, the larger is the average inventory held and thus the larger the carrying costs incurred. To illustrate this point in greater detail, let us make the common—and convenient—assumption that the demand on the inventory is absolutely steady, as is represented in Figure 8–3. Given this constant rate of draw upon the inventory, the average number of units in inventory is half of the order size. So if Q is the order size (see Figure 8–3), the average inventory is Q/2. As we shall discuss later, this is an important simplification in this computation of minimum total costs.

2.   *Order costs.* The order cost for any single order is a constant. The costs of actually placing or setting up the orders for the inventory thus vary inversely with the order quantity. The larger the size of the order (for a fixed annual demand), the fewer the orders that have to be processed, and thus the lower the order costs are. These order costs can be the costs incurred in dealing with

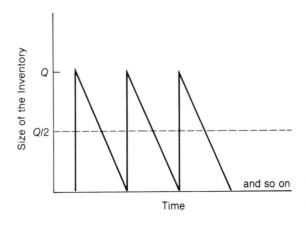

Figure 8–3   Graph Depicting the Assumption of Steady Demand on an Inventory.

vendors or the costs incurred in setting up the order in a manufacturing department of the company. For this case, assume that (1) the time from order to receipt is a constant and (2) no stockouts are deliberately permitted. (In Figure 8–2 stockouts are deliberately permitted.)

It is important to note what is not included as a variable cost associated with changing order quantities. For example, the cost of the inventory itself is not included because, for a fixed annual demand and a fixed price per unit, the cost of the inventory does not vary with changes in the order quantity. However, if a supplier were willing to give discounts on orders above a certain size, for example, the cost of the items in inventory would become a cost that varies with different order quantities and should be included in the total cost calculation. Transportation costs are also assumed not to vary with changes in the order size, nor are any production or other related costs.

Given the assumptions spelled out above, and with the knowledge that the only variable costs we can associate with different order quantities in this case are carrying costs and order costs, we can define the total variable costs in symbols as follows:

Total variable costs = order costs + carrying costs
= (cost per order)(number of orders)
    + (period carrying cost as a percentage)(value of average inventory)
= $S(D/Q) + i[C(Q/2)]$

where

S = cost per order
D = period demand, usually annual demand
Q = order quantity
i = period carrying cost as a percentage (includes opportunity cost, physical costs of handling and storage, obsolescence)
C = variable cost per unit of inventory
$Q/2$ = average number of units in inventory, assuming a steady and constant demand.

We want to solve for the order quantity (Q) for which the total cost is a minimum. Given the particular expressions for carrying cost and order cost, one way to solve for this minimum is to set the order cost equal to the carrying cost, since the intersection of these two lines falls directly below the low point of the graph of total cost (see Figure 8–4).[1]

---

[1]In general, of course, one cannot rely on friendly mathematical functions to solve for the minimum of an expression like that for total costs. One must rely on calculus to develop an expression for the slope and solve for Q, the order quantity, at the lowest point, where the slope is zero. Differentiating total cost (TC) with respect to Q and setting the resultant expression equal to zero yields

$$TC = S(D/Q) + iC(Q/2)$$
$$\partial TC / \partial Q = -SD/Q^2 + iC/2 = 0$$
$$Q = \sqrt{2SD/iC}.$$

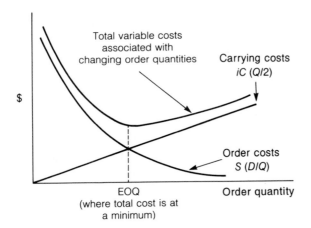

$

Total variable costs
associated with
changing order quantities   Carrying costs
                              iC (Q/2)

Order costs
S (D/Q)

EOQ   Order quantity
(where total cost is at
a minimum)

Figure 8–4 Costs Versus Order
Quantities for the Simple Case of
Carrying Costs and Order Costs Only.

Setting order cost equal to carrying cost and solving for Q yields

$$S (D/Q) = iC (Q/2)$$
$$2 SD = iCQ^2$$
$$Q = \sqrt{2 SD / iC}.$$

What does this solution mean for this simple example? It has the intuitively appealing properties that the cost-minimizing order quantity, the EOQ, rises with increases in period demand and cost per order and declines with increases in the inventory carrying-cost rate and in the variable cost of the inventoried item. Importantly, the EOQ varies by the square root in this simple case. That is, an increase in company sales does not require a proportional increase in inventory to supply it, but merely an increase according to the square root. In other terms, a doubling of demand does not require a doubling of inventories, but merely an increase of 41 percent, all other things held constant.

To reiterate, the key thing about the determination of an EOQ within a reorder point inventory system is not the formulas themselves, but the method by which an EOQ is found—namely, by use of the framework of total variable costs associated with changing order quantities. To see this point more clearly, consider some variations on the simple case just analyzed. The EOQ calculated earlier was simple because of the numerous assumptions that were made. Some of these assumptions can be relaxed easily and a new, modified EOQ can be calculated.

Variation: price discounts.   One important factor that the simple EOQ model does not allow for is price discounts with volume orders. It is common practice for vendors to quote reduced prices for orders of a certain size.

Thus, after certain order-size thresholds, the variable cost of the unit of inventory declines. The lower cost for successive ranges of order volumes naturally changes the total variable cost and thus the computed value of the EOQ. The conventional technique for calculating the EOQ when price discounts are applicable uses the following steps:

1. Compute EOQs for each different unit cost. Compare each with the range of volumes for which it applies to see if the EOQ is feasible (i.e., check to see that the EOQ calculated with a given price lies within the quantity range for that price). Start with the lowest cost per unit range. If its EOQ is feasible, it will be the minimum-cost EOQ.

2. Compute the total costs for each price break quantity and for each feasible EOQ.

3. Select the lowest total cost from step 2. Its quantity is the minimum-cost order quantity.

Figure 8–5 illustrates this situation of price discounts for larger orders. There are three different prices applicable, C_1, C_2, and C_3, as shown in the figure. Associated with each different unit cost there is a distinct total cost curve. These cost curves are designated TC_1, TC_2, and TC_3. As the figure demonstrates, only the first part of the TC_1 curve is applicable because it is only with that first range that the unit cost C_1 prevails. After quantity Q_1, unit price C_2 applies. Thus the relevant total cost curve for quantities lying between Q_1 and Q_2 is the curve TC_2. After Q_2, what is relevant is unit cost C_3 and total cost curve TC_3. The three-step procedure outlined above is a means of investigating each section of the total cost curve systematically to see what lies at a minimum.

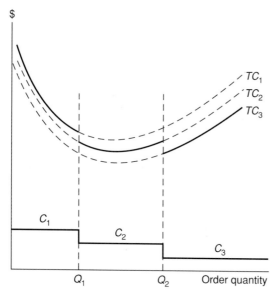

Figure 8–5 EOQs When Price Discounts Exist.

This three-step technique can be tedious, however, especially when there are many price break points. Kuzdrall and Britney have suggested a new method that assumes that the price discount schedule for the vendors' products is composed of fixed costs (setup costs) as well as variable costs. It then calls for the use of regression analysis to estimate the fixed and variable vendor costs. Using this information, the method then dictates several well-defined steps to develop a "critical interval" in which an EOQ of least total cost is identified. There are numerous instances where the EOQ cannot easily be calculated from a formula or even a computer algorithm. In such instances, the framework of total variable costs is essential for keeping things straight.

Choosing Between Periodic Reorder and Reorder Point Inventory Systems

These then are the major elements of both the periodic reorder and the reorder point inventory systems. Both, remember, are non-time-phased systems. Situation 8–1 will help us consider why one might institute one system rather than the other.

SITUATION 8–1

Driscoll Lumber Company

Spurred by some informal conversation at a recent Lions Club luncheon, Aubrey Driscoll was reflecting on the way in which he stocked items for his lumber company. Together with his brother, Burney, Aubrey owned and operated the Driscoll Lumber Company in Devine, Texas. Devine, a small town southwest of San Antonio, depended largely on cattle ranching and peanut farming for its livelihood. The Driscoll Lumber Company was a major retailer of lumber, hardware, construction materials, and ranching supplies (corral gates, posts, barbed wire fencing) for the area surrounding the town.

The Lions Club discussion caused Aubrey to think of dividing his inventory of goods into distinct classes, some of which might be ordered better through a periodic reorder system rather than the standard "order when low" system that prevailed in the lumberyard. As Aubrey saw it, his stock could be classified into several major categories:

1. *Seasonal versus nonseasonal demand.* The lumber and hardware that the Driscoll Lumber Company sold followed no seasonal pattern. Housing construction and repair in South Texas could be maintained in winter, due to the region's mild climate. Sales of barbed wire and steel fencing, however, were higher in the late fall and winter, as ranchers and farmers shifted their attention from the raising of peanuts, hay, and other crops to the repair and construction of fields, pastures, and corrals.

2. *Items easily counted for inventory and items more difficult to count.* Most of the items the lumber company stocked were easily counted for inventory. Lumber, plywood, roofing material,

cement, and the like were kept in open bins in the company's shed; low levels of any of these items were immediately obvious from just a quick glance around the shed. Some items, however, were more time-consuming to count, particularly those that came in many different sizes, shapes, or grades. Some hardware items such as pipes and fittings were among these, as well as special bolts stored in small compartments. Glass was another such item because it often had to be cut to order, and keeping track of the usable remains was difficult.

3. *Ordered lumber versus rolling lumber.* Most of the lumber Aubrey Driscoll sold had been ordered about 30 days in advance. What was shipped to Driscoll Lumber Company was exactly what had been ordered, usually in packaged bundles of standard lengths and a fixed count of pieces. Often however, West Coast sawmills specializing in Douglas fir, spruce, hemlock, and other softwoods dispensed with filling specific orders. Instead, the mill would fill railroad boxcars with just what it was sawing at the time, set the boxcars rolling on the rails toward various regions of the country, and rely on lumber brokers to sell off the boxcars before they reached the end of the line. Retail lumber companies could often enjoy significant purchasing discounts by buying lumber in this way, although it frequently meant that some lengths or grades would be overstocked for a time.

To Aubrey Driscoll's way of thinking, these were the major categories of items that he inventoried. He wondered whether he should continue to order all of them only when they were low (a reorder point system) or whether he should make periodic checks of at least some items and order variable quantities (a periodic reorder system). Which items seemed more suitable to one system or the other?

Discussion of Driscoll Lumber Company. Aubrey Driscoll's three categories of items serve as a useful starting point for a discussion of the pros and cons of either a periodic reorder system or a reorder point system.

1. *Demand seasonality.* The calculation of an order quantity for a reorder point inventory system implicitly assumes that demand is steady. That is, the minimization of total cost generally assumes that over the relevant time period, the draw on the inventory is constant. Thus, using an annual demand figure to calculate an order quantity is inappropriate if marked demand seasonality exists. One could calculate different EOQs for different seasons, but it is often simpler to use a periodic reorder system for items whose demand is seasonal. Other things being equal, the Driscoll Lumber Company would be better advised to use a reorder point system for its lumber and hardware (nonseasonal) and a periodic reorder system for barbed wire and steel fencing (seasonal). If the lumber company placed barbed wire and steel fencing on a reorder point system, it might risk carrying too little inventory in fall and winter and too much the rest of the year.

2. *Ease of taking inventory.* A reorder point system requires that the inventory be monitored constantly. If inventory is difficult or expensive to take, a reorder point system is less desirable. At the Driscoll Lumber Company, lumber and other open-bin items are easily inventoried and thus can be maintained under a reorder point system. Glass and certain hardware items, however, are tough to inventory and thus argue for a periodic reorder system.

3. *Price discounts.* The possibility of price discounts on West Coast "rolling lumber" and their irregular timing disrupts both periodic reorder and reorder point inventory systems. Deciding whether to buy such lumber, once offered, demands a quick inventory of existing stocks and a computation of how much of the purchased lumber will be used during the ensuing time frame. In a sense, this computation lies outside the routine workings of either inventory system. The fact that an inventory of the existing stocks is required suggests that such price discounts are perhaps more compatible with a reorder point system, but they are still compatible with a periodic reorder system.

Consideration of all of these features suggests that the Driscoll Lumber Company may be best off using a reorder point system for its lumber and larger hardware supplies and a periodic reorder system for its small, hard-to-inventory hardware items, its glass, its barbed wire and fencing, and similar items.

In more general terms, a periodic reorder system has a relative advantage over a reorder point system when the costs of taking a physical inventory are high or when there are savings in regard to information (such as seasonal data), production scheduling, price discounts, or transport costs from ordering items on a regular basis. If these cost savings are not significant, however, a reorder point system has the striking advantage of being able to minimize the total variable costs associated with changing order quantities. Broadly speaking, the economics of inventory control favor the reorder point system but only when the important, practical costs of inventory control and administration are not significant.

The saving grace in all of this is that failing to calculate the precisely optimal order quantity under any inventory system is not likely to be devastating. The costs of various order quantities are, in most instances, fairly near one another. In other words, a graph of inventory costs against various order quantities is likely to be shallow (saucer-shaped, as in Figure 8–6), rather than steep (bowl- or cup-shaped). Making some sensible decisions about inventories to get oneself "into the ballpark" is thus more important than landing on precisely the best order quantity. It has been said that order timing is more important than order quantities.

Though prevalent in both manufacturing and nonmanufacturing businesses, non-time-phased inventory systems such as the periodic reorder and reorder point systems described above are perhaps best suited to retail and wholesale situations (Driscoll Lumber Company), where the source and precise timing of demand are seldom known with much certainty. These conditions often apply to manufacturing as well, but there are many manufacturing

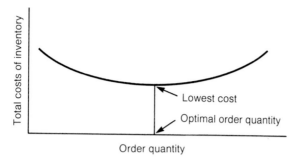

Figure 8–6 Inventory Costs Graphed Against Order Quantities.

businesses that know far more about the source and timing of demand for their products, and hence for the parts that make up their products. It is in these instances of known or easily provided demand that time-phased inventory systems, such as material requirements planning, make good sense.

SAFETY STOCKS

Safety stocks are useful in managing inventories precisely because companies do not know in advance exactly what the demand made on them will be. As long as replenishments to an inventory cannot occur immediately, the lead time necessary for delivery of the replenishment order is an uncertain and problematic period of time. Consult Figure 8–7. At time T, there was a delivery of inventory that replenished the stock up to the level of Q. At time T_2, it was decided to place another order. This new order could have been placed because a reorder point had been struck (level R of inventory) or because T_2 was the appropriate, periodic time to review the status of inventory (per a periodic reorder inventory system). The order is expected to arrive at time A, so the lead time is the time between T_2 and A.

During this lead time, almost anything can happen. If demand proceeds at its usual, expected rate, when the order arrives inventory should be depleted to point B. The safety stock, however, will not have been used. If demand is lighter than expected (something that one might think occurs about 50 percent of the time, if demand is a statistical creature with a distribution that is symmetrical about the mean), then at time A, inventory would stand somewhere between points B and C. If, on the other hand, demand is heavier than expected (typically, another 50 percent probability) the safety stock will have to be used. During the lead time, the quantity AB could be used up before a stockout occurred.

Levels of Customer Service

At issue, then, is how much safety stock a company should hold. How much is enough or desirable? This is sometimes described in terms of determining the level of customer service. There are many, somewhat different measures for

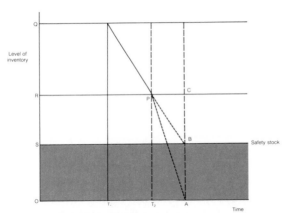

Figure 8–7 The Usefulness of Safety Stock.

customer service, however. Some are more appropriate for some uses than others. Two specific measures of customer service bear mention:

1. The percentage of orders covered by the inventory, or equivalently, the probability of not stocking out. This measure indicates the probability that the company will not stock out during any given order cycle time period. A 95 percent service level, by this measure, indicates a 5 percent chance of failing to fill one or more orders during any given time period. This measure is fairly easy to work with statistically.

2. The percent of all items ordered shipped on time. This is a measure of items and not orders, and it has intuitive appeal. Though similar to measure 1, this measure has some significant distinctions. Indeed, the mathematical correspondence between the measures is not a simple one because stockouts can involve orders for any number of items. For this reason, to match a 95 percent service level by measure 1, measure 2 generally has to be greater than 95 percent. Despite the complex mathematical relationship between the two measures, for many items, rough correlations between the two measures can be devised empirically.

Let's return to the issue of determining the targeted level of customer service, as measured by either measure. The discussion of Figure 8–7 and previous comments suggest several factors that ought to influence the size of any safety stock:

1. *How frequently the order is placed.* The larger the quantity ordered at any time—and thus the less frequent the exposures to potential stockouts—the greater the level of customer service provided.

2. *Lead time.* The longer the lead time, other things being equal, the more safety stock is targeted. Shorten lead times and safety stocks can be lowered.

Typically, there are differences in lead time between the reorder point and the periodic reorder systems. The period of vulnerability is generally shorter with a reorder point system—only the time between the placement of the order and its delivery—than it is with a periodic reorder system. For the latter, the period of vulnerability is the length of the time period itself, not just the delivery lead time.

3. *Stability of demand.* The more erratic the demand, the greater the safety stock has to be to maintain a given level of customer service.

4. *Relative costs of stockout versus inventory carrying.* The greater the penalty to the company of not having enough inventory relative to the cost of holding inventory, the more safety stock is desirable.

For the most part, companies settle on a particular safety stock and accompanying level of customer service on a trial-and-error basis. A service level is established, and then, over time, performance against that service level is monitored as well as customer satisfaction with delivery. If performance is satisfactory, then the safety stock can be lowered somewhat and performance again monitored. By focusing on the service level, companies can improve their performance dramatically over general rules that merely pick a given period's demand as the safety stock. It is important to keep in mind the fact that safety stocks should be used. If a safety stock is not dipped into regularly, then inventory is too high and should be reduced.

Continual trial-and-error adjustments to safety stock levels have a lot to recommend them, especially given an environment of change. There are, however, alternative schemes for setting safety stocks. One fairly simple scheme merits attention as a means to estimate what level of customer service to shoot for, namely the use of the critical fractile.

The critical fractile approach.   This approach to setting the level of safety stock essentially picks out a suitable level of service based on a trade-off of stockout costs and inventory carrying costs. The chosen level of service is then translated into a safety factor that can be multiplied by the computed standard deviation of the distribution of demand to yield the extent of safety stock. Let us work through this process in reverse in order to understand it better.

Many distributions of demand can be approximated by the normal distribution, the familiar bell-shaped graph pictured in Figure 8–8. The two parameters needed to describe a normal distribution are its mean (μ) and its standard deviation (σ). Naturally, a low standard deviation represents a very tight, stable demand, and a large one represents a more erratic demand. No matter what the value of the standard deviation, however, with a normal distribution, there are standard percentages of the distribution that fall within x standard deviations of the mean. This fact permits us to make the correspondence between the percentage of demand covered by a certain size of safety stock (one measure of the level of customer service discussed earlier) and the number of standard deviations

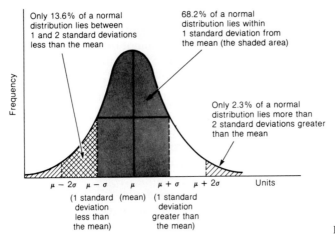

Only 13.6% of a normal distribution lies between 1 and 2 standard deviations less than the mean

68.2% of a normal distribution lies within 1 standard deviation from the mean (the shaded area)

Only 2.3% of a normal distribution lies more than 2 standard deviations greater than the mean

Frequency

$\mu - 2\sigma$ $\quad \mu - \sigma$ $\qquad \mu$ $\qquad \mu + \sigma$ $\quad \mu + 2\sigma$ $\qquad$ Units

(1 standard deviation less than the mean) (mean) (1 standard deviation greater than the mean)

Figure 8–8 The Normal Distribution.

above the mean the inventory represents (the safety factor, or from statistics, the z-score or z-factor, which is defined as $z = (x - \mu) / \sigma$. The z-score gives the value of x for which the area under the normal curve to the left of that point equals the targeted level of coverage). Some relevant safety factors to use, given a normal distribution with a 0 mean and a standard deviation of 1, are as follows:

Coverage of expected demand (percent)	Safety factor (or z-score)
99	2.326
97.5	1.960
95	1.645
90	1.282
85	1.038
80	0.843

Thus, if the demand is normally distributed with a mean of 50 and a standard deviation of 14, a 90 percent level of coverage (i.e., a 90 percent level of customer service) would be given with an inventory of

$$x = \mu + \sigma (z) = 50 + 14(1.282) \approx 68 \text{ units,}$$

of which 18 units constitute the safety stock itself.

The critical fractile calculation helps production managers decide upon an appropriate level of service so that the corresponding safety factor can be applied to the standard deviation of the distribution of demand.

Common sense insists that the level of customer service be higher if the cost of carrying too little inventory and thus stocking out greatly exceeds the cost of carrying too much inventory. The former cost is commonly called the cost of being under or the cost of underage (C_u) and the latter is commonly called the cost of being over or the cost of overage (C_o).

The suitable percentage coverage that a company ought to seek for its inventories subject to uncertain demand is approximated by the following formula:[2]

$$\text{Critical fractile} = C_u / (C_o + C_u).$$

This formula meets the test of common sense in that if the cost of carrying too little and stocking out is high relative to the cost of carrying too much, then the suitable percentage coverage will be high. The formula also makes sense in that it cannot reach 1 in value nor can it fall to zero; it must range in between, just like the range for cumulative probability.

What are costs of underage and costs of overage? Let us consider the costs of overage first since they are a bit easier to think about. The costs of overage are all the costs that would be incurred by carrying one extra unit of inventory for the time period needed to prevent the stockout. These are the costs of holding inventory that were discussed previously:

- Finance charges (opportunity costs)
- Storage and handling costs
- Insurance and taxes
- Obsolescence and shrinkage

---

[2]The ratio of $C_u / (C_o + C_u)$ is the critical fractile (or percentile). Although technically it applies only to single-period holding of inventories and linear costs of underage and overage, it is a useful enough approximation to be applied more generally.

The basic argument underlying the derivation of the critical fractile is, once again, incremental in origin. Suppose we arbitrarily select q^* as the best level of inventory there could be. It must be true then that we receive an incremental gain by inventorying q^* as opposed to one unit more or less (i.e., either $q^* + 1$ or $q^* - 1$). This being the case, we can write formally the following inequality:

$$C_u[P(d > q^*)] \leq C_o[P(d \leq q^*)]. \tag{8-1}$$

By stocking q^* the expected expense of being under when demand is greater than q^* (the cost of underage times the probability that demand is greater than q^*) must be less than or equal to the expected expense of being over (the cost of overage times the probability that demand is less than or equal to q^*); otherwise, it would make sense to stock another unit so that one is not caught being under. Similarly, we can write the following inequality:

$$C_u\{P[d > (q^* - 1)]\} \geq C_o\{P[d \leq (q^* - 1)]\}. \tag{8-2}$$

By stocking q^*, the expected expense of being under when demand is greater than $q^* - 1$ must be greater than or equal to the expected expense of being over; otherwise, it would make sense to stock one unit less in order to save some money.

Using the fact that $P(d > q^*)$ is equal to $[1 - P(d \leq q^*)]$ we can rewrite inequality 8–1 as

$$C_u[1 - P(d \leq q^*)] \leq C_o[P(d \leq q^*)] \tag{8-3}$$

or

$$C_u \leq (C_u + C_o)[P(d \leq q^*)]$$

or

$$[C_u / (C_u + C_o)] \leq [P(d \leq q^*)]. \tag{8-4}$$

In a similar fashion, we can rewrite inequality 8–2 as

$$[C_u / (C_u + C_o)] \geq \{P[d \leq (q^* - 1)]\}. \tag{8-5}$$

Inequalities 8–4 and 8–5 suggest that $C_u / (C_u + C_o)$ is the relevant ratio for picking off the point in the cumulative probability distribution that corresponds to the optimal level of inventories, q^*.

As an example of the cost of overage, this cost for a year could be 30 percent of the cost of the product, calculated as 15 percent for financing costs (such as the company's prevailing borrowing rate or perhaps the rate it expects to earn on any cash freed up by reducing inventory), 10 percent for physical costs, and 5 percent for the risk of obsolescence. In most cases, however, buffer inventory would be vulnerable to depletion for only a short time before the next delivery was due. If the period of vulnerability were only one to two weeks, the cost of overage for the relevant period for this example would be approximately 1 percent of the cost of the product.

The cost of underage is the penalty incurred by failing to have a unit of inventory on hand when demand calls for it. At worst, typically, the cost of underage is the lost contribution to profit and overhead incurred because the unit was unavailable for sale. Again, the concept of opportunity cost intrudes into our thinking—here, in the form of contribution forgone. Forgoing all of a unit's contribution assumes that the buyer goes away empty-handed and will never again return to purchase the item. Often however, stocking out of an item does not mean all of a lost sale, especially if the purchaser is willing to substitute another item for the one out of stock (another color, another model, another size) or if he or she agrees to come back when the item is back in stock. Market research can often determine a reasonable expectation for this cost of underage.

As an example of the cost of underage, the contribution per unit might be 40 percent of the revenue the company receives from it; the probability that the unit will be forgone forever might be 50 percent; the probability that some other unit (with contribution of 30 percent) will be substituted might be 30 percent; and the probability that the customer may return later for it might be 20 percent. In such a case, the cost of underage could be estimated as an expected value of the contribution forgone.

$$0.5(40\%) + 0.3(40\% - 30\%) + 0.2(0\%)$$
$$= 0.5(40\%) + 0.3(10\%) + 0.2(0\%)$$
$$= 23\% \text{ of the cost of the product.}$$

Costs of underage generally greatly exceed the costs of overage for most relevant time periods.

Let us then calculate the critical fractile for this example. The relevant inputs are

$C_o = 1.15\%$ (30% annual rate for a 2-week period)
$C_u = 23\%$.

Suppose, as well, that the demand during the period is expected to follow the normal distribution with a mean of 50 and standard deviation of 10.

Critical fractile (percentile) $= 23 / (1.15 + 23) = 0.95$
Safety factor (or z-score) for 95th percentile $= 1.645$.

The size of the buffer or safety stock is then

$$z(\sigma) = (1.645)(10) = 16.45 \text{ units.}$$

The size of the inventory at the start of the period should be the expected average withdrawal from inventory plus the buffer stock:

$$x = \mu + \sigma(z) = 50 + 16.45 = 66.45 \text{ units.}$$

To reinforce this discussion of safety stocks, consider Situation 8–2.

━━━━━━━━━━ **SITUATION 8–2** ━━━━━━━━━━

DiMarzo Costume Company

The DiMarzo Costume Company rented theatrical costumes of all sorts to theater groups, colleges, schools, churches, and the like. During the Christmas season, one of the most popular costumes (aside from Santa Claus) was Frosty the Snowman. (Data on orders placed for Frosty the Snowman costumes over all 20 years of the company's history are shown below. The company could not detect a trend in orders over the years; orders seemed to be fairly random. The company, however, wanted to be able to fill about 95 percent of all its orders for Frosty and wondered how many costumes it should stock at Christmas.

YEARS AGO	DEMANDED	YEARS AGO	DEMANDED
1	411	11	296
2	347	12	382
3	412	13	473
4	385	14	320
5	441	15	423
6	402	16	354
7	395	17	512
8	370	18	389
9	480	19	378
10	416	20	392

Discussion of the DiMarzo Costume Company. Given no discernible trend in the demand over the years for Frosty the Snowman costumes, the DiMarzo Costume Company can let the past 20 years be its guide in selecting the number of Frosty costumes it should stock.

A Historical Count Approach. The easiest, if not the most scientific, way to select an appropriate stock level so that the company can expect to cover 95 percent of the orders placed on it is to make a count of the data. The company could expect that a stock level at or above the highest number demanded over the past 20 years would be too high. Company history shows that in 95 percent of the years (19 of 20) demand was less than 512 but not more than 480. It would seem reasonable, then, to select a stock level between 480 and 512.

A Statistical Approach. A more formal way of selecting an appropriate stock level is to apply some statistics to the data.

The mean of the distribution of demand for Frosty the Snowman costumes is 398.90 and the sample's standard deviation is 50.63. These summary statistics (sample mean and sample standard deviation) are estimates of the unknown true population mean, μ, and the unknown true population standard deviation, σ, which underlie the demand for costumes at DiMarzo Costume Company. Often, we do not know how the full population of observations is distributed, and we must depend on samples from that full population to draw inferences about the population itself. Such is the case at the DiMarzo Costume Company. The summary statistics, $\overline{X}$ and S, can help us condense the demand data into a more easily digested bar graph of the frequencies with which the data fall into various classes. Figure 8–9 displays such a bar graph. For intelligibility, the classes are set at 25, about half of the standard deviation, and the figure is centered on 400, which is just above the true mean of 398.90.

The bar graph in Figure 8–9 can be approximated by a normal distribution. We know that the data in Situation 8–2 fall roughly into a normal distribution pattern because (1) 70 percent of the 20 observations fall within one standard deviation of the mean (i.e., 14 of the 20 observations fall between 350 and 450) versus 68.2 percent in a true normal distribution, (2) 20 percent of the 20 observations fall between one and two standard deviations from the mean versus 27.2 percent in a true normal distribution, and (3) 10 percent of the 20 observations fall beyond two standard deviations from the mean versus 4.6 percent in a true normal distribution. It seems reasonable, then, to presume that the demand for Frosty the Snowman costumes is normally distributed with a mean of 398.90 and a standard deviation of 50.63.

In a normal frequency pattern, the top 5 percent of the distribution falls above the value of +1.645 standard deviations from the mean. In this case, we can presume that 95 percent of the demand for Frosty costumes will fall below

$$x = \mu + \sigma\,(z) = 398.90 + (1.645)(50.63) = 482.19.$$

We can take this figure, 482 or 483, as a suitable stock level to assure ourselves that 95 percent of our expected orders can be filled.

If we were content to fill only 90 percent of the expected orders, then the proper stock level would be

$$x = \mu + \sigma\,(z) = 398.90 + (1.282)(50.63) \approx 464$$

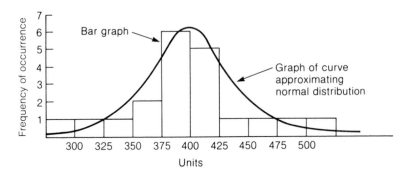

Figure 8–9   Frequency Distribution of Monthly Sales for DiMarzo Costume Company.

because the top 10 percent of the distribution falls above the value of +1.282 standard deviations from the mean.

Trends and Aggregation

The DiMarzo Costume Company had to worry only about stocking Frosty the Snowman costumes for one peak time during the year. Furthermore, there were no clear trends in the demand over the years. The task of calculating an appropriate inventory level for uncertain demand is complicated further when trends are involved or when time periods are aggregated. Consider the following modifications of the procedures we have used to date for coping with demand uncertainty:

1. *Trends.* If sales have grown (or declined) over time, the distribution of demand shifts rightward (or leftward) along the x-axis of units demanded. In the simplest case, the distribution itself remains the same and merely shifts position; the mean changes, but the standard deviation remains the same. In more complex cases, the distribution changes along with the shift, changing both the mean and the standard deviation. When trends are involved, therefore, it is important to ascertain whether the shape of the distribution is changing along with its mean.

2. *Time period aggregation.* Suppose that we wanted to shift the horizon for a periodic reorder system from 1 month to 3 months. All the calculations about the appropriate level of inventory to hold were based on a distribution of demand for a month. How do things change if we are to define everything in terms of 3 months? If demand follows a normal distribution, is the mean of the new distribution simply 3 times as large? What about the variance? If we assume a normal distribution for the demands and if those demands in any month are independent of one another (a reasonable assumption), then the mean of the new 3-month distribution will be three times the 1-month mean, and the variance will also be 3 times greater. The standard deviation, however, will not be 3 times the old standard deviation because it is the square root of the variance. Thus if the 1-month mean is 50 and the standard deviation is 10, the new 3-month distribution can be expected to have a mean of 150 and a standard deviation of $10\sqrt{3} = 17.3$.

In general terms, under the assumptions of normal distribution and independence of demand, both the mean and the variance are additive.

Chapter 9

Issues in Logistics, Location, and Franchising

LOGISTICS

Logistics is chiefly concerned with the movement of products to markets and of materials to facilities. Entwined with the actual movement of material, of course, is its storage and handling. Logistics is a commonly neglected aspect of operations, but one whose potential impact on costs and profits is greater than most realize. Total distribution costs are roughly as high a percentage of sales as direct labor costs, and, for the most part, more amenable to cost cutting.

In managing logistics, several issues are of central concern:

1. What should be the structure of the distribution system? Where should various inventories, especially finished goods inventories, be held within the system?
2. Which geographic locations make sense as stocking points?
3. How much inventory should be held at each location?
4. How should the flow of goods throughout the distribution system be coordinated? Which products should be treated in which ways?
5. Which modes of transportation should be used?

General Motors' service parts network, as mentioned in the service tour of Ogle–Tucker Buick, is a good example of these key issues in logistics. GM's distribution system, as described there, has three tiers to it: national distribution controlled from Flint, regional distribution centers such as Lansing, and local distribution centers such as Chicago. One can expect that the most commonly used parts are abundantly stocked in the local distribution centers, but that uncommon, rarely used parts are available routinely only from the regional or national distribution centers. As that service tour relates, there are several ways orders could be placed with the parts network, some calling for wider searches and faster deliveries than others.

To discuss these logistics issues in greater depth, we can organize them into three broad categories: distribution system structure and operation, distribution center location, and transportation mode choice.

Distribution System Structure and Operation

In deciding how the distribution system should be structured, a critical decision turns on how centralized or decentralized the system ought to be. Should the company keep its inventory in just a few locations, or should it disperse its goods into a number of regional or metropolitan areas? This question can be a subtle one, and an answer to it depends on balancing the costs and benefits of centralization versus decentralization.

The argument for decentralization. The argument in favor of dispersing inventories in a number of locations is clear and compelling: Customer service can be greatly enhanced. The time it takes to fill an order can be cut markedly if sales and service people can call on a nearby facility. Fewer errors are likely to be made because field people can be in close, informed touch with the distribution center. Sales may even be stimulated if customers react favorably to the knowledge of a facility nearby dedicated to serving them.

Moreover, delivery time can be reduced, not only because the order may be filled more quickly, but also because there is less distance to travel and swift modes of transportation can be used. This contraction in delivery time means that safety stocks can be reduced because fewer days of uncertainty need to be covered.

The argument against decentralization. Despite all the advantages decentralized distribution offers field sales and service people, it can be costly. Transportation and handling expenses typically increase with decentralization. Decentralization can also lead to an expansion of inventory to be carried and a loss of control over that inventory. These points against decentralization are argued in greater detail in the following discussions.

Transportation and Handling Expenses. How do the costs of transporting and handling a product differ between a centralized strategy, where the customer is served directly, and a decentralized strategy, where the customer is served through various tiers? The answer is not clear-cut, because there are costs that cut both ways. Naturally, the fewer the number of intervening locations, the lower the transportation expense, suggesting that centralization and direct customer shipments are more economical. On the other hand, shipment of small quantities is invariably more expensive than shipment in bulk, and often, the replenishment of decentralized distribution centers can be done cheaply through bulk shipments. This point argues for at least some decentralization. How these conflicting costs total up naturally depends on the situation—what the full-truckload versus less-than-truckload rates are, where the customer is, where the distribution centers are, and how much the order is for.

Often, however, the telling expense is in the handling. If the product has to be handled from one tier of the distribution system to another, additional costs are incurred. These can swamp any cost savings attributable to freight consolidation.

Administering Decentralized Distribution.   Inventory spread among a number of facilities is more difficult to keep track of than inventory kept in one or just a few facilities. Recordkeeping is more voluminous and thus subject to error. Swaps between facilities may be so informal that records are not even entered. Moreover, the sales and service people may become so possessive of "their" facility that a hoarding mentality takes over, especially with items that are scarce and that a central authority may want to call in for allocation somewhere else. Such items may purposely become "lost" in the distribution system.

Irregular Demand and Buffer Stocks: The Law of Large Numbers.   The demand in any one region of a company's market area is likely to follow a more irregular pattern than the company's overall demand. Greater-than-average demand for a particular product in one region may well be balanced by below-average demand for the same product in another region. Thus, the buffer stock that a centralized facility would have to carry is likely to be considerably less than the sum of the buffer stocks of decentralized facilities for the same level of protection against stockouts. This result is a variation of the "law of large numbers." The variance of demand for a single large service center will almost always be proportionally less than the variance of demand faced by smaller, dispersed service centers offering the same coverage against stockouts.

Scattered Warehousing and the Optimal Inventory Calculation.   The logic of our EOQ calculation can be applied to the case of many, scattered warehouses versus a single, large warehouse. Much as we derived earlier, let

> D = expected period demand over the entire company
> i = inventory carrying cost percentage
> S = cost per order
> C = variable cost per unit of inventory
> N = number of scattered warehouses, all of the same size.

From our calculations before for the simple case where carrying cost and order cost were the only costs that varied with changes in the order quantity, the optimal order quantity, Q, was found to be

$$Q = \sqrt{2\,SD\,/\,iC}. \qquad (9\text{--}1)$$

Now let's consider a small warehouse, one of N identical warehouses that the company operates. The demand that each small warehouse will face during the period is D/N. We can substitute this into our formula to find the optimal order quantity, Q^*, for the small warehouse.

$$Q^* = \sqrt{2\,S(D/N)\,/iC}. \qquad (9\text{--}2)$$

But there are N small warehouses, so the total of all the order quantities would be

$$NQ^* = N\sqrt{2\,S(D/N)\,/\,iC} = \sqrt{N}\sqrt{2\,SD\,/\,iC}. \qquad (9\text{--}3)$$

We can substitute equation 9–1 in to find a relationship between Q^* and Q, namely,

$$NQ^* = \sqrt{N}\sqrt{2\,SD\,/\,iC} = \sqrt{N}\,Q. \qquad (9\text{--}4)$$

Thus, merely by dispersing inventory in N facilities and allowing each to optimize its order quantities under a reorder point inventory system, we find that the order quantities demanded of the supplier—and by implication inventories since in this case average inventory is $Q/2$ or $Q^*/2$—increase by the square root of the number of warehouses. If we establish four small, identical warehouses instead of one, and if we follow a reorder point system for each one, then inventories will be double what they would be if we established a single warehouse.

This argument is meant to be more suggestive than exact. The regional warehouses of most companies are not organized so that individual reorder point systems prevail. But they are organized differently in many cases precisely to avoid the heavy inventory burden that the line of reasoning sketched above leads to.

Tiered Inventories and Pipeline Momentum

Many distribution systems are tiered. They have a centralized inventory that sits above a number of regional inventories; these, in turn, sit above local, metropolitan inventories. In some of these systems, the central inventory feeds products to the regional inventories, and the regional inventories feed the local ones. This kind of division can work quite well. However, if the decision rules for holding inventory are disjointed rather than coordinated, such a tiered system can lead to substantial swings in demand and somewhat higher levels of inventories than a completely coordinated system.

To illustrate what is meant, think of an inventory system of three tiers in which each tier is mandated to hold 2 weeks' worth of demand. For a weekly demand of 20, then, the corresponding levels of inventory and orders on the next tier would look like Table 9–1. Note that in each tier, the desired inventory is twice the weekly sales, and orders on the next tier proceed accordingly. Observe, however, what happens when demand falls by a single unit (5 percent) at the level of tier A (the local level) and stabilizes there (at 19). The period-by-period adjustments implied by the myopic decision rule of "hold two weeks' worth of sales in inventory" are traced in Table 9–2.

As Table 9–2 shows, this tiered inventory system with its myopic replenishment rule takes four periods to settle into a steady state. What is more, the orders placed on successive tiers become more and more erratic and vary wildly from period to period. When the initial demand reduction occurs, it is covered by

TABLE 9-1 TIERED INVENTORY SYSTEM AND DISJOINTED DECISION RULES—THE STEADY STATE

Tier	Item	Amount
A (Local)[a]	Beginning inventory	40
	Sales in week	20
	Ending inventory	20
	Desired inventory	40[b]
	Order on the next tier	20
B (Regional)	Beginning inventory	40
	Sales in week	20
	Ending inventory	20
	Desired inventory	40[b]
	Order on the next tier	20
C (Companywide)	Beginning inventory	40
	Sales in week	20
	Ending inventory	20
	Desired inventory	40[b]
	Order on factory or to be absorbed by buffer stocks	20

[a] Weekly sales demand at level of tier A is 20.
[b] Twice the demand of 20.

TABLE 9-2 TIERED INVENTORY SYSTEM AND DISJOINTED DECISION RULES—REACTION OVER TIME TO 5 PERCENT DEMAND REDUCTION

Tier	Item	Period 0	Period 1	Period 2	Period 3	Period 4
A	Beginning inventory	40	40	38	38	38
	Sales	20	19	19	19	19
	Ending inventory	20	21	19	19	19
	Desired inventory	40	38	38	38	38
	Order on the next tier	20	17	19	19	19
B	Beginning inventory	40	40	34	38	38
	Sales	20	17	19	19	19
	Ending inventory	20	23	15	19	19
	Desired inventory	40	34	38	38	38
	Order on the next tier	20	11	23	19	19
C	Beginning inventory	40	40	29	46	38
	Sales	20	11	23	19	19
	Ending inventory	20	29	6	27	19
	Desired inventory	40	22	46	38	38
	Order on factory or to be absorbed by buffer stocks	20	0	40	11	19

the inventory already in the pipeline and no orders are placed on the factory. However, the pipeline's inventory is soon depleted and the next period's factory order is huge. This is an example of the "pipeline momentum" that can afflict a tiered inventory system or tiers of suppliers in a multilevel supply network. Not only does it cause great variability in period-by-period demands on each tier, but it can sometimes cause more inventory to be held, over time, than necessary.

Avoiding the whiplash of this pipeline momentum effect calls either for more coordination among the tiers (so that tier C can adjust immediately to the problems tier A is experiencing) or more foresight in the lower tiers (so that these tiers can anticipate the erratic demands that will be placed on them). In either case, avoiding the pipeline momentum effect means junking the myopia that is implied by a seemingly innocuous decision rule like "hold 2 weeks' worth of sales in inventory."

In any event, this pipeline momentum effect can be one more argument against a decentralization of distribution centers.

Distribution System Operation

No matter how the network of distribution centers is configured, there are several ways to link the operations of the distribution centers to customer demand. Three major techniques are used to operate distribution systems, all variations of the familiar reorder point, periodic reorder, and MRP techniques already discussed. Let us examine their application to distribution systems.

1. *Reorder point.* Using a reorder point technique is a straightforward, very decentralized way to operate a distribution system. Each distribution center has its established reorder point levels for the products it handles. When they are replenished by the next level up in the distribution network, which could be another distribution center or a factory, the replenishment is an economic order quantity's worth, typically using either past demand or a future projection as its basis.

This technique is decentralized because the inventory records are maintained strictly at the distribution centers and not by some central authority. Often, the setting of reorder points and economic order quantities is left to the individual distribution centers. This decentralization of information and decision-making tends to bloat the level of inventory in the system and to make any allocations of temporarily scarce inventories difficult to achieve. It is sometimes said that the reorder point technique "pulls" inventory out into the field.

2. *Base stock.* The base stock technique is essentially a periodic reorder technique. With this technique, the distribution center is replenished on a regular, periodic basis. The various inventories held are brought up to levels that are expected to hold up, with a given level of customer service, until the next replenishment arrives. The replenishment is thus of variable quantity.

The base stock technique is a more centralized one because the resupply point requires information enough to assemble periodically what each distribution center needs to tide itself over until the next replenishment. The information processing required of the base stock technique is thus greater than that of the reorder point technique, but the field inventories are likely to be lower and better coordinated. This technique "pushes" inventory out into the field rather than "pulling" it.

It is interesting to note that the typical just-in-time manufacturing relationships with suppliers call for frequent, periodic replenishments of inventory to bring the factory inventory back up to some base stock level (the level dictated by the number and size of the standard containers used in the process).

3. *Distribution requirements planning (DRP).* DRP is analogous to MRP (Material Requirements Planning, a computer-based system for planning the acquisition of materials in manufacturing at just the time they are needed, as dictated by the master production schedule) in that the levels of inventory in the field are tied to projected, time-phased demand. The projected demand works like the gross requirements line of an MRP inventory status record, and the conventional MRP logic can be applied to determine how much inventory should be supplied to each distribution center and when it should be shipped. This approach is often also termed the "time-phased order point."

Much as with MRP, various lot-sizing techniques can be applied, often to group differently timed needs together to ship replenishments economically. And, as in MRP, rescheduling can be accomplished easily if forecasts or actual demands change.

Of course, DRP is more information-intensive than either the reorder point or base stock techniques. It can also be linked to MRP in the following way: The demands forecast for individual distribution centers can be summed and used as a basis for the development of a master production schedule, the schedule that drives an MRP system.

Transportation Mode Choice

Transportation mode choice tends to be a very specialized field of inquiry. Mode choice decisions require reams of very detailed information on transportation costs and delivery times by mode for different classes of shipments characterized by weight, volume, and specialized shipping requirements (such as refrigerated trucks, open flatcars, pressurized compartments). Less-than-truckload or less-than-carload rates tend to be much higher than full-truckload or full-carload rates. Mode choice is further complicated by a proliferation of rates. A company's traffic department cannot merely think of truck, rail, water, or air but must think in terms of common truck carrier, owner–operator trucks, own fleet trucking; regular rail service, piggyback (truck–rail) service; ocean, lake, or river barges; commercial jet shipping or private jet shipping; and a number of other variations.

Rates and deliveries vary, as does the impact of federal and state regulation, which can for no good reason dictate substantially different shipping rates from seemingly equivalent shipping points or different rates between two points depending on which direction shipment is made.

Other than to note some of the many peculiarities that afflict the nation's transportation system and thus the mode choice decisions of companies, this text will leave to more specialized and detailed treatments this issue of transport mode choice.[1]

LOCATION DECISIONS FOR SERVICE COMPANIES[2]

Operation relocations are overwhelmingly made by small, growing operations (often independent of particular suppliers, markets, or labor sources) that are pressed for more space. They move to larger, more modern quarters and in the process alter their operations, sometimes in fundamental ways. The vast majority of relocations are over short distances (less than 20 miles), which help to ensure labor force continuity and the retention of customer and supplier contacts. To a lesser degree, relocations also occur to consolidate two or more operations into a single new facility and to escape from high site costs (wages, land values, taxes). As one might expect, however, the operation whose profits are hurting the most sees relocation chiefly as a means to lower costs. These operations are also the ones that are most likely to move further than 20 miles in search of these lower costs.

Operation relocations are trauma-filled experiences for many managers and so are to be avoided if at all possible. Even so, about half of all service operations have moved during the course of their existence, and half have expanded on-site as well.

Selecting Areas and Sites

Many people, including some location consultants, try to simplify the decision by introducing elaborate rating schemes that quantify everything imaginable about a particular location. Much of this is false rigor. There are, of course, a number of costs that can usefully be estimated—among them expected labor costs, construction, rental, or remodeling costs; taxes and other government payments; transportation cost savings or penalties for inputs and finished goods; expenditures for needed services such as energy, pollution control, roads, sewerage, water, and parking; insurance costs; moving costs; and expected operation startup inefficiencies or time delays due to startup or to governmental approvals. Often one or just a few of these costs are so important that they can control the entire site-selection process. For services, the controlling considerations

---

[1]An issue related to mode choice is the determination of when deliveries ought to be expedited, perhaps by using a faster, more expensive mode of transportation. See D. P. Herron, "Managing Physical Distribution for Profit," *Harvard Business Review* 57, no. 3 (May–June 1979): 121–32.

[2]Much of this section is derived from Roger W. Schmenner, *Making Business Location Decisions.* Englewood Cliffs, NJ: Prentice-Hall, 1982.

that occur most often are the quality of the infrastructure (roads, communication, services, utilities), proximity to customers, and the ability to attract qualified labor. Although costs such as these may be important to evaluate (and linear programming can help assess the impact of transportation costs), they do not tell the complete story and sometimes they do not differ enough to ground a location choice strictly on their merits. A company should not expect any quantitative analysis to isolate a single area or site that stands alone as clearly optimal. Rather, a company should expect that a number of sites will show more or less the same cost structure.

Often, the next phase of site selection is an exploration of the intangible and qualitative features of a location that could be expected to contribute to the company's competitive success. Although these factors may be difficult or even impossible to quantify, they are no less real; companies should resist the temptation to let hard numbers drive out reasoned but qualitative analysis. The intangibles can be of many varieties: risks associated with any of the quantitatively evaluated costs or the sales potential of the site; the area's prevailing business climate (which means different things to different people but mainly means long-term competitiveness); educational and training strengths of the area; attitudes of the workforce toward productivity, change, and unionization; the aesthetic and cultural attributes of the area (important aspects for attracting and holding managers); the cooperation of the local and state government for resolving public service or other public matters faced by industry; the commuting distances of workers and managers; and the impact of other, perhaps competitive, industries in the area. Frequently, a careful point-by-point comparison of these difficult-to-quantify factors against the real demands a particular product, area, or process will make on the manufacturing function can argue decisively for a particular site. A site need not rate high on all factors, but it should rate high on those that truly make a difference for the operation's competitiveness.

The company should be prepared for location analyses that, at the end, do not favor one site over another. If careful analysis reveals no preferable option, a company should not feel guilty that a seemingly inconsequential item tips the scale toward one site. After all, in such a case the company stands to gain or lose little by the location choice itself.

One can easily take the location decision for service firms for granted. Many see service firm location decisions as simple site selections that are governed by proximity to the local markets that service firms serve. This is an easy stereotype to fall into, but it is just that, a stereotype. In fact, the geographic markets for service firms are often greatly dispersed. Evidence suggests that, on average, service firms generate half of their sales from a distance of 45 miles or more, a distance greater than the radius of most metropolitan areas.[3]

---

[3]This statistic, as well as others in this section, are due to research on Midwestern service firm locations. See Roger W. Schmenner, "Service Firm Location Decisions: Some Midwestern Evidence," *International Journal of Operations & Production Management*, 1994.

Service firms are much like manufacturing firms in that they approach the location decision first as a decision about where "generally" they should locate and only later, after that decision has been resolved, where in particular they should locate—the specific site. The influences on the one decision (the general area) are somewhat different from the influences on the other (the particular site).

For the general area choice, service firms, in the aggregate, look at three things: infrastructure (roads, utilities, public services), proximity to customers, and the ability to attract qualified labor. There are natural differences from service industry to service industry in what guides this choice. Some services are fairly constrained in where they can locate: hospitals, education and social services, personal and business services (e.g., direct mail, cleaning, graphic arts, temporary employment agencies) and utilities do not have much choice in where they have to locate their facilities; proximity to customers drives them. On the other hand, transportation, warehousing, and wholesaling have many fewer constraints.

For companies that are more footloose—those that serve large territories and do not have to be close to their customers—influences such as quality of life and labor considerations (labor costs and labor climate) take on increased importance.

After deciding on a general area (be it a metropolitan or a rural area), the service firm must decide on a particular site. This choice is governed, in large measure, by the adequacy of parking and by building cost and attractiveness. This is especially true for firms whose sales are more local in character. Retail operations crave adequate parking and high-traffic areas.

Smaller and more labor-intensive services are interested in low rents. Larger firms have more specialized space needs that influence their site selections, and they become concerned with their workers' commutes to work.

Some services benefit by locating close to their competitors, usually to negate their impact on the local market. These decisions are typical for services such as fast-food, motels, auto dealerships, and other retailers.

Branches vs. Single-Location Services

A variety of service companies have spread successfully into geographically dispersed markets, either by franchising or by owning and operating branches. This success prompts some questions about branches: Are such branch operations different in important ways from single-location services? Should one expect that they must be managed in different ways?

In reality, there are many similarities between branch operations and single-location operations: size, how long they have been where they are, the type of space they occupy, their capital–labor ratios, their degree of interaction with customers. Most industries, in fact, share about the same concentrations of branches vs. single-location operations, although there are some industries with somewhat more branching than others—communications, transportation, warehousing, and hotels, for example, have more branching than repair shops, construction, utilities, and amusements.

Statistically, branches are different from single-location operations. They value proximity to customers more and they offer a more standardized service. They see their site selections as depending more on high-traffic, high-population areas. They also are more likely to locate so as to nullify the location choices of their competitors. Such distinctions make sense. We can readily associate branch operations with getting and keeping local customers and with the idea of negating the presence of competitors in, at least, certain markets. That branches offer, on average, more standard service could help explain why branches are successful.

Distribution Center Location

The location decision for distribution centers is dominated by consideration of transportation costs, and this makes it a much easier decision than the location of operations. The distribution center decision lends itself to some mathematical analysis, and numerous studies for companies have been done using mathematical techniques to zero in on low-cost locations.

The heart of the decision is finding the location (or set of locations) that minimizes the cost of transporting goods to customers. This analysis requires information on the quantities demanded by all customers, the quantities that can be supplied from each distribution center, where those customers are located, and the freight rates applicable from the contemplated locations to each customer. Different locations will offer different distances and hence transportation costs to customers, and a systematic way to examine these costs is called for. Simulations can be performed and are often most appropriate for complex, many-factor decisions. For simpler cases, however, linear programming or one of its offshoots is often the most effective tool.

Variations on the simple transportation problem permit the distribution center to be subject to fixed as well as variable costs. Consult a book on operations research topics for a discussion of the sophisticated methods employed to solve these more true-to-life problems.

It should be stressed, however, that for most companies the solution given by these mathematical techniques is frequently modified by some qualitative considerations that could not be incorporated into the formulation.

FRANCHISING

Franchising is often an attractive way to expand a company's geographic presence in the marketplace quickly, perhaps as a mechanism to pre-empt one's competition. With franchising, there is always a franchisor and a franchisee. The franchisor is typically the company that has developed a service task, a set of service standards, and a service delivery system that has proven itself, usually in a specific local market. The company wants to expand geographically but has neither the equity nor the borrowing capacity to establish branches on its own fast enough to fulfill its desires. It enlists franchisees who are required to contribute some of their own equity and borrowing capacity to the venture in return for the right to open up franchise units, typically within a fairly sizable geographic area. For this initial investment, and usually a small percentage of the sales, the franchisee receives a tested service as well as startup help, advertising and promotion, and assistance in meeting the operation's service standards (such as quality, cost, and productivity). If the franchisees are not up to snuff, their contracts can be terminated by the franchisor. If the franchisee does not see continued benefits from an association with the franchisor, it can let the contract lapse, and perhaps go on alone, although without the franchisor's brand name behind it.

The relationship can be a mutually beneficial one. A number of very well-known services operate on a franchise basis: auto dealerships, fast-food restaurants, retail and repair outlets of all types, travel agencies, and a host of others.

There are many good points to franchising:

- Local operators are committed because they have their own capital at risk.
- The service tasks, service standards, and service delivery systems are usually well-defined and structured, and thus they work well. They have been prototyped, and many of the potential problems with the operations have already been identified and ironed out.
- There are usually training materials already developed, for both franchisees and their workers.
- Expansion of the franchise can proceed quickly.
- The franchisor need apply only minimal controls; it does not have to develop as large a bureaucracy to govern the business.
- A franchisor's overhead is lower because the franchisee does hiring, collections, local promotions, etc.
- There are economies of scale to advertising and promotion.
- The franchisee is responsible for most of the cost control.
- There is often less risk attached to franchise expansion than to the creation of new service ventures that may not have been tested as well. Franchises usually have a better record for staying viable businesses than the typical service business startup.

Nevertheless, franchising does not always work. Sometimes the franchisee, especially after several years on the job, begins to feel exploited by the franchisor. The franchisee may not see the benefits streaming to it from its association with the franchisor, and fixes instead on the franchise royalties that it must pay. In addition, there may be disagreements over the nature or effectiveness of advertising and promotion, or changes imposed on the service system by the franchisor. Franchisees always have to be careful to investigate potential franchisors to make certain that the prototype they are selling is really going to be the franchise they will be getting. Sometimes, franchisors spend resources on the prototype to guarantee its success that they are not willing to spend on franchisees.

Franchisors, for their part, need to take the pulse of their franchisees constantly and to adjust what they offer those franchisees (e.g., assistance of all types) on a regular basis. In that way, the benefits from being a franchisee can be maintained in excess of the costs. Otherwise, franchisors may run the risk of franchisees abandoning them in favor of establishing their own, competitive operations, using all that they may have learned from the franchisor. This is sometimes referred to as "the heartbreak of franchising" and it is worth keeping in mind.

The control systems for franchising have to be sophisticated, especially on financial controls. There is always a danger that a franchisee may try to trim its royalty payment or try to cut costs by skimping on the delivery of the service. The franchisor needs to make frequent visits, often unannounced (e.g., quality audits, financial audits), so that the franchisees know just how seriously the franchisor takes the relationship and how committed it is to continued superior service.

Dealing with Capacity Change

Overtime, shiftwork, revamped scheduling, and other "fixes" can often meet peaks in demand, but they usually cannot be sustained over a long period of time. Improvements to the process and information flows, although desirable long-term policies in themselves, often cannot boost service production enough to eliminate an operation's need for more space in the face of sustained increases in demand. Although a company normally looks first to such a list of short-term means of adding capacity, more substantial space additions are generally considered at the same time.

In this chapter we concentrate on the three bricks-and-mortar choices for adding capacity: on-site expansion of an existing facility, the establishment of a new branch operation, and the relocation of an existing operation to larger quarters. Among the issues that surround these choices are: How much should any capacity expansion be? When should it be timed?

AN OVERVIEW OF CAPACITY MANAGEMENT

In most companies, most short-term measures to increase capacity can be planned for in a matter of weeks, involve only limited sums of corporate capital, are studied at the facility (rather than the corporate) level, and originate and are carried through in an informal way. Although they are concerns of top management, such short-term capacity measures seldom absorb much of the energy of the top rank of company managers. These short-term measures are apt to be too routine and too devoid of strategic importance to demand the careful study of the layers of management that sit above the particular concerns of individual operations.

Longer-term, bricks-and-mortar capacity expansions occupy top management time to a much greater degree. This is because they involve considerable expense, usually above the spending authority of even the chief executive officer, and they often have strategic and competitive implications for the company. Moreover, the initiation of capacity expansions is apt to be the result of a formal companywide planning and review procedure rather than the result of a plant's reaction to day-to-day demands.

A typical planning and review procedure is an annual exercise that looks 5 years into the future. This exercise is driven by a marketing forecast for each year (and quarter, perhaps) of the planning horizon and for each service provided. Available capacities are estimated as well and the two are meshed together to determine to what extent capacity is in surplus or in deficit. Naturally, both marketing and operations estimates become much more nebulous the further into the future the company looks.

More than simply identifying capacity shortfalls and their likely timing over a multiyear horizon, the planning exercise concentrates on alternatives for dealing with such shortfalls. The on-site expansion of certain operations, the character, size, and region for possible new branches, or the relocation of some other operations may be considered as viable alternatives for coping with capacity shortfalls. The review of the submitted plans normally comes to some tentative decisions about which avenues for remedying capacity shortfalls ought to be shelved, at least for the time being. It is unlikely that firm commitments will be made on any specific proposal, but the waters will be tested on many.

The planning and review procedure generally works from the bottom up. (See the organization chart in Figure 10–1.) While the particular individuals involved vary from one organization to another, generally operations managers and their staffs work out the lowest tier of corporate needs and priorities. The divisions under which the facilities operate review and expand on the proposals and needs and address more far-reaching issues. The same kind of review and expansion occurs at the group level (groupings of divisions), if such a level exists, before the corporate level operations committee (or some similar body) reviews the refined proposals. For our purposes, on-site expansion is probably initiated at the facility level and approved at successively higher levels in the corporation, although it could also be initiated at the division or group level. New branches and relocations, on the other hand, usually originate not at the facility level (understandably, because the plant itself is not responsible for such an action) but at the division, group, or corporate levels.

As a result of the planning and review procedure, the divisions (and groups) are given a mandate to develop in-depth analyses of the on-site expansion, new branch, or relocation proposals that surfaced during the planning process. These proposals must be translated from ideas and plans into specific projects to be implemented and funded by the corporation. Most corporations have a formal capital appropriation request procedure that roughly parallels the hierarchy through which capacity plans are reviewed. The capital

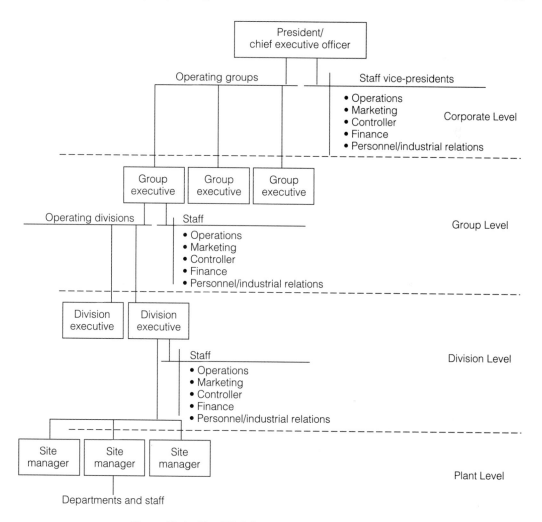

Figure 10–1 Simplified Organization Chart for a Large Corporation.

appropriation request often merely makes formal and explicit what has been discussed during the company's business planning. This request typically consists of a justification for the project and some in-depth analyses of it. These analyses include engineering specifications and cost/timing estimates; specific size, service delivered, equipment needed, worker and manager requirements, and location decisions; and an economic analysis (sometimes called a capital budgeting analysis). The appropriation request, after it has been completed and approved at the group and division levels, makes its way to the company's board of directors for final approval and the authorization to spend the necessary funds.

In broad outline, this planning and review procedure is fairly typical for capacity expansion (or contraction). It may sound straightforward, and in many cases it is, but there are many other cases where the choices and issues are complex and require clear and systematic analysis.

There are some critical features to the typical capacity plan and its analysis: the forecast, gauging capacity, the transition to increased space, economic analysis, dealing with risk, and noneconomic considerations.

The Forecast

The driving force behind the typical capacity planning exercise is a forecast or group of forecasts of sales in the upcoming quarters and years. In most companies, the forecast itself is not the particular responsibility of the operations managers, although they might have a hand in it. More often, the marketing department for a particular product or product line is charged with forecasting sales.

Forecasting the long term is often very uncertain, especially if the market is not well defined or the product is new or highly dependent on the fortunes of a hard-to-predict national economy. Over the years, forecasting techniques have become increasingly sophisticated, although one must admit that an entire arsenal of mathematical techniques may fall short of a single person's gut feeling or refined intuition. (See the Chapter 7 Appendix discussion of forecasting.)

GAUGING CAPACITY

Capacity can be very ambiguous, subject to a host of influences. Nevertheless, capacity management requires some appraisal of present capacity and what can be done to increase capacity by a given amount.

The Transition to Increased Space

It is one thing to recognize the need for increased space in the long term and quite another to manage the transition from the present to that long-term goal. Capacity increases often come in lumps, and in such circumstances managers must devise short-term policies to ease the operation into that capacity increase. The nature of this transition, coupled with the needs of the forecast, often determines the timing of a capacity increase.

Economic Analysis

Finding an economic justification for a particular capacity proposal is an important step in advancing that proposal through approval and implementation. Because capacity plans are almost always multiyear in outlook, the time value of money becomes an important consideration in any economic analysis of a project.

In any analysis of the economics of a project, assumptions have to be made. It is usually worth exploring how the economics vary under different assumptions. This kind of sensitivity analysis can be applied to the time horizon of the project, the cash flows expected in any year, and the rate of discount to be applied to the cash flows. The sensitivity of a project's net present value to such factors is important because the risks involved with a project may be great; whether it should be chosen may rest on how "robust" its economic value is, given a host of different assumptions. Sensitivity analyses help to identify the projects that entail high risks as well as high returns.

Dealing with Risk

A corporation's capacity decisions are among the most uncertain it faces. Although there is no sure-fire way to handle risk, it usually is helpful to know whether adding capacity is cheap or expensive and what penalties the corporation faces by having either too much or too little of it. If, for example, capacity is rather cheap to add and falling short of it would forgo substantial contribution, the corporation is probably better off carrying an excess. Many services involve relatively little capital investment and considerable labor intensity. In such services, it is often the case that some excess capacity can usefully be kept for peak periods of demand and left idle the rest of the time. Its use during the peak periods generates more than enough contribution to finance it for the remainder of the year.

Noneconomic Considerations

Although the economics of a capacity project are important, it is a narrow-minded manager who bases his or her decision solely on the economics. Three nonquantifiable (or at least difficult to quantify) factors deserve special mention:

1. *The impact of particular choices of capacity and facilities on existing operations.* The transition to enlarged capacity or to a new facility can be time-consuming and troublesome; it is seldom as smooth as hoped for or planned. It often pays, however, to make some allowance for the impact of a new project on the existing operation. How much is problematic, but its presence should be considered in the decision.

The nature of these impacts on existing operations is varied. Frequently, a capacity or facilities change will alter the character and extent of materials and information handling and movement within the company. Marketing and sales may have to adjust to such a change as well. Often, too, the startup of the new capacity saps engineering and management attention from the existing operation. Other impacts abound as well, many peculiar to the company or the investment itself.

2. *The competitive reaction of others in the industry to the capacity change.* Many capacity projects cannot be investigated in a vacuum, since their desirability rests in part on how competitors meet a company's particular decision on new capacity. This is particularly true of oligopolistic industries and those that are sensitive to transportation costs. How a competitor reacts may greatly affect the market in a geographic area or the market for a particular product line.

3. *Flexibility and new capacity.* In fast-paced industries, where new services, markets, and marketing approaches are routine, service delivery must stay flexible. The choice of a capacity project in one form or another may hinder or help the company's ability to keep abreast of the latest developments. Flexibility is very difficult to quantify, but its importance to a firm's continued success can be immense.

Common Pitfalls in Dealing With Capacity

The capital appropriation request procedure as outlined at the beginning of this chapter has recently come under increasing attack. The procedure is frequently seen as too rigid in practice and too narrow and confining in its outlook. How ironic it is that purchasing, which accounts for half of the cost of goods sold in many companies, and hiring, where lifetime decisions are often made, are management activities that are taken almost casually in many companies, whereas operations managers are often required to jump through hoops to justify capital expenditures for equipment that may be fairly inexpensive when compared with a worker's capitalized stream of earnings.

Some companies do tend to look at choices involving large expenditures as isolated decisions, not as interrelated parts of an overarching operations strategy. This approach narrows the focus for many capital appropriations. This narrowed focus, coupled with the need for appropriation requests to win approval by the corporation's financial department, leads to several problems with these procedures:

1. Many corporate procedures for capital appropriations are typically used, or even intended, for the study of additional capacity, not replacement capacity. As a result, what needs to be done to shore up existing operations and to keep them fully competitive is sometimes overlooked or not examined very critically.

2. The procedures too often stimulate a weak or narrow list of alternatives to be investigated. Although the stated corporate policy may be to promote fresh, even radical, ideas, in practice the options that are considered tend to be conservative and may even be specifically slanted to what the general manager thinks (or is believed to think by the group making the study).

3. Capital appropriation plans are typically excursions into uncertainty. Benefits from new space, equipment, or process configurations—especially radical ones—tend to be more elusive to quantify than are costs. As a result, options that are safe (such as on-site expansions as opposed to new facilities, known technologies rather than fledgling technologies) often have an inherent advantage, although they may be the worst choices for the company in the long run.

4. To get around the biases of narrowness and uncertainty, project teams that really believe in change often end up fudging their data. Games are sometimes played between project teams and the corporate-level managers who must decide on the appropriations. It is understandable then that capital appropriations that have to meet a certain hurdle rate (rate of discount) often end up with project proposals whose rates of return are just over those hurdle rates. Most companies deliberately set their hurdle rates high as a way of insisting that new capital projects end up better than existing capital projects. Too often, however, these high rates simply stimulate more creative fudging of the data.

From my point of view, capital appropriation projects should be evaluated in the context of the company's formal operations and competitive strategies. Thus individual projects would be seen as involving interrelated pieces of operations, capacity, and technology. The key question for the decision would be how the individual project fits with the plan. This is not to say that the economics of net present value should be ignored. Rather, this point of view argues for all the right kinds of benefits to be included in the calculations. It also argues for the hurdle rates to be realistic and for postaudits of projects to be done so that project teams and top management can recognize the numbers problems that one can fall victim to in developing capital appropriation requests.

AN EXAMPLE OF CAPACITY DECISION-MAKING IN A SERVICE INDUSTRY

Most services are provided on demand, with interaction between the customer and someone who conveys and often provides the service, and without any inventories to help smooth out the supply task. Under such circumstances, it is not difficult to understand why capacity planning and choice are critical elements in the management of service industries. As background for a discussion of capacity management of services, consider the following situation.

================ **SITUATION 10-1** ================

Quaker City Squash, Inc.

So far it had seemed easy, but now Dick Murnane, president of Quaker City Squash, Inc., faced the first tough decision of his young business career: Should he expand operations and, if so, how? For the past two years, Quaker City Squash, located in the business district of Philadelphia, had been selling half-hour blocks of time on its six squash courts to anyone willing to pay the $8 fee. Squash is a racquet sport generally played indoors by two people and is similar to handball. It had been enjoying growing popularity, especially at universities. Once out of college, however, players typically had to join downtown clubs to gain access to squash courts. The club fees were invariably high and covered more than just squash.

Sensing this latent demand, Dick (a former college varsity player himself) used some of an inheritance to purchase a building downtown and convert it into six air-conditioned squash courts, locker and shower rooms, several offices, and a bar and grill area where a bartender/short-order cook served drinks and a limited selection of sandwiches. Business boomed. Soon after opening, Dick extended the hours of operation so that now play began at 7 A.M. and continued to 10 P.M. every day but Sunday. Further, Dick hired a teaching pro who was now drawing a fine salary from teaching and from restringing squash racquets. The squash pro was regarded as a definite asset to the operation. Even the bar and grill was making money, doing a brisk luncheon and cocktail business.

From all Dick could tell, Quaker City Squash attracted mainly young (under 40) professionals who worked in Philadelphia's business district. Most had been introduced to squash while in college or in graduate school and were looking for a way to stay in shape. More than 90 percent of the customers were male. The peak hours lasted from 11:30 A.M. to 2 P.M. and from 4:30 P.M. to 7 P.M.; it was rare that a court was open during those times. Average usage outside these hours ran about 50 percent. The same 50 percent usage prevailed all of Saturday as well. Standard practice was to reserve a court at least a day in advance, although no reservations except permanent ones (a year's worth of time at a particular hour and day of the week) were accepted for any more than a week in advance. There were no assigned or permanent lockers; players brought their clothes and racquets with them.

With business going so well, Dick naturally pondered the opening of another Quaker City Squash Center. Two different options presented themselves:

1. Open another center in the business district, much like the one currently in operation. A building suitable for the necessary remodeling was available in another portion of the downtown area. It could be purchased for $300,000 and the remodeling for six courts could be done for $275,000. Operating expenses (salaries, utilities, necessary maintenance, taxes) could be expected to run about $115,000 per year, the same rate as at the existing squash center. This new squash center would cater to the same market as the old one but because it would be located in a different part of the business district, it would appeal to a different group of customers.

The available building was somewhat larger than the existing center, and that posed some special problems. Dick could add another court, but that would mean paring some space away from the locker rooms and the bar and grill. Or, Dick could expand the locker room space (some of the permanent reservation holders had been clamoring for their own lockers at the existing facility and would gladly pay for them) or expand the space of the bar and grill, making it fancier, perhaps adding a waiter, and permitting the kitchen to expand its limited menu in hopes of attracting more players after their games or of catering to a small band of squash "addicts" who might use the squash center as their own club. The costs seemed roughly comparable; that is, $40,000 more would pay for either the additional court or for the expanded locker room ($10,000) and an expanded bar and grill (between $20,000 and $35,000, depending on decor and modifications to the kitchen).

2. Alternatively, Dick could open a squash center in one of Philadelphia's suburbs. Demand in the suburbs was more spread out and so only a smaller center, say three courts, could be supported at any one location. Building in the suburbs was likely to be considerably cheaper than remodeling a downtown building. For a suburb along the fashionable Main Line, construction estimates, including land, averaged about $200,000 for a three-court squash center. Operating expenses were also likely to be proportionately lower, the best estimate being $48,000 per year.

Much less predictable was suburban demand for the courts. Dick had no good feel for how strong any one of several trends would be and what each would mean for the operation:

Would a suburban location shift demand to more women players than were using the downtown facility?

Was that demand strong enough so that Quaker City Squash should offer nursery services?

Would the peak demand period shift from lunch to the early evening, as was true for many indoor tennis clubs?

Would the time pattern of play support opening up later than 7 A.M. and extending play to 11 P.M. or even midnight?

Three courts would not support a bar and grill, as in the downtown squash center, but Dick wondered whether some vending machines ought to be substituted.

Three courts would not support a full-time teaching pro. Dick wondered whether a part-time pro would be necessary, say in the morning, teaching mainly women.

A further concern of Dick's, no matter which alternative was finally chosen, was how competition would affect all of his operations. Not only was there the threat of new squash centers opening up in either the business district or the suburbs, but there was also the threat of the downtown clubs introducing squash-only privileges at special rates. Dick wondered whether adhering to the same strategy and being first in the market was sufficient, or whether he should try to lock in his clientele by offering club memberships.

Discussion of Quaker City Squash

The situation Dick Murnane finds himself in illustrates many of the unique problems with which service firms have to wrestle, most of which are doggedly difficult to quantify.

The first-cut economics of this situation are actually quite straightforward. For each court, Quaker City Squash now receives $8 per half-hour or $16 per hour of use. There are 5 hours of each weekday when all the courts are occupied; for the remaining 10 hours per day and for all of Saturday only half of the courts are occupied. These figures imply a weekly revenue of $5520 ($920 per court) and a yearly revenue of $287,040, assuming the same level of use as now exists. We can use this revenue figure together with the investment sum required ($575,000) and the expected operating costs of $115,000 per year to analyze the economics of another downtown location. The cash flows in real terms for that investment over, say, 10 years are shown in Table 10–1.

The net present value of the investment (10 years at a high real rate of interest of 15 percent) is a handsome $288,430. We can also calculate the average usage level that must be sustained if the investment is to have a net present value of at least zero. The annual revenues would have to be $229,570 per year to have an NPV of zero, and this in turn implies an average usage rate of 51 percent. Any rate higher than that and the NPV turns positive.

In similar fashion, the economics of the suburban location can be calculated. The investment comes to $200,000 with expected annual operating costs of $48,000. If the revenue per court remains the same as downtown with 5 hours of peak play and 10 hours of 50 percent usage, weekly revenues will total $2760 and the yearly revenues will come to $143,520. The cash flow pattern is shown in Table 10–1.

The net present value of this suburban investment (10 years at a real rate of interest of 15 percent) is $279,390, which is almost as high as for the new downtown location. In fact, shortening the time horizon or raising the discount rate makes the suburban location relatively more attractive. The economics, then, do not argue much in favor of one location over the other.

What must guide the decision are a number of other considerations, most of which are exceedingly difficult to quantify. They are what make the capacity decisions of service industries, in many cases, relatively more troublesome than those of manufacturing enterprises. Among these considerations are the mesh of marketing with operations, competitive reactions, demand modification, and nonspace capacity adjustments. These four considerations can all shape thinking about the need for and the design of capacity in service industries. Although their economic impact is often difficult to assess, their importance to the success

TABLE 10-1 A COMPARISON OF CASH FLOWS (QUAKER CITY SQUASH)

	New downtown location			Suburban location		
Year	Cash outlay(−)	Receipt(+)	Total	Cash outlay(−)	Receipt(+)	Total
0	−$575,000			−$200,000		
1	−115,000	+$287,040	+$172,040	−48,000	+$143,520	+$95,520
2	−115,000	+287,040	+172,040	−48,000	+143,520	+95,520
.	.	.	.	.	.	
.	.	.	.	.	.	
10	−115,000	+287,040	+172,040	−48,000	+143,520	+95,520

of any service firm's operation can be crucial. At the same time, deciding what should be done about each is quite a burden. As we shall see, the course Dick Murnane should follow with Quaker City Squash is far from evident.

The mesh of marketing and operations in planning capacity. Should Quaker City Squash's courts be centrally located in the business district or should it decentralize its capacity? The juxtaposition of marketing and operations is critical in this regard. Is growth to be found in the suburbs? Which is more convenient: squash near home or squash near work? How much a part of the game is camaraderie, and is camaraderie more likely to flourish at a downtown location? Will significant numbers of women be attracted to the game if courts are situated in the suburbs?

Because capacity is often the "product" in a service business, or at least intimately linked to the service provided, knowledge of why a customer purchases the service is a critical item in the plan for the design of new capacity. This is something Dick Murnane must ponder; the answers are by no means obvious.

Related to the issue of increasing the right kind of capacity is the concern about whether new capacity will undercut the service provided by already existing capacity. At Quaker City Squash, will a new downtown location divert players away from the existing downtown site, or will players refrain from downtown play during the day to play at the suburban location in the evening? To answer these questions, one needs knowledge of the customers, where they come from, and why.

Another aspect of the close marketing/operations bond in a service firm's capacity planning is the need to *balance the elements that make up that capacity.* For example, at Quaker City Squash there is the opportunity to build a seventh court, although at the expense of the locker rooms and grill. Alternatively, a private locker room could be installed and the bar and grill expanded.

If one assumes that the new court will attract use just like any of the other courts, the economics are much more likely to support a squash court than to support private lockers or added space in the grill room. What must be questioned is whether a new court, coupled with smaller locker and grill room space, would actually add enough revenue to warrant its construction. It is conceivable that usage would adjust itself not to the number of courts provided but rather to the locker room or grill room space. In that case, adding a seventh court would be a disastrous move because total patronage would actually fall.

Competitive reactions.   We have already discussed the importance of gauging competitive reaction for capacity planning in manufacturing companies. Because capacity decisions (how much, of what type, and where) are so critical to a service firm's competitive stance, the reactions of competitors are usually even more significant in service industries. At Quaker City Squash, for instance, competitive reactions may take the form of other squash centers being opened in downtown Philadelphia or they may be policy changes at some of the existing clubs (say, the addition of separate squash memberships for special fees). In any event, competition can quickly change the earnings potential of all of Quaker City Squash's operations.

Modifying demand.   When a bottleneck is reached in the provision of a service (e.g., during the noon hour at Quaker City Squash), often that bottleneck can be relieved, at least temporarily, by manipulating demand in various ways through pricing policies and service policies.

Pricing can be used as both carrot and stick to shift the extent and the timing of demand. High prices can shut off demand or shift it into other time periods. Low prices can stimulate demand. Whether a price cut will actually lead to more revenue through greater patronage depends on how sensitive the demand by patrons is to price changes. If changes of X percent lead to changes in the quantity demanded of more than X percent, the demand is said to be *price elastic* and revenues can be increased by cutting price. If an X percent change in price leads to less than X percent change in the quantity demanded, the demand is termed *price inelastic* and revenues can actually be increased by raising price. Ascertaining whether demand is in fact price elastic or price inelastic is often hit or miss, however, and it is usually under pressure—severe lack of capacity or embarrassing excess capacity—that prices are altered significantly.

The extension of existing services and the provision of ancillary or complementary services can also have a substantial impact on demand. In terms of the Quaker City Squash situation, the teaching pro, the bar and grill, the private lockers, nursery care, the reservation system, and other extras may all have important implications for demand. One or more of them may be instrumental in attracting demand or in shifting demand from peak times to off-peak times. The reservation system is clearly a tool to apportion demand among peak and off-peak periods, and the timing of the teaching pro and nursery services could also have a bearing on broadening demand away from the peak periods.

Adjusting capacity without altering space requirements.   At Quaker City Squash, space means capacity, but there are a variety of other service industries in which capacity can be increased modestly by employing several techniques:

Using part-time workers for peak times (e.g., think of temporary employment services).

Increasing efficiency via methods improvements, labor specialization, labor cross-training, and the like.

Inducing consumers to provide some of the service themselves (e.g., salad bars at restaurants).

Sharing equipment or other resources with firms or organizations in the same or a related industry.

ON-SITE EXPANSION, BRANCH ESTABLISHMENT, AND RELOCATION

Once a company's managers agree that new capacity ought to be created to satisfy expected future demand, they still must decide how that new capacity ought to be implemented. Should on-site expansion, the opening of a new operation, or the relocation of an existing one prevail?

The Relative Advantages of On-Site Expansion

On-site expansion is by far the most popular way of adding productive space. Its low cost (often no new land acquisition costs), the relatively short time lag associated with it, and its status as a known quantity make it appealing. By expanding on-site, a company can keep its labor force intact and it does not have the difficult task of weeding out pieces of the service delivery system for isolation at another site.

Often, too, on-site expansion is viewed as a way to achieve the benefits of economies of scale. This is an elusive concept, however, and it merits some discussion of its own.

Economies of scale.[1]   It is often stated that large companies enjoy a competitive edge over small companies because of the inherent advantages of economies of scale. The phrase has a strong appeal, and large companies with sizable operations have a certain aura about them. Wal-Mart is no stranger to the observation that its continued cost-competitiveness is the result of its size. The phrase draws nods of recognition, yet few people can define it and fewer still have thought critically about it.

All too often you hear a company president nonchalantly say something like, "If we increase the size of our operations, we'll naturally enjoy some economies of scale." There is nothing natural about economies of scale and certainly nothing to be nonchalant about.

Confusion about the term is understandable because it serves as an umbrella for a number of real but quite distinct concepts. Because it is an umbrella term, *economies of scale* often loses its usefulness in making management decisions on operations size.

Volume, Capacity, and Process Technology.   How do economies of scale relate to operations size? The standard definition declares that economies of scale are reaped whenever higher output volumes lead to lower unit costs. However, the definition only *seems* to be clear.

Consider four different operations, all in the same service industry. Operations A and B are physically identical in every respect. They differ only in that

---

[1]This section is adapted from Roger W. Schmenner, "Before You Build a Big Factory," *Harvard Business Review* 54, no. 4 (July–August 1976): 100–104.

operation B produces just a fraction of the volume of operation A, perhaps because company A's marketing efforts are much more effective than company B's. Operation C is similar to operation A in layout and equipment but is twice the size. Operation D, on the other hand, incorporates an entirely different service process technology from the other three and can produce twice what operation A can produce.

I draw these examples to distinguish among the concepts of volume, capacity, and process technology. As Table 10–2 shows, operations A and B share the same capacity and the same process technology, although their actual volumes differ. Operations A and C share the same process technology, although not the same capacity; operations C and D share the same capacity but not the same process technology.

These concepts of volume, capacity, and process technology are important because they all relate to economies of scale. We will discuss these three specific types of economies.

Economies of Volume. The higher-volume operation A will enjoy lower unit costs than operation B because it can spread its fixed costs (overhead, capital costs) over a greater number of units. If by scale we mean volume, then the difference in unit costs between operations A and B can be an economy of scale.

For some people, however, the spreading of fixed costs seems too trite an example to be labeled a scale economy, so they dismiss it. These people then modify the definition of a scale economy to exclude economies that are really economies of volume.

Economies of Capacity. As the table shows, operation C's unit costs are lower than operation A's and thus much lower than operation B's. Operation C's

TABLE 10–2 DEFINING THE DIFFERENCES IN UNIT COSTS

Operation	Capacity		Volume produced		Process technology		Manufacturing costs per unit produced
A	100	Difference in capacity; same volume to capacity ratio	100	Difference only in volume	Type X		$1/unit
B	100		40		Type X		Higher than $1/unit
C	200		200		Type X	Difference only in process technology	Lower than $1/unit
D	200		200		Type Y		Much lower than $1/unit

Source: R. W. Schmenner, "Before You Build a Big Factory," *Harvard Business Review* 54, no. 4 (July–August 1976): 102.

increased capacity permits it to carry proportionately less raw materials inventory. This may be due to the familiar "economic order quantity" result that optimal inventories need increase only as the square root of volume and not proportionately with volume.

On the other hand, because operations A and C share the same technology, operation C is not likely to enjoy a proportionately lower work-in-process inventory, but its finished goods inventories may well be proportionately lower. For example, suppose that operations A and C both make two different products. If operation A has only one production line that it must change over from one product to the other, it will have to build up proportionately more finished goods inventory to cover its demand than operation C, which can afford to manufacture each product on a separate, dedicated line. Operation A needs to carry enough of an inventory of its first product to tide itself over while it makes its second product. Operation C need not worry about this problem.

In addition to these inventory-associated economies, operation C will have an advantage over the smaller operation A, as its increased capacity allows the luxury of more spare equipment and maintenance capabilities or of additional and useful overhead functions. If scale means capacity, then any differences in unit costs between operations A and C can be appropriately called economies of scale.

Economies of Process Technology. As we can see, operation C enjoys some cost advantages over operation A. However, operation D enjoys even lower costs, for two major reasons: capital-for-labor substitution and labor specialization. Operation D has automated more (substituted more capital for labor) than operation C. Using more, better, and different procedures and equipment, operation D has been able to produce as much as operation C, but it employs fewer workers. As a result, its costs are lower. The increased automation and the process changes at operation D may or may not be an advance in the state of technology, but the increase in capital certainly alters the process in operation D as compared with operation C. Moreover, often a company cannot make small additions to its operation's stock of equipment and space; large additions (often called *indivisibilities*) have to be made and are perhaps the classic explanation for economies of scale. Such indivisibilities are usually substantial alterations to an operation's process technology and so are more than just scale changes. They are changes in process technology, and should be recognized and managed as such.

Operation D also has lower unit costs because it has altered its process technology to specialize its labor for particular tasks. In order to make its process more continuous, jobs are "deskilled." That is, instead of large numbers of highly skilled workers each doing a number of operations to form the product, the process is organized to link together less skilled workers doing a small number of specific operations. The time and responsibility any one worker devotes to a particular service is reduced in an effort to increase productivity through repetition and specialized competence.

To reiterate, both capital-for-labor substitution and labor specialization alter process technologies. Thus, if by scale we mean process technology, then we can appropriately call these two means of cost reduction economies of scale.

Avoiding Ambiguity.   As pointed out in the preceding paragraphs, the term *economies of scale* suffers from irredeemable ambiguity. It can take a variety of meanings depending on one's interpretation of "scale" as volume, capacity, or process technology. Even then, there are a variety of ways to effect the economies. Instead of inviting confusion by using the term *economies of scale,* people should think of volume, capacity, and process technology separately.

Size Decisions over Time.   The operation size decision depends on the careful balancing of a number of alternative technologies, costs, and risks. Over time, these alternatives become more and more blurred. Technological advance is unpredictable, and it is not clear whether new capital equipment with smaller or with larger break-even volumes will predominate. A lot of new technology is sophisticated, expensive, and large scale; and yet microcomputers and telecommunications advances are persuasive examples of some small-scale technological change.

In sum, the term *economies of scale* is vague enough to provide easy justification for any number of decisions on operation capacity. Because it is so vague, its usefulness to managers is minimal. Instead, two areas should be carefully scrutinized: (1) the cost reductions a company can achieve through specific changes in an operation's volume, capacity, or process technology and (2) what those changes mean for management control, logistics, inventories, and the ability to respond to service or process innovations.

These cautions about economies of scale notwithstanding, on-site expansion has some very attractive features. Nevertheless, it is not an all-purpose remedy for space shortages and there are a host of circumstances where either a new branch or a relocation would be preferred.

The Disadvantages of On-Site Expansion: Building the Case for Branching and Relocation

Although often attractive, on-site operation expansion can usher in a host of diseconomies, particularly if on-site expansion has been a repeated practice. For example, as more and more space is added on-site, the layout of the operation typically becomes less and less optimal. Rarely is an entire operation reconfigured during an expansion; rather, only portions of the operation are shifted around. The result, over time, is that departments, once close together, become separated. Materials handling and storage become more difficult, with more chances for delay or error. Managers find themselves isolated from one another or from the work groups they are supposed to oversee. In short, transportation and communication become strained and this strain is likely to impede service delivery and quality.

Staying at the same site often postpones the introduction of new process technology as well. Old equipment is kept in use, old methods are followed, and the advantages of new equipment and techniques are forgone, with consequences for future costs and innovation.

Continued on-site expansion means that more and more workers and, often, more and more products, must be managed. Such a layering of expanded responsibilities creates real complexities for managers at all levels. The existing cadre of managers may be asked to supervise more than they are readily capable of, thus lessening the attention certain problems should receive. With more products and output from the same operation, decisions on the levels, composition, and uses of inventories are likely to become more difficult and prone to error. Decisions on control are likely to become vastly more complex as well. As more and more services are added to the operation, the cost accounting system is likely to become more arbitrary and thus less helpful.

With more services in the operation, management runs the risk not only of complicating supervision, inventory, control systems, and the like, but also of placing incompatible demands on managers, workers, and systems. For example, services delivered in low volumes but with special performance features demand a different mode of management, worker effort, and control systems than services delivered in high volumes with few special features. If both are delivered from the same facility with common management, workforce, and operating policies and systems, the likely result is that both services may suffer in the individual dimensions (price, performance, delivery) that make a service competitive.

Besides this incompatibility problem, the addition of more workers to an existing site is apt to require the increasing formalization of the workforce–management relationship. The workforce is less apt to identify strongly with the company, and labor relations within the operation may become strained. Old management concessions to the workforce may come back to haunt operations.

For these reasons, continued on-site expansion becomes less and less desirable. The alternatives—the establishment of a new branch operation and operation relocation—can prevent many of these long-term and often subtle pitfalls of on-site expansion, although their abilities to surmount certain of these pitfalls differ. Table 10–3 outlines some of the relative advantages of new branches and relocations.

New branch establishment, for example, is at a relative advantage if the operation's problems run more to service proliferation, workforce size, or meeting expected future growth. By branching, a company can avoid overloading one operation with either too many different services or too many workers. At the same time, the new branch can exploit the latest production technology and the most sensible operation design. The operating policies and systems of the branch can also be meshed carefully with the services chosen and with the competitive priorities attached to them.

TABLE 10-3 ADVANTAGES OF BRANCHES AND RELOCATIONS VS. ON-SITE EXPANSION

Problem area	New branches	Relocation
Facility layout and materials handling	Radical improvements possible with operations placed in branch; some possibilities of improving base facility as operations are placed in branch	Radical improvements possible
New process technology	New technology for branch possible; likely that base operations will keep much of old technology	Scrapping of old operation, equipment, and methods possible; new technology can supplant it readily
Control	Can mean radical change to control procedures and policies in new facilities, although not much change to be expected for old operations; inventories can build up by adding branch	Can mean radical changes to controls of all types; inventory levels not likely to be affected
Managerial impact	Additional managers needed to open and run branch: staff demands increased to coordinate operation interactions	Old set of managers can generally run new operation without stretching themselves too thin
Service proliferation	Can easily manage new services, especially if branch operations are organized as distinct services	New products less easily managed
Size of workforce	Keeps workforce levels at all operations under desired ceilings	Little or no effect on workforce size
Financial burdens	Extra overhead demanded to cover more than one location, new operation startup expenses	Moving costs, new operation startup expenses
Ease of meeting future growth	Relatively easy; geographic growth met best with new market area operations, service introductions with new operations	Not easy; shares many future capacity problems with on-site expansion alternative

Operation relocation, on the other hand, is at a relative advantage if the operation's problems are more involved with operation layout, materials and information handling and storage, new process technology, control, and lack of management depth. Relocation, by definition, means closing one facility and opening another at roughly the same time, which means that relocation can readily scrap old capital, technology, and policies for new. Thus relocation gains in standing when the operation's problems are less related to large size and more to process technology and control.

Chapter 11

Managing Projects

A project—constructing the World Trade Center or sending a man to the moon—shares many characteristics with other types of production processes. We can picture a project with the same kind of precedence relationship with which we pictured the line flow process. Certain activities must be completed before others begin, and each activity can be expected to take a given period of time, just as in other process types. But our concern for balance in the factory, so prominent in our thinking about production processes, does not trouble us in thinking about a project because a project is, by definition, a one-time endeavor and workers can generally expect to work only so long on it and then move on to something else. It is typical for a project to employ wildly fluctuating numbers of people, many with different skills. We do not worry about idleness—construction workers move on to the next project as do space scientists and engineers.

What does trouble us in a project is getting it done on time, for projects often have important deadlines to meet. Scheduling is thus absolutely critical to the management of a project. Several techniques have been developed to highlight the project activities that must be accomplished on time (or else risk delaying the entire project) and the activities that can be delayed somewhat. One such scheduling technique is called the critical path method; what follows is a brief description of its rationale and workings.

THE CRITICAL PATH CONCEPT

As an illustration, let us consider the simplified example of a project many companies face—the startup of a new facility. The major tasks involved in a facility startup are arrayed and described in Table 11–1. The table makes clear

TABLE 11–1 A FACILITY STARTUP PROJECT

Job name	Job description	Immediate predecessors	Time (months)
A	Selection of facility manager and management personnel	—	3
B	Site survey soil test	—	1
C	Extension of roads, water, utilities, sewer	—	6
D	Selection and purchase of equipment	A	2
E	Final engineering plans for construction	B	3
F	Employment interviews and hiring	A	3
G	Equipment delivery	D	9
H	Construction of facility	E	11
I	Precise layout of plant	D, E	1
J	Institution of management systems for control of production, inventory, purchasing, accounting	A	4
K	Worker training	F, G, H	2
L	Equipment and system installation	G, H, I, J	1

that some tasks cannot be started until other tasks (predecessors) have been completed.

The precedence relationships of the startup can be depicted in a graph or network, as shown in Figure 11–1. This network follows a particular convention known as *activity-on-node*. This convention is intuitively appealing and somewhat less confusing than the alternative convention, known as *activity-on-arrow*.

The key principle of the critical path concept is that a project cannot be completed any faster than the longest time path between the project's start and its finish. In Figure 11–1, the longest path from the start (project approval) to the finish (facility startup) involves the following activities—B, E, H, and K; they take a total of 17 months. The longest path between project approval and facility startup is termed the *critical path*, primarily because any delay along this path of activities sets back the entire project. It is this critical path that merits the most management attention.

All the other paths from start to finish enjoy at least a month's slack time, so they can experience delays and still not harm the 17-month completion schedule. For example, the next two longest paths after the critical path involve the following activities:

B-E-H-L	16 months
A-D-G-K	16 months

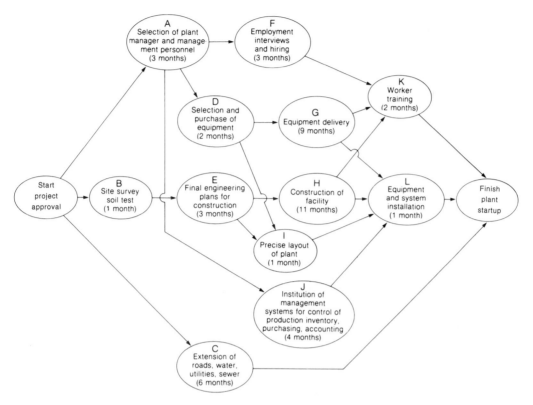

Figure 11-1   Precedence Diagram for a Facility Startup Project.

There can be delays of up to a month on these two paths without setting back the entire project. However, note that the first path is very much like the critical path itself; it differs only in that activity L is substituted for activity K. The slack in this path then can be taken only on activity L (equipment and system installation). If a delay occurred on any other activity, say H (construction of the facility), the critical path would also be affected, and the entire project would be delayed.

The second path is much more flexible about where its slack can be used up. Only one of its activities, K (worker training), is shared with the critical path. Thus, its month of slack can be used up on activities A, D, or G without affecting the critical path in any way.

Other paths, of course, have considerably more slack and can be accomplished at a more leisurely pace, if need be. For example, the uppermost path in the diagram (A-F-K) is expected to take 8 months, with only activity K on the critical path. Activity F could be delayed as much as 9 months without making the project late. However, activity A could not be delayed that long because it is on one of the second longest paths and can be delayed only a month before it would affect the project's completion time.

This example raises an important point about critical paths and project scheduling. As time wears on in a project's life, delays and even some speed-ups can be expected. What may look like the critical path at a project's start may not remain the critical path if many delays (or speed-ups) strike the project. This means that the project manager should periodically recalculate the critical path to check that he or she is focusing on the activities that really matter to finishing a project in the least time.

Gantt charts can capture some of what the critical path gives us, but not all. A Gantt chart of the table above could be constructed. (See Tour A for both a Gantt chart and a precedence diagram of the same project steps.) Whereas the precedence characteristics can be depicted, and some feel for the slack in the system can be shown, the links between activities are missing and the critical path itself is not evident from the diagram itself; it must be imposed on it from an outside calculation.

Calculating the Critical Path

To this point, we have calculated the critical path solely by inspecting all the paths and choosing the one with the longest duration. In simple cases, such as this generalized facility startup, inspection is a perfectly feasible and reasonable way of selecting the critical path. When projects get more complicated, with many more activities, inspection as a means of computing the critical path bogs down. Happily, there is an alternative procedure or algorithm, which can cut down the speed of solution markedly.

In essence, the critical path algorithm is a procedure to identify which activities have some slack time and which do not. Those with no slack time, of course, make up the critical path or paths. Before describing the algorithm, however, it is helpful to define some terms:

Early Start (ES)—The earliest time a job can begin, which is the latest time that any of the job's predecessors are finished.

Early Finish (EF)—The earliest time a job can finish, which is the early start time plus the time it takes to do the job.

For any job i, the early start and early finish can be represented symbolically.

$$ES(i) = \max [EF \text{ (all of } i\text{'s predecessors)}],$$

or the start time of the project if we are considering the beginning jobs.

$$EF(i) = ES(i) + t(i),$$

where $t(i)$ is the time to perform job i.

Late Start (LS)—The latest a job can start without causing the entire project to be completed any later, which is the late finish time less the time for the job.

$$LS(i) = LF(i) - t(i).$$

Late Finish (LF)—The latest time a job can finish, which is the earliest time that any of the job's successors have to be started. These can be represented symbolically, as well, for any job *i*.

$$LF(i) = \min [LS \text{ (all of } i\text{'s successors)}],$$

or the earliest finish time for the project if we are considering the ending jobs.

Total Slack (TS)—The difference between the early and late starts for a job, or the early or late finishes. Total slack is the time a particular job could be delayed without delaying the completion of the project. Symbolically,

$$TS(i) = LS(i) - ES(i) = LF(i) - EF(i)$$

The critical path algorithm involves calculating ES, EF, LS, and LF for all the jobs in the network and then comparing them to discover which nodes have zero total slack.[1] These nodes are the ones comprising the critical path(s). The calculation and comparison involve three steps:

1. *Forward pass.* The forward pass through the network calculates the early start (ES) and early finish (EF) times. It does so by moving from start to finish, figuring first the early start time and then adding the job's duration to figure the early finish. The early start for any job is calculated by scanning all of its immediate predecessor activities (those with arrows pointing into it in the path) and choosing as the job's early start the latest of all the predecessors' early finish times. The ES and EF times for our facility startup example are noted in Figure 11–2.

2. *Backward pass.* The backward pass through the network calculates the late start (LS) and late finish (LF) times. It does this by moving from the finish back to the start, figuring first the late finish times and then deriving the late start times by subtracting the job's duration from the late finish time. The late finish for any job is calculated by scanning all of its immediate successor activities (those with arrows leading away from it on the path) and choosing as the job's late finish the earliest of all the successors' late start times. The LF and LS times for our facility startup example are noted in Figure 11–3.

3. *Comparison.* The comparison of either early start with early finish or late start with late finish is the way to figure whether the job has any total slack (TS) associated with it. If the LS(*i*) – ES(*i*) or LF(*i*) – EF(*i*) calculations are zero, the job has no total slack and is on the critical path. Figure 11–4 combines all the times in one diagram and displays the critical path.

---

[1]Or a minimum total slack if there is some discretion about the completion time possible for the project. Note the later discussion of windows of time.

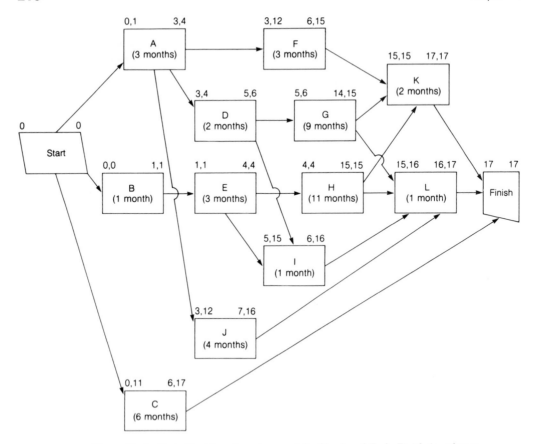

Figure 11–2 Early Start (number at upper left of box) and Early Finish (number at upper right of box) Months for the Facility Startup Project Depicted in Figure 11–1.

For very large projects, of course, and ones that go into significant detail, even the critical path method can become tedious. To aid in the analysis, there are computer programs that calculate the critical path (See Tour A). These can be used easily to determine how differences in expected completion times for various activities (and even the introduction of variations in the network of activities itself) affect the critical path(s). Because so many things can go awry in a project, it is advantageous to compute the critical path on a regular basis so as not to be caught napping.

Project Costs and Timing and the Critical Path
Often, actual projects (such as the new facility startup outlined in Figure 11–1) need not be finished in the least time possible but, rather, can be finished during any portion of a window of time. When during the acceptable window of time

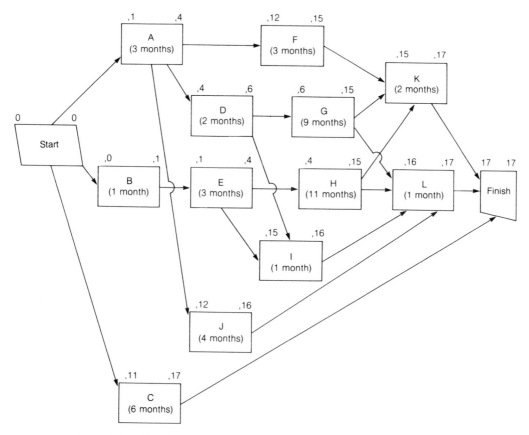

Figure 11–3 Late Start (number at upper left of box) and Late Finish (number at upper right of box) Months for the Facility Startup Project Depicted in Figure 11–1.

the project's finish ought to be targeted depends largely on the project's managers. Often they are influenced by cost considerations, because it is not uncommon for a project's contract to stipulate rewards for an early finish and penalties for a late finish. These rewards and penalties must be weighted against the costs that hurrying up any of the project's activities could impose on the project's budget.

Windows of Time and the Critical Path

Windows of time can be easily incorporated into the calculation of the critical path; in fact, the terminology is already in place to handle them. The acceptable window of time can be denoted as the difference between the early finish and the late finish (or between the early start and the late start). To return to our example,

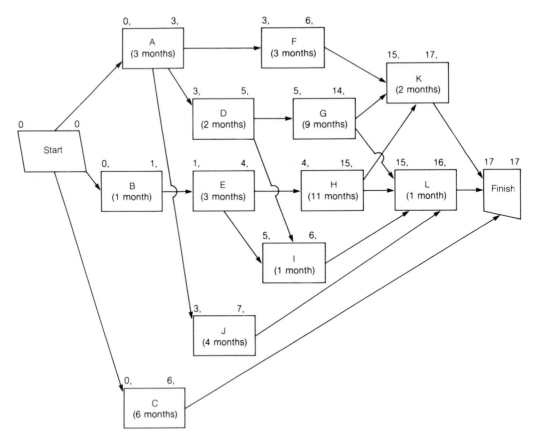

Figure 11–4   Composite of Starting and Finishing Months Given in Figures 11–2 and 11–3 for the Facility Startup Project.

if the facility startup could be completed between 17 and 21 months from the start, the values for Figure 11–4 would be recast as in Figure 11–5.

Building a window of time in the critical path computation makes it important to distinguish between two different kinds of slack time during the project: total slack and free slack. Total slack, as discussed previously, is the difference between the early and late finishes (or early and late starts) for any activity. An activity's total slack time is the maximum time that activity may be delayed beyond its early start without forcing the delay of the entire project. As previously noted, this notion of total slack can be used to define the critical path; the critical path is composed of the activities that have the lowest total slack (the smallest differences—possibly zero—between early and late starts or finishes).

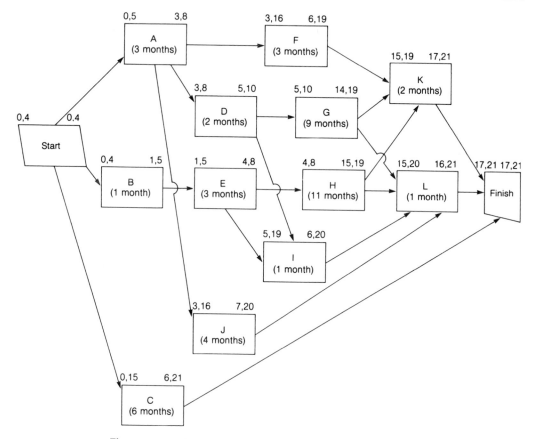

Figure 11–5 The Addition of Four Months (a window of time) to the Facility Startup Project.

Free slack, on the other hand, is the time by which an activity can be delayed without delaying the early start of any other activity. Free slack is defined as the difference between an activity's early finish time and the earliest of the early start times for all its immediate successor activities. Symbolically, the free slack (FS) for any job i can be defined as

$$FS(i) = \min [ES \text{ (all of } i\text{'s immediate successors)}] - EF(i)$$

Consider path A-J-L in Figure 11–5. Activity L can be delayed at most a month without risking the delay of the entire project; as it is, its early finish time (16 months) is but 1 month shy of the project completion's early start month (17 months). Its free slack is 1 month. Activity J, on the other hand, has more free slack. Its early finish time of 7 months is 8 months shy of its only successor activity's (L's) early start time of 15 months; its free slack is thus 8 months. Activity A, the predecessor to activity J, has no free slack because its early finish time (3 months) is equal to the early start time of activities D, F, and J.

This lack of any free slack does not mean, however, that if activity A were inadvertently delayed, the entire project would be delayed. Activity A, after all, does not lie on the critical path. It has a positive total slack and thus could be delayed by one month without necessarily delaying the project. It is often useful to employ a network-based Gantt chart as an aid in tracking and scheduling noncritical activities (see Figure 11–6). Such charts usually display two panels, one depicting all activities at their earliest starts and the other depicting all activities at their latest starts. Network-based Gantt charts can also include data on workforce schedules per time period and cost incurred per time period. Figure 11–6 refers back to Figure 11–4's network, where there is no window of time for the completion of the project. Note how the activities on the critical path coordinate with one another on the chart.

Trading Off Time Against Cost

Suppose up to two months could be shaved off both the time it took to construct the new facility and the time it took to deliver the necessary equipment,

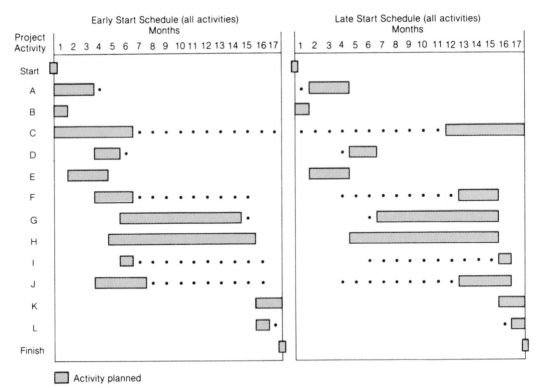

Figure 11–6 A Network-based Gantt Chart for the Facility Startup Project.

although at a cost. The costs that would have to be incurred to "crash" each of these activities are shown in Table 11–2. Suppose also that having the new facility finished a month or two early was estimated to be worth $70,000 per month, because the new facility promised capacity that was unobtainable any other way. Should these activities be crashed by 1 or 2 months? How can the critical path aid in the analysis?

As should be increasingly evident by this point in the text, this decision is one for which marginal analysis is appropriate. That is, it pays to speed up the project if the additional benefits enjoyed are greater than the additional costs incurred. If the costs outweigh the benefits, it is best to keep the project on its original schedule.

This use of marginal analysis to decide which activities are to be crashed, and how, is a central element of the critical path (CPM), which is one of the key tools for project management. It is particularly popular with construction companies, although it has a wide following elsewhere.

The use of the critical path is important for this kind of analysis, for it indicates, for any project length chosen, exactly which activities have to be speeded up and which can be left on the original schedule. Ideally, of course, we would like to leave slack all that can be left slack and speed up only what must be speeded up (and if a choice exists, to speed up the least costly activities). Put another way, to the extent possible, we would like every path to be a critical path because in so doing, the least expenditure for project speedup will be incurred. What does this mean for our example? To complete the facility startup in 16 months rather than 17, activity H (facility construction) must be crashed because it (not activity G, equipment delivery) lies on the critical path. Activity G can be left as originally scheduled. The costs incurred for speeding up the project to 16 months are thus only $50,000 and the expected benefit from the early completion is $70,000. It is clear that the project ought to be speeded up by at least 1 month. Note that there are now two critical paths: B-E-H-K and A-D-G-K.

What about speeding up the project from 16 months to 15 months? To complete the facility startup in only 15 months would require that facility construction (activity H) be speeded up an additional month (for critical path B-E-H-K) and that either equipment delivery (activity G) or personnel selection

TABLE 11–2   COSTS TO "CRASH" THREE ACTIVITIES IN THE FACILITY STARTUP PROJECT

Activity	Cost to crash first month	Cost to crash second month
Construction of facility (H)	$50,000	$75,000
Equipment delivery (G)	20,000	40,000
Selection of facility manager and management personnel (A)	5,000	Impossible

(activity A) be speeded up by one month (for critical path A-D-G-K). The additional cost would be at least $80,000 ($75,000 for crashing activity H again and $5000 for crashing activity A), which exceeds the benefits of $70,000 for being another month early. Speeding up the project from 16 months to 15 months is thus not advised. Note that the critical path and marginal analysis are both called for in analyzing trade-offs of time and cost in project scheduling.

AN ALTERNATIVE: PROGRAM EVALUATION AND REVIEW TECHNIQUE (PERT)

At about the same time as the CPM was developed in the late 1950s, a similar technique called PERT (program evaluation and review technique) was also developed. Both CPM and PERT require the construction of a network diagram, and they both share the concept of the critical path as determining the least time for project completion. In contrast to our discussion so far, PERT offers a different graphical technique and an added wrinkle.

Graphing PERT

Where the networks we prepared previously place activities to be performed at the nodes of the network diagram and use arrows only to indicate which activities follow others, PERT uses a different convention. Activities are placed on arrows and the nodes of the network serve as events—the starts and completions of various activities. In order to preserve the proper precedence relationships when using this graphical convention, dummy activities and events must sometimes be introduced. Figure 11–7 illustrates this with a portion of the precedence relationships from the facility startup example. As Figure 11–7 implies, PERT is more cumbersome to graph than the activity-on-node networks.

Time Estimate Variations

PERT can be used to provide some insight into likely variations in the completion time of the project. Individual estimates (an optimistic one, a pessimistic one, and a most likely one) of the variance in performing each activity are made. This is accomplished by assuming a certain distribution for these variances—the *beta distribution* (a skewed distribution that permits the possibility of occasional very late events, but no very early events—and by insisting on the independence of each activity from others. An estimate of the time variance in accomplishing the entire project (and thus the probability for completing it by various dates) can be made by summing the variances along the critical paths. The assumptions ensure that the distribution of the summed variances will be normal.

The expected value of the time for each activity is

$$T = \frac{oe + 4ml + pe}{6},$$

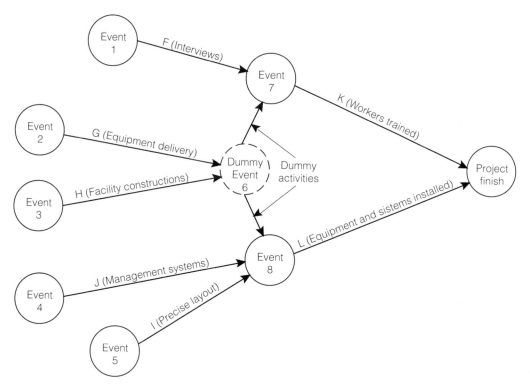

Figure 11–7　A Sample PERT Network Using a Portion of the Facility Startup Example. The dummy event and activities are used only to clarify that both activity G and activity H must precede activities K and L.

where oe is the optimistic estimate, pe is the pessimistic estimate, and ml is the most likely estimate. The variance of the time for each activity is

$$\sigma^2{}_T = ((pe - oe)/6)^2.$$

It is the sum of these variances along any path in the network that is normally distributed. By using the summed variance for the path (e.g., the critical path) and the fact that the summed variance is distributed normally, a probability of completion of any event can be computed.

As may be surmised, using PERT in this way to calculate a project completion time variance and probabilities of completion by specified dates can be a bit concocted. The variance for the entire project can be only as good as the variance estimates for individual activities, and often there is little information on which to base such variance estimates. Using PERT in this way can be more trouble than it is worth. Nevertheless, PERT does make explicit a concern for time variations and the fact that the critical path itself cannot be known with certainty. These insights are useful reminders to any project manager.

SOME PRINCIPLES FOR PROJECT MANAGERS

Although critical paths, the critical path method, and PERT have been exceedingly useful to managers in scheduling projects, effective project management means more than the adept use of these techniques. Drawing on his own vast experience in project management, Herbert Spirer has arrived at a dozen principles that serve as a useful checklist for project managers:[2]

1. A project has to have a clear objective or set of objectives, and these objectives ought to be stated in terms of specific items (tangible or intangible) to be delivered to the project's sponsor.

2. The project manager ought to be able to structure the project clearly, detailing which bundles of major activities (work packages) are required and how they comprise the deliverable items that meet the project's objectives. Spirer calls this a "work breakdown structure," and he sees it as a hierarchical representation of the project.

3. The work packages making up the work breakdown structure are composed of individual activities. These activities have to be listed and organized into groups that can be overseen by specific people. The specific activities for a major project can number in the thousands. Spirer recommends, however, that no one manager have direct responsibility for more than 50 specific activities. Top-level management itself should not be responsible for more than 30 to 50 aggregations of these activities, a precept that highlights the need for an effective work breakdown structure.

4. These activities should then be placed in a precedence diagram or network, and a critical path developed with the concomitant early and late start and finish times and slack calculations. The development of the precedence diagram or network is an important task in itself; analyzing such a network can lead to various suggestions or to resequencing activities. Calculations of the critical path need to be done periodically as the project proceeds.

5. The calendar of activities and times that comes out of the network creation and the critical path analysis must be combined with some knowledge of resource constraints to produce a schedule that tells management when activities will be done, not simply when they must be done.

6. Managing the resources needed to meet the schedule is eased by making use of Gantt charts and plots of cumulative resource use such as are applied in manufacturing situations.

7. Activity times can be estimated often by analyzing similar activities and modifying their times by using common sense. Sometimes more analytic methods (regressions, cross tabulation) can also be used. The estimation of

[2]Adapted from Herbert F. Spirer, "The Basic Principles of Project Management," *Operations Management Review* 1, no. 1 (Fall 1982): 7–8ff.

activity time is often helped by referring explicitly to the network and the critical or near-critical paths that are implied by the first-round estimates.

8.   Use pessimistic, optimistic, and most likely estimates for as many activities as possible. It is always helpful to recognize the uncertainty inherent in projects.

9.   Tracking the progress of a project is helped by establishing milestones, which are easily grouped events. Such milestones can help serve as motivation for the project as well as checkpoints for the project's progress.

10.   Assign one and only one person to be accountable for every activity.

11.   Use the plan to control the project. This is done by keeping the plan current and monitoring the actual performance in timely fashion. Determine how the actual performance measures up to the plan and what variances are implied by that contrast. Take any corrective action that is necessary, assessing the likely consequences of any corrective action and adjusting the plan accordingly.

12.   Assess the status of the project by using various "earned value concepts" such as the budgeted cost of work scheduled, the budgeted cost of work performed, and the actual cost of work performed. By comparing the budgeted cost of work scheduled against the budgeted cost of work performed, one can come up with a general measure of the on-schedule performance of the project. Similarly, by comparing the budgeted cost of the work performed with the actual cost of the work performed, a measure of the cost variance of the project can be ascertained.

A PROJECT
Geupel DeMars, Inc.
Indianapolis, Indiana

Geupel DeMars, a subsidiary of the DeMars Corporation, was an Indianapolis-based construction management firm for industrial and commercial properties. The company was formed in 1927 and first worked on department store construction. Since that time, it had gradually broadened its client base. In 1991, the firm employed 250 people. See the organization chart in Figure A–1.

Geupel DeMars (GDI), as a construction management firm, acted as the agent for an Owner. It did no actual construction itself, but rather planned for the construction of the building, arranged for Owner-held contracts for the different aspects of the job, oversaw the work, and reported to the Owner. For its effort, the Owner paid Geupel DeMars a fee to cover the salaries and benefits of its employees on the job, plus a percentage markup.

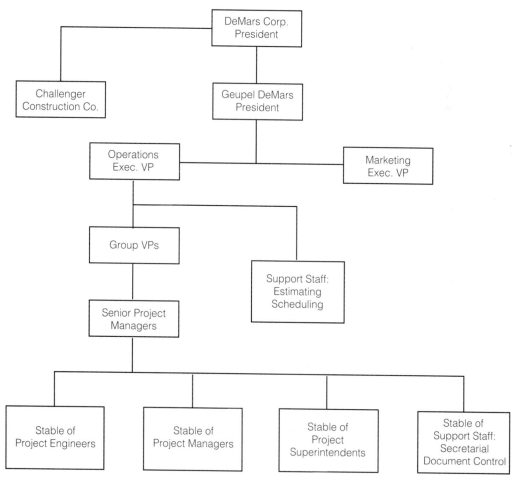

Figure A–1 A. Simplified Organization Chart for Geupel DeMars.

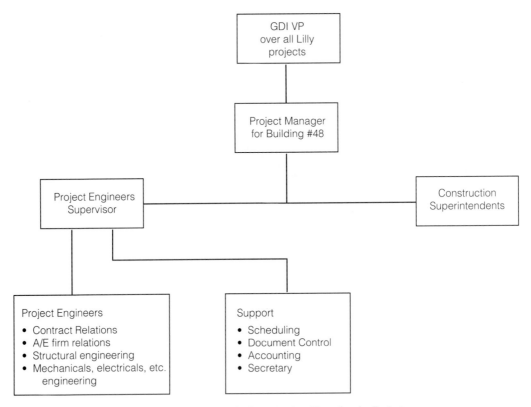

Figure A–1 B. Organization Chart for the Project.

As a construction management firm, Geupel DeMars was distinct from (1) an architectural/engineering (A/E) firm that designs buildings and does the engineering required to translate the design into documents that serve as the basis of contractor bids on the project, (2) a design/build firm that combines the design, engineering, and construction of a building into a single one-stop package for the Owner, or (3) a contractor that only builds.

The workings of a construction management firm are best seen by examining a particular project. For this tour, the project is the construction of Research Building No. 48 for Eli Lilly & Company. This building (see Figure A–2) of 550,000 square feet was slated for completion in early 1993 at a total cost of $135.2 million. The design envisioned a building of four stories, laid out in three wings (Biology, Chemistry, and Animal) tied to a central administrative section. The nature of the building called for features that were distinct from typical office buildings: special ventilation for the 162 labs, greater capacity HVAC (heating, ventilation, and air conditioning), purified water sources, and special drainage systems, among others.

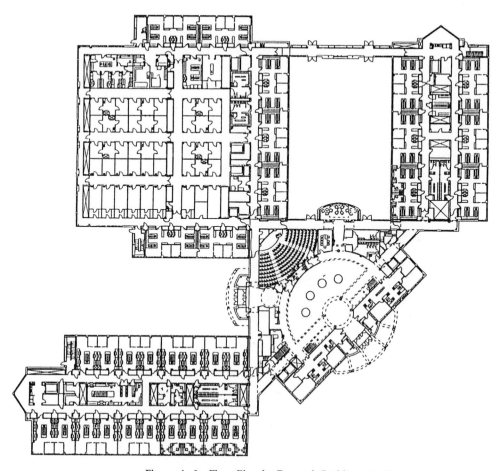

Figure A–2 Floor Plan for Research Building 48's First Floor.

PROJECT ORGANIZATION AND TIMETABLE

Research Building No. 48 was scheduled to take roughly three years to build from groundbreaking to completion. Before that time, considerable planning had to be done. Geupel DeMars became involved with the project about two years before construction began. The nature of its involvement in the project changed over time. To wit:

YEAR ONE, 1988

Personnel: 0 in field; 2 in the office.

Tasks: Gather data; estimate costs and constructability; develop overall schedule.

When Geupel DeMars entered the project, Lilly had already engaged the architectural/engineering firm (CUH2A of Princeton, New Jersey) and the building's design was proceeding. Although the location for the building was set, there was still considerable fluidity to the design: how many stories, how stretched out, how the various research wings would be connected. Geupel DeMars's role in this conceptual phase of the project involved the following tasks:

- Reviewing the plans and estimating the costs of various alternative designs.
- Reviewing the constructability of the building and identifying the cost–feature tradeoffs that the Owner (Lilly) would have to make, tasks known as value engineering.
- Identifying schedule parameters and inputs. Preparing and presenting alternative schedule strategies for delivery of the project.

In this conceptual phase, GDI provided cost estimates to the Owner with an accuracy of within 10–20 percent of actual costs for each of the building configurations seriously considered. These estimates were based on costs per square foot of interior space, costs per square foot for the face of the building (stone, glass, concrete), and costs for HVAC, plumbing, electrical requirements, etc.

YEAR TWO, 1989

Personnel: 0 in the field; 2 in the office.

Tasks: Continue Year One tasks but with further refinement; establish budget.

The second year of the project continued the tasks begun in Year One. Over time, decisions were made that refined the project more and more. The project moved from conceptual drawings of the building to schematic drawings, which were half to two-thirds complete and on which materials began to be specified. These schematic drawings required renewed cost estimation and value engineering.

The character of Geupel DeMars's value engineering could include the following types of suggestions:

- *Selection of materials.* The choice of materials can often affect the cost of the project by five to ten percent. Such choices can include the use of concrete versus structural steel, the type of roofing materials to use, and the choice of pipe materials for purified water systems.
- *Design modifications.* The construction manager can suggest which design details are likely to be expensive to render and which are not. Examples include roofing details such as flashings and eaves, structural concrete details on how the concrete is to be formed, and finish details such as door jambs and lighting fixture wiring systems.

The schematic drawings were followed by the even more specific design development drawings and the first of the construction documents upon which supplier and contractor bids could be made.

YEAR THREE, 1990

Personnel: 1 in the field; 4 in the office.

Tasks: Supervise excavation and initial construction; begin bidding procedures for contractors; establish procedures for scheduling, quality control, and cost control.

Excavation of the site began in February 1990. During the rest of that year, the foundations were poured and the erection of the steel superstructure for the building was started. One superintendent in the field oversaw this work.

This year also saw the start of what was termed the *fast-track construction design*. This process called for the identification of sequential "bid packages" of work, the scheduling of the design process to support this sequence, bidding, the award of initial contracts, and the subsequent commencement of work. The development and awarding of bid packages was done on a rolling basis and would continue for a year and a half. Major parts of the construction were treated in this way: excavation, foundation, concrete, structural steel, enclosure packages (skin, roof, doors); elevators, mechanicals (HVAC, fire protection, plumbing); electricals; and various interior finishes (painting, flooring, carpeting, ceiling, partitions, wall coverings). Likewise, as part of this process, came the purchase of equipment for the building by the owner.

This was also the year to establish the balance of the procedures that would govern the construction of the project as time went on. These procedures were essential to the control of the project (schedule, cost, quality) so that the Owner actually received what was designed and specified. These controls are explained in more detail later.

YEAR FOUR, 1991

Personnel: 5 in the field; 9 in the office.

Tasks: Continue construction supervision; continue the development and award of bid packages; monitor project schedule, costs, and quality and report to the Owner.

In this year, the building took shape and the need for field monitoring and supervision escalated dramatically. Bid packages continued to be assembled, bid, and awarded.

The year also saw more administration and management of the project as opposed to the earlier planning and estimating work that dominated the efforts of Geupel DeMars. This management essentially consisted of pursuing the control procedures that had been laid out in the previous year, reporting on progress to the Owner, and dealing with the myriad field questions and problems, both large and small, that inevitably accompanied the work of the contractors as they built the research building and as procurement proceeded.

YEAR FIVE, 1992

Personnel: 8 in the field; 10 in the office.

Tasks: Continue supervision of the construction; continue management of the project; startup of major systems

YEAR SIX, 1993

Personnel: 8 in the field; 10 in the office.

Tasks: Close out the project for the Owner.

In this final year, the construction was completed and the project closed out. Closing out a project meant several things:

- All contractors had completed their work, including their "punch lists" (i.e., the lists of repairs and inadvertent omissions that are identified before the Owner takes possession).
- The contractors had supplied the as-built drawings, warranties, and guarantees.
- All paperwork had been finished, including all letters answered and items resolved.
- The project file was completed, including all copies of correspondence, all shop drawings (the detailed drawings from the contractors, of which there were thousands of pages), all as-built drawings, all quality control documents, and all test reports.

The Manual and Its Controls

Before the start of construction, Geupel DeMars and Lilly prepared a procedures manual that outlined the specific duties of each party. This manual was the basic control document for the project. In it, procedures were described for such items as bidding, materials substitutions, submittals, quality control, requests for information (usually from a contractor to the A/E firm and the Owner), design changes, and progress payments to the contractors.

Submittals were a particularly important point of control. A submittal was the contractor's submission for review of any of several types of documents:

- Catalog and performance data for the materials to be used
- Shop drawings—the contractor's drawings detailing what actually was to be done

- Guarantees
- Job standards, consisting of certifications or approved samples that could be used as field examples
- Maintenance data and operating instructions
- Installation instructions
- Physical samples of material and assemblies

Once the submittals were reviewed and approved by the A/E, the contractor could procure and install the material and equipment. Submittals thus led to the approval of materials, and materials were seen as driving both the schedule and the budget. Geupel DeMars insisted that contractors follow a submittal schedule so that they performed on time with the proper information.

Substitutions were another important item to control. Substitutions of materials were usually made to reduce cost, to provide a better product (perhaps as a result of value engineering), or to speed up an aspect of the project that had fallen behind schedule. Substitutions required the approval of the Owner and the A/E firm.

There were a host of other controls on quality. For example, the superintendents completed reports each day on the work accomplished. There were reports on nonconforming work, which typically would necessitate repair. Independent tests were made to verify that items such as the soil, concrete, structural work, roofing, HVAC, and high voltage met design requirements. A periodic report was distributed to the Owner on the construction progress, the topics at morning meetings, and, most importantly, a listing of "open issues."

Contractor Bidding

Geupel DeMars did no real construction on Building No. 48, acting only as the agent for the Owner. A major task for the company was to assist the owner in assembling the best available stable of contractors who had the expertise, met the Owner's financial requirements, and were aware of the Owner's high quality standards. Working from the plans and engineering specifications of the architectural/engineering firm, Geupel DeMars assembled about 30 bid packages for the diverse pieces of the construction. A bid package contained a summary of work that spelled out all that the contractor was to do, a manual detailing procedures used by Geupel DeMars and Lilly, and the applicable construction drawings and technical specifications by the A/E firm. A bid package took about a week to assemble. Once assembled, the bid package was sent to four to six contractors that had been invited to bid on the job. These contractors were generally well-known to Geupel DeMars, either from past work or from the formal approval process, and were all considered to be capable of performing high-quality work of the scale required. (Often, the Owner would have its own preferred list). New or previously unknown contractors would be visited and their operations and financial conditions reviewed.

After the bidding documents were out for 2 weeks, Geupel DeMars held a prebid meeting with the invited contractors. At this meeting, GDI reviewed the manual and the summary of work and then, with the assistance of the A/E and the Owner, answered questions. Following the meeting, an addendum with meeting minutes and revisions was issued.

It took the contractors three to six weeks to prepare their bids. After review of the bids, the apparent low bidder was invited to attend a precontract meeting between the contractor, the Owner, the A/E (if necessary), and GDI. This was a technical meeting that sometimes involved Geupel DeMars's field superintendents. If all issues were resolved, the Owner then signed a contract with the successful bidder. Construction then began on that contracted work.

Dealing with Contractors on the Job

Once construction began, Geupel DeMars's passed on information between contractors and the Owner and the A/E firm. (The Lilly team for this project numbered about 10 people. The A/E firm, at one point, had as many as 300 on the design effort, with about 10 on the continuing supervisory team.) Sometimes, the contractor would have questions about particular details of the construction, questions that were generally overlooked by all parties before then. These questions triggered a formal RFI (Request for Information). Geupel DeMars's role was to follow up on the RFI, to distribute the information to the appropriate people, and to communicate any decided changes to the scope of work.

Geupel DeMars felt that it had failed if any major problems occurred. The company was always looking ahead to such things as the schedule of submittals, approved materials, and test results. Fortunately for all concerned, there were few problems of any magnitude with the Research Building #48 project.

Field Supervision

As the building progressed, more and more attention was devoted to planning and supervising the daily construction activities. This was the responsibility of the field's construction superintendents and field engineers. Initially, there was only one to supervise the excavation and foundation work. As the superstructure was set in place, more superintendents joined the project and a greater division of labor ensued. For Research Building #48, there were different superintendents for each of the major trades represented by the contractors (e.g., structure, mechanicals, electricals).

The superintendents oversaw the quality of work being done, any testing of materials, and the coordination of the contractors' work. They reviewed requests for information. They also determined the percentage completion of various aspects of the job, which affected scheduling and the progress payments Lilly made each month.

Scheduling

After quality control in importance came the control of the project's schedule. The schedule affected both quality and cost. Although keeping on schedule was everybody's concern, there was a scheduler whose task was to document the schedule and the project's conformance to that schedule.

The schedule was derived in backwards fashion. The Owner had a completion date in mind. From that date the scheduler worked back to the relevant start dates.

The raw data for the schedule were the numerous activities that had to be accomplished. Some of these activities had to precede others, although many activities could be accomplished simultaneously. For the most part, the activities comprising the schedule followed the various bid packages. The contractors responsible for each bid package detailed their construction schedules, floor-by-floor, and this information served as a basis for the schedule. Geupel DeMars then applied its own experience and its knowledge of supplier timetables, especially for long-lead-time items.

A computer program, Primavera Primavision, was used to document, monitor, and make changes to the schedule. Primavera kept track of all the designated activities, their expected times-to-completion, and their relationships to each other. The input to Primavera was built up bit by bit as GDI developed each bid package. The program's input began shortly after excavation was begun. By the end of the project, its was expected that 2000 activities would be captured. Of those 2000 activities, for example, 640 would pertain to mechanical and electrical installations. Only about 20 percent of the activities pertained directly to actual installation; the other 80 percent referred to various reviews, approvals, bidding, comments, documentation, etc.

Primavera Primavision generated several documents that helped with the project's scheduling:

1. **Gantt Charts.** Figure A–3 is a Gantt chart generated by Primavera. Gantt charts, discussed in Chapter 11, are simply bar charts that plot time for each activity. They show expected start and stop times, and the bars could be filled in to show the extent of actual progress at each point in time. Note that in Figure A–3, the project is up-to-date. All of the activities that should have been accomplished by the time of the chart's date, April 1991, have indeed been accomplished.

   The solid bars represent activities that are designated as critical. More formally, these are activities that lie on the "critical path" (See Chapter 11.) Activities on the critical path are those that, if delayed, will delay the entire project. For them, there is no spare catch-up time available. They must be accomplished on time or the project is delayed.

   Sometimes, of course, an activity might be hurried up in order to put a delayed project back on track. Often, such hustling costs money in addition

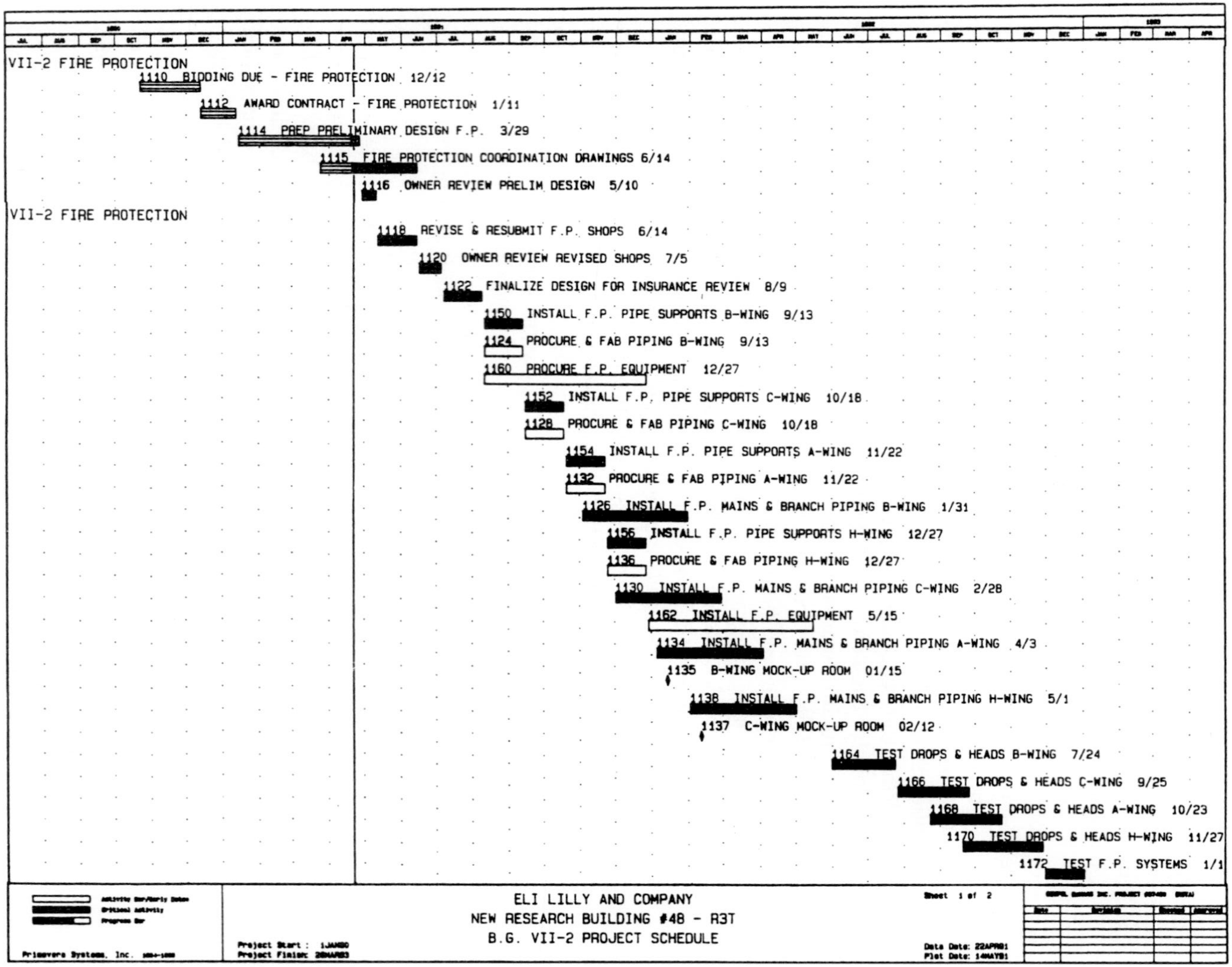

Figure A-3   A Portion of the Project Schedule for Research Building 48—Gantt Chart.

ACTIVITY ID	ORIG DUR	REM DUR	PCT	CODE	ACTIVITY DESCRIPTION	EARLY START	EARLY FINISH	LATE START	LATE FINISH	TOTAL FLOAT
VII-2 FIRE PROTECTION										
1110	37	0	100	44	BIDDING DUE - FIRE PROTECTION 12/12	23OCT90A	12DEC90A			
1112	22	0	100	44	AWARD CONTRACT - FIRE PROTECTION 1/11	13DEC90A	11JAN91A			
1114	75	5	93	44B	PREP PRELIMINARY DESIGN F.P. 3/29	14JAN91A	26APR91		26APR91	0
1115	60	40	33	44B	FIRE PROTECTION COORDINATION DRAWINGS 6/14	25MAR91A	14JUN91		14JUN91*	0
1116	10	10	0	44B	OWNER REVIEW PRELIM DESIGN 5/10	29APR91	10MAY91	29APR91	10MAY91	0
1118	25	25	0	44B	REVISE & RESUBMIT F.P. SHOPS 6/14	13MAY91	14JUN91	13MAY91	14JUN91	0
1120	15	15	0	44B	OWNER REVIEW REVISED SHOPS 7/5	17JUN91	5JUL91	17JUN91	5JUL91	0
1122	25	25	0	44B	FINALIZE DESIGN FOR INSURANCE REVIEW 8/9	8JUL91	9AUG91	8JUL91	9AUG91*	0
1150	25	25	0	44 BB	INSTALL F.P. PIPE SUPPORTS B-WING 9/13	12AUG91	13SEP91	12AUG91	13SEP91	0
1124	25	25	0	44B	PROCURE & FAB PIPING B-WING 9/13	12AUG91	13SEP91	16SEP91	18OCT91*	25
1160	100	100	0	44	PROCURE F.P. EQUIPMENT 12/27	12AUG91	27DEC91	26AUG91	10JAN92	10
1152	25	25	0	44 CC	INSTALL F.P. PIPE SUPPORTS C-WING 10/18	16SEP91	18OCT91	16SEP91	18OCT91	0
1128	25	25	0	44C	PROCURE & FAB PIPING C-WING 10/18	16SEP91	18OCT91	21OCT91	22NOV91*	25
1154	25	25	0	44 AA	INSTALL F.P. PIPE SUPPORTS A-WING 11/22	21OCT91	22NOV91	21OCT91	22NOV91	0
1132	25	25	0	44A	PROCURE & FAB PIPING A-WING 11/22	21OCT91	22NOV91	25NOV91	27DEC91*	25
1126	65	65	0	44 BB	INSTALL F.P. MAINS & BRANCH PIPING B-WING 1/31	4NOV91*	31JAN92	4NOV91	31JAN92*	0
1156	25	25	0	44 HH	INSTALL F.P. PIPE SUPPORTS H-WING 12/27	25NOV91	27DEC91	25NOV91	27DEC91*	0
1136	25	25	0	44H	PROCURE & FAB PIPING H-WING 12/27	25NOV91	27DEC91	30DEC91	31JAN92*	25
1130	65	65	0	44 CC	INSTALL F.P. MAINS & BRANCH PIPING C-WING 2/28	2DEC91*	28FEB92	2DEC91	28FEB92*	0
1162	100	100	0	44	INSTALL F.P. EQUIPMENT 5/15	30DEC91	15MAY92	13JAN92	29MAY92*	10
1134	65	65	0	44 AA	INSTALL F.P. MAINS & BRANCH PIPING A-WING 4/3	6JAN92*	3APR92	6JAN92	3APR92*	0
1135	0	0	0	44 BB	B-WING MOCK-UP ROOM 01/15	15JAN92*	15JAN92	15JAN92	15JAN92*	0
1138	65	65	0	44 HH	INSTALL F.P. MAINS & BRANCH PIPING H-WING 5/1	3FEB92*	1MAY92	3FEB92	1MAY92*	0
1137	0	0	0	44 CC	C-WING MOCK-UP ROOM 02/12	12FEB92*	12FEB92	12FEB92	12FEB92*	0
1164	40	40	0	44 BB	TEST DROPS & HEADS B-WING 7/24	1JUN92*	24JUL92	1JUN92	24JUL92	0
1166	45	45	0	44 CC	TEST DROPS & HEADS C-WING 9/25	27JUL92	25SEP92	27JUL92	25SEP92*	0
1168	45	45	0	44 AA	TEST DROPS & HEADS A-WING 10/23	24AUG92	23OCT92	24AUG92	23OCT92*	0
1170	50	50	0	44 HH	TEST DROPS & HEADS H-WING 11/27	21SEP92	27NOV92	21SEP92	27NOV92*	0
1172	25	25	0	44	TEST F.P. SYSTEMS 1/1	30NOV92	1JAN93	30NOV92	1JAN93*	0

Figure A–3   A Portion of the Project Schedule for Research Building 48–Gantt Chart. (*Continued*)

231

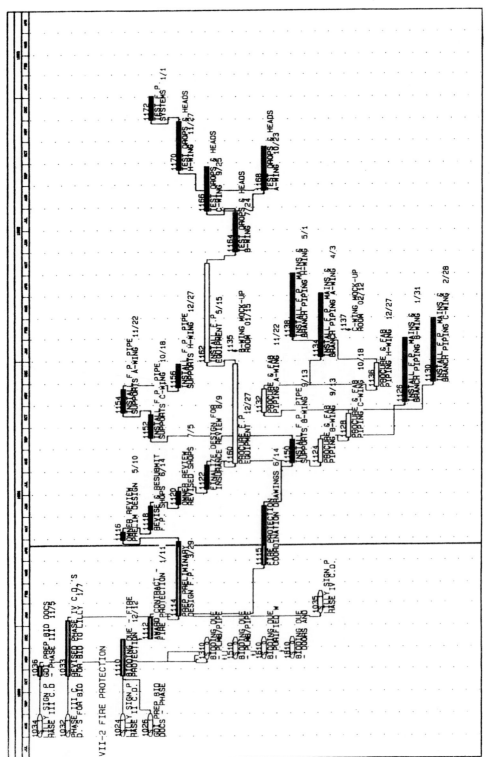

Figure A–4 A Portion of the Project Schedule for Research Building 48—Activity Descriptions.

VII-2 FIRE PROTECTION

ACTIVITY ID	ORIG DUR	REM DUR	PCT	CODE		ACTIVITY DESCRIPTION	EARLY START	EARLY FINISH	LATE START	LATE FINISH	TOTAL FLOAT
1110	37	0	100		PRED	BIDDING DUE - FIRE PROTECTION 12/12	23OCT90A	12DEC90A			
1024	4	0	100	C 6	PRED	LILLY SIGN PHASE II C.D.'S 10/12	9OCT90A	12DEC90A			
1026*	10	0	100		PRED	GDI PREP BID DOCS - PHASE II 10/22	9OCT90A	22OCT90A			
1112*	22	0	100		SUCC	AWARD CONTRACT - FIRE PROTECTION 1/11	13DEC90A	11JAN91A			
1112	22	0	100		PRED	AWARD CONTRACT - FIRE PROTECTION 1/11	13DEC90A	11JAN91A			
1110*	37	5	93		SUCC	BIDDING DUE - FIRE PROTECTION 12/12	23OCT90A	12DEC90A			
1114*	75	5	93		SUCC	PREP PRELIMINARY DESIGN F.P. 3/12	14JAN91A	26APR91		26APR91	0
1115	60	40	33	C 50	SUCC	FIRE PROTECTION COORDINATION DRAWINGS 6/14	25MAR91A	14JUN91		14JUN91*	0
1114	75	5	93		PRED	PREP PRELIMINARY DESIGN F.P. 3/29	14JAN91A	26APR91		26APR91	0
1112*	22	0	100		PRED	AWARD CONTRACT - FIRE PROTECTION 1/11	13DEC90A	11JAN91A			
1116*	10	10	0		SUCC	OWNER REVIEW PRELIM DESIGN 5/10	29APR91	10MAY91	29APR91	10MAY91	0
1115	60	40	33		PRED	FIRE PROTECTION COORDINATION DRAWINGS 6/14	25MAR91A	14JUN91		14JUN91*	0
1112	22	0	100	C 50	PRED	AWARD CONTRACT - FIRE PROTECTION 1/11	13DEC90A	11JAN91A			
1150*	25	25	0	C 40	SUCC	INSTALL F.P. PIPE SUPPORTS B-WING 9/13	12AUG91	13SEP91	12AUG91	13SEP91	0
1116	10	10	0		PRED	OWNER REVIEW PRELIM DESIGN 5/10	29APR91	10MAY91	29APR91	10MAY91	0
1114*	75	5	93		PRED	PREP PRELIMINARY DESIGN F.P. 3/29	14JAN91A	26APR91		26APR91	0
1118*	25	25	0		SUCC	REVISE & RESUBMIT F.P. SHOPS 6/14	13MAY91	14JUN91	13MAY91	14JUN91	0
1118	25	25	0		PRED	REVISE & RESUBMIT F.P. SHOPS 6/14	13MAY91	14JUN91	13MAY91	14JUN91	0
1116*	10	10	0		PRED	OWNER REVIEW PRELIM DESIGN 5/10	29APR91	10MAY91	29APR91	10MAY91	0
1120*	15	15	0		SUCC	OWNER REVIEW REVISED SHOPS 7/5	17JUN91	5JUL91	17JUN91	5JUL91	0
1120	15	15	0		PRED	OWNER REVIEW REVISED SHOPS 7/5	17JUN91	5JUL91	17JUN91	5JUL91	0
1118*	25	25	0		PRED	REVISE & RESUBMIT F.P. SHOPS 6/14	13MAY91	14JUN91	13MAY91	14JUN91	0
1122*	25	25	0		SUCC	FINALIZE DESIGN FOR INSURANCE REVIEW 8/9	8JUL91	9AUG91	8JUL91	9AUG91*	0
1122	25	25	0		PRED	FINALIZE DESIGN FOR INSURANCE REVIEW 8/9	8JUL91	9AUG91	8JUL91	9AUG91*	0
1120*	15	15	0		PRED	OWNER REVIEW REVISED SHOPS 7/5	17JUN91	5JUL91	17JUN91	5JUL91	0
1124*	25	25	0		SUCC	PROCURE & FAB PIPING B-WING 9/13	12AUG91	13SEP91	16SEP91	18OCT91*	25
1150*	25	25	0		SUCC	INSTALL F.P. PIPE SUPPORTS B-WING 9/13	12AUG91	13SEP91	12AUG91	13SEP91	0
1160*	100	100	0		SUCC	PROCURE F.P. EQUIPMENT 12/27	12AUG91	27DEC91	26AUG91	10JAN92	10
1150	25	25	0		PRED	INSTALL F.P. PIPE SUPPORTS B-WING 9/13	12AUG91	13SEP91	12AUG91	13SEP91	0
1115*	60	40	33	C 33	PRED	FIRE PROTECTION COORDINATION DRAWINGS 6/14	25MAR91A	14JUN91		14JUN91*	0
1122*	25	25	0		SUCC	FINALIZE DESIGN FOR INSURANCE REVIEW 8/9	8JUL91	9AUG91	8JUL91	9AUG91*	0
1152*	25	25	0		SUCC	INSTALL F.P. PIPE SUPPORTS C-WING 10/18	16SEP91	18OCT91	16SEP91	18OCT91	0
1124	25	25	0		PRED	PROCURE & FAB PIPING B-WING 9/13	12AUG91	13SEP91	16SEP91	18OCT91*	25
1122*	25	25	0		PRED	FINALIZE DESIGN FOR INSURANCE REVIEW 8/9	8JUL91	9AUG91	8JUL91	9AUG91*	0
1126	65	65	0		SUCC	INSTALL F.P. MAINS & BRANCH PIPING B-WING 1/31	4NOV91*	31JAN92	4NOV91*	31JAN92*	0
1128*	25	25	0		SUCC	PROCURE & FAB PIPING C-WING 10/18	16SEP91	18OCT91	21OCT91	22NOV91*	25
1160	100	100	0		PRED	PROCURE F.P. EQUIPMENT 12/27	12AUG91	27DEC91	26AUG91	10JAN92	10
1122*	25	25	0		PRED	FINALIZE DESIGN FOR INSURANCE REVIEW 8/9	8JUL91	9AUG91	8JUL91	9AUG91*	0
1162*	100	100	0		SUCC	INSTALL F.P. EQUIPMENT 5/15	30DEC91	15MAY92	13JAN92	29MAY92*	10
1152	25	25	0		PRED	INSTALL F.P. PIPE SUPPORTS C-WING 10/18	16SEP91	18OCT91	16SEP91	18OCT91	0
1150*	25	25	0		PRED	INSTALL F.P. PIPE SUPPORTS B-WING 9/13	12AUG91	13SEP91	12AUG91	13SEP91	0
1154*	25	25	0		SUCC	INSTALL F.P. PIPE SUPPORTS A-WING 11/22	21OCT91	22NOV91	21OCT91	22NOV91	0

Figure A-4 A Portion of the Project Schedule for Research Building 48— Activity Descriptions. (*Continued*)

to the extra effort of those involved. This hustling is typically called *crashing* an activity. For example, for Research Building 48, the erection of the curtain wall began seven weeks late. The contractor, however, recaptured some of the lost time by putting more people on the task than was originally planned.

2. **Time Logic Diagrams.** Another output of Primavera is a time logic diagram, such as depicted in Figure A–4. This diagram depicts the precedence relationships among activities. In the diagram and the accompanying sheet of detail, the ties between activities become clear. For example, Figure A–4 relates to Bid Group VII-2 (Fire protection), and among its first set of activities, there are these ties to other activities:

Activity 1110—The bidding was due on December 12, 1990. Before the bidding, two things had to happen: Lilly had to sign the Phase II construction documents (Activity 1024), and GDI had to prepare the bidding documents themselves (Activity 1026). These two steps were completed in October. The successor activity (1112) was the awarding of the contract. The expected duration of the activity, 37 days, is given in the ORIG DUR (Original Duration) column.

Activity 1112—This is the successor activity to Activity 1110. It was accomplished by 1/11/91. We know this is so for several reasons: the progress shown on the chart's bar, the 100% completion shown in the PCT column, the "0" in the REM DUR (Remaining Duration) column, and the "A," for Actual, after the early start and early finish dates. Activity 1112 has two successor activities: preparing a preliminary design and working up fire protection coordination drawings.

Activity 1115—This activity is one of the successors to Activity 1112. It is on schedule, but it has not yet reached its conclusion. The percentage completed is 33 percent, with 40 of the expected 60 days' worth of work remaining. It has one successor activity, installing the fire protection pipe supports in the B-wing, slated to begin on August 12, 1991.

Observe that not all of the activities noted in the diagram have bars shown. The complexity of the relationships has forced Primavera to show them on a different sheet. This diagram is useful for depicting the relationships. Also observe that the bars for some of the forthcoming activities are solid, indicating that they are critical activities, but that some are not filled in. These latter activities are not on the critical path and thus have some slack associated with them.

Primavera was able to generate other useful documents and to sort the activities in different ways. Sorts could be done by contractor or by floor of the building. By examining the scheduled activities in these ways, conflicts among contractors, and any subsequent rescheduling, could be held to a minimum.

Weekly meetings were held to track the schedule. Data for the schedule monitoring were provided by the superintendents on the site and by the GDI project engineers who followed the submittals and other paperwork. Every two weeks, a rolling four-week summary schedule was generated.

Budgeting

The budget's major components included the following:

	Original Budget (in millions)
Construction (building materials, labor, Owner-furnished equipment)	$ 99.4
Engineering (Owner's cost, A/E firm, GDI)	23.8
Contingency	12.0
	$135.2

Geupel DeMars monitored these costs and managed the construction costs, the contingency costs, and its own costs closely.

DISCUSSION

Geupel DeMars, Inc. is in no way responsible for the following views and presentation. They remain solely the responsibility of the author.

The Flow of the Process and of Information

Figures A–5 and A–6 display process flow and information flow diagrams for a project like the construction of Building #48. The diagrams are fairly general and include numerous entries that can be repeated. For example, there is a whole sequence of the process flow diagram that repeats for each of the 30 bid packages. With the information flow diagram, the interactions of RFIs, submittals, and approvals are repeated almost a countless number of times as the project continues. Geupel DeMars is really an intermediary for a lot of these transactions, filtering information, monitoring progress and costs, and making recommendations to the various parties. Coordination and communication are essential to the smooth running of the project.

This is an example of so-called fast-track construction that is completely analogous to concurrent engineering in a factory setting dealing with new product development. Fast-track construction overlaps the phases of construction so that detailed design aspects of the building proceed even as the initial construction is being done. Such management of the process calls for a great deal of coordination among the players, and that is just what Geupel DeMars provides.

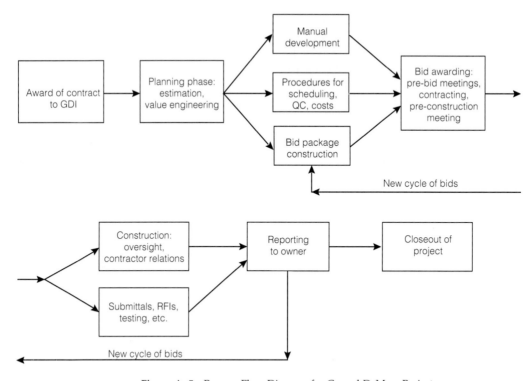

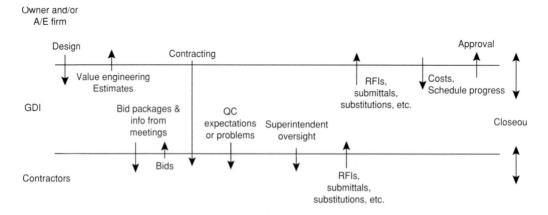

Figure A–5   Process Flow Diagram for Geupel DeMars Project.

Figure A–6   Information Flow Diagram for Guepel DeMars Project.

Features of the Process

There are a number of interesting and distinctive aspects of the project that differentiate it from the other processes investigated in this book:

1. The workforce in this process is constantly changing. Not only are there varying numbers of construction workers on site, but there are variable numbers of architect/engineers, and importantly, varying numbers of GDI workers as well. There is a constant ebb and flow of people of various skills and in various quantities as the project progresses.

2. A variety of specialized talents are called for. Again, these are talents not only in the architecture/engineering and construction trades themselves, but also in GDI itself as it manages the project. GDI, for example, needs specialists for construction superintendents, cost estimation, scheduling, and contractor and A/E firm relations.

3. Projects take a significant degree of up-front planning in order to be carried out well. The budget for Building #48 reveals this degree of planning. So much of the project involves one-of-a-kind design that such planning cannot be avoided.

4. Constant coordination is required among the parties.

5. The means by which resources can be conserved is generally by stretching out the timetable. The contractors do this to save costs, and only when forced by slips in the schedule do they apply more labor or equipment to "crash" an activity. It is the same for GDI. Not all of the bid packages are prepared at the same time or bid on at the same time. Rather, because the job does not require it, and because it would tax GDI too much at the same time, the schedule of bid packages is spaced out. Such smoothing out of the work helps all concerned.

Demands of the Process on Management and the Workforce

At GDI, the workforce and management are almost indistinguishable, as one could look at the project engineers as lower levels of management. For everybody, the demands of the process are quite similar. The process demands extraordinary planning skills of its workforce as well as tremendous attention to detail. The days of nearly everyone at GDI are filled with the follow-up and communication of details and, when called upon, the development of future needs and controls of all sorts. People live by their calendars, beepers, voice mail, and faxes.

Planning and Control

The project lives and dies by the excellence of the planning that has gone into it and by the efficiency and thoroughness of the controls it has in place. The following controls have to be planned for in advance, so that all parties are clear about what is required of them:

Quality (knowing in advance what the requirements of the job are and what constitutes satisfactory performance)

Schedule (knowing when the job has to be started and stopped)

Cost (knowing what the flow of expenses is)

Documentation (keeping a paper trail about everything decided, everything accomplished, and everything changed)

The planning and control required for the project are much greater than those required for the job shop or other kinds of processes. Similar kinds of documentation are kept (drawings, process and routing sheets or their equivalents, tests of materials, change documents, quality documents, and schedules), but the quantities of them and care with which they are handled are typically extraordinary. After all, with a project you only get one shot at it, and it must be right the first time, or other projects are not likely to come one's way.

Drawings are an example. Consider the different kinds that are maintained: conceptual drawings, schematics, shop drawings, and as-built drawings. Everything about the building's construction is captured in these drawings. Everybody pores over them, communicates through them, and formally approves or changes them. They number in the hundreds and thousands.

A SERVICE FACTORY
Burger King Restaurant
Route 37,
Noblesville, Indiana

The Burger King Restaurant on Route 37 in Noblesville, Indiana, was one of more than 6000 fast-food restaurants operated worldwide by Burger King Corporation, a wholly owned subsidiary of Grand Metropolitan, and by the corporation's franchisees. Service was available from 6 A.M. to 2 A.M. every day. The dining room was open from 6 A.M. until 11 P.M. Sunday through Thursday and from 6 A.M. until midnight on Fridays and Saturdays. Breakfast was available from opening until 10:30 A.M. and consisted of a choice of bacon, ham, and sausage bagels, biscuits, and croissan'wiches, with or without eggs or cheese, French toast sticks, mini-muffins, breakfast buddies, biscuits with gravy, hash browns, and a scrambled egg platter. The regular menu consisted of a wide selection of hamburger sandwiches (regular hamburger and cheeseburger; a special Whopper sandwich with or without cheese; hamburger deluxe; double burger, double cheeseburger, and double Whopper; and a bacon double cheeseburger) as well as some specialty sandwiches (chicken, ham and cheese, fish), BK broilers (broiled chicken sandwiches), chicken tenders, and prepacked salads. To accompany these selections, the restaurant offered various choices: french fries, onion rings, soft drinks, shakes, Breyer's frozen yogurts, Snickers ice cream bars, Kool Aid cool pops, apple pie, cherry pie, and lemon pie. Occasionally, there were promotional items such as Burger Buddies.

The restaurant, the highest sales volume Burger King in Indiana, was located on Route 37, a busy thoroughfare between Marion and Indianapolis. The restaurant was opened in May 1987 on the site of a former farm. The restaurant was owned and operated by a franchisee, Douglas Brucker of Marion.

The restaurant was rectangular, freestanding on 2 acres, and was constructed mainly of wood planks, bricks, and glass. The building was situated toward the front of the lot, freeing the sides and rear for 64 parking spaces. A drive-thru was operated on one side of the restaurant, with the order board at the rear and the pick-up window toward the front. Inside the restaurant 96 seats (either benches or freestanding chairs) were arranged in groups. There were 16 tables of four, 1 table of three, 8 tables of two, and 13 single places within the restaurant. The eating area was tastefully appointed in oak wood, with a handsome color scheme, an atrium off to the side of the main eating area, ceiling fans, and many hanging plants. In the eating areas there were service counters for napkins, straws, and so on, and several large trash cans for customer use. The rest rooms were located next to the main door. The eating area occupied about half of the restaurant's square footage; the other half was occupied by the counter, the kitchen, and the storage area.

PART ONE PROCESS DESCRIPTION

Restaurant Operations Order Taking
(The Front Counter)

After entering the restaurant, customers walked between the railings of the queuing line (or, as Burger King calls it, the "customer guidance system"). While

The Front Counter as Seen from the Dining Room. (*Courtesy of Burger King Corporation*)

awaiting their turns to state their order at the counter, they could consult the brightly lit menu above the counter area. At the right-hand side of the counter were two cash registers with screens (point-of-sale devices). An order-taker greeted each customer there and took the order. As the customer spoke, the order-taker keyed the contents of the order on a register (e.g., pressed the key for the Whopper—a large hamburger with lettuce, tomato, onions, pickles, ketchup, and mayonnaise), read the printed total for the order, took the customer's payment, and gave the customer change and a receipt that listed the order. Each register could accommodate one or two cashiers simultaneously and could handle up to three transactions at the same time.

At the other end of the counter, a printer printed a duplicate copy of the order. Using this copy, an expediter proceeded to assemble the order. Assembling the order meant going to the counter and the chutes that lay between the front counter and the kitchen to gather the sandwiches, fries, or other items that flowed from the kitchen. When shakes were ordered, the expediter was responsible for drawing them from the nearby dispensing machine. After assembling the kitchen items of the order, the expediter presented them to the customer either on a tray (for inside use) or in a bag (to go). The expediter also gave cups to the customer so that he or she could fill them with the desired soft drinks, tea or coffee.

The Front Counter as Seen from the Kitchen. (*Courtesy of Burger King Corporation*)

Several features of the front counter's operation were comparatively new and merit highlighting. The most important innovation was the split made in the duties of the order-takers and expediters. The system in use at the Noblesville Burger King was known as the *multiconventional lineup*. It was a throwback to the early years of Burger King, when the *conventional lineup* was used. That system consisted of a single line of customers served by a single cash register where orders were taken. Expediters assembled the orders and presented them to the customers farther along the counter. The present system operated in much the same way, although up to six orders could be taken at the same time, and several expediters could handle those orders. The new, multiconventional system was thus much faster than the old system.

The multiconventional lineup was a more radical change from the *hospitality lineup* that had replaced the old conventional system. With the hospitality lineup, cash registers were evenly spaced across the entire front counter and customers had to choose which of several lines they wished to wait in. Cashiers both took orders and assembled them. The hospitality lineup, although somewhat more labor-intensive than the conventional lineup, could handle peak hour demand more efficiently than the older system. With the advent of the multiconventional lineup, however, the labor intensity of the hospitality lineup was reduced without sacrificing its peak-period capacity advantages. Customers preferred the new lineup as well. With a single line, they did not risk becoming annoyed because some other line was moving faster than theirs. In addition, they were often better prepared to give their order to the order-taker, and this speeded up the process for everyone.

Another innovation involved the self-service drink dispensers. With their installation, customers could fix their drinks precisely the way they wanted (with lots of ice or no ice, for example). By moving the drink dispensers out of the kitchen, time and some labor costs were also saved. Because free refills were possible, materials costs were somewhat higher, but not appreciably so.

Order Filling (The Kitchen)

Burger King differed from McDonald's and some other fast-food restaurants in that comparatively little finished-goods inventory was kept; sandwiches were assembled continuously. Certain orders might not have been delivered as quickly as when larger inventories were kept, but this approach offered the distinct advantage of producing to order when appropriate. As an old Burger King slogan put it, you can "have it your way," say, by ordering a Whopper with double cheese and mustard but no pickle, or a hamburger with extra onions.

Providing this kind of customer order variation with minimum customer waiting demanded a production system that was extraordinarily flexible. In fact,

The Kitchen. Preparation for the peak period is important. (*Courtesy of Burger King Corporation*)

two kinds of flexibility were required: flexibility to meet special customer orders and flexibility to meet large surges in customer demand during lunch or dinner hours. Many aspects of the production system contributed to this flexibility.

The "Line": Layout and Job Descriptions

The process of making sandwiches and filling orders at Burger King was explicitly recognized as an assembly line. Production of the hamburger sandwiches (burgers, for short) followed a straight path from the back of the kitchen to the front counter. Along this path were a series of workstations (see Figure B-1).

Any of the various burgers was begun either by taking a broiled meat patty and toasted bun out of an environmentally controlled holding compartment called a steamer or by placing a frozen meat patty (Whopper size or regular) and bun onto the chain drag at the feed end of a specially constructed gas-fired broiler at the back of the kitchen. The meat patties were drawn from a freezer below the broiler. The broiler cooked the meat at approximately 800°F, allowing the grease to drip into a special compartment, and it also toasted the bun.

Next in the assembly line came the *board*, where buns and meat were transformed into Whopper sandwiches, burgers, hamburger deluxe sandwiches, double cheeseburgers, and the like. This was the key portion of the line, where the burger could be assembled "your way." The board itself was a long, stainless-steel table in the center of which were bins of condiments (cheese slices, bacon, pickles, onion, sliced tomatoes, shredded lettuce, mayonnaise) kept at

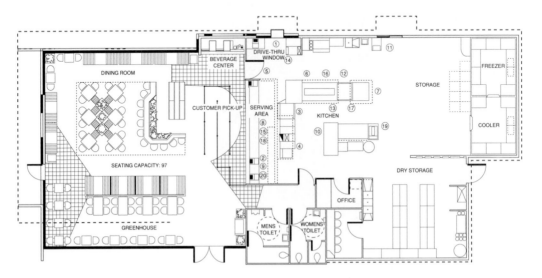

Figure B–1 Layout of the Noblesville Burger King. The circled numbers indicate the sequence of additions of workers to the kitchen as demand increases.

room temperature. Below the table were racks for holding spare condiments and supplies and also places for waste disposal. There were two work areas, one on each side of the center inventory of condiments. Above each side were two microwave ovens that could be used for keeping assembled sandwiches hot, stacks of various wrappers into which the sandwiches were placed, and a special series of touch controls that were part of the information flow system of the kitchen (more on this later). Beyond the board, on the pick-up counter, were chutes that held completed sandwiches ready for assembly into customer orders.

On one side of this main burger assembly line were the frying vats and the specialty sandwich board. The four frying vats were computer controlled, two just for french fries and two for other products (such as onion rings, chicken sandwich portions, chicken tenders, or fish portions). Near the frying vats were racks of thawed or thawing french fries (1- to 2-hour thaw times maximum). Behind the frying vats was the specialty sandwich board, which had its own assortment of condiments, buns, and wrappers. To one side of the specialty sandwich board were two warmers (one for items such as cooked chicken patties and the other for chicken tenders) and to the other side was a bun toaster.

The Fry Station. (*Courtesy of Burger King Corporation*)

On the other side of the main burger assembly line were the automatic drink machines for the drive-thru operation. A worker simply placed an ice-filled cup under the appropriate drink spout and pressed a button for small, regular, or large drinks; the machine then dispensed the proper quantity of soft drink, freeing the worker to do something else while the cup was being filled. The shake machine (for chocolate, vanilla, and strawberry) was located nearby, close to both the drive-thru window and the front counter.

Around the periphery of the kitchen were sinks and storage areas for food and supplies. There were also cooler and freezer rooms, an office, a training room, and a crew room where workers could congregate.

The Drive-Thru Operation

Because the drive-thru at the Noblesville Burger King accounted for approximately 50 percent of the restaurant's business, its smooth operation was critical. Work assignments at the drive-thru depended on how busy the restaurant was. In very slow times, a single worker (order-taker/expediter) could handle the drive-thru alone. When business picked up, two people were assigned to the drive-thru—one as an order-taker and one as an expediter). At peak times, five workers were assigned to the drive-thru: order-taker, window pusher, expediter, drink assembler, and cashier. (The Noblesville Burger King had two windows in the drive-thru lane, the first to handle the money and the second to "push out" the order.)

Peak Versus Nonpeak Operation

Employees were allocated to the workstations at the restaurant according to the pace of demand. When demand was slow, a smaller crew operated the restaurant: an order-taker/expediter at the front counter, a drive-thru order-taker/ expediter, and two kitchen workers. One worker took the broiler and the burger board, while one worked at the fry station and the specialty board. At peak times, there were as many as 24 employees working in the restaurant plus two or three managers. Management knew from historical data exactly when the peak hours would be at the Noblesville restaurant and so could plan worker arrivals.

Before the daily peaks in demand at lunch and dinner, considerable preparations were made, such as stocking the freezer under the broiler with hamburger patties, taking frozen fries out for thawing, and slicing tomatoes. If things worked as planned, minimal restocking would be needed during the peaks.

As demand picked up, more workers were added and job assignments became more specialized. In slow times, for example, one worker split duties between the fry station and the specialty sandwich board; during peak periods there were separate workers for these two work areas. During slow periods, one worker handled the broiler and all burger sandwich preparation; during peak times, one worker "fed" the broiler, one or two "caught" patties and buns and monitored the steamer, and up to four workers assembled sandwiches at the burger board. At the Noblesville Burger King, the burger board was divided during peak times into cheese and noncheese sides. (At other Burger Kings, this division might be Whopper-sized sandwiches on one side and small sandwiches on the other. Such a split frequently depended on the composition of demand at the particular restaurant.) During peak periods as well, two workers helped keep the dining area clean.

During very slow periods, much of the sandwich and drink production was triggered by the customer order itself. The burger given to the customer might actually be the one placed on the broiler chain in response to punching in the order. Some items could be held in inventory. An inventory of the most popular sandwiches (such as regular burgers and Whoppers) was usually kept in the chutes, but only for 10 minutes; if no customer requested them, they were discarded. Each sandwich wrapper was marked with a "time to discard." The system used the numbers pointed to by the minute hand on the clock. Thus a Whopper wrapped at 20 minutes after the hour (the 4 on the clockface) would have a 6 marked on the wrapper, because at 30 minutes after the hour (the 6 on the clockface) its 10-minute hold time would have expired. French fries were handled in a special way. Fries took approximately 2 minutes and 30 seconds to cook—too long to have a customer wait. As a result, fries had to be waiting in

At the Burger Board. (*Courtesy of Burger King Corporation*)

finished goods inventory. Here, too, the restaurant kept track of the time fries were waiting. If no one claimed fries within 7 minutes, they were discarded. (The fry station computers helped by keeping track of the time between batches so that fries were not sitting out too long.)

As demand picked up, it became more and more likely that a finished goods inventory of the major burgers and specialty sandwiches would be kept and that the broiler feeder would be loading the broiler in response to the inventory situation rather than in response to the particular orders displayed on the video screens. To guide production and to maintain inventory levels as demand increased, the Noblesville Burger King operated *stock-level charts.* There were four stock-level charts—one each for the broiler-steamer, sandwich board, specialty sandwich board, and specialty sandwich warmer. The chart featured a stock-level light indicator on which there were seven lights. Corresponding to each light was a volume of sales range to which were pegged inventory standards for the various items. Each change in the level (e.g., from level 4 to level 5 or from level 6 to peak) was announced by a special bell and the light switched so that all workers could infer, for example, how many sandwiches of particular types should be in the finished goods chutes and how many patties and buns should be in the steamer. The workers at the board were constantly tracking how many sandwiches were in each chute as well as keeping an eye on the video screen for any special order variations entered by the cashiers. When a worker finished such an order, he or she pressed one of the special touch controls above the station (mentioned earlier), which removed the call for that sandwich from the video screen. The worker then marked the wrapper to identify it to the expediters.

For the manager, the choice of a level represented a trade-off between meeting service standards with quick deliveries on one hand, and keeping too much in inventory and risking waste on the other. The manager always wanted to raise the level just before a surge in demand and to lower it just before the surge evaporated.

Coping with Bottlenecks

Surges in demand or runs on particular items could strain the production system and cause it to miss its established service standards. Three service standards were routinely tracked: (1) door-to-door time—the time elapsed from the moment the customer entered a line to place an order until the customer was served, (2) drive-thru time—the time elapsed from the arrival of a car in line until the customer was served, and (3) drive-thru transaction time—the time elapsed between a car's arrival at the pick-up window and its receipt of the order. The Noblesville Burger King restaurant tried to keep these service standards at company-mandated levels: 3 minutes average for the door-to-door and drive-thru times and 30 seconds average for the drive-thru transaction time. This last time was tracked automatically by the store's computer.

To reach these goals consistently, the restaurant's managers had to avoid bottlenecks in production. By providing both guidance to the crew and a set of spare hands, a manager could help ensure a smooth operation. (The Noblesville Burger King's sales volumes were high enough to warrant the creation of a production leader position for work in the kitchen, and a head cashier position. These workers were active in guiding the crew and anticipating bottlenecks.) During peak hours especially, it was not uncommon to see the production leader or a manager stepping up to the board to assemble a sandwich or drawing a shake from the machine or bagging fries or replenishing materials. The managers also encouraged crew teamwork. For example, workers with some slack time helped those who were overloaded—a cheese sandwich worker might assemble some non-cheese burgers. In fact, the manager's mandate for each of the workers was (1) to be aware of which level was being operated and what was on the video screen, (2) to be aware of any materials that would soon be out of stock, (3) to keep the workstation clean, and (4) to help anyone needing help. This mandate to keep production smooth and efficient placed special demands on a manager. The manager's job was not only to break any current bottlenecks but also to anticipate any potential ones. The manager constantly sought information from the workers on where bottlenecks were, how many cars were in line, and which

The Drive-thru Window as Seen from the Kitchen. (*Courtesy of Burger King Corporation*)

materials were running low, and encouraged the workers to handle surges in demand themselves without intervention.

Adequate prepeak period preparation also meant a great deal in coping with bottlenecks. If the shake machine was not completely filled with ingredients or if the cash register tape was close to running out, the operation was in danger of some bottlenecks that might affect service adversely. The restaurant manager had to check the status of items like these to be sure that incomplete preparation did not detract from the success of the operation.

Purchasing and Materials Management

For any item, the quantity ordered was the amount needed to bring the restaurant's existing inventory up to a certain established level. This level was the quantity of the item the manager expected to be used between receipt of the order and receipt of the next order (3 to 5 days at a maximum) plus a safety stock amount equal to 20 percent of the expected usage. This safety stock helped ensure that the entire menu was always available. The expected usage was calculated from the previous week's demand but was adjusted to reflect special trends or such conditions as holidays, school vacations, and newspaper promotions.

Orders were typically placed 1 day in advance of delivery. Materials were generally received in the afternoon. All materials were dated on receipt, and the oldest materials were always used first. However, usage levels were so high that the restaurant never needed to worry about spoilage, even for produce or dairy products. Orders for meat, paper products, and certain other supplies were placed three times a week with the Chicago regional office of Burger King Distribution Services, Burger King's supply subsidiary. Fresh produce was ordered from either Burger King Distribution Services or an independent supplier 6 days a week. Baked goods were ordered 6 days a week and dairy products 5 days a week.

The Workforce

The restaurant employed 45 workers. A typical worker put in 35 to 40 hours each week, spread over 5 or 6 days. Most lived in the area of the restaurant. At night and on weekends, high school students and second-job workers were often employed. The area was considered one that was hard to find staff for.

The crew for the Noblesville Burger King was hand-picked by the assistant managers. Almost none had worked at a Burger King before. Workers were paid for the hours worked, with overtime given after 40 hours each week. The average hourly wage was $5.20, with some workers receiving a minimum wage of $4.25 and the best-performing worker receiving $5.80. The fringe benefit package was modest. Labor turnover at the restaurant ran at 40 percent.

A worker's hours were likely to differ from day to day, although there was a set crew for the breakfast shift. The schedule for any week, however, was worked out about a week in advance. The schedule did try to reflect worker preferences about the amount and timing of their work. Most work assignments were shuffled daily. The prime reason for shuffling assignments was to promote worker cross-training, which increased the operation's flexibility. A manager might also be forced to shuffle assignments because of worker scheduling or absentee problems. For these reasons, the order-taker knew how the kitchen operated, and the kitchen knew how to take orders. The cross-training also had the welcome benefit of heightening the tolerance any worker had for the momentary troubles of other workers.

The daily rise and fall of peak and off-peak demand required continual changes in crew size so that neither too few nor too many workers worked at any one time. The flexibility needed in the schedule was achieved by using the part-time labor force and by scheduling their arrivals and departures at different times. Some, for example, reported to work just 15 minutes or so before the noon rush hour. Workers worked at least 3 to 4 hours at a time. A worker's departure from the restaurant was at the discretion of the manager. If sales were light, the manager could let some of the workers out early; if demand was heavy, it was understood that workers would be asked to stay past the scheduled departure time. The best crew, however, was generally scheduled for the peak times on Friday and Saturday.

The production leaders and the head cashier were responsible for training new workers. There were seven main stations on which to be trained (sandwich board, specialty sandwich board, fry station, broiler-steamer, order-taker/cashier, drive-thru, and hostess/clean-up). Training for any one of these stations took about 3 hours and consisted of reading some prepared material, watching a videotape on the station's work, doing a worksheet based on that video, reading a manual on procedures on the workstation, watching the trainer demonstrate procedures at the workstation, performing on a trial basis for 1 to 2 hours, taking a written test, and then having performance evaluated by the trainer. A new worker trained first on the broiler and steamer and then progressed to every station in the kitchen, finally winding up at the front counter and drive-thru operations. The fry station and the burger sandwich board were generally acknowledged to be the toughest tasks at the restaurant.

Quality

Periodically, about once a month, a team from the corporation would visit the restaurant unannounced to perform a quality inspection. They used a form for rating the food, the service, the appearance of the restaurant, and some other factors. In addition, the district manager for the franchisee made weekly visits to the restaurant to audit quality. Twice a year, management performed a three-day restaurant operations consultation during which every aspect of the restaurant's operation on every shift was analyzed. The results of such audits were taken very seriously. In addition, much of the managers' time was spent in the dining room talking with customers and assessing how well the service was being delivered.

Management

The Noblesville Burger King was a franchise store. It was part of the company's Chicago area. Supervising the Noblesville Burger King were a manager and five assistant managers. One of these six was always at the restaurant. During peak times managers would overlap, so that two or three sets of extra hands and eyes were available for breaking bottlenecks. The five assistant managers worked five days a week, but on a rotating shift.

Any manager's primary responsibility was to ensure that a good-quality product was promptly served in a clean environment within company guidelines. Although a manager's ability to control costs was valued, meeting the corporation's service, quality, and cleanliness goals came first. Meeting these goals meant developing the capabilities of the production crew and maintaining its morale. Thus the manager was first and foremost a crew chief, teaching new hires, guiding work assignments, checking quality, breaking bottlenecks, and providing an example for the crew. Layered on these responsibilities were others—ordering materials, receiving deliveries, checking and posting standards of performance (such as the door-to-door or transaction times), checking on the preparations for the day and for the peak periods, and scheduling the part-time workforce. Of the restaurant's five assistant managers, three specialized in the functions of ordering, scheduling, and breakfast operations.

Burger King headquarters provided restaurant managers with a number of aids. Chief among these aids for the week-by-week operation of the restaurant were the charts, formulas, and decision rules for scheduling the workforce, given the restaurant's particular configuration. The corporation had developed aids that showed, for different sales levels and hours of operation, how much labor each restaurant should have and where that labor ought to be assigned. These charts, formulas, and decision rules greatly aided the managers in controlling labor costs, which was the second highest cost that could be controlled.

The restaurant's POS system (computer/cash register network) was also a useful management tool. From the computer, the manager could obtain information, by half-hour increments, on sales, product mix, and discounts. The POS system also kept track of the restaurant's service standard performance.

Facilities and Technology

This Burger King was a design called BK87. According to Larry Levensky, the franchisee's district manager, the BK87 was an excellent design for a high-volume restaurant. The layout was very efficient, workers did not waste many steps in performing the tasks required of them, materials were readily available, and there was ample storage space. Workers at nonpeak times could easily cover more than one workstation.

In addition, the Noblesville Burger King included several technological improvements that had been initiated by the corporation. For example, computerized frying vats had been installed with temperature probes that automatically adjusted the frying times so that french fries or other fried foods were cooked perfectly. Buzzers indicated when the fries should be shaken or removed from the vats. The automatic drink machines were another advance; these permitted workers to engage in other tasks while soft drink cups were being filled automatically. A new shake machine mixed shakes automatically as well. The addition of TV screens to indicate variations on the standard sandwiches was another advance; these reduced the cacophony that could strike the kitchen during peak periods. The kitchen included a new breakfast grill and hood, a specially designed unit that could be set up for the breakfast business and then transformed into a work area the rest of the day. The heat chutes for finished sandwiches were coated with Teflon and were enclosed to keep the sandwiches warmer. The extra window for the drive-thru was still another innovation, helping to cut 12 seconds off the line time for drive-thru customers. Burger King was always inventing new ways to deliver better service.

PART TWO DISCUSSION

The Burger King Corporation is in no way responsible for the following views and presentation. They are solely the responsibility of the author.

THE FLOW OF THE PROCESS AND OF INFORMATION

In most service industries, the time delay between service provision and service consumption is necessarily very short. Put another way, one can rarely inventory a service, at least not for very long. Hotel room-nights cannot be inventoried, nor can timely tips on the stock market, nor can tasty hamburgers. Hence a whole degree of freedom is removed from the service manager, which heightens the importance of capacity choice in most service industries.

It is also often the case that services must be particularly flexible so that they can be customized to individual consumer needs. Think of the travel agent, the salesperson, the cab driver, and, yes, the fast-food restaurant.

These two basic features of many service businesses place substantial demands on the process design and information systems of an enterprise such as Burger King. Flexibility in both product and volume is paramount, and Burger King has adopted some classic policies for yielding such flexibility.

Figure B–2 is a process flow diagram for assembling an order. It is simple, and that is one of its advantages. Responsibilities are clearly demarcated, and yet all of the key tasks for customizing the hamburger or specialty sandwich rest with the worker who actually assembles the sandwich at the board. This fact, in turn, simplifies the information flow so that only one worker need pay strict attention to the punch-in of a special order. (An information flow diagram is found in Figure B–3.) In this way, with a clear delineation of tasks and direct information flows, rapid product changes can be facilitated.

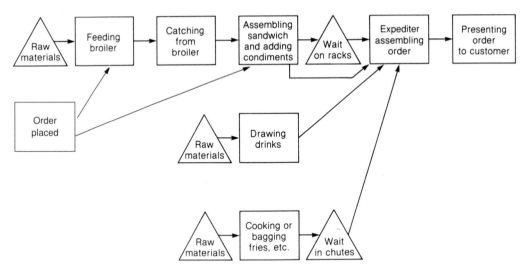

Figure B–2 A Process Flow Diagram (nonpeak period) for the Noblesville Burger King Restaurant's Kitchen Operations.

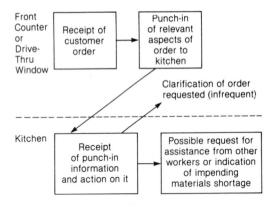

Figure B–3 An Information Flow Diagram (nonpeak period) for the Noblesville Burger King Restaurant.

Flexibility in changing production volumes is achieved by a continual rebalancing of the sandwich production line. The time pattern of demand is well known from past experience, and this knowledge has permitted the staggering of work hours for the part-time workforce so that varying numbers can be on hand at any one time. The workforce ebbs and flows from 3 during slack periods to 20 during peak periods. As more workers are added, the job contents narrow and, importantly, the flow of information changes. No longer is production keyed completely to the punch-in of the order. More and more, production is keyed by the levels of the finished goods inventory and of the work-in-process inventory of broiled burgers and toasted buns. Instead of reacting to the order punched in, the broiler feeder reacts to the manger's posted list of burgers to be held as work-in-process, feeding the broiler so as to maintain the desired inventory level. Similarly, the board workers respond to the level of finished goods inventory, although these board workers must also respond to any special orders that are punched in. Special orders, of course, must take precedence over the maintenance of the finished goods inventory. The peak period changes in the process and information flow diagrams are pictured in Figure B–4.

Demands of the Process on the Workforce

The flexibility of the Burger King fast-food operation demands flexibility from its workers. The job contents and the production pace vary markedly throughout any worker's shift during the day, requiring a special tolerance. Workers on a machine-paced assembly line get used to the rhythm of the conveyor. But, on a worker-paced line, and particularly one in a service industry, any rhythm may soon dissolve.

What is especially true of worker-paced lines is that the crew on the line views itself as a team, largely because they are so dependent on one another. This

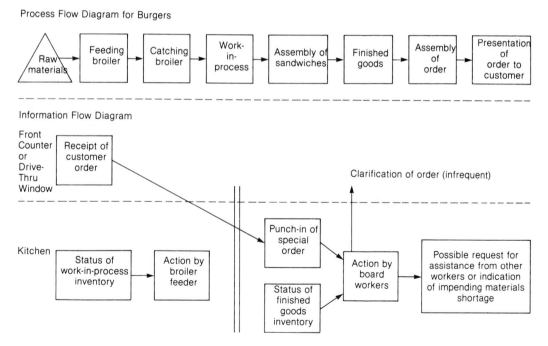

Figure B–4 Process and Information Flow Diagrams (peak period) for the Noblesville Burger King Restaurant.

fact often permits worker-paced lines where the demand is steady (unlike at a fast-food restaurant) to be paid according to a group incentive scheme. Some standard of production—X units per time period—is established and the crew on the line, if it can better the standard, is paid extra for doing so. This kind of group incentive pay scheme can tie a crew together as a team even more than usual.

Demands of the Process on Management

An operation such as a Burger King restaurant places specific demands on management both because it is a service operation and because it is a worker-paced line flow process. As a line flow process, many issues surface:

Balance of the line
Materials management
Technological advance
Capacity planning
Product design
Workforce management

Managers of worker-paced lines should be sensitive to all these issues, because falling down on any one could seriously jeopardize the entire operation.

The issue of technological advance is particularly acute, because such an advance may enable a smoother, more regular flow of the product. After all, a worker-paced line flow usually remains worker- rather than machine-paced because there is as yet no easy way to guard against a succession of overcycle conditions striking a worker all at once (such as a run on "Whoppers, hold the pickles"). If the mix of product options can somehow be smoothed out or if particular advances can be made in product or workstation design, a worker-paced line can easily be transformed into a machine-paced line. In other words, the worker-paced line is somewhat more vulnerable to radical, rather than incremental, change than is a machine-paced one.

The technological changes evident at the Noblesville Burger King all contributed to a smoother flow of products. The automatic drink machines, the computerized frying vats, the TV monitors of information, and even the new BK87 layout all act to speed up and smooth the delivery process.

A Burger King's status as a service operation only heightens the importance of capacity planning because service firms cannot ordinarily inventory their product. The new BK87 design is testament to the importance the corporation assigns to planning capacity. The importance of workforce management is also heightened because the worker–customer interaction is part of the service. Ordinarily, one cannot hide the service process as readily as one can hide the manufacturing process. Keeping the workforce productive and interested in their jobs is a key challenge for managers in service operations.

QUESTIONS

1. Visit a fast-food restaurant with a friend to perform an experiment. While one of you times the other's entry and exit and the time from the placing of the order to its receipt, the other should observe how many workers are actually involved with the order. Visit the fast-food restaurant at a slack time and at a peak time, and compare the differences in time and number of workers.

2. Watch for bottlenecks the next time you are in a fast-food restaurant (or any worker-paced service operation). Where do they arise and why? How might they be remedied?

3. Suppose that Burger King were to introduce a new type of sandwich. What aspects of the restaurant's operations would be affected, and how?

4. Why is flexibility one of the key features for success in a worker-paced assembly line operation such as Burger King?

5. How would you define capacity at a Burger King? What factors influence the establishment of a limit to capacity?

6. Would you prefer to work on a machine-paced assembly line or a worker-paced one? Why? Which would you prefer to supervise? Why?

7. Visit a Burger King close to you. It is unlikely to be a brand new one with all the advances incorporated into the Noblesville Burger King. Consider the ways in which the Burger King you visit could be modernized. Consider as well what could be done at the restaurant to increase capacity as sales increase. Prepare plans of action that specify which things ought to be done, and in what order, to modernize the restaurant and increase its capacity. Defend your choices.

8. Consider an alternative kitchen layout to the one at the Noblesville Burger King. In what ways is your alternative better or worse than the one discussed in the tour?

=========== **SITUATION FOR STUDY B–1** ===========

Legacy Homes

Tom Stoddard had been employed part-time as a "rough carpenter" by Legacy Homes while he completed his degree at Interstate Tech University. After his graduation, Legacy hired Tom as a construction superintendent; this job combined the duties of foreman, scheduler, and expediter.

By building only to order, Legacy took a conservative approach to the ups and downs typical of the home construction industry. Legacy offered a limited number of home designs; Tables B–1 and B–2 show the work involved on most of them—usually about 90 days' worth.

When a buyer arranged a home loan from a lending institution, the local practice was to allow the construction company to receive the money in partial payments (cash draws) depending on the degree of completion of the home. Thus, for Legacy to receive the money, Tom needed to finish a home as fast as possible.

Legacy had a nucleus crew of highly skilled workers that it wanted to keep working most of the time. Other workers could be hired to supplement this crew when necessary. Table B–3 shows this crew and the various tasks they were capable of

TABLE B-1 CREW SIZE AND TIMES FOR VARIOUS TASKS (LEGACY HOMES)

Task description work type[a]		Minimum/maximum crew size	Days to complete (with minimum crew)
1 Concrete footer	A	2–4	1.00
2 Foundation	F	Subcontract	1.00
3 Grading	A	2–4	0.50
4 Framing	B	5–8	2.60
5 Roofing	F	Subcontract	1.00
6 Concrete	A/B	3–5	1.50
7 Wiring	C	2–4	1.00
8 Furnace and ducts	C	2–4	2.25
9 Plumbing	C	2–3	2.50
10 Insulation	B	1–3	2.25
11 Dry wall	F	Subcontract	1.00
12 Siding	F	Subcontract	5.50
13 Sewer line	A	2–3	2.00
14 Painting	F	Subcontract	1.50
15 Finish carpentry	D	2–4	2.50
16 Tile	D	1–2	5.00
17 Electrical trim	C	1–2	1.50
18 Finish plumbing	C	1–2	3.50
19 Heating trim	C	1–3	2.50
20 Carpeting	F	Subcontract	2.00
21 Cleanup	E	1–3	2.00

[a]A, excavate; B, rough carpentry; C, plumbing, heating, electrical; D, finish carpentry; E, part-time clean-up; F, subcontract.

TABLE B-2 PRECEDENCE RELATIONSHIP (LEGACY HOMES)

Job	Preceding operation(s)
1	
2	1
3	2
4	3
5	4
6	2
7	4
8	5
9	5
10	7, 8, 9
11	10
12	10
13	9
14	11
15	14
16	14
17	14
18	15
19	14
20	6, 12, 13, 16, 17, 18, 19
21	20

TABLE B-3 LABOR FORCE (LEGACY HOMES)

Type of work	Current labor available	Tasks performed[a]
A Excavate	3	1, 3, 6, 13
B Rough carpentry	5	4, 6, 10
C Plumbing, heating, electrical	4	7, 8, 9, 17, 18, 19
D Finish carpentry	2	15, 16
E Part-time cleanup	1	21
F Subcontract		2, 5, 11, 12, 14, 20

[a]See Table B–1 for an explanation of these numbers.

performing. Each crew member knew well a primary function such as plumbing but could be counted on to help with other functions such as rough carpentry. The crew who installed the plumbing, for example, also installed the heating and electricity. This overlap of skills was possible for two reasons: (1) most of the work on a Legacy house was rather straightforward and did not entail the total skill requirements of worker in any of the trades, and (2) Legacy hired nonunion workers.

Table B–1 shows the minimum and maximum crew sizes for completing each task. For example, task 8 requires a minimum of two workers because one person working alone cannot position the furnace or handle the ductwork; two people working on separate houses would take much longer to complete their work on both houses than if they worked together on one house at a time. At the maximum crew size, of course, it can happen that workers interfere with each other's work. Tom assumed that additional workers could work at the same rate as workers already on the job; he therefore scaled the number of workers up or down proportionately. For example, in task 1 if two workers can do the job in 1 day (i.e., 2 labor-days are required), three workers can do the job in 2/3 day (2 labor-days divided by three workers available), and four workers can do it in 1/2 a day. All operations have been designed to require a low level of skill; thus, any worker can shift to another operation with only a negligible loss of efficiency. Usually one worker is used as parts chaser and relief. The supervisor can help with the parts chasing but is not expected to take part in operations except as a troubleshooter.

Although the products (houses) do not move, Tom feels that the principles of worker-paced lines can be applied with beneficial results.

1. Design a process flow for Tom.
2. What is the minimum time requirement to build a house? How many houses should be being built to keep the permanent crew busy? What is the maximum number of houses that should be under construction at one time?
3. Is the workforce balanced? If not, which crew sizes should be changed?
4. Design an information flow for Tom.
5. Set up a sequence for raw material flow for Tom.

SITUATION FOR STUDY B–2

Small City Newspaper

Small City Newspaper (SCN) was a family-owned paper with a circulation of 43,000 in the morning and 22,000 in the evening. There were three editions of the morning paper and two editions of the afternoon paper; the earlier editions of each paper were for delivery further away.

Newspapers have two content inputs: news and advertising. For *SCN*, as with most daily newspapers, advertising determined the size of each issue, which in turn affected the length of the production run. To maintain an average of 43 percent news content and 57 percent advertising, the number of columns of news was allocated according to the number of columns of advertising sold for a particular issue. A minimum number of news columns (front page, sports, editorial, comics, and so on) was required for the morning paper (96 total columns) and for the evening paper (80 total columns). Information about the number of columns of advertising was communicated to the editors and the production manager by the advertising department.

Advertising was divided into three categories: display, classified, and national. Display was used primarily by local retailers and ad agencies, who often had camera-ready copy prepared for the paste-up department. On occasion, the advertising and art departments worked with the customer in preparing the advertisement. Three days' lead time was generally required of the client when placing a display ad; however, flexibility in this procedure allowed for changes to be made until press time. Classified ads had to be submitted by 5:00 P.M. the previous day and could be prepared for paste-up on the computer. National advertising copy was usually camera-ready and followed much the same procedure as the display ads. To expedite the use of both display and national ad copy, an inventory of these ads was maintained.

The morning news department had a staff of 40: city desk, copy desk/AP wire service, sports, style, editorial, and cartoon. The afternoon paper had a staff of 22 (no cartoonist). The library kept microfilmed copies of newspapers, publicity brochures, and a master file of news clippings (filed alphabetically) on important individuals. A personal computer that was tied into the Associated Press news retrieval system was also located in the library.

The managing editor assigned reporters and photographers to cover newsworthy events. Editorials as well as style and feature articles had the earliest deadlines (5:00 P.M. for the morning paper and 9:00 A.M. for the afternoon paper) and so were often written the day before they were to be published. Front-page stories and sports coverage demanded up-to-date reporting; the deadlines for these articles were 11:00 P.M. for the morning paper and 11:00 A.M. for the afternoon paper.

Flexibility in the entire operation was a must, to allow for reporting late-breaking news. Because these stories could significantly disrupt the process, reporters were encouraged to prepare as much of their other copy as far in advance of press time as possible. To facilitate this, the newspaper had adopted a flexible time schedule for its reporters, who were generally on the job from 3:00 P.M. to midnight (for the morning paper) and from 7:00 A.M. to 4:00 P.M. (for the afternoon paper). In spite of this effort, half of the newspaper was made up in the two hours before press time.

Generally, a reporter composed a story at a video display terminal (VDT). The story appeared on a screen (CRT) as it was typed. Errors could easily be corrected, and additions and deletions did not affect the rest of the story. Typewritten copy could enter the computer through the use of an optical character reader (OCR), which sensed typewritten copy if it was prepared in a compatible typeface. Once the reporter was satisfied with the story, a single key command put the story in the story queue in the computer. If this was done close to the deadline and the reporter considered the story to be especially important, the reporter could supersede this queue by notifying the editor.

The editor had a list of all stories in the queue. He or she accessed the stories and made revisions using special keyboard commands. Once satisfied, the editor added the headline via the keyboard, specifying the type size of the heading (in points), and designated where the story should go in the paper. The story was then transferred by computer to page paste-up, where a hard copy was printed.

Syndicated features and wire service copy were transmitted to the paper in a form compatible with the VDT system, replacing the old teletypewriter and eliminating the need for rekeyboarding. At the copy desk, these stories were reviewed and a determination was made concerning which stories to use; then the copy was forwarded by computer to page paste-up. The laser photo service was another external input. Photographs were beamed to the newspaper along with a subtitle or a short explanation. The photo came to the paper ready for paste-up.

Advertising copy, news stories, and photographs were pieced together on a page the size of a newspaper page. Reusable bylines and photos of syndicated columnists were kept at the paste-up tables. Efforts were made to smooth the flow through paste-up by having advertising, feature articles, and as much of the news as possible in paste-up as early as possible. The paste-up operation for the morning paper normally ran from 5:30 P.M. to 11:00 P.M. Paste-up for the afternoon paper generally ran from 8:00 A.M. to 11:30 A.M. The time difference for the papers was due to the latter's smaller size and the advance preparation the morning paper paste-up had to do for its Sunday edition. Changes for the final edition of each paper could be made after the presses began the earlier edition(s).

Once the pages had been laid out, they were photographed. An aluminum-backed, polymer-coated plate was placed in an exposure unit beneath the page negative. After a 45- to 70-second exposure, it was put through a wash unit, which used water and a small amount of biodegradable defoaming agent to remove the non-exposed polymer areas. After drying, the plate had a raised mirror-image surface, which was curved to fit the rotary press cylinder. One page could pass through the engraving process in 22 minutes standard time, although several plates could pass through simultaneously. Once the plates had been prepared, a press room employee picked them up on the fourth floor and carried them to the press on the first floor.

The current printing process replaced several steps of the old letterpress system. It was compatible with both the rotary press and the offset press systems. An offset press, although it wasted as much as 4 percent newsprint per run, offered computerized printing capabilities, better quality of print, and flexibility with the use of color.

Press runs for the morning paper were approximately as follows: first edition (outlying counties) 12:10 to 12:40 A.M., second edition (adjacent county) 1:00 to 1:25 A.M., and final edition (city) 1:45 to 3:20 A.M. Press runs for the afternoon paper were approximately as follows: first edition (all counties, except the immediate one) 12:50 to 1:30 P.M., and final edition 2:15 to 3:15 P.M. The capacity of the press was 80 pages (16 per deck) per run. When full color was used, only 64 pages could be printed per run because two half-decks had to be devoted to overlap the four colors necessary for full color. To circumvent this bottleneck, the Sunday feature section was printed on Saturday and many of the inserts were preprinted during slack time. The Sunday comics, for example, were printed externally and were delivered early in the week.

The press cylinders were on the first floor. Rolls of newsprint were loaded on the press in the basement, and the cutting and folding mechanism was on the second floor. The newly printed newspaper was carried by conveyor to the mailroom.

Maintenance could be performed by disconnecting the individual decks; however, all five were operated simultaneously by a central drive system. A problem with the electrically powered drive unit, which had happened recently, could prevent the press from operating. Fortunately, this situation was corrected in time to get the paper out, but it pointed up a weakness in the functioning of the entire operation.

In the mailroom, the sections and inserts were assembled. The papers were counted, bundled, labeled, and dropped through a chute to an alley, where they were picked up by carriers or were trucked to drop points.

Timely delivery was very important. The evening newspaper had to reach the customer before the evening TV newscast, or it would not be read. The morning paper had to be to the carriers (who usually held day jobs) in time for them to make deliveries before they went to work. In meeting these objectives, the earlier editions of the morning paper were to leave the headquarters by 2:00 A.M. and the final edition was to be to the drop points by 4:00 A.M. The earlier afternoon edition was to be ready to go by 1:30 P.M., with the final edition due at the drop points by 3:30 P.M.

1. Diagram the process and information flows for this process.

2. In what ways is this a worker-paced line flow operation and in what ways, if any, is it not?

3. How do the concepts of line balance and rebalance apply to this situation?

A SERVICE SHOP
Ogle–Tucker Buick Auto Service and Repair
Indianapolis, Indiana

Tour C

Ogle–Tucker Buick was located on Keystone Avenue in northeast Indianapolis. It was located on 7.25 acres of land and occupied 43,000 square feet of space. The service department consisted of 27 stalls available in the service area, 24 stalls in the body shop, 6000 square feet dedicated to parts storage, and the associated office space for these operations.

The dealership was owned by Robert Ogle and Thomas Tucker, who had grown up on farms and had moved to Indianapolis after World War II. The dealership had been at its current location since 1969. It sold Buick cars exclusively.

PART ONE PROCESS DESCRIPTION

Writing the Service Order

The service operation began at 7:00 A.M., Monday through Friday. At that time, the two service advisors who were responsible for developing the repair orders began greeting the customers who had lined up for service. The service advisors' responsibilities were to detail the symptoms of the problem experienced by the customer and the work the customer wanted to have performed. This called for skillful listening by the service advisor and the knack for asking the right questions to glean the proper symptoms to explain to the mechanic. The service advisor was also responsible for suggesting additional services the customer might want but had not thought of, such as oil changes, new brake linings, or front-end alignments. The service advisor was the operation's chief contact with the customer through the service process. If the customer needed to be informed about the progress on his or her car, or that additional work was needed, or that the car might not be ready in time, the service advisor communicated that information.

Upon greeting the customer, the service advisor logged in necessary identification information to the service department's computer, and a customized repair order form was generated (Figure C–1). When the customer finished detailing the work to be done on the car, he or she signed the repair order, giving the service operation authorization to work on the car. The service advisor then assigned a control number to the job and placed an oaktag control number on the rearview mirror of the car and also attached a tag with the same number on the keys to the car.

The repair order consisted of four paper "soft" copies plus an oaktag "hard copy." The four soft copies were of different colors. The top sheet, white copy, was the accounting copy. The yellow sheet was the customer's copy. The pink sheet was kept by the service advisor. The green sheet was a control copy that was used by the person who followed up with customers on their repairs, and was then routed back to the service manager, whose secretary filed them. After the service advisor filled out the repair order, he or she detached the green sheet and sent the other soft copies, together with the hard copy, to the dispatcher in the "tower."

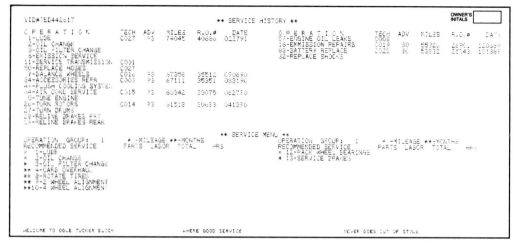

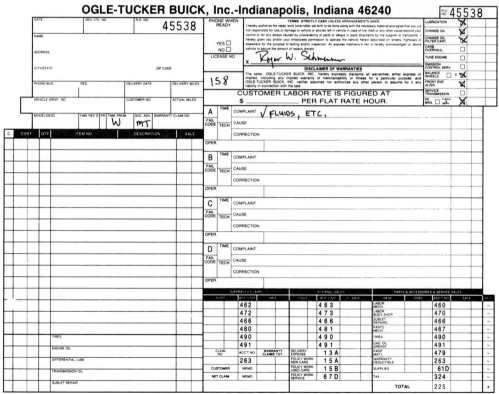

Figure C–1 A Repair Order.

The Customer Service Area With the Dispatcher's Window Looking Over the Shop. *(Courtesy of Ogle–Tucker Buick, Indianapolis, Indiana)*

Dispatching

By keeping the soft and hard copies together,[1] Ogle–Tucker was able to reduce some double entry of information by the tower and yet still keep control over what was done, so that mechanics could not enter work that was not ordered by the customer. The service advisor sent the repair order into the dispatching office (the tower), the nerve center for the service operation. Here the dispatcher (the tower operator) logged in the control number, the name of the customer, the type of car, the time the service advisor promised the car for delivery, the repair order number, and the work that was to be done, together with the number of the mechanic who was supposed to do that work. Figure C–2 shows a dispatcher's route sheet.

Jobs were classified by category. The categories included lubrication and filter changes, tune-ups, front-end work, rear-axle work, transmission work, brake work, and the like. Ogle–Tucker's mechanics (called *technicians* at the dealership) were specialized by task. For example, one did transmission work exclusively, two did front-end work, three handled tune-ups, and others devoted themselves to other tasks. When the tower operator logged in a repair, he or she noted which technician in which specialty was to do the job. When that job was

---

[1]Many dealerships separated the soft copies from the hard copy that went to the mechanic.

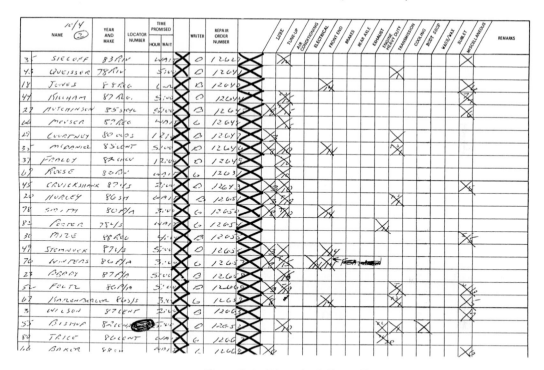

Figure C–2 Dispatcher's Route Sheet.

completed, another technician might take over the car to work on a different aspect of its service or repair. A crossed-out entry on the route sheet meant that the technician had completed the work.

Routine items such as tune-ups and oil changes could be assigned to technicians without a diagnosis about what was wrong. For a number of cars, however, some diagnostic work had to be done before the car could be fixed. Whether diagnostic work was needed was generally determined from the service advisor's wording on the repair order. Key words such as "hesitating sometimes," "occasionally stalling," and so on, were tip-offs. Technicians were responsible for diagnosing problems as well as fixing them. On particularly tough assignments, the service manager was consulted. The dealership referred to the "3 C's" of "complaint, cause, and correction" that were listed on the repair order. The service advisor was responsible for detailing the complaint and the technician was responsible for determining cause and performing the correction.

Shop Operations and the Workforce

The service floor had 27 stalls that were divided among the 13 technicians currently employed. Most technicians were assigned two stalls. Most of the shop's technicians (mechanics) had some post-secondary school education, generally technical school training, and they often had a rich family heritage of

A Service Bay. *(Courtesy of Ogle–Tucker Buick, Indianapolis, Indiana)*

working on mechanical things. The better-established mechanics could make more than $30,000 a year and carried at least $20,000 worth of their own tools. Established technicians earned a higher total income than younger technicians who did not have as many tools or as much knowledge. Younger technicians built up their collections of tools on a continual basis. Tool salespeople came to the shop every week to peddle their tools and collect payments from any technicians who were buying tools on credit.

The technicians were paid on a flat-rate basis. A manual indicated what the time standard should be for every particular kind of job. The technician was paid according to the standard for the job, not according to the time spent on it. Thus, if he or she spent less time than that indicated in the manual, the technician could "beat the book" and earn increased wages. If he or she spent more time at the job than indicated, the technician would not earn as much. Any rework was directed back to the technician on an unpaid basis, and the shop's policy was that any rework had priority over other work. There were also some skill-level differences incorporated into the wage structure. The most inexperienced worker received $10.50 for every "flag hour" (standard hour), and the most experienced worker earned $14.50. Thus a technician could earn more annually in two ways: by improving his or her skill level or by being more efficient. When technicians had to wait for a part, it was to their advantage to go to the tower operator and get assigned some quick work that they could perform while waiting. In this way, technicians were able to convert more of the time they were in the shop into flag hours for which they earned income.

After finishing work on a car, the technician road-tested it, and if satisfied, wrote the mileage on the back of the repair order's hard copy and filled in both the cause of the complaint and the correction made. The technician then returned the repair order to the tower. There, the dispatcher reviewed what the technician had written, and in consultation with a standard reference, determined what the flag hours should be for the repairs made. The dispatcher then filled in and attached a gummed segment of the time sheet (Figure C–3) to the back of the hard copy.

The repair order was routed to the cashier for payment and accounting, the pink copies were retained by the service advisors, and the hard copies filed. White and green copies were filed by repair order number; hard copies were filed by car serial number. Customers returning for their cars went to the cashier to pay, and there received the yellow copies of the annotated repair orders and the keys to their cars. Within a few days of repair, customers were called by the dealership and asked to comment on the quality of their repair. If customers were not at home, a letter was sent. Postcard surveys were also left in each car repaired, with customers encouraged to mail their responses back in. The service manager viewed these customer surveys as an important aspect of the service department's operation.

Cars typically arrived during the morning. On an average day, 70 cars might be worked on, with a typical range of 40 to 85. The day's chief period of stress came after 4:00 P.M., when most people came to pick up their cars. This was when customer complaints surfaced about cars not being ready or about the bill being too high. The service advisors were pulled in many different directions during this time.

Quality Control

Quality was enhanced in several ways. Of course, the road tests were done on each car. And because technicians had to do rework for no pay, there was an incentive to do things right the first time.

Shoddy work was grounds for termination. If, in the opinion of the service manager, there were three instances in one month where poor work was involved with no mitigating circumstances, the technician was terminated. The technicians, of course, were alert to this policy, and each instance of shoddy work was discussed between the service manager and the technician.

From time to time, technicians were sent to training schools, usually either in Indianapolis or in Cincinnati, where the zone's main training center was located. Most schools lasted between 2 and 4 days. The dealership paid for the school's fees plus food, lodging, and transportation. Technicians were also encouraged to take the twice-yearly Automotive Service Excellence tests for accreditation in major aspects of automotive service and repair.

The Parts Department

The parts department employed six people: a manager, a computer operator, a truck driver, and three countermen. The parts department was charged with purchasing all the parts used by the technicians, maintaining that inventory, handling damaged parts, and filing claims and other returns. The department maintained an inventory of $320,000 worth of parts, an inventory that turned over three times a year. In a typical day, perhaps 300 parts would be used to serve the needs of the technicians in the shop, but only two or three of those parts would be out of stock and have to be special ordered.

The parts department could place orders with General Motors Service Parts Operations (GMSPO), outside jobbers, or other dealers. The parts department liked to turn a part around (sell it) every 30 days, but with an actual inventory turn ratio of around three, they were only able to turn parts on the average every 120 days. Exactly which parts should be purchased at any time was determined jointly by the parts department and a computer program developed by Reynolds and Reynolds. The computer system and its software were fairly standard for the industry. This computer software used past sales histories to generate suggestions for which items should be purchased to replenish the inventory. Each day, the parts department manager made sure that parts that had been used or sold were removed from the perpetual inventory record kept by the computer. In this way, the computer knew what was needed for replenishment, although the parts

The Parts Counter. (*Courtesy of Ogle–Tucker Buick, Indianapolis, Indiana*)

department manager could override the suggestions made by the computer to take into account special circumstances.

There were several ways by which parts were ordered:

1. *Stock orders.* The stock order was the regular way to order parts. Parts were ordered every week at a set time (Tuesdays). Parts ordered through GMSPO by stock order received a 7 percent purchase discount and an 8 percent credit on returned parts. The credit was useful because it permitted Ogle–Tucker to return slow-moving parts at no cost, thereby improving the way the dealership's inventory dollars were spent. Stock orders were issued for regularly used parts and for parts whose demands were known with considerable lead time. There were also "target orders" (placed on Mondays) for the fast-moving parts. Extra discounts were available for these parts. Target orders could mean a 22 percent extra discount, and on special promotions the discount could be 27 percent plus 16 percent return privileges.

There were several other ways to order parts. These were more costly than stock orders, but provided faster service.

2. *Car Inoperative Orders (CIOs).* CIO orders were handled faster than stock orders and, consequently, no discounts or returns were given. For CIO orders, GM checked the six closest depots in that region for parts. The distribution channel for parts went through three types of depots. The most local were termed Parts Distribution Centers (PDCs), the closest being in Chicago. The next level up, Field Processing Centers, carried more inventory. Lansing, Michigan, was the nearest Field Processing Center. The last resort was the parts plants themselves, controlled from Flint, Michigan. If the part could be located in any of the depots checked, it was sent. If the part could not be located, the dealership was so informed and would have to either wait for the part or give it higher priority.

3. *VIP (Very Important Parts) Orders.* VIP orders called for all depots in the country to be checked for parts. The cost charged was $2.00 per item plus the dealer cost plus 5 percent.

4. *SPAC (Special Parts Assistance Center) special orders.* If all else failed, and if GM had a formal customer complaint, SPAC could be initiated. A SPAC special order called for action within 48 hours and dealers across the country could get involved.

5. *Partech.* For problem parts, Partech could be consulted. Partech helped with part number problems such as no part number or part number misprints in catalogs.

6. *Other dealers.* Ogle–Tucker also bought parts from other dealers through informal relationships. The parts manager sometimes phoned other dealerships and asked whether they had specific parts that could be shipped by bus or some other means. Typically, the cost was dealer cost plus 22 to 25 percent.

Within the first-floor storage area of the parts department, there were both small bins and large bins. In the upstairs area, bulk materials such as sheet metal parts were stored. Parts were stored in numerical order by group number. For example, 2000 series numbers were for electrical parts, 3000 series numbers for fuel and exhaust, 4000 series numbers for transmission and brake parts, and so forth. Ordering parts, however, depended not on the group number, but on a specific part number six to eight digits in length. The workers at each counter were responsible for identifying the proper part for the job, tracking it down in the storage room, and delivering it to the technician or the purchaser, with the proper paperwork done. At each counter, there were manuals for each model or body type of Buick. Each manual had text and illustrations to aid the search. Prices were kept on the computer. When a part was billed out, the computer automatically deducted it from inventory and kept its accounting straight.

Body Shop

The body shop's major task was to repair cars that had been in accidents. These cars had smashed some sheet metal parts or even the car's frame itself. The shop employed nine: a manager, four bodymen, a painter, a painter's helper, a car washer, and a porter (who did waxing and detailing and kept the shop clean). There were 15 stalls designated for the four bodymen and 9 stalls for the painter.

The body shop was a full-service body shop that could handle both ordinary sheet metal tasks and framework—the shop was equipped with the hydraulics, chains, and other equipment necessary to straighten automobile frames. The dealership provided benches, welding equipment, painting equip-

In the Body Shop. *(Courtesy of Ogle–Tucker Buick, Indianapolis, Indiana)*

ment, some special tools and the consumables such as sandpaper that were used in the course of the shop's work. Each bodyman, however, owned his own tools, which were valued between $15,000 and $20,000.

The bodyworkers typically worked on two cars at any one time, one that could be classified as a "heavy hit" and one that demanded much lighter work. Often the major job proceeded in fits and starts as parts became available. The smaller job thus served to keep the workers fully occupied. The painter often worked on six or seven cars in a day.

Within the body shop, the bodyworkers continually helped one another with problems, such as opening smashed doors or attaching frame-straightening equipment. Although they were paid for their individual work, they recognized the need for assistance when one of them ran into trouble. Within the paint shop, the painter was aided by a helper who did much of the required sanding and the masking of the parts of the car that were not to receive paint. The painter was primarily responsible for "shooting" the paint and ordering supplies. The other two were mainly cleanup people.

The typical car spent one or two days in body repair and two to three days in painting. (Painting required the application of a base coat and a clear coat, with time in between for drying, sanding, and rubbing out.) Some cars with major damage spent much longer in the shop. They required much more work and were sometimes delayed until parts were received. Typically, the body shop did not begin work on an automobile until all the parts were received. Thus, if the owner could still drive the automobile, he or she continued to drive it until all the parts were received and an appointment was scheduled. However, if the car had sustained major damage and could not be driven, it remained outside the shop until all the parts were available. With major damage, however, there was always a substantial chance that hidden damage would be revealed as the car was worked on. Hidden damage took even more time to fix and often required the purchase of additional parts. This took time, especially if the car was a foreign make.

The body shop had two constituencies: car owners and their insurance companies. Almost all of the shop's work was paid for out of insurance claims, which meant that the shop had to agree with the insurance companies about how much a particular job was worth. The estimates by both the insurance companies and the shop itself were aided by reference to standard books that periodically updated prices and gave standards on the time it should take to remedy certain problems. The shop, in particular, followed the *Mitchell Crash Book* and had very few disputes with insurance adjusters. Most of the disputes centered around which parts ought to be straightened rather than replaced. (It was standard practice to replace a smashed part with a brand new one on new cars, whereas on older cars, the existing parts were more often straightened or replaced with used parts of the same kind and quality. The shop contacted insurance adjusters either by telephone or when adjusters came by to check jobs in progress or to obtain estimates for potential jobs.

Adjusters could not insist that repairs be made by a particular body shop, but they could recommend shops. Thus, keeping the insurance adjusters happy was an important aspect of the body shop's efforts. The body shop manager kept the adjusters up to date on what was happening and indicated when hidden damage was found. They could check this type of damage themselves and then reach agreement with the shop on a supplement to the original estimate. The shop tried to do its work quickly. Often, the insurance company had to pay for rental cars for inconvenienced owners. Thus, the quicker work was done, the more likely the insurance company would not have to pay extended rental charges. To make life easier for the adjusters when they came to visit, the body shop maintained a small office and stocked it with supplies and a telephone.

The body shop manager also spent considerable time with car owners. Typically, there were many occasions for such customer contact. The first occurred if an estimate of the damage was requested. An estimate was made by systematically examining the car in the same fashion as an insurance adjuster and by using the pertinent information in the crash book. Once the owner received the estimate, the body shop manager typically followed up by phone to answer any questions about the estimate or about the insurance process itself. Often in these follow-up calls the shop was informed that it or some other shop had been selected to do the work. However, sometimes it took two or three follow-up calls before a determination was reached about what to do with the car.

After the car was brought in, the body shop manager went over with the owner what was going to happen and what the probable time for repair would be. The body shop manager instructed owners to call the shop before the car was due in case there were any schedule problems, hidden damage, or the like. When the car was ready, the manager went over the car in detail with the owner, telling the owner what had been done and letting the owner check the quality. The shop delivered cars to owners in as close to showroom condition as possible. Every car was road-tested and thoroughly cleaned.

How Workers Were Paid

Workers were paid in different ways. As discussed previously, technicians were paid on the basis of a flat-rate hour. The best technicians generally were the fast ones. They were the best at diagnosing problems, they did not squander time, and they knew exactly how to do each job. Technicians could also receive *spiffs*, bonuses for working more than a set number of flat-rate hours. A bonus of 25¢ per hour was paid each week to technicians who had more than 35 hours time logged. A bonus of 50¢ per hour was paid to those with more than 40 hours, and a bonus of 75¢ per hour went to those with more than 45 flat-rate hours for the week.

The bodyworkers and painter were paid in a similar way. If they were able to beat the standards set for their work, they were able to make more money. If they could not meet the standard, they made less. Some standards naturally were looser than others. In the body shop, for example, sheet metal standards were generally looser than other types of work: thus, sheet metal jobs were the most prized. The parts countermen were paid a salary, although they received a bonus if sales reached some target level. Service advisors were paid commission; that is, they got a set percentage of the service business brought in. This was an incentive for them not only to do a good job so that people were satisfied, but also to suggest additional repairs that the owner might not have thought of. They also received spiffs for special sales (e.g., tires, antennas) that were documented on their job-order sheets.

The Duties of the Service Manager

The service manager was constantly on the move. In the early mornings and in the late afternoons the service manager's main interactions were with customers. The service manager helped the service advisors at the start of the day in order to handle particularly concerned or aggressive customers personally. This saved time for the service advisors and contributed to a routine flow of cars into the shop. In the late afternoon, the service manager spent time with customers who complained about work or registered dissatisfaction with the size of the bill. He listened to customers and then, typically, educated them as to the real problems with their cars and the reasons for the costs charged.

During the day, the service manager made the rounds of the repair floor, the body shop, and the parts department, checking the dispatching and the efficiency of technicians. He did diagnostic work and road tested completed cars. On heavy days, the service manager was particularly stressed. The tasks were the same, but heavier days were more demanding on everyone, especially if the shop was short-handed.

Promotions and Specials

The flow of work into both the service area and the body shop was not even from day to day or month to month. People drove their cars more during the summer months and thus incurred more repair problems during that time. Periodically, in an effort to smooth the flow of work it received, the dealership publicized some service specials. These were typically cut-rate prices on services such as oil changes and lubrications, cooling system winterizing, or total paint jobs. These specials were timed so that they did not interfere with normally busy periods.

PART TWO DISCUSSION

Ogle–Tucker Buick is in no way responsible for the following views and presentation. They remain solely the responsibility of the author.

The Flow of the Process and of Information

Figures C–3 and C–4 display process flow and information flow diagrams for a car in the course of its repair at Ogle–Tucker Buick. Similar diagrams could be drawn for the operation of the body shop or for the operation of the parts department. (Those diagrams are left as exercises at the end of this tour.) Note

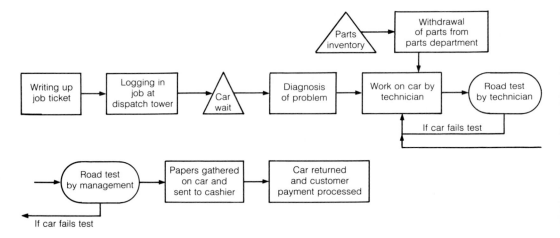

Note: The car may wait between any of the process steps shown and not simply between the log-in of the job and the diagnosis of any problem.

Figure C–3   Process Flow Diagram That Follows a Car in the Course of Its Repair at Ogle–Tucker Buick, Indianapolis, Indiana.

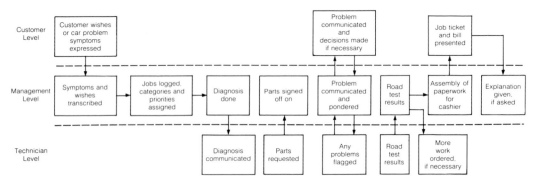

Figure C–4   Information Flow for a Car in the Course of Its Repair at Ogle–Tucker Buick.

that the customer's car may wait at almost any point in the process. The only wait shown in the diagram is between logging in the job and its diagnosis; it is but one of many such waits that could exist. What is most striking about the flow of the process and information at Ogle–Tucker versus a service factory such as Burger King is the extent to which there is communication between customer and management and between management and technicians. Because of the customization that is required in auto repair, the flow of information at Ogle–Tucker is much more frequent and less structured than that at Burger King.

Management is very much an intermediary between the customer and the technician. At the same time, management is also very much the source of control for the process.

One can see from this information flow diagram why peak days are so tough on management. There are no shortcuts in the information flows that must occur on busy days. The only source of help is to draw on others, such as calling on the service advisors to do road tests or to give diagnostic work to technicians themselves.

Of interest is the fact that Ogle–Tucker represents an example of a fixed position layout, where materials are brought to a particular location. Chapter 4 discusses this type of layout more and contrasts it with other types.

Demands of the Process on the Workforce

Most of the repair workers at Ogle–Tucker Buick are paid on an incentive basis. The technicians, bodyworkers, and painters all are paid according to the ratio of their performance relative to a time standard. The base wage against which that ratio is applied depends on their level of skill, which in turn depends on their willingness to learn and the experience they have accumulated. If a technician wants to get ahead and wants to be able to be promoted to more prestigious jobs in the shop, he or she must be willing to go to school. The increasing sophistication of cars demands this. The increasing sophistication of auto repair work is reflected in the fact that Ogle–Tucker's mechanics are not called mechanics but technicians. The use of that term is a reflection on how the workforce and management alike consider the demands of the job.

Working hard as a technician means more than simply beating the standard as set in the book. Working hard also means being able to juggle several different jobs at once so that little time is spent waiting for parts or otherwise removed from the actual repair job. In this regard, the technician is responsible for the pace of the work. That pace is not dictated by the dispatcher or by the flow of work along a line. The pace is dictated solely by the technician and his or her level of skill and effort.

The high level of individual responsibility for the technician job carries over to the considerable inventory of tools everyone is expected to carry. Indeed, the capital-to-labor ratio implied by this tool inventory nearly equals 1 (about $20,000 in tools and somewhat more than $20,000 in annual wages for an average technician) without counting any of the plant, equipment, or parts that are made available to the technicians by the dealership itself. As owners of their tools, technicians are almost like independent operators rather than employees of the company. They have considerable freedom to come and go on their own, for they are paid only for what they do and not for how many hours they spend in the shop per day. Nevertheless, being part of a dealership's service operation has its advantages. The work is steady, training is provided, and the technician does not have any of the headaches that would be involved in establishing and directing a business.

Ogle–Tucker represents a significant contrast to a Burger King. The jobs involved in auto repair are more individual and varying, and, despite some specialization within the workforce, there are fewer job niches. Although some teamwork is required, the element of teamwork at the dealership is much less than that which applies in a service factory.

Demands of the Process on Management

As the information flow diagram leads one to suspect, auto repair places some significant demands on management. Some of those demands deal with the control of the process, which essentially means control over the rather independent operators. The elements of control include dispatching, diagnosis, the periodic checking of efficiencies, and the quality checks made for both part ordering and road testing. Control over the workforce is a continual endeavor, and one that is fairly loosely defined.

In addition, management must deal with complaints from technicians about their pay or the work that has been assigned to them. Management must also keep track of the training possibilities for the technicians and who should be assigned to which school.

Monitoring technician training is just one aspect of keeping up to date. Other aspects are equipment and information. The use of computers is now standard in most auto dealerships, and computer facilities are steadily being improved. This permits more of the paperwork and information to be put on computer. Keeping up to date with the increasing sophistication of cars requires added investments in plant and equipment and in manuals and documentation. It is important for management to have the right kind of equipment and enough of it so that workers are not cramped for space or equipment and thus do not impede the capacity of the shop. An important aspect of the capital requirements of the dealership is the parts department. Dealers want to have enough of the right parts available so that they do not stock out too often, but they do not want to drown in inventory. The use of the computer helped to strike this balance, as did the discipline that was applied in keeping track of the parts on hand.

Another whole realm of management effort is devoted to dealing with customers. Managers were in repeated contact with customers—taking orders, handling complaints, and explaining the shop's actions. Senior managers, in particular, were safety valves for the service advisors so that when all the service advisors were occupied with customers, the flow of the process could continue unabated.

Management is also responsible for generating a steady flow of work into the shop. That means trying to perk up business in the off-peak times of the year through promotions and specials. Once a customer does come in, the service advisor informs the customer about other services that his or her car could really use.

QUESTIONS

1. How does the payment scheme for the shop's technicians compare with other incentive pay schemes discussed in previous tours?

2. How does the Ogle–Tucker Buick dispatcher compare with the foreman at Norcen Industries?

3. Why are the hard and soft copies of the repair order split the way they are?

4. What kinds of parts orders suggested by the parts department's computer program would likely be overridden by the parts manager?

5. Why was the parts manager so dedicated to updating each day the perpetual inventory records kept of each part?

6. In what ways was managing the body shop similar to managing the service shop? In what ways were they different?

7. In what ways is the Ogle-Tucker service manager's job like that of the Noblesville Burger King manager? In what ways is it different?

8. Develop process and information flow diagrams for the body shop.

9. Develop process and information flow diagrams for the parts department.

SITUATION FOR STUDY C-1

Big City Hospital Emergency Room

The emergency room of the Big City Hospital served about 100 patients a day. Some patients' arrivals were unannounced. Others, however, were announced through communication with ambulance drivers or physicians. The pattern of admission was routine except for patients who were obviously in medical distress.

Each patient entering the emergency room was met by one of two clerks at the front desk. The clerk was the first to assess whether the patient needed immediate medical attention. The clerk would announce "Patient here" over the loudspeaker and a triage nurse would take over, reviewing the paperwork that had been done, taking the patient's vital signs, and gathering additional information. The triage nurse then determined whether the patient had to be seen by a physician immediately or whether he or she could wait. If a patient arrived by ambulance, the communication

from the ambulance would indicate an estimated time of arrival and some word of the patient's condition. If the patient could give some preliminary information on arrival to the clerk, that would be done; if not, the patient was wheeled directly into the emergency room treatment area.

There were several treatment areas to the emergency room. These included the acute trauma room; a large open area with seven bed slots with curtains to close off each of the slots; four other, separate holding slots; an ear, nose and throat (ENT) room; an OB/GYN room; a cast room; and a family room. The acute trauma room was kept always set up in anticipation of a patient with a severe problem. Up to 20 people could be mobilized to help stabilize a patient in acute trauma.

The open area with the seven bed slots was used for general admission patients. If the patient's condition warranted continual observation, he or she was placed near the nursing station. Patients not needing constant surveillance were placed at more of a distance. The ENT, the OB/GYN, and the cast rooms were used for isolating patients with those conditions. The family room was used either for psychiatric patients or for the families of patients who were critically ill.

Once patients were seen by the triage nurse and then by the resident nurse, they were evaluated by a surgical or medical intern, and, if necessary, by an attending resident or physician. Upon examination, the patients were either treated and discharged or admitted to the main part of the hospital. The time goal for admitting, treating, and discharging a patient was four hours. Nurses handled any transfers to other areas of the hospital.

Each patient generated substantial amounts of paperwork: personal medical history, notes from physicians and nurses, diagnoses, orders and instructions, laboratory tests performed, and any supplies used. This paperwork was necessary for recording instructions to be used by other hospital personnel, or by departments for billing and for the creation of a permanent medical record. Given these various purposes, the record forms included space for personal data, the nature of the complaint, the physician's name, the type of insurance, notes from the physician, orders from the physician, diagnosis from the physician, and instructions for the discharge. Separate records were kept for nursing, the physicians, and insurance. Lab work was tracked using individual tickets that were kept grouped with the emergency room reports. After a specific time, these reports were entered in the hospital computer for storage.

1. Diagram the process flow.
2. Diagram the information flow.
3. How would you determine how the emergency room ought to be staffed with clerks, nurses, and physicians?

MASS SERVICE
Thalhimers—
Cloverleaf Mall Store
Richmond, Virginia

The Cloverleaf Mall store of Thalhimers was one of 25 that the company operated in Virginia, North Carolina, South Carolina, and Tennessee. Thalhimers was a general department store chain, begun in Richmond in 1842, and the fifth generation of the Thalhimer family was in the senior management of the corporation. Through the years, Thalhimers grew both by acquiring stores and by building new ones. In 1978, the firm merged with the Carter–Hawley–Hale group of stores, headquartered in California. By dollar volume, the firm's largest store was at Cloverleaf Mall, located in one of the fastest-growing areas in the Richmond market, and situated in one of the 15 fastest-growing counties in America. The store was built in 1972 and had been remodeled twice—extensively in 1978, when a second floor was added to the initial one-floor layout. It now occupied 130,000 square feet. As a general department store, Thalhimers carried a broad selection of merchandise for women, men, children, and the home.

PART ONE SERVICE PROCESS DESCRIPTION

Layout

The ambiance and design of the store were recognized as an important feature in attracting and appealing to customers and generating sales. A good layout accomplishes several things. It provides entertainment and excitement for the shopping experience. The customer is led in a logical pattern from one area to another. A good layout allows a store to present fashion merchandise in an accessible manner with proper adjacencies, to change the fashion statements each season, and to present the merchandise assortment in a meaningful manner and thereby maximize each area's sales potential.

Traditionally, department stores were designed with long central aisles that effectively divided the store into large quadrants of merchandise of a particular category. Through the years, the old-fashioned layout was supplanted by more architecturally pleasing designs. The Cloverleaf Store, for example, did not have the straight aisles. It was an open store with aisles that led the customer from one fashion world to another, using soft wall treatments to designate particular areas or shops. The adjacencies of the areas and the merchandise presentations created the feeling that the customer was shopping in an area with a complete assortment of women's, men's, children's, or home merchandise. It incorporated shops—small, distinctly identified, sometimes partially enclosed areas that dramatized particularly important fashion statements. The Cloverleaf layout did not follow the "world concept." (In that concept of department store design, the consumer enters a well-defined arena or "world" of a particular category of merchandise—such as a "children's world," a "juniors' world," or a "men's

NOTE: This tour describes operations at Thalhimers in the summer of 1988. Since that time, Thalhimers was purchased by the May Department Stores.

The Cosmetics Counter. *(Courtesy of Thalhimers—Cloverleaf Mall Store)*

world." A world concept surrounds the customer with one category of merchandise and catches the customer's eye with dramatic wall treatments, color schemes, and fixtures.)

When Thalhimers designed a new store, space requests would be submitted by the Merchants as well as the Stores Division. For example, a request would be submitted for women's accessories for a certain square footage, based on a history of sales from other stores. Similar requests would be submitted for men's furnishings, the home division, and other areas, each broken down to the level of detail of individual departments within each area. Management then examined the current sales trends for the various segments of the business and the sales per square foot that were generated in each area in the current stores. Decisions were then made concerning space allocation for the new store. Together with the Thalhimers' architects, management then decided on the character of the store's environment; a store in Charleston, South Carolina, would probably be different aesthetically from one in Fayetteville, North Carolina. At this point, decisions were also made about which departments should be adjacent to one another and what the proximity should be to the various store entrances. The different entrances generated different levels of traffic and it was important to keep that in mind in developing the plan for the store. Plans and space allocations were

Signature Sportwear with the Liz Claiborne Shop in the Background. *(Courtesy of Thalhimers—Cloverleaf Mall Store)*

changed from one store to the next, depending on the performance expectations of the various areas of the business.

There were substantial differences in the sales per square foot generated by the different departments. For example, fragrances enjoyed an annual sales volume per square foot that was 12 times the store's average. Men's ties produced sales per square foot of 7 times the store's average. Electronic sales were well above the average also. On the other hand, some areas, such as infants' clothing or men's robes, generated sales that were substantially lower than the storewide average. Nevertheless, all elements of the store were important to the image of a department store with broad assortments of merchandise.

A tour of the store can help dramatize the importance of the layout. On the first floor, the Cloverleaf store had four entrances. The entrance with the most traffic was the north or mall entrance. The cosmetics department was located there. The cosmetics counters produced high dollar volumes per square foot. It was an area that created excitement and generated impulse purchasing. To capture the attention of the customer entering the store, immediately adjacent and to either side of the cosmetics counters were fashion shops featuring well-known designer sportswear (Liz Claiborne, Anne Klein II, Chaus, and Pendleton). These designer fashion shops were appropriate complements to the excitement generated at the cosmetics counters.

As demonstrated by both the cosmetics counters and the designer sports-wear shop, the interior design of the store was dramatic, creative, and yet very pleasing to the eye. One could look at the presentations of the merchandise and sense a statement of fashion. The distinctiveness of these statements of taste and fashion were important aspects of the sales performance of the store.

Moving west from the cosmetics counters and the designer sportswear shop, a customer would find both fashion and fine jewelry, and on the right, a large selection of moderately priced and career sportswear, blouses, sweaters, and active sportswear. In general, designer fashions and the more expensive labels were located closer to the front of the store. As one continued moving west toward the west entrance (the third most important entrance) (see Figure D–1), one could see the bodywear and accessories departments on the inside of the aisle and women's coats, dresses, and petites' clothes on the other side of the aisle. Each of these areas maintained its own fashion statements.

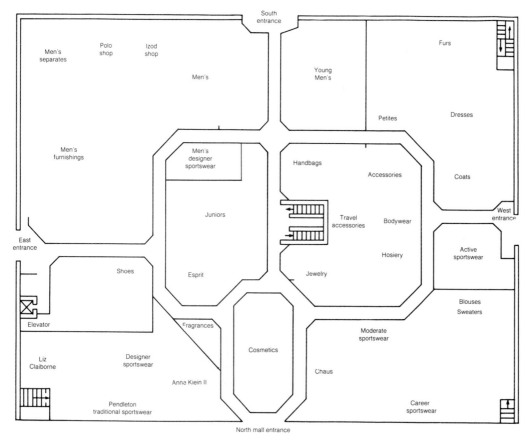

A. First floor layout.

Figure D–1   Thalhimers—Cloverleaf Mall Store.

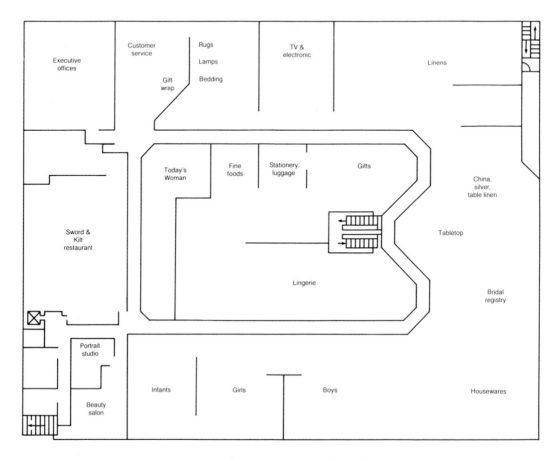

Figure D–1   Thalhimers—Cloverleaf Mall Store (*Continued*).

The men's area was located between the south and the east entrances. The south entrance was the second most important entrance, and the east entrance was the least trafficked entrance. As in the other areas on the first floor, the fashion statements were presented both on the aisle and with important wall treatments in the rear of the department, acting to draw the consumer's eye into that area of the store. The menswear area had its own brand-name shops, including Izod and Polo.

Several areas in the store served as "swing" areas. Some, for example, offered sweaters for the fall and winter seasons and bathing suits for the spring and summer seasons. Other areas of the store were assigned even more temporary space, such as seasonal merchandise for Christmas. These trends and seasonal changes meant that the layout changed constantly.

The Juniors Area. *(Courtesy of Thalhimers—Cloverleaf Mall Store)*

The South Entrance. *(Courtesy of Thalhimers—Cloverleaf Mall Store)*

The store's second floor was as fashion-conscious as the first. On entering the second floor the customer viewed a broad assortment of fine china, silver, and glass stemware from around the world in the tabletop area. To the right of this area was the gourmet housewares area, which dramatically presented a broad selection of imported and domestic merchandise. Other areas on the

The Polo Shop for Men. *(Courtesy of Thalhimers—Cloverleaf Mall Store)*

second floor were the children's departments, gourmet foods, women's lingerie, large-size women's clothes, the restaurant, television and electronics, and the linen and bedding shops.

Management and the Workforce

The organization chart for the Cloverleaf store is displayed in Figure D–2. Reporting to the store manager were the assistant managers, the operations manager, and the personnel manager. The store manager also supervised the home and children's areas. Reporting to the assistant manager were the sales managers for the other sales areas within the store. Reporting to the operations manager were the lease departments, the restaurant manager, the customer service supervisor, and the supervisors for housekeeping and merchandise handling. Each selling center (made up of multiple complementary departments) of the store was managed by a sales manager, and selling center sales associates reported directly to their sales manager. Also reporting to the sales manager could be an assistant sales manager (three intern-interim training positions for sales associates working their way up through the ranks).

Ensuring customer satisfaction was the primary focus of all associates. Each level of management periodically attended training seminars devoted to teaching, reinforcing, and perpetuating the culture of customer satisfaction of the

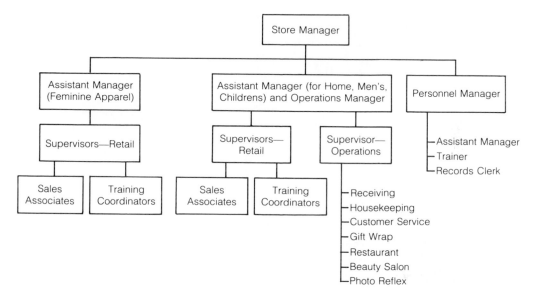

Figure D–2 Organization Chart for the Cloverleaf Mall Store of Thalhimers.

Cloverleaf store. Monitoring and evaluating all elements of customer satisfaction for all associates was an ongoing function of management. Customer service was an element on which each employee was annually reviewed.

There were 250 employees in the Cloverleaf store, roughly half of whom worked full time and half part time. The store was open from 10:00 in the morning until 9:30 in the evening, Monday through Saturday, and from 12:30 to 5:30 on Sundays. With the store open so many hours during the week, employing part-time personnel was essential to providing maximum staffing. Full-time people were required to work two nights a week and to work every other Sunday. The part-time people worked a fixed schedule: mornings, evenings, and weekends.

During the Christmas season, additional temporary employees were hired (180 for the 1988 Christmas season). This temporary workforce was hired in late September and early October, trained at the end of October, and began work on the floor in early November. This hiring and training process ensured that every temporary employee had sufficient experience on the floor before Thanksgiving, the beginning of the strongest part of the Christmas buying season.

In addition to the store's part-time employees, there was an additional group of sales associates. The group was known as "flyers," and they formed the "flying squad." These substitute employees on the flying squad were called on short notice to work a particular day or period of time. Depending on their individual schedules, they would or would not be available to work. They were all fully trained to fill in, in various departments throughout the store.

The China and Crystal Area. *(Courtesy of Thalhimers—Cloverleaf Mall Store)*

The store's employees were paid in different ways, although the same employee benefit package applied to all. Support personnel were paid between $3.35 and $7.00 an hour, based on experience and background. Sales associates, on the other hand, were paid a commission based on their individual sales. The commission rate varied from one department to another. The typical commission was 6.5 percent for most areas of the store, but it could reach 8.5 percent for accessories and 10 percent for shoes and the bridal gift areas. Each employee was paid a base hourly rate depending on experience and their ability to generate sales, which was applied against the commission earned. In other words, each associate was paid a commission on the merchandise they sold, which constituted their total earnings. The commission arrangement was new for the store except for shoes and electronics. It showed great promise for generating higher sales for the stores, encouraging individual effort, and using product knowledge and individual selling expertise.

Both hiring and training were extremely important activities. The right sales associate for a particular department was critical to that department's sales performance. Different personalities were required for different departments. For example, cosmetics required sales associates who were aggressive and enthusiastic as well as highly knowledgeable about the products. China and silver, on the other hand, required sales associates of good taste and great patience, capable of serving the bride and the mother of the bride. Younger sales

The Market Place Shop. (*Courtesy of Thalhimers—Cloverleaf Mall Store*)

associates could interact more effectively with teenagers in the juniors' department. If certain clothes were selling well, it was advantageous to have sales associates who could relate to the merchandise and enjoy wearing that style of fashion.

For these reasons, the hiring decision was important and took on elements of theatrical casting. There were three required visits before a new employee could be hired, after which the employee was given 24 hours of training off the floor, 2 weeks of training on the floor, and then a 90-day period of evaluation. In addition, training sessions for sales associates (meetings and videotape viewings) were held weekly. Training was important not only for acquiring knowledge about the merchandise and the operation of the department, but also for learning selling skills. Thalhimers engaged in several innovative programs to train its sales associates. Everyone played the Selling Game, a Monopoly-like game specifically developed to teach selling skills. Through playing the game and viewing accompanying videotapes, sales associates learned the best ways to approach the customer, to interpret verbal and nonverbal buying signals, to present the merchandise, and to close the sale, among a host of other things. Sales associates also attended product seminars that Thalhimers hosted from time to time. At these seminars, the store's vendors displayed the merchandise Thalhimers had ordered for the next season and provided the sales associates with the latest product knowledge.

The sales managers were essential to successful operation of the store. Each year for a week they attended a sales leadership development seminar, focusing on the latest in store operations and in motivation and communication techniques. The 15 sales managers were responsible for a number of important activities, including the following:

1. Scheduling the sales associates in the department, both full- and part-time, and determining when to use the flying squad.
2. Overseeing the training of sales associates.
3. Monitoring all sales transactions.
4. Receiving inventory, checking it against the paperwork, and reconciling any errors in its shipping or paperwork (explained later).
5. Adjusting prices and preparing the department for sales and promotions.
6. The store's management was very supportive of sales manager initiatives to make the Thalhimers shopping experience as enjoyable as possible. Fashion shows, cosmetics make-overs, special senior citizen promotions, focus group meetings with customers, and clientele books with customer preferences noted, among other things, were routinely used to enhance Thalhimers' already enviable reputation in the community as the fun place to shop. Figure D–3 displays two courtesy notes that Thalhimers' sales associates sent customers.

Some of the sales managers began their careers as sales associates. Others were management trainees, employed out of college, who served in the store for two years before entering the merchandising arm of Thalhimers as assistant buyers.

The Transaction—and Supporting It

At the heart of the store's operations was the sales transaction itself and the information it generated. Scattered throughout the store in the various departments were point-of-sale devices or registers. These registers were all tied into the store's computer, and via that computer, they were tied to the computer at Thalhimers in Richmond and the computers of Carter–Hawley–Hale in California. All transactions, once they were rung on the register, were immediately sent to the computers in California and in the Richmond headquarters. Each transaction consisted of the following items of information: the type of payment to be made (cash or charge), the personnel identification number for the sales associate (the "pin number"), the department's number, the class of merchandise being sold, the stockkeeping unit number for the item (the "SKU number"), and the price of the item (see Figure D–4). Once these bits of information were entered into the register, the sale could be completed, the drawer opened, and change returned to the customer if necessary. With these registers, immediate credit information was available. Credit card numbers could be traced immediately and information relayed to the register on whether to complete the transaction. With

Figure D–3 Courtesy Notes Sent to Customers by Sales Associates.

the registers tied in to the company's computers, up-to-the-minute sales reports, or return reports, by department, could be generated at any time.

Supporting the store's transactions was a staff in the customer service area. The customer service department was responsible for opening up each register each day (including supplying it with $75 reserve change). Sales associates were required to log into the register upon arrival and to log out of the register when they had finished working for the day. At the end of the day, the customer service staff was responsible for accounting for all cash and charges and for checking any discrepancies. The money and the charge slips were taken to the registers by a sales associate and returned to the credit office in the evening by a sales associate. They were verified by the sales managers before being turned in to the customer service office.

The customer service department also ran the customer service window, through which it received payments, adjusted bills, sold tickets to various theater

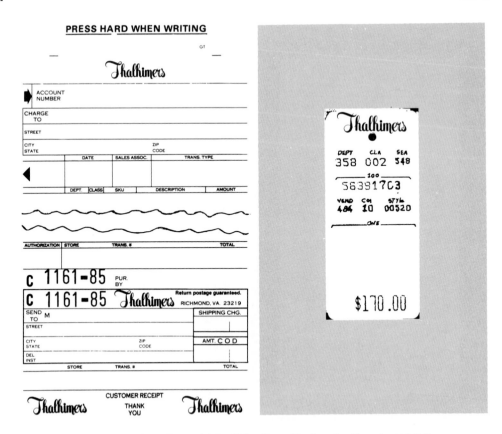

Figure D-4   A Price Tag and Sales Ticket Form Used at the Cloverleaf Mall Store of Thalhimers.

events, provided extra coins or cash to registers throughout the store, handled some customer satisfaction issues, and cashed checks. Customer service was a vital center for the store's transactions.

Managing and Controlling the Inventory

Providing the merchandise for the Cloverleaf store was the responsibility of Thalhimers' merchandising staff located at the Richmond headquarters. The buyers determined how much merchandise was to be purchased, when the merchandise was to be delivered, and for what price the merchandise would sell. Many of the items in Thalhimers were fashion-sensitive, with lead times between ordering and receiving of 6 to 12 months. Thus, a buyer often had to make decisions months in advance on what would sell during a particular season. If the buyer bought the wrong merchandise or ordered too much, the store's sales and profits suffered. If the buyer erred on the other side and did not order enough merchandise, the store lost potential revenue. The buying decision was thus a very important one, but one that was essentially outside the control of a branch store such as Cloverleaf. Of course, the store could provide feedback to the buyers on what merchandise was selling well, the type of customers who seemed to be buying it, and how it could be effectively presented, but the merchandising decision rested with those at the corporate headquarters.

Thalhimers' new computer system, dubbed IMIS (Integrated Merchandise Information System), was a key resource that helped relieve the store of its past labor-intensive burden of recordkeeping. IMIS kept up-to-the-minute track of every item in stock at all of the company's stores, including such information as the quantity on hand or on order, sales, returns, price changes, and transfers to other stores or returns to the vendor.

Even automatic reordering of merchandise was possible, with the system to maintain inventories within a minimum-to-maximum range that was prearranged by the buyer and the store manager.

Receiving

All items received at the store were sent from Thalhimers' Distribution Center (DC). At the DC, items were checked, sorted, priced, and marked. Deliveries to the Cloverleaf store were made between 4 and 6 A.M. The receiving crew started work at 6 A.M. and delivered all of the merchandise that was received that morning to the floor by 9 A.M. Several checks were made of the merchandise received to ensure that the merchandise received and accounted for was what was expected and had, in fact, arrived. Each truck was physically sealed and the number on the metal seal had to match the manifest that accompanied the shipment (see Figure D–5). After the seal was broken, the crew grouped the boxes that were shipped together and checked their numbers against the manifest. Hanging garments in canvas rollers, termed "hampers," were similarly checked. Each group of boxes or "hampers" was accompanied by a movement tag (Figure D–6). The movement tag indicated the store department to receive the merchandise, the purchase order number, the hamper number, and the seal number (which indicated the truck shipment). The movement tags came in triplicate; the white tags stayed with the hamper or box, yellow tags were kept by the receiving store, and pink tags were kept by the service building.

After the truck was unloaded, the merchandise was moved onto the selling floor. The merchandise handling group knew exactly where each department received its merchandise, usually near its register. The merchandise moved out to the floor was accompanied by the white movement tag and the paperwork on the purchase, typically the purchase order (see Figures D–7 and D–8 for examples of this paperwork).

Every morning, the sales manager and the sales associates in each department checked the merchandise delivered against the accompanying paperwork to ensure that all of the items they expected to receive were, in fact, received. Each department checked the seals on their hampers and boxes, circled the

THALHIMERS RELAY TRANSFER MANIFEST 292101

DATE			TIME OUT		TIME IN		
DRIVER							SEAL No.
FROM			TO				TRUCK No.
DISPATCHER					RES. CLERK		

NO.	DEPT.	RECEIVING NO. OR ROSTN. NO.	HAMPER NO.	SEAL NO.	NO. OF CARTONS	NO. OF UNITS	Chk.
1							
2							
3							
4							
5							
6							
7							
8							
9							

Figure D–5 A Shipment Manifest Used in Transporting Merchandise at the Cloverleaf Mall Store of Thalhimers.

counts to indicate agreement, stamped the paperwork "received," and then filed that paperwork appropriately. The stock was then displayed in the appropriate place in the department.

The records of the inventory received were kept in a journal room. The journal room was also next to the office of the inventory controller and the mailboxes for all the supervisory personnel. It was the nerve center for processing the merchandise paperwork for inventory.

Variations on the Standard Receipt of Material

Although most of the merchandise received at the store followed the standard procedure, there were a number of errors and changes that had to be recorded. These errors and changes were generally kept on the computer, although some hard-copy "books" were kept as well.

1. *Interstore transfers.* Often items of merchandise were transferred from one store to another. When this occurred, the stores involved entered the information on the store's computer and the appropriate records were updated (see Figure D–9).

DEPT.	Receiving Apron No.	RTW Pieces	SPECIAL INSTRUCTIONS

MOVEMENT LABEL

SERV. BLDG.

RICHMOND, VA.

| | | | This   of   Cartons
is   -Pieces |

Wheeler Container **NO.**

Sent by	Location	Date

Figure D–6 A Movement Tag That Accompanies Merchandise Between the Service Center and the Store.

2. *Errors in shipment.* If there were errors in a shipment received by the store (what was received did not match the paperwork), these errors were noted.

3. *Report of changes in retail price.* This computer record tracked changes that had occurred to the retail price, such as missed markdowns or markups and month-end special sale liquidation of inventory.

4. *Merchandise transfer.* If merchandise had been incorrectly charged to the store or had been incorrectly charged to another department, these errors were corrected on the computer records.

Through the use of computer records for changes and errors, the store kept excellent track of exactly what inventory it had and for what it should be credited. The sales managers and the inventory controller also kept track of price changes. Figure D–10 offers an example of a price change document.

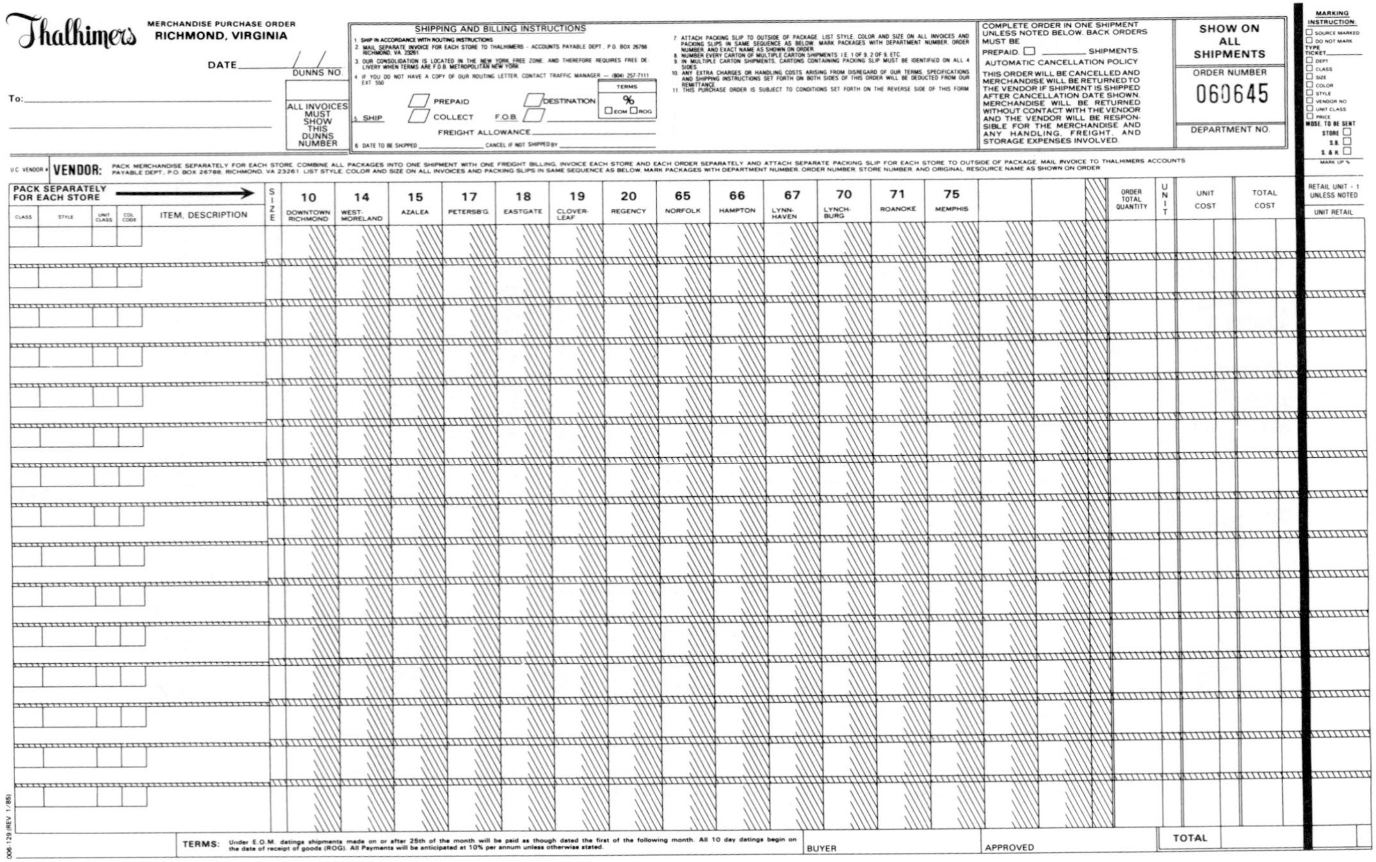

Figure D-7 A Purchase Order Sheet That Is Filled Out by a Buyer and That Accompanies Merchandise to the Cloverleaf Mall Store. Note that Cloverleaf is Store 19.

```
  11      99999      11      99999    •••••• MARKING AND TRANSFER ••••••      PRINTED 12/17/85  TIME 06:22    PAGE    1
 111     99  99     111     99  99
  11     99  99      11     99  99    MRKNG SEC/LOC _____ MRKNG LINE _____ MRKER ID ___ TKT PRT T3C®      OP ID TP00021
  11      99999      11      99999    RCV 12/16/85                   DOC : N         DOC TYPE P
  11         99      11         99
1111         99    1111         99    VENDOR   878 . JOSIAH WEDGWOOD AND CO

DEPT   281 # OF STYLES    2  SKUS       2
RCVNG   281530              UNITS       2

PO  20155396

  MFG-STYLE STYLE CD COLOR     SIZE   RCVD   REA LINE   SSKU    DESCRIPTION      RTV  CLASS   RETAIL UM    EXT-RTL
         6 00006 00                     1    ___ 0601 56147314 OCEANSIDESANDWICHTRA   0     5    25.00 EA    25.00
         8 00008 00                     1    ___ 0801 55948658 OCEANSIDETANKARD       0     5    17.50 EA    17.50
```

Figure D–8 A Computer-Generated Marking and Transfer Sheet that Performs the Same Function as the Purchase Order Sheet. It, or the purchase order sheet, accompanies goods to the store. It is generated by a buyer and is store-specific. Note the 19 in the upper left corner.

Shipping Items out of the Store

It was Thalhimers' policy not to ship items between stores or back to the service building unless the dollar value of the transfer justified the expense. In general, unless a shipment was worth $1000 or more, no transfers were made. One day a month was allocated to transferring merchandise to other stores to balance inventories. There were some exceptions to this policy; vendor returns, damaged goods, alterations, and monograms could be returned to the service center or moved between stores on a daily basis. Shipping of this merchandise involved the same care and controls that were shown for the receipt of the merchandise.

Evaluating the Store's Performance

The store was evaluated as a profit center. The profit plan for the store involved the determination of sales for each department and a calculation of the proposed selling cost. (Selling cost was calculated as the compensation paid divided by the sales in the department for the time period under consideration.) The sales for each department were forecast by the merchandising arm of the company. The merchandisers were responsible for analyzing the sales trend for the store as a whole and any trends for individual areas within the store. A sales plan was developed for each department of the store and stock levels were planned to vary seasonally. Different "thrust" areas were also singled out for unusual attention; separate plans were developed for increased inventory, increased promotional activity, and additional personnel to achieve a substantially larger-than-normal increase in volume. There were daily, weekly, and monthly reports that monitored the progress of these departments and any variances from the projected sales and profit plan.

The store carefully monitored the *penetration* of particular departments. Penetration of a specific area was calculated by dividing the sales of the area by the total sales of the store. If this fraction for a particular area at Cloverleaf differed significantly from those of other Thalhimers stores, the store manager

DIV: THALHIMERS   I N T E R - S T O R E   T R A N S F E R   S Y S T E M   PAGE: 1 OF: 2
ON-LINE REPORT   ID: HNAS0600   TRANSFER DOCUMENT   REPORT DATE: 09/23/88
RUN DATE: 09/23/88

STORE: 22

DEPT: 7521   TRANSFER NO: 10362192   X-REF:
REASON: 26 CENTRL STK VERSION: SEND-BY DATE: 09/23/88
MSG:

TO STR	
11	99999
111	99 99
11	99999
11	99
1111	99

CUST: PHONE: EMP:

DESCRIPTION:	CLASS:	VNDR:	STYLE:	***COLOR*** NUM:	DSCRPTN:	**SIZE* NUM:	DESC	SSKU/UPC NUM:	MFG/STYLE:	RETAIL:	RQST QTY:	SENT QTY:	RCVD QTY:
LIBERTY 5 PC.PL	30	82	1207	0		0		59901524	99999	105.00	1	1	0
STERL.COVE CUP	50	142	5702	0		0		72479750	5 99 99	24.50	1	1	1
STERL.COVE SAUC	50	142	5703	0		0		72479769	5 99 99	12.00	1	1	1
STERL.COVE SALA	50	142	5704	0		0		72479777	5 99999	17.00	1	1	1
STERL.COVE BREA	50	142	5705	0		0		72479785	5 99	12.50	1	1	1
STANFORD CT.20	50	709	1708	0 0		0		59320432		340.00	2	2	2
STANFORD CT.OVA	50	709	1711	0		0		59278142		65.00	1	1	1
STANFORD COURT	50	709	1712	0		0		59287591	1	105.00	1	1	1
ROTHSCHILD 20 P	50	709	3308	0		0		59320351		278.00	1	1	1
CARLYLE 5 PC.PL	60	134	1007	0		0		70968029		198.00	12	12	12
CARLYLE 20 PC.S	60	134	1008	0		0		59910868		792.00	2	2	2
CARLYLE COMPLET	60	134	1009	0		0		70968037		520.00	1	1	1
CARNATION GRAVY	60	134	1119	0		0		71781364		48.00	1	1	1
SHERBROOKE DINN	60	134	1301	0		0		59623370	1	34.00	4	4	4
SHERBROOKE CUP	60	134	1302	0		0		59282026	1	24.00	4	4	4
SHERBROOKE SAUC	60	134	1303	0		0		59282093	1	18.00	4	4	4
SHERBROOKE OPEN	60	134	1311	0		0		59505874		78.40	1	1	1
SHERBROOKE COVE	60	134	1317	0		0		72471342		160.00	1	1	1

Figure D–9 A Transfer Document.

```
BATCH REPORT HMMS5411-01              P R I C E   C H A N G E
   DIVISION: BOYLE 27-TABLE TOP
DEPT    PC NUMBER    XREF NUMBER    XREF TYPE    REASON
7521    5556503                                    12
COUNTED BY --------J.Kotes--------DATE-08/34/88
MESSAGE: NORITAKE PRICE INCREASE - PATTERN EDGEWATER

____DESCRIPTION_____  CLASS FRM TO   _____VENDOR_____  STYLE __
                        SEA SEA         NAME      NUM   NUM  NU

5PC.PLSETTING           50          NORITAKE CO I  142  6207

DINNER (((              50          NORITAKE CO I  142  6201

CUP (((                 50          NORITAKE CO I  142  6202

SAUCER (                50          NORITAKE CO I  142  6203

SALAD ( (               50          NORITAKE CO I  142  6204

B&B ((                  50          NORITAKE CO I  142  6205

14IN PLATTER            50          NORITAKE CO I  142  6212

SUGAR                   50          NORITAKE CO I  142  6213

CREAMER                 50          NORITAKE CO I  142  6214

20 PC.SET               50          NORITAKE CO I  142  6208

5PC.COMPLETER           50          NORITAKE CO I  142  6209
```

```
W O R K S H E E T            DATE 08/23/88 PAGE    1 OF  1
                                STORE:  19
PC TYPE     EFFECTIVE DATE    CANCEL DATE    REPRINT
              08/30/88                          N

    MARKED/APPROVED BY_____DATE __/__/__

__COLOR____   SIZE UOM   OLD        NEW  C __QUANTITY___

M  DESCRPTN   DESC       RETAIL     RETAIL R SEAS TKT MRKD LN IT
              EA         77.50      81.50  --- ---- _0_ 01
              EA         24.50      25.50  --- ---- _3_ 02
              EA         23.50      24.50  --- ---- _3_ 03
              EA         11.50      12.00  --- ---- _1_ 04
              EA         16.00      17.00  --- ---- _2_ 05
              EA         12.00      12.50  --- ---- _2_ 06
              EA         95.00     100.00  --- ---- _0_ 07
              EA         54.00      55.00  --- ---- _(_ 08
              EA         35.50      37.00  --- ---- _)_ 09
              EA        310.00     326.00  --- ---- _/_ 10
              EA        249.50     257.00  --- ---- _(_ 11

                     QUANTITY TOTALS:    ____ _11_
```

Figure D–10   A Price Change Worksheet

could then investigate reasons for that difference. In this manner, the store manager could move more aggressively to direct business opportunities.

The Cloverleaf store manager spent a great deal of time on the selling floor, observing the operation and communicating personally with the employees. His or her priorities for ensuring the store's profitability were clear: ensuring complete customer satisfaction in all areas of the store, monitoring sales, selecting the proper personnel and developing those personnel, presenting the merchandise in an appealing way to attract customers, and finally, monitoring expenses.

PART TWO DISCUSSION

Thalhimers is in no way responsible for the following views or presentation. They remain solely the responsibility of the author.

The Flow of the Process and of Information

During the course of a day, the sales associates at Thalhimers do many things. The two chief processes in which they are involved are stocking, which occurs in the morning, and the sales transactions themselves, which occur all day long. Figure D–11 diagrams both of those key processes. For the most part, these processes are fairly well-structured. There is interaction between customer and sales associate during the transaction, particularly in the presentation of the merchandise and the closing of the sale, but for the most part the process is a fairly standard one, well-known to both parties. Similarly, the stocking process is a routine occurrence, day in and day out.

Information flows are also fairly standardized, although many different kinds of information can be passed down from management to the sales associate and up from the sales associate to management. Figure D–12 indicates some of the key information flows that go both down and up in the organization. For the most part, the information flowing downward relates to merchandising shifts, whereas the information flowing upward deals with irregularities in the routine of the inventory and sales transactions.

Demands of the Process on the Workforce

Because Thalhimers is open so many hours, one key demand on the workforce relates to the scheduling of everybody's work hours. Evening and weekend work are sometimes required.

Another key demand relates to coping with the change that goes on around the employees all the time. Layouts are changing, inventory stock levels are changing, the character of the inventory is changing, and the workforce must cope with all of these changes. To help them cope with these changes, there is considerable training. Workers are not only trained initially, but spend appreciable amounts of time week in and week out in training, both to improve their skills and to educate them about the merchandising changes in the store.

A. Material Receipt

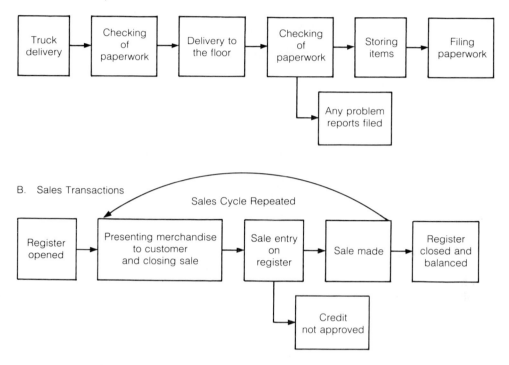

B. Sales Transactions

Figure **D–11**   Rough Process Flows for Material Receipt and for Sales Transactions at the Cloverleaf Mall Store of Thalhimers.

A. Information flowing down from management
Merchandising shifts
 • sales and promotions
 • changes to merchandise presentations
 • layout and space allocation changes
B. Information flowing up from the sales associates and support staff
Irregularities
 • in transactions
 • in inventory status
 • in paperwork
 • in cash balances
 • other errors
Inventory counts

Figure **D–12**   Examples of Information Flows at the Cloverleaf Mall Store of Thalhimers.

Another demand on the workforce is accuracy, both with respect to the transactions made and the inventory overseen. Such accuracy is crucial to the success of the store, and it is a routine to which they must apply themselves all the time.

Demands of the Process on Management

Like the sales associates and other employees, management must also adhere to and foster the importance of controls on transactions and inventory. The customer service department and the journal room are the store's nerve centers for control, and they must be supported.

Personnel functions are also extremely important, as indicated by the personnel department's status within the organization chart. Hiring (perhaps better termed "casting"), training, and advancement all consume a lot of management time and care. Sales associates' skills are critical to the sales volume that the store generates, and thus hiring and training are key functions of management.

The other key elements to sales increases are the layout itself and the presentation of merchandise. Good layout and good merchandise presentation depend not only on the analysis of sales per square foot figures, but also on intuition and feel for the psychology of the sales situation. The value of powerful fashion statements throughout the store is a clear indication of the art involved in a store's design and operation.

Because fashion can be so fickle and people's tastes can change so abruptly, it is important for the store to monitor sales and costs on a continual basis. Thus, not only are there controls on the transaction and inventory levels themselves, but also controls on sales and selling costs. Store management has to be ready to examine these costs and use them to make decisions about staffing levels and the responsibilities of sales associates and support personnel within the store.

QUESTIONS

1. Visit a department store near you. In what ways is its layout similar to that of Thalhimers? In what ways is it different?

2. One might suppose that theoretically, at least, departments ought to be given space in such proportions that the sales per square foot would be roughly the same anywhere in the store. Why is that point of view impractical?

3. Express some of the fashion statements you have observed at department stores. How do the store's layout, fixtures, and decor contribute to those statements?

4. What kinds of questions would you ask of a prospective employee to work in the Liz Claiborne shop? What characteristics would you look for? How would those characteristics and questions differ for someone working in the jewelry department?

5. What is the argument for paying sales associates on a commission basis? What is the argument for paying them on an hourly basis?

6. Outline the various controls that exist on the store's inventory. Why are there so many controls?

SITUATION FOR STUDY D–1

Adams Convenience Store

The Adams Convenience Store, located on a major state artery, was open from 6 A.M. until midnight every day and sold grocery items, fast food, and gasoline. Gasoline, dispensed through self-service pumps, represented about 50 percent of total sales. Customers paid first and pumped afterward. All of the gasoline pumps were multiproduct dispensers that handled both leaded and unleaded gasoline.

The store was laid out as in Figure D–13. Seventy percent of the people who entered the store to do something other than to pay for gasoline bought some sort of beverage. The fast food available at the rear of the store was the highest-margin item for sale; gasoline was the lowest-margin item. The Adams Convenience Store offered hot dogs, sandwiches, pastries, coffee, and other food items. There were two peaks for food item demand: breakfast and the 4 P.M. to 6 P.M. after-work period. Sales slowed in mid-morning, early afternoon, and late at night.

The store operated two shifts. The store manager was there to open the store in the morning and stayed during the first shift; the store's assistant manager handled the second shift. During the busiest period of each shift, there were a total of four working in the store: two to handle the fast-food area and two to tend the registers. In addition to the manager and the assistant manager, there were two full-time workers and the remaining were part-time employees. Pay averaged just above the minimum wage, and turnover rates often ran as high as 300 percent a year.

The manager and the assistant manager trained the others and determined which items met the company's definition for being short in supply and needed to be reordered. Orders were placed to a central Adams warehouse. The managers were also responsible for controls on cash and inventory so that everything was accounted for.

1. Why is the layout designed as it is? Give a rationale and explain what you think the typical traffic flow would be.

2. Why would the Adams Convenience Store invest in multiproduct gasoline pumps?

3. What do you see as the biggest challenges for the store's owners?

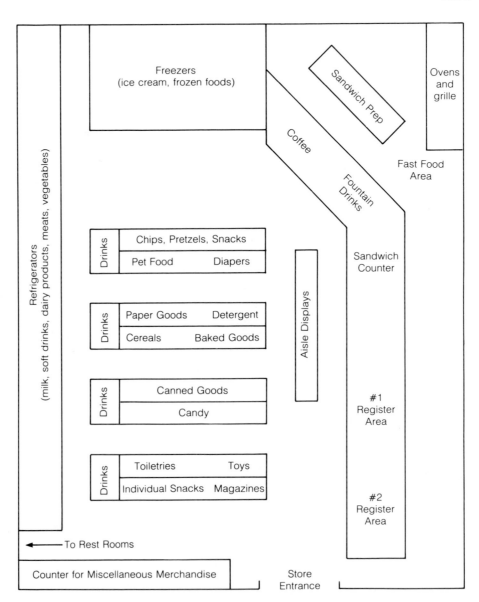

Figure D–13 Adams Convenience Store Layout.

A PROFESSIONAL SERVICE
Arthur Andersen & Company Accounting and Auditing Services Charlotte, North Carolina

Tour E

Arthur Andersen & Company was one of the world's leading accounting firms, with headquarters offices in Geneva, Switzerland, and in Chicago. As of the end of 1990, the firm employed 56,800 people worldwide and operated 299 offices in 66 countries. In the United States, Arthur Andersen was the largest of the so-called Big Six accounting firms. The firm was operated as a partnership; that is, the firm was owned and managed by a group of partners (in 1990 the partners totaled 2292) who had been elected by other partners in the firm.

The Charlotte office was the administrative office that coordinated the practice for the two Carolinas, including Columbia, South Carolina; Greensboro, North Carolina; and Raleigh, North Carolina. These four offices combined employed about 400 people, of whom 325 were professionals and 75 were support personnel. Of the 400, 290 worked in the Charlotte office. The office served more than 450 clients in a variety of industries.

PART ONE PROCESS DESCRIPTION

Lines of Business

Although Arthur Andersen & Co. was known as a Big Six accounting firm, it did more than provide classic auditing attest services (described in detail later). Its practice also included tax, consulting, other accounting services, and a series of specialized services for smaller businesses. In fact, the auditing and enterprise groups accounted for a little less than half of revenues; the tax and consulting divisions accounted for the remainder. Although this tour examines mainly the accounting and auditing practice of Arthur Andersen & Co. in Charlotte, the tax, consulting, and enterprise practices merit brief separate attention.

The Tax Practice

The tax practice in Charlotte employed 29 professionals. It was an important component of the office's business, and was well-established in the firm at large. There were two major components to the tax practice. One dealt with client compliance issues: preparing returns for clients, representing clients at Internal Revenue Service reviews, and providing defense for any clients in legal matters involving taxation. The other component involved advice on business transactions that had significant tax implications, such as mergers, acquisitions, and syndications. This kind of work typically complemented that of investment bankers and lawyers. Tax work consisted of many short-term jobs that often had to be done quickly but that typically did not involve substantial resources over extended periods of time; consulting or auditing services were longer term. Although there was considerable demand for tax services all through the year, the peak demands naturally occurred each February through April.

The Consulting Practice

The management information consulting practice was now formally known as Andersen Consulting. For the Carolinas, it was concentrated in Charlotte; of the

169 professionals employed in the consulting practice, 145 worked in the Charlotte office. The mission of the practice was to help clients obtain the information they needed to plan and manage their organizations. The practice was broad-ranging and included the development and installation of computer systems for financial and operations control of both manufacturing and service businesses. Much of this work was customized for the client and thus called for skill in drawing together the disparate elements of each project.

Consulting revenues were evenly divided among banking, manufacturing/textiles, health care, government work, and some miscellaneous businesses. The projects performed by the consulting division varied widely in their scope and duration, although many were accomplished for repeat clients. Typical projects included the development of a new deposit system for bank customers and the installation of management information systems for a group of trucking companies.

Enterprise Practice

The enterprise practice was technically a part of the audit practice of the firm; however, attest services accounted for only about half of the entreprise practice's revenues. The remaining revenues were generated by a diverse array of services: assistance in preparing financial forecasts and cash-flow projections, development of long- and short-range business plans, consultation in approaches to minimize taxes and maximize after-tax cash flow, evaluation of lease vs. buy decisions, breakeven analysis, capital budgeting, assistance with purchase, merger, or divestiture plans, and an assortment of other services. The enterprise practice had been created nearly 45 years before and had grown in Charlotte since the office opened in 1958. By 1990, there were 70 clients, and some of the original clients' businesses had grown so much that they were no longer served out of the enterprise practice.

For the professionals in the enterprise practice, the demands were quite diverse. Each professional had fine auditing skills, but they also had to foster other skills so that the wide-ranging demands of enterprises could be met: use of the microcomputer, preparation of business plans, private placements for company stock, and so on. For these reasons, the enterprise practice was often difficult to schedule and manage, but it had been a significant source of growth over the years.

Auditing Attest Services

All publicly held companies (those regulated by the Securities and Exchange Commission) are required to have independent certified public accountants report whether their financial statements fairly represent their financial positions and results of operations. These reports are usually found in company annual reports (see Figure E–1). Usually, these opinions are unqualified, but occasionally, accounting firms have to qualify them to alert shareholders to particular risks or problems in the financial statements of the company. Thus, reports are important safeguards to company shareholders. The audit was the procedure by

Report of Independent Public Accountants

To the Shareholders of International Paper Company:

We have audited the accompanying consolidated balance sheets of International Paper Company (a New York corporation) and subsidiaries as of December 31, 1990 and 1989, and the related consolidated statements of earnings, common shareholders' equity and cash flows for each of the three years in the period ended December 31, 1990. These financial statements are the responsibility of the Company's management. Our responsibility is to express an opinion on these financial statements based on our audits.

We conducted our audits in accordance with generally accepted auditing standards. Those standards require that we plan and perform the audit to obtain reasonable assurance about whether the financial statements are free of material misstatement. An audit includes examining, on a test basis, evidence supporting the amounts and disclosures in the financial statements. An audit also includes assessing the accounting principles used and significant estimates made by management, as well as evaluating the overall financial statement presentation. We believe that our audits provide a reasonable basis for our opinion.

In our opinion, the financial statements referred to above present fairly, in all material respects, the financial position of International Paper Company and subsidiaries as of December 31, 1990 and 1989, and the results of their operations and their cash flows for each of the three years in the period ended December 31, 1990 in conformity with generally accepted accounting principles.

Arthur Andersen + Co.

New York, N.Y.
February 8, 1991

Figure E–1 An Opinion.

which Arthur Andersen & Co. developed and substantiated reports about the financial records of the client companies.

Arthur Andersen & Co.'s auditing methodology was designed to identify and concentrate on the risk areas of greatest exposure to a company's financial statements and the related key control elements put in place by management to mitigate the risks. It was a top-down approach that addressed risks in two stages.

The first stage focused on the principal external and internal factors influencing the client company's operations, such as the industry in which it operated, the nature and complexity of its businesses and products, the operational and financial planning and control activities of management, and management's attitudes toward risk control and financial reporting.

The second stage provided a systematic basis for evaluating individual internal controls over an organization's significant cycles of activity.

Much as a manufacturer is concerned about the integrity and capabilities of the manufacturing process, so, too, an Arthur Andersen & Co. auditor is concerned about the integrity and capability of the internal controls in the client company for capturing accurately all of the accounts billed and collected, the invoices to be paid, the expenses authorized, the inventory, and other data.

The audit attest process could be broken into three major phases: the planning phase, the specific risk analysis phase, and the final phase. These different phases required different amounts of time and attention from the various members of the engagement team working on the audit.

The planning phase, for example, accounted for about 10 percent of the typical audit's effort, although much more than 10 percent of the time of the senior members of the engagement team. The senior members of the team were the partner or partners in charge and the manager (the professional with rank just below partner, who had anywhere from 5 to 12 years of service. The manager was actually in charge of the day-to-day progress of the audit). The planning phase was concerned with defining the scope of work to be done and its timing. It identified the risks that seemed to be important and the changes in the character of the business that ought to be scrutinized. Once the planning phase was over, the partners returned periodically to review progress, to help work through particular problems, and to monitor the quality of the work in progress.

The specific risk analysis phase was concerned with fact-finding. In this phase, the junior members of the engagement team (i.e., the staff accountants, and the "seniors") investigated the paperwork and controls of the client company. They checked to see that the controls actually worked. Sometimes, they identified substantive problems that had to be dealt with by the senior members of the engagement team. This phase could range from perhaps 30 percent of the time and effort in a small audit to 60 percent of the time and effort in a large audit.

The final audit phase led to the generation of the report. This phase updated the results of the specific risk analysis phase, involved substantiation of year-end balances, and included a review of the client company's financial statements and their accompanying footnotes. For large audits, this final phase might account for only 30 percent of Arthur Andersen & Co.'s time and effort, whereas for smaller audits it could account for 60 percent.

The total professional time devoted to an audit by the Charlotte office could vary dramatically, from 80 hours each year for the smallest audits to more than 4000 hours each year for the largest. The median amount of time consumed for an audit was estimated at about 500 hours each year. The calendar for an audit varied somewhat. For the largest audits, Arthur Andersen & Co. professionals were in and out of the client company all the time; they were often part of quarterly reviews of the client's business. At more typical audits, however, the planning phase was done about 6 months into each fiscal year, the specific risk analysis work was accomplished in months 7 through 11, and the final work was done in the first 3 months after the close of the fiscal year.

Although two-thirds of the Charlotte office's audit work was repeat business, the office was always eager to attract new business. It secured this business by drafting a proposal to the target client company. This proposal discussed the key aspects of Arthur Andersen & Co. and what differentiated it from other accounting firms. It introduced the firm's other major clients in Charlotte and the services the entire office could provide a client company. It discussed in some detail the audit approach that Arthur Andersen & Co. planned to take. It profiled the personnel making up the engagement team, and it discussed how those personnel would be managed over time to provide the kind of continuity that was valued by clients. The proposal also established the fee schedule.

Managing the Practice: The Pyramid

Arthur Andersen & Co.'s auditing practice in the Carolinas totaled 140 professionals. Of this number, there were 10 partners, 22 managers, 38 seniors, and 70 staff accountants. These different classifications could be depicted as a pyramid, with the staff as the base and the partners at the top. Each engagement had its own pyramid, as well, with one or two partners at the top, one or more managers, and various seniors and staff accountants.

Staff, seniors, and managers were all salaried positions. The partners were not salaried; their compensation depended on the profitability of the firm. If the partners were to make money, they had to use the salaried personnel of the firm effectively. This placed several demands on the partners: (1) effective scheduling of personnel so that everybody was working as much as possible but without excessive overtime (scheduling will be discussed later), and (2) fostering as much responsibility in the lower ranks as possible. Firm profitability was enhanced to the degree that effort and responsibility were thrust to lower levels of the pyramid (this was termed as having a broad-based pyramid). If the higher-paid senior members of an engagement team were free to perform other duties, such as bringing in additional business, everyone benefited and the firm as a whole would be profitable.

If a job could be run with a broad-based pyramid, it would likely be profitable. If, however, the pyramid were slender, it was likely not to be as profitable because the time of the senior members of the engagement team would not be as effectively used as when the pyramid was broad.

Accounting firms such as Arthur Andersen & Co. primarily operated on an *up-or-out* basis: professionals within the firm were either promoted to the next-higher rank or they left the firm. In a sense, the partners were the survivors, those who had proven themselves over the years by their performance and had demonstrated the qualities that made for effective partners.

Arthur Andersen & Co. was continually looking for innovative ways to keep highly trained individuals within the firm, even though they could not rise to partnership rank. In 1991, the firm created the "national partner," a senior-level position just short of the equity partner rank, as a way to hang on to talented people.

There was considerable turnover at the lower levels of the pyramid. If one followed the path of new recruits in the Charlotte office, for example, one typically found that only 50 percent of each new cohort of college recruits were still with the firm after 3 years, and that only 25 percent of them were still with the firm after 6 years. After 10 years, the figure was 14 percent. Only about 9 percent reached partnership.

About three-quarters of the time, professionals left the firm of their own volition. Some left for more attractive, higher-paying positions in other companies. Others left because of personal incompatibilities with the degree of overtime or travel, or because of other elements of life on the job. Some returned to school. The remainder left at the suggestion of the firm itself; those were split between professionals who lacked the technical ability to do the job and those who lacked some other personal qualities that were required. Although an up-or-out system might be viewed as harsh, Arthur Andersen & Co. was famed for its concern for the placement of its accountants in other jobs, often with valued clients.

The pyramid concept raised several issues. Broad pyramids meant lower costs, but because they encouraged the delegation of responsibilities to lower levels of the pyramid, there were quality control and cost-effectiveness issues associated with doing business that way. For example, staff might not have the ability or the training to do all that is requested of them, or they might take a longer time than some more senior professionals in doing some job, thus raising the specter of cost-effectiveness.

Another issue involved client perceptions. The accountants at client companies were knowledgeable about firm operations, because they were often former Big Six professionals themselves. Often, they would prefer experienced personnel and staff continuity. The Charlotte office was careful about making its assignments and had to consider each client's perceptions on staffing.

The Cycle of Business Planning

Given the labor intensity of auditing, business planning for the Charlotte office was very much an exercise in determining labor needs. The business plan for the audit practice started with a forecast of chargeable hours for the Carolinas' four offices. The area had been growing and Arthur Andersen & Co. had been developing additional clients, so chargeable hours were growing at a healthy clip.

Once a defensible forecast of chargeable hours was developed, productivity factors (i.e., average chargeable hours per person per year) were applied to determine how many people would be needed. In general, the Charlotte office averaged between 1400 and 1500 chargeable hours per person per year. That number differed by level within the pyramid: Partners generally had the fewest and seniors the most. Nonchargeable hours were taken up in a variety of activities, including training, marketing and sales promotion, community service, administrative tasks, recruiting, and, of course, inefficiently used time. Given the application of the productivity factors to the forecasted chargeable hours, the office figured out how many people it needed. This, in turn, determined how many new recruits were needed to make up for any personnel shortfalls.

The business plan's forecast of profitability depended on the fee structure as well as the staffing plan. With the growth of business in the Carolinas, there was heavy competition for new business. The Charlotte office took this into account in developing its fee structure to match its chargeable hour plan and its staffing plan.

Scheduling

As mentioned previously, personnel scheduling was a key determinant of the office's profitability. The Charlotte office had responsibility for scheduling not only its own operation but coordinating those of Greensboro, Raleigh, and Columbia as well. One manager-level professional was assigned full-time to scheduling and other division administration functions.

The scheduling process began with the managers in charge of the office's engagements. For each engagement, the manager indicated how many hours of which levels of professional were required (see Figure E–2). The manager was

Figure E–2 A Sample Master Job Scheduling Sheet, as Used at Arther Andersen & Co.—Charlotte.

also permitted to request specific people to be part of the engagement. This planning could often be done far in advance, due to the recurring nature of much of the office's business. Each December and January, a rough-cut schedule for the following May through April period was devised.

The allocation of people to jobs was depicted on two different schedules: (1) the long-range schedule that planned people's assignments for an entire year, by week, and (2) the 20-week schedule, which showed the assignments of all staff persons, by week, for the next 20 weeks. The 20-week schedule used the same database as the long-range schedule. Both of these schedules were known in the office as the "railroad," largely because the schedule itself looked like tracks on paper (see Figures E–3 and E–4).

The scheduling manager was responsible for pulling together the original schedule and then adjusting it as time wore on and inevitable changes occurred. Naturally, the Charlotte office's profitability was greatest when everybody was fully scheduled and working effectively. The inexperienced staff accountants tended to have the most "open holes" in their schedules, and thus they were a constant concern for the scheduling manager. He reviewed the schedule continually to see whether all of the jobs being worked on were properly staffed. Was the pyramid broad enough for them? Were some projects in need of help? Were the Greensboro, Raleigh, and Columbia offices busy? Could professionals be

```
CAROLINAS                               PERSONNEL SCHEDULING                   PAGE-  2        AS OF-20 NOV 85
DIVISION: CHARLOTTE AUDIT                PERSONNEL ASSIGNMENTS                                 PREP-20 NOV 85
TO: 450561                                                                                    RPT-EC01000
FOR: CC, ASR, 206440
HOME ADDRESS:
                             LOC         SCHED
JOB NUMBER/JOB YEAR END      OFF  PTR MGR   **  HRS TO 11    12           01       02       03          04       05
   JOB NAME/DESCRIPTION      DIV  SENIOR  STAT DATE  18 25 02 09 16 23 30 06 13 20 27 03 10 17 24 03 10 17 24 31 07 14 21 28 05 12
-----------------------------  ---  ------  ---- ----- -- -- -- -- -- -- -- -- -- -- -- -- -- -- -- -- -- -- -- -- -- -- -- -- -- --
                                  FGJ DLW   I    140:40  :     36:40 24:32  :     :50 50:50 50:50 50:    :     :     :     :     :
COMPANY 234                   CC                  :     :     :     :     :     :     :     :     :     :     :     :     :     :
                                  PAG RDG   I    240:   :     :     :     :     :     :     :     :10   :24   8:    :     :40 40>
COMPANY 345                   CC                  :     :     :     :     :     :     :     :     :     :     :     :     :     :
                                  FGJ JCH   I    260:   :     :     :     :     :     :     :     :     :     :40   :     :
COMPANY 456                   CC                  :     :     :     :     :     :     :     :     :     :     :     :     :     :
4310000                           BRG            :     :     3:    :     :     :     :     :     :     :     :     :     :     :
AUDIT DIV MEETING                                :     :     :     :     :     :     :     :     :     :     :     :     :     :
555                                              : 2   :     :     :     :     :     :     :     :     :     :     :     :     :
P/M MEETING OR OFFICE MTG                        :     :     :     :     :     :     :     :     :     :     :     :     :     :
815                                              :     16:   :     16: 8  :     :     :     :     :     :     :     :     :     :
HOLIDAY                                          :     :     :     :     :     :     :     :     :     :     :     :     :     :
•TOTAL ASSIGNED HOURS                            42 16    39 40 40 40        50 50 50 50 50 50 10    24  8        40    40 40
•TOTAL CHARGEABLE HOURS                          40       36 40 24 32        50 50 50 50 50 50 10    24  8        40    40 40
•TOTAL NON-CHARGEABLE HOURS                      2 16      3    16  8
•TOTAL OVERTIME HOURS                            2                           50 50 50 50 50 50 10    24  8        40    40 40
 TOTAL TENTATIVE HOURS
 TOTAL UNASSIGNED HOURS                             24 40  1     40 40 40              30 40 16 32 40 40    40
----------------------------------------------------------------------------------------------------------------------
SCHEDULING CONSIDERATIONS:

----------------------------------------------------------------------------------------------------------------------
•  INCLUDES TENTATIVE HOURS                                                  ••••••••••••••••••••••••••••••••
•• STATUS -  I • INCHARGE PERSON, R • REVISED SCHEDULE, T, X • TENTATIVE ASSIGNMENT,    • CC                     •
            C • STAFFING CONTINUITY, O • OUT OF TOWN                         • 18 NOV 85    WEEKS 1 - 26    •
                                                                            ••••••••••••••••••••••••••••••••
```

Figure E–3   A Long-range Schedule, as Used at Arthur Andersen & Co.—Charlotte.

CLT.RR RR-PGM
RAILROAD-PRINT

AUDIT DIVISION PERSONNEL ASSIGNMENTS
TWENTY WEEKS REPORT

DATE: 10/06/88
PAGE: 1

DIVISION: CHARLOTTE AUDIT

EMPLOYEE	CLASS	10/10/88	10/17/88	10/24/88	10/31/88	11/07/88	11/14/88	11/21/88	11/28/88	12/05/88	12/12/88
AA	AESR	CO1 -40						HOLI -16		CO1 -40	CO1 -40 CO37 -16
BB	AESR	CO2 -8 CO3 -8	CO2 -40	CO2 -40	CO2 -40	CO14 -40 CO2 -20	CO14 -40	VACAT -24 HOLI -16	CO2 -40 CO5 -40	CO14 -30	CO14 -50
CC	AESR	VACAT -40	VACAT -40			CO20 -40		CO23 -24 HOLI -16	CO23 -40		CO38 -24
DD	AESR	CO4 -40	CO4 -40	CO4 -40	CO17 -8		CO17 -40	HOLI -16	CO27 -40	CO27 -40	CO32 -40
EE	AESR							CO24 -24 HOLI -16			
FF	AESR				CO4 -40	CO4 -40	CO4 -40	HOLI -16		CO31 -40	
GG	ASR	CO5 -16 VACAT -8 CO6 -16	CO12 -50	CO12 -50	CO12 -50	CO6 -16 CO12 -24	CO6 -40	HOLI -16	CO6 -40	CO6 -40	
HH	ASR	CO7 -40	CO7 -40	CO15 -40		CO21 -24	CO21 -40	CO21 -24 HOLI -16		CO1 -40	CO1 -40
II	ASR	VACAT -16 CO8 -24			CO18 -24 CO19 -16	CO19 -40	CO19 -24	HOLI -16			CO33 -40
JJ	ASR							HOLI -16			CO34 -40
KK	ASR	CO9 -16 CO10 -8 CO11 -16	CO10 -32	CO10 -50	CO10 -50	CO10 -24		HOLI -16	CO36 -32		CO11 -16
LL	ASR		CO13 -40	CO13 -40	CO13 -24	CO14 -40	CO14 -40	CO25 -24 HOLI -16	CO29 -40	CO14 -30	CO14 -50
MM	ASSR	VACAT -16	CO14 -40	VACAT -16 CO14 -8	CO18 -24		CO22 -24	CO25 -24 HOLI -16	CO30 -24	CO14 -30	CO14 -50
NN	ASSR			CO16 -40	CO16 -40	CO16 -40		HOLI -16	CO5 -40		
OO	AEST	CO1 -40 CO10 -24	CO1 -8 CO10 -50	CO10 -50	CO10 -50	CO19 -40	CO19 -16	CO23 -24 HOLI -16	CO23 -40	CO1 -40	CO1 -40
PP	AEST	CO35 -8 TEACH -16 VACAT -16	CO13 -40	CO13 -40	CO18 -16	CO14 -40	CO14 -40	CO26 -8 HOLI -16		CO14 -30	CO14 -50

Figure E–4 A 20-week Schedule, as Used at Arthur Andersen & Co.—Charlotte.

swapped between offices? The Charlotte scheduler acted as the central clearing-house for the staffing needs of all of the Carolinas' offices. In trying to fill the open holes in the schedule, the scheduling manager relied most on the 20-week schedule, which was painstakingly updated with all the changes and was the office's controlling document for the next 20 weeks. That document was organized by individual and displayed the open holes for each professional in the Carolinas, as well as which engagements everyone was scheduled for. An associated document was generated automatically to show the converse—which professionals in the office were available in each week. This document identified candidate professionals who could help with a new or existing engagement (see Figure E–5).

As might be expected, there were continual inconsistencies in the schedule that had to be resolved. These inconsistencies resulted from many things—new work, changes in personnel, or changes in the scope of an existing engagement. Consider the following situation. The Greensboro office not only had been very busy but was short of seniors as well. The existing seniors there were working too much overtime and needed to be relieved in some way. As it happened, a new senior had been transferred to the Charlotte office from Dallas and was due soon. The scheduler's dilemma was how to help the Greensboro office without giving them the new senior for too long a time, because, after all, she had been transferred into Charlotte, not Greensboro. The scheduler knew that it would be toughest to adjust the schedule during the peak time of the year (February and

```
CAROLINAS                              PERSONNEL SCHEDULING                    PAGE-   1      AS OF-20 NOV 85
DIVISION: CHARLOTTE AUDIT                                                                    PREP-20 NOV 85
TO: 450561                        PERSONNEL AVAILABILITY (CONDENSED)                         RPT-EC03100

               PERS                   AVAIL 11    12              01          02          03          04          05
CLASS GROUP  NUMBER CLAS  PERSONNEL NAME  TENT  18 25 02 09 16 23 30 06 13 20 27 03 10 17 24 03 10 17 24 31 07 14 21 28 05 12
------------ ------ ----  --------------  ----  -- -- -- -- -- -- -- -- -- -- -- -- -- -- -- -- -- -- -- -- -- -- -- -- -- --
SENIORS      115312 ASR  AA              AVAIL:     24:    :     :     :  40:     :  40:40 40:40 40:40 16:        :40 40:40 40:
             206440 ASR  CC              AVAIL:     24:40 1:     : 40:40 40:     :     :     :30 40:16 32:40 40:    40:
             295868 ASR  DD              AVAIL:38 24:40 37:40 24:32 40:24   :    :40 40:40 40:    :24 32:40 40:40 40:40 40:
             374725 ASR  EE              AVAIL:38 24:   1:    24:32 40:     :    :40   :    :40 40:40 40:40 40:40 40:40 40:
             595772 ASR  HH              AVAIL:     :    1:    24:32 40:     :    :     : 40:40 40:    :40 40:40 40:40 40:
             657221 ASR  JJ              AVAIL:     24:40 37:40   :16 40:     :    :     :     : 40:    40:40 40:40 40:40 40:
             692981 ASR  KK              AVAIL:     : 37:40 24:32   :     :     :    :     : 40:40 40:40 40:40 40:40 40:
             743739 ASR  LL              AVAIL:     : 37:40 24:24   :     :     :    :     :40 40:40 40:40 40:40 40:40 32:
             778001 ASR  MM              AVAIL: 6   :   1:40   :     :     :     :    : 40:40 40:    40:40 40:40 40:40 40:
             941701 ASR  NN              AVAIL:38 24:40 37:40 24:32 40:40 40:40 40:40 40:40 40:40 40:40 40:40 40:40 40:

             STANDARD WORKLOAD   40 24 40 40 40 24 32 40 40 40 40 40 40 40 40 40 40 40 40 40 40 40 40 40 40 40

                                                                                    • 20 NOV 85  WEEKS 1-26 •
```

Figure E–5 A Personnel Availability Chart, as Used at Arthur Andersen & Co.—Charlotte.

March), so he concentrated on helping Greensboro during those two months. By consulting the schedule, he knew that the new senior could be used on the Company 792 engagement for the weeks of February 17, February 24, and March 3. That engagement also called for a senior's time during the week of December 2, which was fine, as the new senior was going to be in Charlotte at that time. In addition, Greensboro needed help on the Company 409 engagement for the weeks of February 3 and February 10. That also called for work in the week of December 23. This, too, fitted well into the new senior's schedule.

However, there were two other engagements, Company 642 and Company 322, that would need additional professionals and could not be assigned to the new senior. The scheduler looked to the 20-week schedule for holes and then also looked at the personnel availability sheet. No one senior had time available in all of the time periods required for the jobs under consideration: Thus there were some incompatibilities that the scheduler had to check into and resolve. Upon investigation, two seniors' schedules showed some promise. In evaluating the jobs assigned to each of them during this period, it looked as if one would be more available. However, he would not be free for all of the 3 weeks slated for those jobs. He was available during the weeks of December 9 and December 16, but he was not available during the week of January 20, as he was scheduled on another job in the Greensboro office. The scheduler then had to do some negotiating. In order for him to assign the senior to the Greensboro office for the 642 and 322 jobs, he needed to take the senior off his other assignment at Greensboro. By calling around to the interested parties, it was agreed that the senior could be taken off the Greensboro job for the week of January 20 and thus assigned to the 642 and 322 jobs that were coming up immediately. The hope was that the Greensboro office could delay work on that job until sometime later, or if that was not possible, perhaps use another senior for the week of January 20.

The scheduler continually made trade-offs in this way, for the most part following a hierarchy of preferences: (1) Substitute a similar-level professional for the professional initially planned for (possible for preliminary audit work but not for final audit work), (2) substitute an available professional from a different level, if he or she were qualified, and (3) let the schedule slip so that the desired personnel could perform the job at a more convenient date. During the course of any week, there might be two or three problems that consumed up to four hours each to resolve. In addition, there were a host of smaller problems that might be resolved much more easily, say within an hour's time each.

The scheduler was in repeated contact with the managers who oversaw the office's engagements. Those managers informed the scheduler of changes in their needs, and they occasionally lobbied for particular professionals to work their engagements. Sometimes, particularly with new clients, staff and seniors would also lobby the scheduler for those jobs. An important task for the scheduler was balancing the training and development needs of staff accountants and seniors against the practice's need for their services and the client company's desires for continuity in the personnel assigned to them.

Personnel Policy

Although profitability was tied to the pyramid and to the efficient scheduling of people, the Charlotte office's managing partner believed that in the long run, Arthur Andersen & Co. would be successful only if it served its clients well. The major concern was the development of the professionals in the office and the culture in which they worked. Culture, of course, is an elusive concept, but a variety of indications of the Arthur Andersen & Co. culture could be cited:

> The Arthur Andersen motto was Think straight, talk straight.
>
> No secrets were kept around the office.
>
> Teamwork and attention to detail were highly valued.
>
> Prompt client service was highly valued. There was a "code red" program that called for some member of the engagement team to return a client's phone call within 60 minutes, no matter where the engagement's lead partner or manager might be.
>
> Arthur Andersen took pride in having the most highly regarded training program of any of the Big Six.
>
> To ensure that everyone had fun doing their jobs, Charlotte's managing partner worked to see that every professional was assigned to the industry of his or her preference at least half the time.
>
> All the office's professionals were reviewed each year. They filled out a form (Figure E–6) and then met with a partner to discuss their performance and career development.

Training

One of the partners was responsible for monitoring the training of all the audit professionals. Training at Arthur Andersen & Co. was done either within the

TO: _____
                    Reviewing Partner

FROM: _____

DATE: _____

SUBJECT: ANNUAL REVIEW _____

1. Am I satisfied with the assignments I have had? What particular assignments (industry, technical specialization, research, compliance, etc.) would I like in the next year?

   _____

   _____

   _____

2. What, if any, particular training would I like to receive during the next year?

   _____

   _____

   _____

3. Are the demands made upon me as a professional (overtime, travel, work pace, etc.) acceptable?

   _____

   _____

   _____

4. Am I progressing at a pace satisfactory to me?

   _____

   _____

   _____

5. Is my performance being evaluated currently and adequately?

   _____

   _____

   _____

6. My interests in professional and civic activities are:

   _____

   _____

   _____

7. Ideas or suggestions for the Firm:

   _____

   _____

   _____

8. Any concerns:

   _____

   _____

   _____

Figure E–6 An Annual Review Form Used at Arthur Andersen & Co.—Charlotte.

local office or at the firm-wide level. To this end, the firm operated a training center in St. Charles, Illinois, and brought professionals from all over the world to it on a regular basis. Continuing professional education was required of all CPAs by the national and various states' accounting societies (120 hours over 3 years with no less than 20 hours in any year), so even partners and managers spent time in training. For the most part, partners and managers averaged at least 40 hours per year; for example, most staff accumulated between 150 and 200 hours of training, with 100 to 120 hours spent locally, and the balance at either the regional level or at the St. Charles campus. Seniors did not spend quite that much time, but they too spent a considerable amount of time in training.

Training was considered as important as a client assignment for the professionals in the office. The training plan was usually developed well in advance, and put out "on the railroad." Good attendance was viewed as important for career development. The slow period from April through August was the best time of the year for training, although training programs were scheduled throughout the year.

The training program was considerably varied. Some of the programs were basic for the first- and second-year professionals, but other programs were termed either intermediate or advanced. Some of these courses dealt with interpersonal relationships, marketing, effective presentations, and other aspects of management development. Still other courses had industry orientations so that professionals could be better steeped in the nature and problems of the specific industries they served.

Recruiting

Recruiting was another important function that was overseen by a partner and that demanded considerable time from the senior professionals in the office. Recruiting concentrated on local schools, although all the recruiting was done for the firm at large and not just for the Charlotte office. Recruiting was done at both the undergraduate and MBA levels.

The Manager's Life

Managers oversaw the day-to-day operations of each audit engagement. It was their job to see that the audit was done well and on time and that the fee level was appropriate. They were responsible for developing the staffing plan and budget for the engagement and for billing and collecting from the client. Managers wanted to avoid any surprises on an engagement, and thus it was in their interest to have seniors and staff who could be trusted and whose competence and capabilities would be unquestioned.

Managers spent a good deal of their time outside the office — perhaps 55 to 65 percent. Most of that time was spent at existing clients, attending to their needs and solving any problems that cropped up. About 20 to 25 percent of the manager's time was spent with administrative chores. And because managers were partners-in-training to a large degree, they spent some of their time developing new clients and new business for the firm.

In the main, managers were pleased with their lives at Arthur Andersen & Co. Their jobs were viewed as challenging, motivating, and educational, and the partners gave them a good deal of autonomy. The partners were also regarded as fair, and the up-or-out nature of the business was not unduly confining because the managers felt that they could easily leave the firm for attractive jobs elsewhere.

The Partner's Life

Many duties fell on the partners in the Charlotte office. The typical partner incurred about 1000 hours each year that were charged to the engagements on which he or she was the senior member. Of that time, perhaps two-thirds was spent at the client, discussing the client's business and supervising the audit there. Other chargeable hours were spent in the planning phase and final report phases of the actual audit. As an accountant and auditor, the partner was responsible for solving problems, for analyzing risk, and for monitoring quality.

The other 1400 to 1500 hours of a partner's year were spent in many different activities: recruiting; training, including teaching the junior people; practice development, which was the marketing and sales function for generating new business; personnel matters, such as counseling junior professionals and reviewing their progress; and providing counsel to other Arthur Andersen & Co. professionals on matters of the partner's own expertise (e.g., the Charlotte office was viewed as the firm's source of expertise for textiles).

The partners, as a group, were responsible for a multitude of functions. Not only did they have line responsibility for the audits being done, but they had to divide up the overhead functions necessary to further the practice: training, recruiting, expertise in special industry specializations (such as health care, manufacturing, closely held businesses), practice development, administration, and quality control.

Partners were well-compensated. Their high incomes were a motivation for many of the junior people. Arthur Andersen & Co. partners were paid by splitting the worldwide profits of the company according to how many "units" they held. Each unit was stated in U.S. dollars. All partners started with a fixed quantity of units, and over time, these units were added onto, based upon seniority and merit. In keeping with the no-secrets aspect of the firm, files were kept on all partners, and all partners knew what everyone else in the firm made.

A manager was not promoted to partner based solely on the evaluations of the office in which he or she served. There were uniform standards for the promotion to partner that were overseen by a firm-wide committee. Upon becoming partners, managers were required to contribute some capital to the firm, but this was a rather modest amount relative to the partner's income.

PART TWO DISCUSSION

Arthur Andersen & Co. is in no way responsible for the following views and presentation. They remain solely the responsibility of the author.

The Flow of the Process and of Information

Figure E–7 is a very rough process flow diagram of the audit process. It shows the degree of involvement by the various levels of the engagement team. This process flow also includes the proposal stage and the selection and scheduling stage for the development of the audit team. The diagram depicts only the major phases of the audit process. One could, of course, develop a more detailed schedule of the work for any engagement, but that detailed schedule would be very particular to the client, and complex as well. It would include many of the work elements of Arthur Andersen & Co.'s audit procedures; thus it is beyond the scope of this service tour.

Similarly, constructing a diagram of the information flow in a process such as auditing is almost impossible. The flows of information are so numerous and so idiosyncratic to the client and to the needs of the engagement team itself that it is not worth characterizing here. A Big Six accounting organization simply lives on information, and that information flow must be swift, it must involve all layers of the company, and it must carry differing quantities of information.

There are no real distinctions in either the process or information flows during peak versus nonpeak times. During peak times, of course, a lot of overtime is put in and people are perhaps more charged-up about work, but all of the steps must still be done, and all of the information must still flow as it does at nonpeak times.

	Proposal Writing	Engagement Team Selection and Scheduling	Planning Phase	Specific Risk Analysis Phase	Final Audit Phase
Senior Members of the Engagement Team (Partners and Managers)	High involvement with client and among themselves	High involvement, especially by managers. Scheduler is very much involved	High involvement	Little involvement by partner(s), except for periodic troubleshooting and for quality reviews Day-to-day involvement by manager	High involvement
Junior Members of the Engagement Team (Seniors and Staff)	Little or no involvement	Some preferences for work are stated	Little involvement by staff High involvement by seniors	High involvement. Much work done at client	High involvement

Figure E–7   Rough Process Flow Diagram for Auditing Services at Arthur Andersen & Co.—Charlotte.

Demands of the Process on the Workforce

The workforce at Arthur Andersen & Co. is composed of the salaried professionals (managers, seniors, staff) and the less numerous support people. The process demands on them are essentially a high degree of training and a tremendous amount of flexibility. The firm's accountants have to move from job to job, to put in long hours when called upon, and to be out in the field for, perhaps, long stretches of time. Some of the work is tedious, although much of the work can be challenging and rewarding.

The firm's accountants, at all levels, must make decisions all the time. Even in the preliminary phase of an audit, there are decisions to be made and many issues that need to be resolved. Thus, the members of an engagement team have to be constantly on the lookout for problems or opportunities (e.g., add-on business) that they should bring to the senior members of the engagement team for resolution. This is one reason why so much continual training is required to keep everyone fresh and knowledgeable as times and clients change.

Accountants must also face the up-or-out nature of advancement within the firm. Happily, the alternatives to employment are generally good. Arthur Andersen & Co. accountants are typically in high demand by client companies and others. The care with which advancement decisions are made and the counsel given accountants through this process helps to ease any stress that this kind of advancement places on the accountants proceeding through the ranks.

Demands of the Process on Management

The partners in a professional firm such as Arthur Andersen & Co. have a number of responsibilities that they alone must shoulder. Many of these responsibilities relate to the workforce. Managing the pyramid well, as discussed earlier, is an absolute requirement. Partners must take the lead in recruiting new accountants, training them, and managing their advancement through the firm. These activities take up tremendous chunks of partner time.

Partners must also use that pyramid well in order to make money. Thus, the assignment of accountants to engagements and the scheduling of those accountants are important areas of partner concern. Even though the actual schedule itself is developed by a manager-level professional, the partners must develop the strategy underlying the schedule.

Partners are also primarily responsible for procuring new business. They are the ones who must contact the clients, develop proposals, and establish fees. Of course, the partners must also be excellent accountants themselves. They must be intimately involved in the general risk analysis and the final phase of each audit. They are called on to troubleshoot and to review the quality of any audit through all its phases, particularly the preliminary phase. In addition to this line management authority, they are also called on by others in the firm as experts in certain areas (e.g., specific industries and certain accounting practices). Partners must wear many hats and are pulled in many different directions.

QUESTIONS

1. What advantages do you see to the hierarchical structure of an accounting firm such as Arthur Andersen & Co.? Do you see any disadvantages?

2. What kinds of factors do you suppose would affect the fee schedule advanced in a proposal to a client?

3. In a partner–manager–junior type of organization, as described in the discussion of this service tour, suppose the time commitments were changed from a 60–140–400 breakdown to one of 100–200–300. Assuming the same utilization rates, how would the pyramid change if it were to remain perfectly balanced?

4. What benefits and costs are involved in increasing the average chargeable hours in the office from its current level of 1400 to 1500 hours per year?

5. What kinds of trade-offs are the hardest for the office's scheduler? What kinds are the easiest?

6. What are the characteristics you would look for in the typical recruit for a staff accountant position?

===================== **SITUATION FOR STUDY E–1** =====================

Johnson and Trotter Advertising

The Johnson and Trotter Advertising Agency was a large, New York–based agency with a wide variety of clients. J&T was organized into six functional departments: account management, research, creativity, production, media, and legal. The account management department was charged with client relations and was responsible for coordinating the efforts of all of the other departments on the client's behalf. The research department was responsible for uncovering useful facts about the products and services advertised for use in developing new ads, and they were also charged with substantiating the advertising claims made by the ads. The creativity department was the lead department in developing new ideas and the means by which the client's products and services could be advertised. The production department was responsible for making the print, radio, and TV ads that had been conceived by the creativity department. The media department interacted with all of the media in which the agency's clients advertised, and the legal department handled any legal issues raised by the agency's efforts.

The agency worked in teams. Members of the various departments generally worked on more than one account at the same time except for the account executive, who was charged with keeping all members of the product team informed about such things as the client's situation, research findings, creative ideas, production status, and any other information on the account. The account executive was also charged with keeping the entire effort on the established timetable and within budget. Members of each product team could expect to spend several years working for a client before being rotated off. Any differences of opinion were generally dealt with by compromise within the product team. Account executives did not have the authority to overrule a specialist on a question involving that specialist's realm of expertise. If a difference of opinion persisted, the team could take its dispute to its superiors within each department, where it was usually resolved.

There were three quality control mechanisms at J&T: a strategy review board, a creative review board, and a media review board. At key stages of the firm's process, these quality control mechanisms could be invoked.

Promotion for the professionals of the agency came from within each department.

For example, within account management, one typically started as an assistant account executive, moved up to account executive, then on to account supervisor, management supervisor, and then executive vice-president for client services. A general manager oversaw all of the six functional groups.

1. What strengths do you see in the organization of Johnson and Trotter?
2. What potential disadvantages exist with this operation?

Cases

DESROCHERS, INC.

For Bob Desrochers, the chorus of complaints from his managers had risen high enough that he felt he had to do something more about it. All four of his operating managers had gripes, and they all related to space. They either had too little of it or it was configured in the wrong way. The facilities issue had been investigated in preliminary fashion, and Bob thought that this summer of 1992 was the time to rethink the topic. But he had just spent too much time and way too much money getting the Trademarks showroom up and running in the new National Bank Center building. It was gorgeous, but what a drain on him. He didn't want that kind of effort to drag down his managers. They should be free to concentrate on what Bob called "the absolute quality and the overwhelming customer service" that had grown the business. Playing architect might be too much of a distraction from this vision for any one of them. What should he tell them? How should he handle their legitimate concerns?

Desrochers, Inc.

Desrochers was a horticultural and floral services company located in Northern Virginia. It provided a full line of turf, plant, and floral services to commercial accounts. In addition, the company operated three retail floral stores that provided a full menu of floral and gift services to residential and commercial customers. The company did everything from planting and maintaining exterior shrubs, trees, and lawns to leasing tropical plants for lobbies and offices, from planting and maintaining intricate flower beds in front of company buildings to designing distinctive cut-flower arrangements for corporate banquets. Sales for 1992 were running at an annual rate of about $8 million and employment during the May peak ran about 170 people. Desrochers was the largest firm of its kind in the area and one of the few with the capability of servicing events such as major golf championships. The company had just designed and installed floral and potted-plant displays for each of 23 corporate tents at a recent PGA Tour event.

Desrochers was a family-owned company begun in 1932 by M. M. Desrochers. In its early history, the company grew rapidly as a nursery, landscaping, and tree service firm for wealthy private clients, most prominently Fred Holland at his Woodfields residence (now part of the local Museum of Art property) and his Bluebird farm and hideaway. After the untimely death of M. M. Desrochers, the company's revenues dropped, reaching a low of $20,000 in 1955. The older son, Walt, then took over the company's reins. During the next twelve years, Walt built up the Exterior Department of the company (turf and exterior plant sales and maintenance). Walt also recruited his younger brother, Bob, now 51, into the firm. Bob concentrated on the exterior landscape maintenance portion of the business and, at that time, the fledgling Interior Department (interior plant leasing and maintenance). Bob took over the presidency of the company when Walt left for the academic life. (Walt, now dean of a business school in Virginia, retained an ownership position in the company.) By 1985, the Interior Department had grown to be two-thirds of the business and the brothers had long since decided to specialize on commercial customers and not to deal with the residential market.

In 1989, Desrochers bought Wade Florist, the seventeenth-largest FTD florist in the nation, from Mark Wade, 62. Wade operated three retail stores in Northern Virginia. Within a few years of retirement and with none of his children interested in continuing the family business, Mark Wade decided to sell the business to Desrochers, whose reputation for commercial horticulture matched Wade's enviable reputation as a florist.

Within six months of the acquisition, Desrochers created a new division, Trademarks, to deal with their commercial business clients' floral needs. Trademarks specialized in design leadership with very contemporary floral arrangements and services to make things easy for commercial customers. With the advent of Trademarks, the company was now organized into four profit centers: Exterior, Interior, Wade Florist, and Trademarks. See Exhibit 1 for an organization chart.

The Exterior Department.

The vestiges of M. M. Desrochers's original business were housed within the Exterior Department, but since that time, the business had changed dramatically.

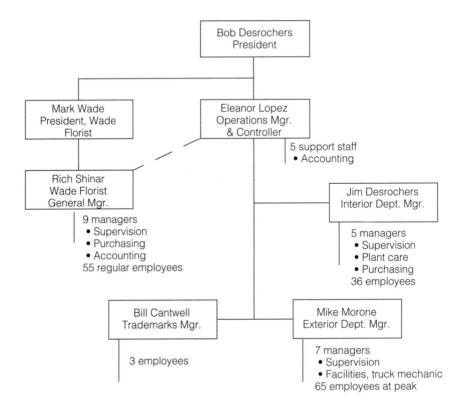

Exhibit 1 Desrochers Organization Chart.

About the only common thread was that the Exterior Department was still housed on the 8.6 acres in McLean that was originally purchased by M. M. Desrochers in 1937 for his nursery.

The Exterior Department offered a program of regular care for shrubs, trees, and turf, some of which had been installed by its teams of workers. The department's flower program (flowers planted in beds at various company locations and maintained throughout the summer and fall) represented an increasing portion of sales.

The Exterior Department was organized in matrix fashion. There were four landscape maintenance account managers and one landscape installation manager. Supplementing these account managers were two others: one to handle the turf needs for all clients (chemicals, mowing) and one to care for the company's facilities and equipment (trucks, mowers, tillers).

During the May peak, the Exterior Department might employ as many as 65 people, many of them temporaries, to install flowers and to do the other necessary springtime and summer work. That number dropped off in the fall to about 45 and could be as low as 20 in the dead of winter. From time to time, the

Exterior Department lent its workforce to the other departments of Desrochers, including crews for the installation of interior plants and the peak needs of Wade Florist.

Facility Problems for the Exterior Department.

Especially during the spring, the Exterior Department suffered because its current site was inadequate. See Exhibit 2 for a layout of the site. According to Mike Morone, 36, the Exterior Department's manager, parking for cars and trucks was a scarce resource that, together with the arrangement of the buildings, led to significant congestion. There was congestion near the barn and even worse congestion near the flower beds as workers picked up the necessary implements

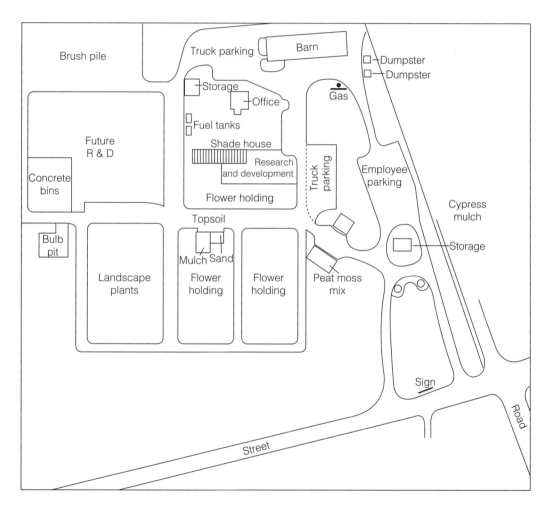

Exhibit 2   Layout for Desrocher's Exterior Department.

and materials for the various jobs that had been laid out in rows and identified by client. Coordination for the site's seven managers (Morone's direct reports) was difficult because they were housed in two different buildings on the site. A normal beginning of the day would see managers and employees outside, in various, shifting huddles, as the day's signals were barked out. The managers preferred to be located right next to one another in an interior space big enough so that they could run their operations and still be easily accessible to one another. The Desrochers corporate office (where Mike Morone had his office) was 3 miles from the Exterior Department's acreage. Letters, timesheets, and phone calls had to be handled at a distance from the Exterior Department, and this meant that those materials and information had to be shuttled between locations.

Plant holding space was also an issue. In some instances it was not enough, although Mike Morone felt that the property could accommodate a doubling in sales with some rearrangement.

The McLean site was bare-bones. There was no pavement, so the trucks kicked up dirt and dust during dry weather and wallowed in mud during wet weather. The space in the old house and the barn was reminiscent of a church summer camp. The Exterior Department paid rent of $12,000 per year to Walt and Bob Desrochers for the use of the site.[1]

Interior Department.

The Interior Department's chief business was the ongoing lease and maintenance of tropical plants. Desrochers typically installed a variety of tropical plants in businesses and then maintained them every week or two. If plants failed, they were replaced. Desrochers's enviable reputation rested not only with the quality of their plants and the care given them, but also with the company's ability to install or replace plants on short notice, often within a week. The ongoing lease and maintenance program accounted for about 80 percent of the Interior Department's revenues. The other 20 percent, and the most profitable 20 percent, came from short-term rentals of plants to meetings, conventions, weddings, and the like. An inventory of hardier plants was kept for this purpose. In some instances, Desrochers had to buy a plant and rent it out specifically for a one-time occasion. Naturally, it was advantageous if the company could rent out plants for more than one occasion. The summer of 1992 was particularly good; a series of significant events in the Northern Virginia area kept the company rotating hundreds of ferns and other plants. For the short-term rental business, scale was important. A company had to be big enough to install many plants quickly and with a balance sheet strong enough to inventory those plants for months.

The bread and butter of the Interior Department, however, were the 900+ weekly contracts that Desrochers maintained. The speed with which the com-

---

[1]The land was zoned for residential use, minimum 10,000-square-foot lots, and had a value of about $12,000 per acre, judging from an adjacent parcel of 8 acres that was up for sale.

pany could react depended upon both the pottery that was used and the type of plant. Only modest inventories of plants and pottery were kept. Most pottery was plastic and Desrochers used an outside vendor that in a day or two could deliver the seven sizes and the nine different colors that were used. For ceramic or metal pots, however, there was a time delay of two–four weeks. These pots came in more styles and many more colors and Desrochers simply could not inventory enough of the right ones.

Plants came from a broker in Florida. Desrochers placed orders on Wednesday and Thursday of one week and the plants arrived by truck the following Monday. There was not a week in the year when Desrochers did not receive plants from this broker. Inventory was taken every Wednesday before plants were ordered from Florida. If things were right, the only inventories of plants were those corresponding to client rejects, extras that were part of a regular shipping lot that were not fully used for an order, and any errors made by the Florida nurseries.

Because of the speed with which Desrochers could receive its plants, no plants were ordered until the pots were in hand. Once pot and plant were in house, installation was scheduled. After installation, the plant was visited every week for the next six weeks. Most plants had a subirrigation reservoir installed in the bottom of the pot. This innovation allowed Desrochers to water only every other week and still maintain a very healthy plant.

The Interior Department employed 36 people. The department's 26 route technicians met between 7:00 and 7:30 A.M. at the company's Glebe Road site, about three miles from the McLean site, and spent 5 to 20 minutes with their supervisors. There were two supervisors for the 26 technicians, and they split the Northern Virginia area into an east and a west segment. (The department also employed sales and warehouse personnel and installation crews.) From the morning meeting, the route technicians made the rounds of their clients and returned back to Desrochers between 3:30 and 4:00 P.M. for another 5 to 20 minutes of debriefing at the end of the day.

The Interior Department occupied about 14,000 of the 18,000 square feet at the Glebe Road location; the remaining 4,000 square feet was used for corporate offices. Of this space, about 7000 or 8000 square feet were taken up by plants in three plant holding areas: one each for trees, hanging plants, and floor plants. See Exhibit 3 for the layout for the Glebe Road facility.

The Glebe Road Facility.

Desrochers had moved into the Glebe Road facility in 1974, initially occupying a section of 5,400 square feet. Over the years it had been able to expand piecemeal by taking over space left vacant by other tenants, to the point where the company occupied 18,000 square feet.

Jim Desrochers, 35, the manager of the Interior Department and Walt's son, saw a number of problems with the existing layout and space.

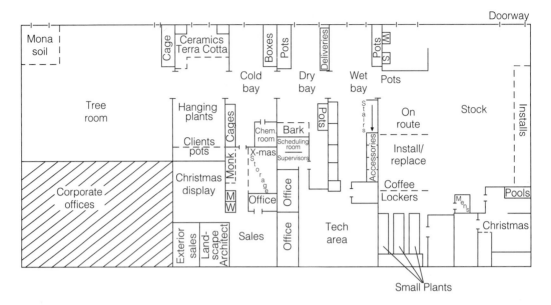

Exhibit 3   Desrochers Layout for Glebe Road Facility (excludes new storage area).

1. *Light.* The Glebe Road facility had no natural light. All of the plants were held in rooms with a combination of fluorescent, sodium, and halide lighting. Such artificial light provided the full spectrum of light needed, but these areas were not conducive to long-term holding of plants; greenhouses with natural light, better ventilation, and underfloor heating were needed.

2. *Temperature.* Tropical plants have to be held in temperatures greater than 55°F or they face damage. When outside temperatures dipped into single digits, it was so risky trucking plants that Desrochers scheduled no installations then. At the Glebe Road facility, there were only two truck docks that could be used in cold weather, and in neither case could the truck be backed into the building. This made it more difficult during the winter months.

3. *Inventory.* The Interior Department kept inventory almost everywhere. There was hardly a room in the chopped-up facility that did not carry inventory of one sort or another. The company had just secured some additional space (1800 square feet) at the end of the building, space that came free with renewing the lease.[2] That space, with more than 20 rooms, was quickly filling up with odds and ends. It was increasingly difficult to

[2]Desrochers paid $78,600 per year in rent for the Glebe Road facility. The lease was to expire in 1994. The prevailing rent in the area for buildings such as Desrochers's was between $4.50 and $5.00 per square foot per year. New space could be built for about $22 per square foot.

control this inventory and the handling that was required was both time-consuming and inevitably led to some damage.

4. *Layout Inefficiency.* New plants that typically came in on a cold day went to a stockroom, were then transferred to the wet bay for cleaning, then back to the stockroom, (or, during the summer, perhaps to the cold bay or the dry bay), and then back to the cold bay for shipping. This led to inefficiencies in handling plants and in staging them for delivery. Such inefficiencies contributed to some unallocated plant costs (essentially "disappearances") that amounted to $52,000 a year, about 2 percent of the Interior Department's sales.

5. *Communication.* Communication was more difficult because people were in nooks and crannies of the building. There was not enough space for the supervisors to be able to talk to employees individually. Individual spaces for employees were just barely adequate and often there was not enough parking. Jim Desrochers admitted that the company could grow somewhat at the existing facility, but not a lot, before things would be too cramped to perform well.

Jim Desrochers was of the opinion that nothing more should be done to the existing Glebe Road facility until a decision was made about facilities for the longer term.

Wade Florist.

Wade Florist's 37-year history began in Arlington in a building owned by Mark Wade's father. The building had been used for road paving after World War I and was made of spare paving bricks. The site was located about two or three blocks from the main Arlington shopping area and was surrounded by residential properties.[3] This location was the company's largest store, and although the other two retail outlets (Tysons Corner and Alexandria) did some limited production themselves, most flower production (70 percent) occurred at the Arlington site. All the telephone and wire orders came to the Arlington location. That site also handled all the major event and holiday production.[4] The Arlington location was responsible for processing, pricing, and distributing products to the other two stores.

Wade Florist currently leased 13,800 square feet of the 17,000 square feet in the building; the remainder was leased to an outside tenant. The building occupied a four-acre plot, some of which lay vacant.[5] Wade was open from 8:30

[3]The Arlington location was about eight miles away from both the Glebe road and the McLean sites of Desrochers.

[4]There were six major holidays for florists: Valentine's Day, Easter, Secretary's Week, Mother's Day, Thanksgiving, and Christmas.

[5]Rent in Arlington was comparable to rent on Glebe Road. The lease was to expire in 1994.

to 5:30 Monday through Saturday. Workers worked five days a week. Since the acquisition, Wade had been operated as an independent profit center.

Floral production entailed the following steps (for small orders, steps 1, 6, and 8 might be omitted):

1. *Product list.* The product list specified the hard goods (vases, pots, etc.), whether they had to be procured, what types of props, and the flowers to be used. It served as the basis for ordering.
2. *Ordering.* Through two or three local wholesalers, flowers for Wade's routine daily business were ordered and received daily. Special orders could be procured in one to four weeks. Hard goods took longer to obtain, generally two–six weeks.
3. *Receiving.* The flowers and hard goods were received by different people at the store and stacked in different areas.
4. *Processing and conditioning.* The same people who received the flowers processed them (removed excess foliage, cut stems) and conditioned them (placed them in preservative water, having first sterilized the buckets, and refrigerated them, usually overnight, to retard their development).
5. *Design.* The containers were prepared (cleaning, soaking, foam put in place), usually several hours before, and then the designers proceeded with the design. The specific designs to be followed could be communicated to the various designers assigned by sketch, by model of the design, by written order, or by verbal order. Sometimes Wade had as many as 12 designers working at the same time.
6. *Storage.* Sometimes completed designs had to be stored (refrigerated) before delivery.
7. *Delivery.*
8. *Cleanup.* Sometimes, for events, the designs and props had to be cleaned up and carted back to Arlington.

A paperwork trail followed this process. It included the product list, the order itself, a router that included a description of what needed to be done, and, if needed, a pick-up router that detailed what had to be picked up after the event.

Although the building worked well enough for Wade, it forced a number of compromises on the firm (see Exhibit 4). For example, there were many separate storage areas and the flower production facilities were separated into three distinct rooms. The receptionist was separated from the telephone sales area, and certain of the facilities were cramped, particularly the telephone sales and some of the production and storage areas. There was some segregation of the kinds of work done in each of the production areas. The design area at the front of the store did most of the every day flower arranging. The assembly area specialized in dried arrangements, silk arrangements, and most of the wedding work. The

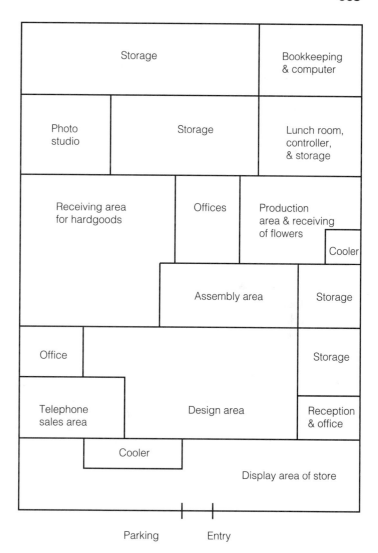

Exhibit 4 Wade Florist—Arlington Building Layout.

production room in back handled holiday work and larger production work. All of the fresh flowers were received in the production area and were conditioned there, as it was adjacent to one of the coolers. During the peak holiday seasons, there was not enough space for everything; two refrigerated truck trailers were typically brought in to handle the overflow.

Concerns About the Arlington Facility.

Rich Shinar, 36, general manager of Wade Florist, had many concerns about the current space. Wade's growth over the years took up more and more space within the Wade building. Because the building had many differently sized rooms, the layout became less and less satisfactory. Workers generated extra steps in gathering materials. There were added steps between the receipt of flowers or hard goods and their conditioning and storage. Sometimes, workers had to hunt for items, particularly hard goods. Flowers were less of a problem, but only because they could not hide in boxes. Still, there was cramped space for conditioning, and the carts did not fit into the existing coolers. About the only thing the Arlington facility had going for it was its homey atmosphere. Workers felt comfortable there and, unlike the Glebe Road facility, every worker could easily look out a window to the outside.

Trademarks.

The Trademarks concept was one of the principal reasons for seeking the Wade acquisition. Within six to eight months after the acquisition, Bob had tapped Bill Cantwell, 32, to handle this startup. Bill was a designer and store manager with Wade and had been with the company for 10 years. He had a fine reputation for dramatic and contemporary floral designs. Trademarks was to concentrate on the business community, to provide design leadership, and to develop some specialized services.

In its first year, Trademarks came near to achieving its ambitious revenue objectives, about 70 percent of which was in events (e.g., corporate tents for the PGA Tour event, and symphony flowers). The other 30 percent of Trademarks's business was more what a traditional florist does, but it was done for business customers, some of whom would have ordered through the National Bank Center gallery that Trademarks had set up. Typically, Trademarks was chosen rather than a traditional florist because of its ease of use, its design distinction, or the quality of its flowers.

In the summer of 1992, Trademarks employed only four people: Bill Cantwell, a sales and marketing consultant who was charged with drumming up business, the downtown gallery manager, and a salesperson downtown who took phone and walk-in orders. Most of Trademarks's production was accomplished at the Arlington location under Cantwell's tutelage. Because of this, Bill Cantwell spent most of his time in Arlington.

Bill Cantwell's Concerns.

Although Trademarks could make do with the present arrangements, there was certainly much to be desired. Trademarks had no production and office space of its own except for a tiny backroom space in the very expensive National Bank showroom in the heart of the area's business district. Production and a desk for Cantwell were squeezed into the Arlington facility. There was no specific staging area for event work at the Arlington site. Some of Trademarks's prop inventory was kept in Arlington, but some had to be kept with the Desrochers operations on Glebe Road in its newly acquired space.

Although space was a concern, the organization of Trademarks' production was Bill Cantwell's major worry. He wanted more formal control over the production of Trademarks' work than was possible by subcontracting it to Wade. Everything to date had been friendly, but Bill was concerned that his goodwill, earned over ten years at Wade, would shortly run out because of the demands he placed on Wade's workers. Wade's designers received no personal benefits from satisfying Trademarks' production requests. From Bill's point of view, all they received was more and more work that came in spurts, depending upon the size and frequency of the events Trademarks was responsible for. This was particularly important to Bill Cantwell, given his admitted fussiness. His concerns were not that Wade's designers were not up to the task but that it would always be difficult for Wade's designers to switch back and forth between their traditional style and the more contemporary arranging that characterized Trademarks.

Eleanor Lopez.

Eleanor Lopez, 44, had been with Desrochers about five years as operations manager and controller. Although she recognized the inefficiencies in each location, she believed that Desrochers's obsession for quality and customer service could be supported with almost any facility. Moreover, just-in-time manufacturing techniques were gradually making an inroad with service operations; Desrochers had to store many fewer plastic pots than it used to. She envisioned that storage space would be less of a facilities issue in the future. Indeed, being a bit cramped was a good thing, if it led to more discipline in the process flow. She had seen a lot of time and energy burned up with the creation of the Trademarks gallery downtown and she was not eager for managers to get drawn into that swamp.

Her concerns about facilities were not financial. The company's finances were strong enough to ensure that any reasonable facilities alternatives could be funded.

Bob Desrochers's Dilemma.

Especially with the advent of Trademarks and its events work, Bob Desrochers began to see more and more synergies among the four departments of the company. The recent PGA Tour event was a good example, as was the Christmas display at the Mall. There, an Interior Department customer used not only Interior Department plants and labor, but also Exterior Department live evergreens and labor in a design that was a combination of Trademarks' work and that of the company's landscape architect, rendered in part by Wade Florist's production staff.

Bob wondered how the departments should be tied together and how their growing facilities needs could be handled. He fretted about the pride of ownership that each part of the company had displayed and pondered how Desrochers' small team atmosphere could be sustained while the company grew.

STOCKER & DRISCOLL: COPING WITH THAMES VALLEY CONTROLS (A)

The Client Service Review[1] form stared Will Andrews in the face. He was new to this. Indeed, he was new to Stocker & Driscoll, having come from a smaller accounting firm that had merged with Stocker & Driscoll a year and a half earlier. Yet, this Client Service Review process held out hope for a thorough airing of the problems he had been living through with his largest client, Thames Valley Control Systems. In particular, he wanted help in sorting out how the London office ought to handle the poor service given Thames Valley by the Milan office and what more should be done to repair, once again, the firm's chronically wobbly relationship with this client.

He had spent the last eight hours spilling out the story of the firm's relationship with Thames Valley on the form, and now it was time for some conclusions. What actions should he advocate, and who should take charge of them? How would the Advisory Panel react?

Stocker & Driscoll.

In the spring of 1992, Stocker & Driscoll stood as one of the Big Six accounting firms, a firm whose practice spanned the globe. Although headquartered in the United States, Stocker & Driscoll had a significant presence in just about every major country. Nevertheless, the firm was, in reality, a collection of nationally based partnerships. Partners drew their compensation from the revenue pool of their particular practice, rather than from a multicountry or worldwide revenue pool.

Several policies and procedures facilitated the international aspects of the practice. (Consult the organization chart in Exhibit 1.) Partners in each country were designated as the liaison or coordinating partners for other countries. Thus, for example, there were liaison partners in London for about thirty other countries with member firms in Stocker & Driscoll, including the United States, Japan, Germany, and so on. For the major economies, sometimes partners from another country were relocated. There were, for example, three American partners in the London office who took charge of the inbound work of American

---

[1]The Client Service Review entailed the completion of a 20-page form on the status of each of the top 50 or so clients in a national market. The review detailed the personnel on the account, the comparable personnel for the client and its other financial advisors, the billing history, and assessments of the quality of the service given the client, the risks posed by the client, and the potential for additional business. The identification of problems and their resolution were critical aspects of the review process. The form was reviewed by a special committee of three senior partners that was termed the Advisory Panel. The partner responsible for the account and the Advisory Panel were charged with the development of an action plan to remedy any problems with client service and to take advantage of any possibilities for new or enhanced business for the firm.

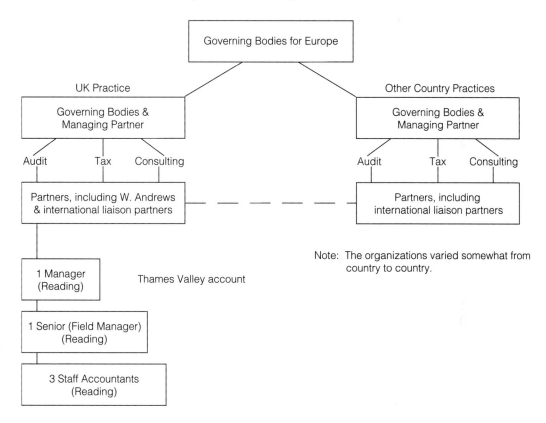

Exhibit 1 Stocker & Driscoll—European Organization Chart.

clients operating in the United Kingdom and of the outbound work of U.K. clients operating in the United States. Relocations of partners rarely occurred within Europe, however. What was more common was the temporary transfer of seniors (or supervisory-level accountants) or managers (the level above seniors, just short of partner status) from one European country to another. There were, of course, committees and managing partners that crossed national boundaries in their responsibilities, but these people were in essence wearing multiple hats, always with one hat being their base in a particular national practice.

For the most part, however, dealing with accounting issues in other European countries was largely done in an informal way, requiring heavy reliance on the firm's continually updated internal directory and the use of a vast, informal network of contacts with other partners whom one had gotten to know over the years, or by referrals from colleagues who had done business with them.[2]

---

[2]Getting to know international partners was generally done through working relationships. There were few international conferences of partners, as this was typically viewed as a "cost."

Will Andrews and Thames Valley.

Will Andrews, 42, a jovial native of the north of England with the direct, speak-your-mind style associated with that part of the country, was an audit partner based in London. He had come to the firm in 1990 with the merger of his old firm, B. C. McCormick, into the much bigger Stocker & Driscoll. He had been quite successful with McCormick, making partner at 31 and rising in later years to be a member of that firm's Management Committee for the United Kingdom. His work with the Management Committee forced him to withdraw from some of the consulting work he had specialized in. Thus, the shift to Stocker & Driscoll had saddled him with the task of building up a portfolio of clients.

Andrews had inherited the Thames Valley account. Since its founding in the early 1970s in Newbury, about 90 km west of London, Thames Valley Control Systems had been a client of B. C. McCormick. It had been served out of the Reading office. McCormick had long been strong in one or two regions of the United Kingdom, and they had dominated the admittedly small area around Reading. It was natural for a high tech startup such as Thames Valley to seek its accounting advice from the local market leader.

Thames Valley Control Systems Plc began in 1972 as the brainchild of Nigel Spear, who had conceived of an improved means of sensing and controlling high-speed, repetitive production processes such as are found in consumer goods, food processing, and materials handling. With some venture capital help, Thames Valley grew steadily. By the mid-1980s, it was a darling of the London Stock Exchange, and by 1990, it was number four in the world in its particular market segment. McCormick's involvement with Thames Valley grew along with the growth of the company. The firm audited Thames Valley and advised it on taxation, helped with its initial public offering, and did some work on Thames Valley's first overseas acquisition. However, McCormick's service to Thames Valley trailed the true needs of that burgeoning enterprise. This was in part because the Reading office had become complacent and in part because it had little experience with the issues that were surfacing at Thames Valley, such as the impact of the various acquisitions on Thames Valley's accounts. The Reading office had little depth of expertise in handling large audit assignments and major client relationships with overseas connections. Also, it had not allocated a suitable partner and manager team to give pro-active corporate and international tax planning advice to Thames Valley until two years after Thames Valley's international expansion had started.

The Sweet and Sour Relationship with Thames Valley.

The previously sweet relationship began to sour in early 1988, some eighteen months after the arrival at Thames Valley of a new chief financial officer (CFO). Patrick Flanagan, a tough Irishman in his late forties who had in the past worked for another Big Six firm, came onto the scene with little regard for McCormick's Reading office. By that time, the 1988 year audit had already been contracted for, but, for the 1989 year audit, McCormick was essentially given a year's probation.

Indeed, by September 1989, McCormick had lost the account in Flanagan's eyes. The only thing that "stayed McCormick's execution" was the fortuitious announcement the day before the Thames Valley audit committee meeting of the merger of the firm Flanagan was going to recommend with another Big Six rival. To Flanagan's way of thinking, the first few years after a merger would not likely be good ones for clients needing extra service, so B. C. McCormick was given another year's grace.

During the spring of 1990, McCormick rose to the occasion and shifted the account to the London office. A senior partner, Aubrey Earle, was engaged to repair the relationship.[3] The firm did some commercial research for Thames Valley's German acquisition, and, early in the summer, Will Andrews was brought in to be the new audit partner for the account. In addition, a new audit manager (still from the Reading office) was named, as was a tax partner, Nelson Dorly. A couple of months later, McCormick announced its own merger with Stocker & Driscoll, but by that time, Flanagan was stuck; he had no choice other than to go with the newly merged partnership for still another year. (Consult Exhibit 2 for a timeline of events in the relationship.)

During his first year on the account (1990–91), however, Will Andrews began to refashion the firm's approach to the audit (a less classically mechanical audit, especially given Thames Valley's increasing sophistication, more oriented to analyzing the true audit risks associated with Thames Valley's business and the systems it had in place) and to develop presentations to the company that were splashier and more wide-ranging. Andrews spent 150 hours on the account in his first year, double the initial budget, but fee increases were deliberately kept down. The 1991 audit went smoothly, helped by it being a record year for Thames Valley. These efforts were received favorably by Flanagan and the board, and the relationship began to mend.

In the latter half of 1991, Stocker & Driscoll performed work on a disposal for Thames Valley.[4] It was the first disposal to a management team that Flanagan had been involved with. It went off without a hitch, for which Flanagan was extremely grateful to Andrews and the firm. In addition, Nelson Dorly provided special tax and treasury advice that was also well-received. The relationship in the United Kingdom was thus mended still further and fee recovery[5] improved. Still, Will Andrews wondered if the audit for next year could be better managed

---

[3]Earle was involved with the account as the partner responsible for the firm's relationships with the Thames Valley board. Thames Valley was unusual in that only half of the board's six members were executives of the company (the company president, the production director, and Patrick Flanagan, the CFO).

[4]The disposal involved the sale of one of Thames Valley's noncore U.K. subsidiaries to its local management—a management buyout.

[5]Fee recovery referred to the percent of costs, at standard, hoped-for rates that were actually covered by the fees charged. Overall, Stocker & Driscoll had a fee recovery of almost 85 percent for the United Kingdom. The fee recovery for Thames Valley U.K. was 83 percent and for Thames Valley worldwide, 80 percent. Naturally, 100 percent recovery was the goal, but for one reason or another this was often difficult to achieve.

Timeline of the Thames Valley relationship	
1972	Thames Valley is founded by Nigel Spear; McCormick's Reading office takes on the account.
1981	Thames Valley becomes a publicly traded enterprise.
1985	Thames Valley makes its first acquisition, in the United States.
Summer 1986	Patrick Flanagan becomes the Chief Financial Officer.
Fall 1989	McCormick is almost replaced by a Big Six firm, but given "stay of execution."
Spring 1990	Reading office signs off on the 1989 audit and then Aubrey Earle of the London office brought in to save account. McCormick does work for Thames Valley on German acquisition.
Early Summer 1990	Will Andrews is named as the new account partner and Nelson Dorly as the new tax partner.
Late Summer 1990	McCormick merged into Stocker & Driscoll.
Fall 1991	Disposal of noncore subsidiary to local management effectively accomplished; UK audit goes smoothly.
Winter 1991/1992	Milan office changes the audit partner and manager of the Thames Valley account; Patrick Flanagan of Thames Valley visits Milan office and receives what he considers less than acceptable service; Nelson Dorly takes on Italian tax work in effort to remedy the situation.
March 1992	UK audit goes smoothly; Thames Valley audit committee meets and agrees to review their tax advisors for Continental Europe.
March 1992	Letter framed and sent to Milan office. No response as of 2 months later.
Spring 1992	Opportunity develops for Thames Valley acquisition in Spain.

Exhibit 2   Stocker & Driscoll: Coping with Thames Valley Controls (A).

with an audit manager based in London, with easy access to him, rather than in Reading, with easy access to Thames Valley.[6]

Over the years, Flanagan had proved himself to be a picky and difficult customer. Will Andrews met with him about eight times a year and as he related it, "Flanagan is a typically dour accountant, and probably overworked. He is an intelligent man and quick to grasp any subject. He is well-organized at an overall level but is not a man for detail. He is very demanding, often to the point of instilling nervousness in his own staff and sometimes his advisors. But, at the same time, he sometimes seems rather insecure. He doesn't like surprises, especially in anything that goes before the Thames Valley board, and he is quite willing to blame others for things that go wrong. He's driven by only one thing: earnings per share."

Still, Flanagan was very good at his job and knew what was good accounting service and what wasn't. Andrews could check off the kinds of things that Patrick Flanagan viewed as important:

---

[6]In any event, the audit staff accountants were likely to be retained in Reading.

- Good technical advice. Indeed, Flanagan was unusual for a CFO in his high interest in keeping up with the technical developments in the accounting profession.
- Integrated tax and audit advice. That is, no solutions proposed that did not combine audit and tax information.
- Proactive service that tried to anticipate the CFO's follow-up questions and that considered the issues broadly.
- Service that took a "commercial" approach, truly asking what was material to the audit and what was not, taking into consideration the sophistication of the client.
- Cost-justification of professional fees, which were always examined closely, and often argued, before agreement, but always paid promptly.

The Global Relationship.

Starting in the early 1980s, Thames Valley began acquiring or establishing subsidiaries in other countries. In 1985 it was the United States, and then subsequently Belgium, Germany, France, Denmark, and Italy. For each of these, McCormick provided some assistance. After the merger into Stocker & Driscoll, all of the subsidiaries' audits were changed over to Stocker & Driscoll except for Belgium and Denmark, which retained the remnants of the McCormick national partnership in those countries. At the time of the changeover, a briefing pack about Thames Valley was provided to each of the new Stocker & Driscoll audit firms. This was followed up by a telephone call from Will Andrews to each audit partner on the nature of the client and its key people.

The extent and nature of Stocker & Driscoll's relationships with Thames Valley operations around the world were as follows:

United Kingdom—Firm did audit, tax, and advisory work for Thames Valley. Relationship now viewed as a good one, but still with room for improvement.

United States—Thames Valley was, in general, delighted with the U.S. service. Stocker & Driscoll's U.S. firm pulled out all the stops in performing a timely audit for 1990, just after the merger. (No Americans were part of the merger of B. C. McCormick into Stocker & Driscoll.) Moreover, the American partner was a former colleague of Flanagan from his days as a Big Six staff accountant in London, and one for whom Flanagan had always had considerable respect. (Fees: £25,000 for audit and £10,000–£15,000 for tax work)

Germany—Firm did only audit work; tax work was retained by another firm. Relationship was viewed as adequate but not inspiring. Flanagan viewed the German audit as expensive for what it did. (Fees: £12,000 for audit)

Italy—Firm did only audit work. (Fees: £7,800 for audit)

France—Firm did both audit and tax work. Thames Valley was very pleased with the service, some of which had been special project in nature. (Fees: £20,000 for all work done)

Belgium and Denmark—Work retained by former McCormick partners in each country, with apparently no problems encountered.

Thames Valley was continuing to expand in Europe, and there was potential for more and more business for Stocker & Driscoll. In the offing was an acquisition in Spain that held hope for being the first opportunity to rebuild Stocker & Driscoll's reputation on the continent since the debacle in Milan (see below). Andrews had introduced Flanagan to Stocker & Driscoll's newly formed European Acquisitions department, which had been established to coordinate accounting projects such as acquisitions across country boundaries, and this new department was gearing up to help Thames Valley with its acquisition.

The Mess in Milan.

In late 1991, for tax purposes, Patrick Flanagan wanted to increase the capitalization of Thames Valley's Italian subsidiary. He needed Italian tax advice for this and sought Stocker & Driscoll's help. Nelson Dorly, as the tax partner for the account, arranged for a meeting with the Milan office the next time Flanagan visited the Italian operation. Dorly did not know any tax partners in the Milan office personally, but given that Milan already performed the audit for Thames Valley's Italian subsidiary, the Milan office was the logical choice.

Thus began a seeming comedy of errors. The tax partner allocated to the project left the firm several weeks before the meeting. Andrews was not informed of this, nor had he been informed that both the audit partner and the audit manager for the account had been changed earlier in 1991. The substitute tax partner assigned to see Flanagan took sick, so that on the day of the visit, Flanagan could only speak to an audit manager. From Flanagan's point of view, this was thoroughly unsatisfactory, and he notified Andrews of the problem in a forceful manner.

Upon hearing of the disastrous Milan meeting, Dorly and Andrews talked things over. In an effort to save the day, Dorly embarked on his own research of the issue and faxed his research conclusions to Milan for comment. There was no timely response, so Dorly took the problem to an old acquaintance in the Rome office who was able to provide quick feedback. Dorly recognized that the tax job for Thames Valley represented only several thousand pounds sterling of business, but, as he put it, "Why jeopardize the almost £300,000 in business that the entire account is worth?"

As a result of the Thames Valley audit committee meeting in March 1992, after the December 1991 year-end, Will Andrews was informed by Patrick Flanagan that Thames Valley's board would be reviewing the use of Stocker & Driscoll for some of its business on the continent. Will Andrews had to agree. As he put it, "This client is a perfect one for us—continually growing and requiring ever more sophisticated work. But we can't keep blowing things in the small bits of the account or we'll lose it all."

In March 1992, in response to the audit committee meeting, Andrews framed a letter to the Milan managing partner (Exhibit 3) that was sent under the

---

I am writing in my capacity as the senior partner dealing with the Board of Directors of Thames Valley Control Systems Plc to report the comments made at the Audit Committee meeting held recently.

Your office undertook audit and tax work for Thames Valley's subsidiary in Milan and a number of problems arose during last year that were highlighted at the Audit Committee meeting. The main points made were the lack of responsiveness on tax matters and changes of both the partner and manager on the client's work without suitable warning or communication.

On the audit, Giulio Vialli—the partner—and Giacomo Cesare—the manager—both changed during the year and your office did not advise Will Andrews, here, who services Thames Valley on a regular basis. It was very embarrassing for Will that Patrick Flanagan, the CFO, made a point of telling him of changes in our own team serving the client.

On the tax side, personnel changes again did not help. A tax adviser was introduced who we then heard only a few days later was leaving your office. I admit that his replacement's absence through sickness could not be avoided. However Patrick Flanagan, who had made a special trip to Italy to discuss among other things difficult taxation issues, was left with a meeting to discuss these points with the audit manager who could not really help him.

I believe Nelson Dorly, who is the UK tax partner for this client, has managed to resolve some of the tax issues, and is now getting his tax assistance from the Rome office; even so, the client has decided to reassess the position for future tax work in Europe, which is disheartening from our point of view.

Although the Italian subsidiary is small at the moment, there are significant plans for its expansion. They have moved to new premises and are looking for acquisitions in Italy. Patrick Flanagan has indicated that Pietro Ronza, the new General Manager, is a commercial man who has instructions to expand the operation and will want a good commerical business relationship with his advisers. There will, I am sure, be further opportunities to do work for Thames Valley if a little investment is put into the relationship.

Also, Thames Valley has recently arranged facilities to make acquisitions, especially in Europe, and is an important growing client for Stocker & Driscoll. In 1991 Thames Valley provided £280,000 of fees (£80,000 of which was outside the UK). It is, therefore, important that we provide a quality service in every location; otherwise, they will use other Big 6 firms in Europe and we may then be threatened in the UK and USA.

Thames Valley is a difficult client and expects a standard of service well beyond its size. However, it is an important growing client and Thomas Leslie [the UK managing partner] thought I should write to you to ensure we improve the delivery of our service in the future and thereby secure more work. I understand that procedures have now been put in place for this particular client to improve communication and avoid a recurrence of the problem, but Thomas felt sure you would wish to be informed of the client's comments.

Note: This letter was also copied to the Italian national managing partner.

Exhibit 3   Body of Letter Sent in March 1992 to Milan Managing Partner from Aubrey Earle, London Office.

signature of Aubrey Earle, now one of the merged firm's "grey-hairs" who had initially been brought in to save the account when he was with McCormick and who still had the responsibility for Stocker & Driscoll's relationship with the Thames Valley board. In the two months since, there had been no response to the letter to Milan.

SULFADYNE CORPORATION: CORPORATE FACILITIES DEPARTMENT

It was a hot July day in 1991, exactly five years since planning for the new research building had begun. The sounds of construction could be heard outside, providing an appropriate backdrop for this meeting. Mike Arnold, the director of Corporate Facilities (CF), remained calm as he attempted to satisfy his customers' concerns about this and other CF projects.

"We're not here to tell you how to run your business, Mike, but it looks to us like something drastic needs to be done!" Dr. Coleman's large face seemed to redden with each word he spoke. "After all, didn't the benchmarking study show some rather large gaps between how we run CF here at Sulfadyne and how the best companies run theirs? Maybe they have something. I mean, come on—seven years to deliver a facility!? By the time it gets here, your 'state of the art' technology will be obsolete. Besides, we have a lot of pressure to get new products to development. You know we can't do that without adequate facilities!"

Mike graciously acknowledged their concerns while pointing out that the drastic change in the research organization from a functional to a "product-group" orientation, accompanied by a major change of the proposed occupants, should not be overlooked as a potential source for delay. He tried not to come across facetiously, but could not help his amazement at how his research customers tended to overlook the obvious. He realized that they would all have to get out of this fingerpointing mode and get busy on solutions. But for now, it was Mike on the hot seat and he had to figure out a better way to deliver facilities.

Sulfadyne.

Sulfadyne was a wholly-owned subsidiary of a major oil corporation. A research-based petrochemical company, Sulfadyne boasted annual sales of $2.5 billion and employed 11,000 throughout the world. Its headquarters was located on the outskirts of Houston, Texas, and housed most of the company's administration

This case was written by Christopher Irpino under the direction of Professor Roger W. Schmenner of the Indiana University School of Business. Copyright © 1991 by Roger W. Schmenner.

and manufacturing and almost all of its research component. Because of its emphasis on research, there was steady growth in terms of the number of research personnel. This created a frequent need for new or renovated facilities to accommodate its current and future personnel. In addition to being functional, research facilities were seen as a means of attracting talented scientists.

Facility Delivery Organization.

The purpose of CF, according to Mike Arnold, was to "deliver facilities and technology to enhance our customers' growth, quality, and success."

The customers referred to in the above statement were the various research, manufacturing, and administration components housed within Sulfadyne's facilities. Periodically, new or renovated facilities on both a small and large scale were required. CF was a crucial internal business in a company whose survival lay in its ability to develop new products and bring them out to market faster than the competition. Of particular importance was not only the quality and cost of a new facility but the speed of delivery.

Although broad in scope, CF was part of an even larger framework called Corporate Facilities and Engineering Operations. It consisted of Facility Strategy, Facility Delivery, and Maintenance. Exhibits 1 and 2 display the organizational chart and the interrelationships affecting CF.

The four basic components to CF were Planning, Design, Construction, and Startup. Although Mike Arnold's group was called Corporate Facilities, he was directly responsible only for the first two components. Construction Services was managed by Joe Rinella. Responsibility for Startup was shared by both managers. Before the fairly new label of Corporate Facilities, the two groups were titled Design Engineering and Construction Engineering, respectively. It was hoped that the new name would begin to create the image of a single business rather than two separate entities.

Planning for the New Research Building (1986).

Brett Ferguson bolted into Don's cubicle even faster than his normally quick pace. Brett, a strategic planner, strongly believed that a key to success was always looking like you were in a hurry. This time he was.

"Don, I think we have a whale of a project on our hands! I just got out of a meeting with Dr. Coleman, and you are not going to believe the growth projections he is forecasting between now and '95—he's talking about recruiting at a 5 percent growth rate. With the number of people in his component, do you realize the impact that's going to have on facility needs??

"No," said Don, furling his grey brows, "but I think I can guess who they have assigned to figure it out!"

Don Bravin had been a research facilities planner for 17 years, this being his fifth position within the company. He had had his share of experience in planning new facilities, and he resented the new breed of strategic planners who

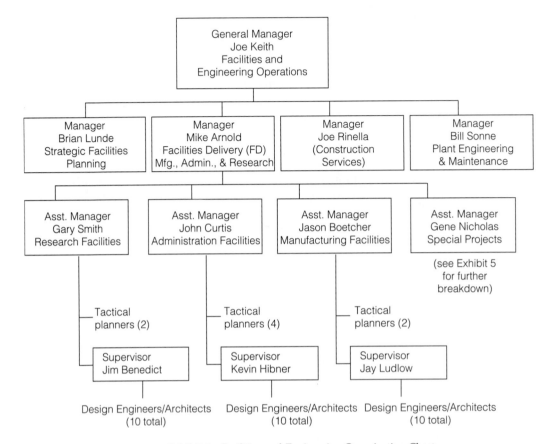

Exhibit 1 Facilities and Engineering Organization Chart.

seemed to major in politicking and knew nothing about what went into delivering a facility.

Planning in CF could be broken down into strategic and tactical planning. Although there was plenty of gray area between the two activities, strategic planning, staffed in the Facility Strategy group, leaned more towards long-term facility forecasts based on personnel growth projections and master site lands for those facilities. It was visionary in nature, focusing not just on facility needs but the business of the internal customers served by the facilities. Tactical planning, staffed in CF, came into play when a vision was established for a particular facility project, at which time facility scenarios were developed. A consensus was then reached on the one that appeared to be most appropriate.

In addition to developing alternative scenarios and rough cost estimates, Don helped to determine the approval strategy needed to get a project rolling. This involved a high degree of customer contact, and Don was generally seen by

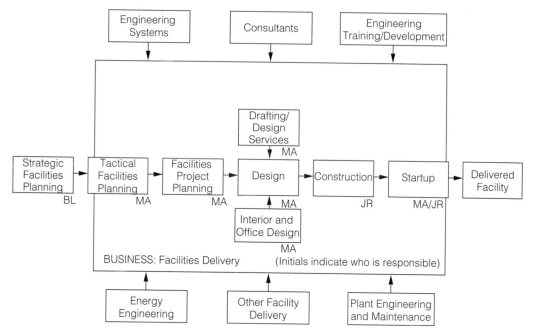

Exhibit 2 Facilities Delivery Business Diagram.

customers as the project leader during this phase. He usually headed selection of the Architectural/Engineering (A/E) firm that would "program" the building (i.e. determining room sizes and adjacencies based on customer needs) and the selection of the design team that would eventually, in conjunction with the outside A/E firm, give the building its shape and size.

NRB.

The new research building (NRB) was intended to be a state-of-the-art research facility located on the campus of Sulfadyne's world headquarters. NRB was to provide chemistry and physics labs, an engineering plastics wing, and administrative support facilities. It was to support Sulfadyne's research program throughout the 1995 planning horizon, at which time it was expected to be at full capacity.

After months of planning, it was determined that the facility would contain a total of 400,000 gross square feet, about 60 percent of which was considered usable net square feet, (i.e. not including mechanical equipment space, corridors, etc.) The building was to be 3 stories high, with basement. The actual programming document from which this summary was taken totaled 90 pages, representing months of customer interviews regarding space requirements.

NRB, like other large CF projects, followed the process flow diagram shown in Exhibits 3 and 4.

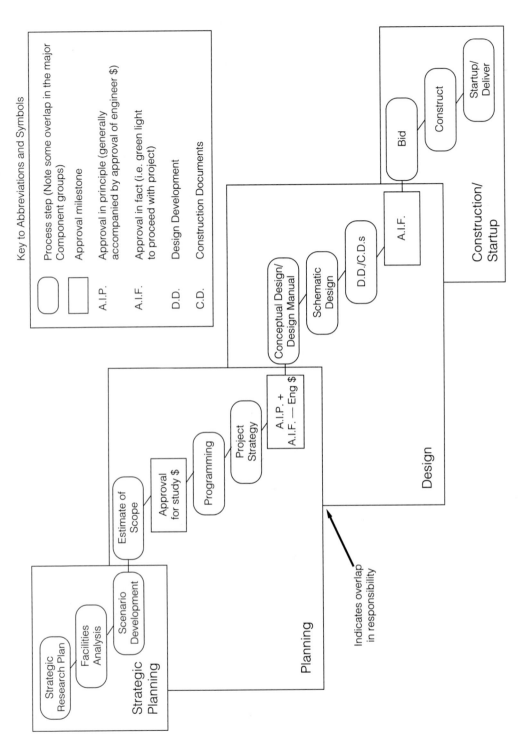

Key to Abbreviations and Symbols

Process step (Note some overlap in the major Component groups)

Approval milestone

A.I.P.   Approval in principle (generally accompanied by approval of engineer $)

A.I.F.   Approval in fact (i.e. green light to proceed with project)

D.D.   Design Development

C.D.   Construction Documents

Strategic Planning

Strategic Research Plan → Facilities Analysis → Scenario Development

Planning

Estimate of Scope → Approval for study $ → Programming → Project Strategy → A.I.P. + A.I.F. — Eng $

Indicates overlap in responsibility

Design

Conceptual Design/ Design Manual → Schematic Design → D.D./C.D.s → A.I.F.

Construction/ Startup

Bid → Construct → Startup/ Deliver

Exhibit 3   Facilities Delivery Roadmap (simplified).

350

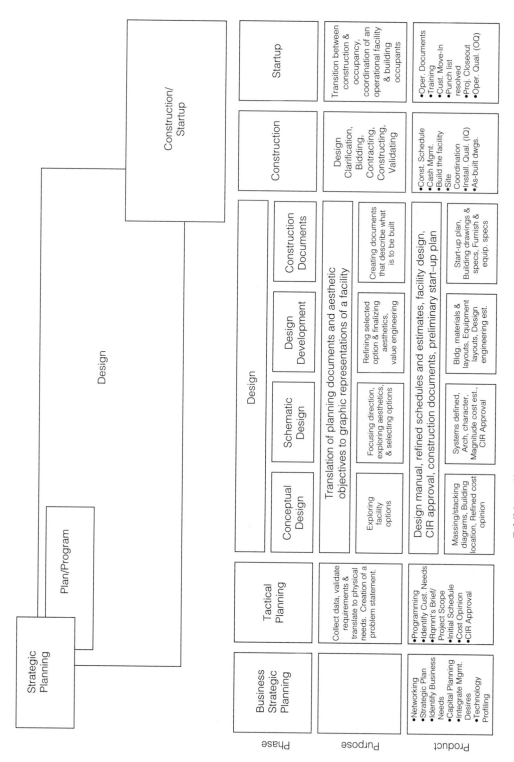

Exhibit 4 Phase Definitions (from FD Roadmap—Exhibit 3).

	Business Strategic Planning	Tactical Planning	Conceptual Design	Schematic Design	Design Development	Construction Documents	Construction	Startup
Phase	Strategic Planning → Plan/Program		Design				Construction/Startup	
Purpose		Collect data, validate requirements & translate to physical needs. Creation of a problem statement.	Exploring facility options	Focusing direction, exploring aesthetics, & selecting options	Refining selected option & finalizing aesthetics, value engineering	Creating documents that describe what is to be built	Design Clarification, Bidding, Contracting, Constructing, Validating	Transition between construction & occupancy, coordination of an operational facility & building occupants
			Translation of planning documents and aesthetic objectives to graphic representations of a facility					
Product	•Networking •Strategic Plan •Identify Business Needs •Capital Planning •Integrate Mgmt. Desires •Technology Profiling	•Programming •Identify Cust. Needs •Rqmnt's Brief/Project Scope •Initial Schedule •Cost Opinion •CIR Approval	Massing/stacking diagrams, Building location, Refined cost opinion	Systems defined, Arch. character, Magnitude cost est., CIR Approval	Bldg. materials & layouts, Equipment layouts, Design engineering est.	Start-up plan, Building drawings & specs, Furnish & equip. specs	•Const. Schedule •Cash Mgmt. •Build the facility •Site Coordination •Install. Qual. (IQ) •As-built dwgs.	•Oper. Documents •Training •Cust. Move-In •Punch list resolved •Proj. Closeout •Oper. Qual. (OQ)
			Design manual, refined schedules and estimates, facility design, CIR approval, construction documents, preliminary start-up plan					

351

Design.

After planning was complete, most CF projects were transferred to a design team led by any one of the engineers and architects on the design staff. With few exceptions, the staff consisted mainly of engineers with less than five years of experience with the company. In fact, the recently appointed department head, Jim Benedict, had only about seven years with the company. As department head, he was expected to fulfill the role of Project Manager for all of the projects in his department. The most recent count was 30 projects in various stages.

Placing considerable responsibility on new engineers was typical at Sulfa-dyne. One of the long-standing values of the corporation was its emphasis on its employees' long-term careers. It was generally expected that new engineers, for example, would stay in their present assignments for only one or two years before moving on to a related but new challenge. The company placed a high value on managerial skills, and those who learned to develop them moved up rapidly. Those who were more technically oriented either developed into senior engineers within CF or consultant engineers outside of CF, or left Sulfadyne altogether. The consultants were responsible for writing up specifications used in facilities design, and were available to advise newer engineers on major engineering issues for designing facility systems.

The design portion of CF was where much of the action, albeit hidden from public view, took place. The design process translated the planning documents and rather loosely defined objectives of the customers into graphic representations of the facility. Design projects took place in several phases, as shown in Exhibit 3, with the commitment of resources increasing throughout as the projects moved from conceptual design through construction documents. Generally speaking, the design team consisted of one of each of the major engineering disciplines (e.g., mechanical, electrical, chemical, civil, and industrial).

On large projects, an A/E firm was selected to perform the bulk of the engineering work. The CF design team worked alongside the A/E firm. This often created confusion in terms of individual responsibilities and often seemed to many of the designers to result in duplicated costs. However, the company did not have enough engineers to carry on large projects without help from A/Es. However, engineering management did not want projects to be handled by the A/E without close monitoring from its own designers. It was felt that this arrangement would be the best way to maintain consistency in designs throughout the corporation.

Design of NRB.

For the new research building, upper-level management in engineering decided upon a different project management strategy. Instead of using resources within the existing matrix organization chart, they decided that the magnitude of this effort called for a dedicated team with its own project manager. Seventeen engineers were pulled from within the existing CF group and moved to a different area on the floor. The leadership went to Gene Nicholas, a manager

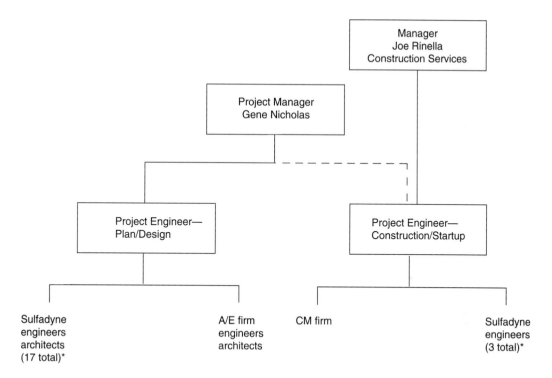

*Actual headcount numbers varied throughout the project depending on project phase.

Exhibit 5   NRB Project Organization.

from Plant Engineering. Although Gene had no experience in design/construction, it was felt that his sensitivity to plant engineering and maintenance issues would close a long-standing gap between the two groups. Besides, at Sulfadyne, managers were expected to be able to manage any group regardless of how close of a match there existed between a given department and the manager's background.

Gene was given experienced project engineers in design and construction to help manage the details. The resulting temporary organization chart is shown in Exhibit 5.

The Aftermath—Design Issues.

"I got involved in the project in 1987" recalled Gene. "I remember that first day well, because I saw the presentations given by the two top-choice A/E firms to upper management. Generally the Project Manager gets involved early in the A/E selection process, but the way these things go, I was happy to get on board when I did.

"When the A/E firm we selected walked on to the job site, they did something that impressed me a lot. They had us all get together with our top research management personnel and senior management in engineering, up through our General Manager, Joe Keith. They put on a good session to review the vision for the site and what the expectations were for the facility. That was supposed to help smooth out the programming and schematic design steps. Looking back on it though, I wish we had included our Executive V.P., Mr. Boyd. As it turned out, it took us three different schematic designs to come up with one he liked. That cost us an entire year and a bunch of engineering money. First he did not like the footprint,[1] saying it took up too much real estate. We had four wings, each of two stories, and it was a design that everyone else agreed on. So it was back to square one that time.

"The second time was not quite as bad but substantial nonetheless. It turned out that based on the personnel growth projections used up to that point, the building would contain almost 500,000 gross square feet. Well, for some reason there was a lot of disagreement about the accuracy of those projections. They finally got the projections down to where the building would be no more than 400,000 square feet—the original estimate of the building size! I really think management was scared about going over that. It was already the largest single capital expenditure to date. Besides, the original target completion date was 1990, which would have given us at least five years of excess capacity. They felt that if growth projections were on the high side we could have idle building space for the entire decade, thereby wasting capital dollars that could have gone elsewhere.

"I think a lot of our schedule delay problems are due to poor planning. We go around and around questioning growth projections and then all of a sudden we run out of space and they say "Hey, we need a new facility!" By then it becomes a rush project that we tactfully label fast-track and, naturally, we run into problems."

Other points of view were expressed by some of CF's designers on the project.

"Originally we did not feel a need to identify the specific customers who were to occupy the building. We knew they would change anyway. So, for the most part, we tried to design generic labs that could be used by any research group. Along the way we ended up designing specific space for certain groups that could not fit into the mold. Sure enough, we were right—the intended occupants changed late in the design process. But guess which ones changed—the ones we designed specific space for and are the most expensive to redesign! In fact, we are still waiting for final decisions on who is going to occupy the building. Now that the building is being constructed, the changes are becoming even more expensive. It is not easy to say to a contractor—'Hey, remember the money we gave you to build those labs? Can we have it back—we changed our minds?'

---

[1]*Footprint* refers to the two-dimensional area of the building as seen from the air.

"We really had two customers—the research groups and Mr. Boyd. The research people thought that a lot of the building characteristics were driven by CF. Actually, a lot of the expensive decisions were made by the Executive V.P., and of course we had to implement them. For example, there was the decision on which brick to use. We had selected a good and fairly inexpensive brick that was consistent with the rest of the site. Mr. Boyd was not happy with it and personally selected an exquisite imported brick, the most expensive that money could buy. That decision was basically a $2 million premium."

An interior designer cited further examples of the chairman's active role in the design process: "He personally selected the wallpaper for the auditorium, at five times the normal price! Worse yet, every entrance within the administration and research areas had to be marble entryways rather than standard drywall. In addition, the research group badly wanted to select the chairs for their own auditorium. Although we presented several varieties to Mr. Boyd, he could not accept the lack of aesthetics of the chairs they chose. He had us get the ones he wanted, which were much more expensive yet less functional. In effect, he was saying, 'I don't care about functionality if we cannot get an aesthetically pleasing look.' "

Gene resumed, "My vote for the biggest contributor to delays, however, was the lack of clear direction. Once we had the direction, we were able to move along well. And it's not like we didn't try. Months went into getting customer input on the various aspects of design, but we were always one rung too low on the approval ladder and it came back to haunt us time and time again. Maybe we should have made Boyd a full-time member of our team. It is kind of strange to me that the other projects supporting NRB, like the utility center and materials transport system, are on time and under budget. And we are not talking about small budgets—they add up to about $60,000,000, but Boyd did not seem to be very interested in those."

Construction.

Construction was, of course, the bricks and mortar of the entire project. During the construction phase, it became readily apparent whether the designers were successful in translating the planning documents into usable construction drawings and specs. If not, costly changes were made that often resulted in budget and schedule overruns. A brief summary of the activities of the construction group were as follows:

- Review construction documents from the design team.
- Prepare bid documents.
- Select contractor through bidding process (low bidder gets the job of general contractor).
- Estimate construction costs (based on bids).
- Obtain approval from Capital Budget Committee (if not already done in design phase).

- Finalize construction schedule.
- Manage field construction.
- Conduct construction meetings.
- Track costs and progress.
- Close out the project.

In theory, project leadership transferred from the design team to a construction team during this phase. The design team was to stay involved in a consultant role, assisting in solving field problems and startup problems as well as doing design changes where required. Most of the time, however, the transition was not that smooth.

On projects such as NRB, the design and construction were much more of an iterative process. For example, the foundations were designed first. Then, while foundations were being laid, the design team would design the steel frame and roof systems, and then the utilities while the steelwork was going on, etc. This was known as phasing or fast-tracking. However, the customer would generally have to face a new (or at least another) contact person when the transition was made.

Another transition point, although subtle, occurred during the startup phase. This had formerly been the responsibility of the construction group, but as of July 1991, a shift was being made to make it a dual responsibility between design and construction. An attempt was being made to develop a formalized checklist that could help track what needed to be done by whom. The vast number of systems in a building such as NRB created the need for a rather lengthy matrix that took the form of a manual. (Exhibit 6 highlights the systems designed into NRB.) It was hoped that focusing more attention on the details related to occupying the facility would give customers a better overall impression of the delivery and a better understanding and ownership of what "their" building contained.

Construction Management of NRB.

About the time an A/E firm was selected for NRB, it was decided by upper management, at the recommendation of the planners, that a Construction Management (CM) firm be used to manage the budget and schedule as well as other aspects of construction, such as the bidding process. As in design, this was fairly typical for projects of this magnitude. In light of the $60 per hour internal engineering rate charged to capital budgets, it was considered a cost-effective approach. A Sulfadyne project engineer, reporting to Gene Nicholas, would be expected to interface and oversee the work of the CM as well as the work of the few Sulfadyne construction engineers. The CM became involved early in the life of the project, once again with the assumption that the project would flow more smoothly. As one might expect, "smooth" was not one of the adjectives used by the people associated with the project:

"I think that a good part of our cost problems came from the A/E firm. I have never seen so much mechanical equipment space in a building! And it kept growing throughout the design process. We coined something that we called the

Mechanical Systems: HVAC, air balancing, hydronic, sanitary sewer, storm water sewer, waste solvent, chilled water piping, steam, purified water, ultra filtered water, soft water, domestic water, clean steam, nitrogen gas, carbon dioxide, compressed air, natural gas, vacuum, medical compressed gas, glycol laser cooling, pumps

Electrical Power Systems: 5KV feeders, 480 V double-ended substations, 480 V distribution, 208 V distribution, emergency generator and transfer switch, motor control, isolation transformers, building ground

Fire Protection: Wet sprinklers, fire rating maintenance, atrium smoke evacuation, hazardous location familiarization, star pressurization, foam deluge, halon, preaction sprinklers, fire pumps Kidde panel programming, smoke and heat detectors, fire pulls and strobes, atrium smoke evacuation system, fire pump controller

Electronic Systems: Johnson BMS, structured wiring, data systems wiring, PA system, rim panel, closed-circuit TV, intercoms, door and gate controls, allen Bradley programming, fiber-optic system, telephone system, variable-frequency drives, audio–visual equipment, IBT frame room, lab equipment alarms, autocall system

Miscellaneous: Cleaning familiarization, fume hoods, biosafety cabinets, balancing enclosures, autoclaves, cage washers, glass washers and dryers, freight and passenger elevators, dock leveler equipment, environmental cold rooms/labs, neutralization system for lab waste, biocab and fume hood exhaust fans, trash compactor, bottle washer, bottle filler, X-ray machines, iodination hoods

Exhibit 6   Building Equipment Systems.

Penthouse rule—any design changes automatically increased the size of the mechanical penthouse geometrically. It's no wonder they had to skin it with matching brick—it looks like a fourth floor!"

"I don't think that upper management understands enough of the facility delivery process. They 'asked' us to slow things down by six months to delay capital outlays. Well, that may help the financial report, but it cost us $1.6 million. You cannot just put the brakes on a construction project without cost. We had contractual obligations. And the only way we could recoup that cost and still stay within the original budget was to 'shell' more labs.

"When a new building is built, it is generally planned that some of the space, say, 10 percent is 'shelled' for future expansion," he explained. "In other words, the walls and utilities are there but roughed in rather than finished out, and of course no furniture or equipment is included. The drawback of shelling is that it costs about twice as much to go in later and finish them out, for a variety of reasons. To make a long story short, we are shelling 25 percent of the building. In essence, we are trying to save a little capital now by spending a lot later."

Another engineer in the group expressed concern about the inexperience of the CF design engineers:

"They really do not understand how the building actually comes together. More often than not, the result is drawings that are either wrong or incomplete and have to be changed in the field. It is a big waste of time and creates friction between those involved. It does not help their credibility one iota. We in construction have the opportunity to review the drawings before we send them out for bids, but we really have just enough time to make sure we know what is in the package of drawings so we know which contractors would be needed. For NRB there are over 1400 drawings. There is no way we have time to check the accuracy of the drawings themselves. And if the drawings are not right, we don't have a leg to stand on because the contractors are only obligated to do what is on the drawing. So then it's hello change notice, goodbye budget. In a job the size of NRB, a million here and a million there and pretty soon it adds up to real money problems," he chuckled sarcastically.

Another construction engineer followed up with a slightly different perspective. He felt that most of the engineers, particularly in design, were learning just enough technical information to get by. Instead, most of their energies went into getting as much exposure and management visibility as possible so as to be seen as candidates for positions outside of engineering. There were very few instances that he could cite where any significant promotions were obtained within engineering. He also volunteered his opinion regarding communications between design and construction:

"You know, I keep hearing rumblings about our customers being dissatisfied with our communications and the lack of timeliness of our deliveries. Well, it's no wonder. We lack an overall communication point for projects. We don't have anybody customers can really count on for answers and support throughout the project life. NRB is the first time that I am aware of that we have tried a form of overall project management, but even so, it fell short. For one thing, we have a project manager who did not have a good overall grasp of the construction industry. Second, there has been a lot more attention given to design issues, especially aesthetic ones, than to construction detail, and I think that is showing up in delays and overruns. Third, the customers still had to face a change in project engineers when the we shifted from design to construction. I don't know what the right answer is, but I know we didn't hit it on this one. The most positive thing I can say is that I think we are getting warmer."

Benchmarking Study.

Early in 1989, special project teams were being formed in the corporate Internal Management Consulting group (IMC) to analyze various internal businesses within the company to see whether there was any need for improvement.

One project team was assigned the responsibility of identifying and developing recommendations for the improvement of CF by using the concept of benchmarking. This involved interviewing several other companies in related fields, selecting those that were considered the best in the area to be studied, and comparing notes with those companies. The object was to see how Sulfadyne measured up to the others and to see if there were pertinent differences in operations that might lend themselves to improvement. Paramount in this process was obtaining appropriate measures based on customer input. This was achieved by means of a series of customer focus groups. The results are summarized in Exhibit 7 for the various areas included in CF.

Planning:

Bring upper management in earlier.
Accuracy of estimate.
Schedule length.

Design:

Too many design changes.
More user involvement during design.
Aesthetics versus functionality.
Innovation, standardization, flexibility of labs.

Construction:

Construction cost too high.
Understanding construction process.

Project management:

User lack of knowledge and involvement of cost control.
Organization is confusing to user.
Transfer of project from design is not done smoothly.

Exhibit 7 Customer Feedback Summary.

Aside from general comments, the customers also gave input on the criteria that they used to measure CF performance. The first three criteria were selected by the group as the ones to focus on during the benchmarking process—functional quality, communication, and timeliness. Upper management in engineering was also concerned about some of the more operational "scorecard" measures, particularly total cost per square foot and engineering costs as a percentage of construction on new facilities.

The next step was benchmarking. Of approximately 30 "very good" companies, 6 were picked as the "best" in the area of CF by the team, and were chosen as the benchmarks. A survey was given to each of the six companies before a visit. These visits were basically mutual sharing sessions with no initial attempt at analyzing differences, which were significant both in customer criteria measures and in "scorecard" measures. (Exhibits 8–10). It became rather obvious that Sulfadyne's facilities were running higher in cost and longer in delivery time than most of their counterparts.

Low-Cost Approach.

Mike had already begun to see a need to be proactive in reducing costs and lead time even though the benchmarking process was not yet in full swing. In August 1990, he sent his new department head, Jim Benedict, and a small group including the director of product development to tour a competitor's new research facility. Mike was surprised to learn that the cost was roughly three

	Sulfadyne	Benchmark Companies
Engineering Cost as % of Construction $	20%	16%
$ / S.F. — Research Facilities	$250	$212
Delivery Time	66 mo.	44 mo.

Exhibit 8 Facilities Delivery Benchmark Study.

times lower on a per-square-foot basis yet, although the aesthetics were certainly not as high, there was no real decrease in the functional quality of the facility. The A/E firm was not one that Sulfadyne had ever considered working with; they were small and somewhat unknown to Sulfadyne engineering.

A decision was made to use this A/E on a new temporary development facility located some distance from the headquarters. Still under construction at the time of this writing, the building was scheduled to take 1.5 years total delivery time. Although much smaller than NRB, the delivery time and cost were still impressive.

Although not complete yet, the building had been a subject of much controversy. Although management was delighted at the prospect of saving money and getting a first-hand look at how to save on future CF projects, many engineers, particularly in the Plant Engineering group that had to maintain the buildings, had another opinion:

"It may be cheaper on the surface, but not when you add up all the hidden costs. They are specifying equipment and materials that we have not used in the past. That means buying a bunch of new spare parts and getting a bunch of guys trained on how to maintain this stuff. Some of it is O.K., but a lot of it is not going to last. Again, that means more maintenance costs. You can bet that none of those costs show up on their dollars-per-square-foot calculations! Besides, it goes against our whole image. We have always bought the best quality materials both inside and out and hired the best firms to design it. I do not understand where we are headed."

"We would like to nip these kinds of mistakes in the bud if we could," said another, "But we were not informed about many of these decisions. Most of the time, when these engineers are asked to review drawings from the A/E, they

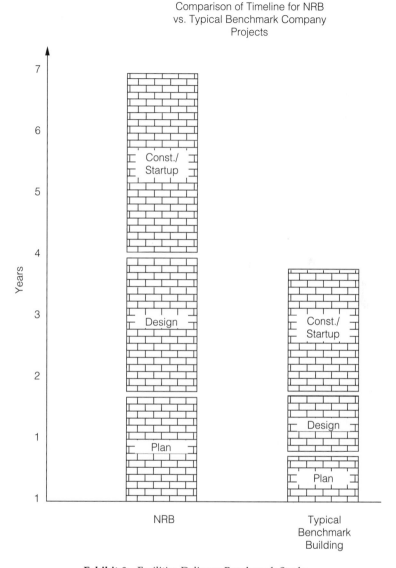

Comparison of Timeline for NRB
vs. Typical Benchmark Company
Projects

Exhibit 9   Facilities Delivery Benchmark Study.

come to us because we can generally guide and redirect them to ensure that the building is maintainable. For this new one, I guess the engineers felt like they could take it solo. I don't think they were quite ready. One could chalk it up to experience, but then again, three of the six designers have moved to new assignments already."

Item	Sulfadyne	Company A	Company B	Company C	Company D	Company E	Company F
Planning done by	Corporate engineering	Division engineering	Division engineering	Division & Corporate engineering	Corporate engineering	Divisions/ functions	Divisions/ functions
Estimates done by	Design team	Project engineering thru A/E or CM	Separate group in each discipline	Estimating group	Project engineer	Project engineer with consultants	Project manager with consultants
Project approval by	Corporate engineering	Division engineering	Division engineering	Division engineering	Not uniform, moving that way	Div./Function	Div./Function
Space utilization database	No	Yes, not in engineering	Yes, not in engineering	Yes, not in engineering	No	No	No
Design strategy	Project management & design	Project management	In-house design	Project management & design	Project management	Project management	Project management
% Engineering	20%	20%	15%	20%	15%	11%	12%
Chargeout rate used per hour	$65	$59	$57	$62.50	$144,000/engr.	$56	$57.50
% Engineers time charged to project	70%	81%	70%	N/A	No charging	75%	76%
Leadership change during project?	Yes	No	No	No	No	No	No
Historical cost data system	Yes	No, developing spreadsheet	No	No	Yes	No	No, starting one
Customer satisfaction measurement?	No	No	No	No	No	No	No
Office standards (sq. ft.):							
Secretary	80	50	—	60	—	—	—
Associate	100	80	90–120	80	80–120	80–100	64
Manager	150	150	100–150	100	120–192	120	120–140
Executive	200+	300	216–324	150–200	288	—	180
CADD system	Autotrol	Integraph	Computer Vision	Integraph	Autocad	Integraph	Integraph/ Autocad
Central CADD group?	Yes	Yes	No	Yes	No, site-based	Yes	Yes
Require CADD on all projects?	Yes	No	No	Yes	No	No	No
Rigidity of drafting standards: 1–5 rating with 5 high	5	1	3	3.5	1	1	
Typical contract strategy/construction approach (Outside const'n mgrs. unless noted)	Phased multiple bid	Phased multiple bid	Own general contractor, multiple bid	Phased multiple bid	Phased multiple bid	Phased multiple bid, own construction manager	Phased multiple bid, own construction manager

Exhibit 10 Benchmark Comparison Data.

Customer Relations.

The benchmarking study brought to light some of the concerns customers had about CF. In addition, various other rumblings could be heard among the research clientele that CF served:

"There are too many redos because CF didn't listen to what we wanted in the first place."

"No matter how much time gets spent on these projects, there always seems to be a time crunch and we get a compromised design. And no two designs are alike! No consistency."

"There doesn't seem to be a whole lot of communication between planning and design, and almost no communication between design and construction."

"I think they are competent designers. I just wish they could stay on the project awhile. I get dizzy trying to keep track of who replaced who."

"I guess it makes sense to have a break between design and construction, but I sure don't enjoy having to switch gears. It is very hard not to feel like the ball gets dropped. Worse yet, on these fast-track projects, no one in CF lets us know when the transition takes place. If you ask me, I don't think they even know!"

Some researchers expressed concern that some of the functional aspects of the facilities were sacrificed for the more aesthetic features.

"I get tired of seeing marble entryways and at the same time hearing about capital budget constraints. I cannot help but think that my new $-80°$ freezer that I was promised is sitting there on the floor disguised as marble tiles. Personally, I find it embarrassing to walk my colleagues through these gilded halls. You know, some of our external customers are small-scale entrepreneurs who can barely make ends meet. I wonder what they would think of our magnificent research palaces."

Conclusion.

Mike grunted under the force of the weights piled high on the machine as he carried on with his traditional morning workout. As the weights slapped down they released the burden. He wished it could be that easy at work. Right then, his burden consisted of how he was going to live up to his group's commitment to having "all our customers want us back!"

"At the moment," he thought to himself, "it might be more accurate to say 'All our customers are on our backs!' " And, as if that were not enough, there was the territorial infighting among the various engineering groups both within and outside of CF.

Would the benchmarking study provide the answers they were looking for? If so, how could he reconcile them with the company's long-standing values? At any rate, Mike knew it would not be long before research personnel recruiting would pick up again, along with an abrupt need to begin planning the next NRB. How was he going to set the stage for this one in such a way that he could meet customer needs and improve his "scorecard" measures?

METROPOLITAN TRANSIT SYSTEM

Dan Blocher, Director of Maintenance for Metropolitan Transit System (MTS), sat troubled at his desk over the recent November roadcall performance report (Exhibit 1). The number of roadcalls during November was up again for all maintenance garages in MTS. For the period, the average number of miles between roadcalls for the month was 4,773, compared to the industry average of 5,300 to 5,500 miles. The roadcall measure was an important performance yardstick and MTS management wanted to be near or above the industry average. To add to the concern, the monthly performance for the last two years did not have a positive trend (See Exhibit 2). Dan wondered whether the early snow storms for the winter had some influence on the roadcall experience. Heavy snows influenced some breakdowns of the bus fleet, but these problems normally involved failed transmissions. A closer review of the data in Exhibit 1 by Dan suggested the proportion of failed transmissions during November was out of line with historical experience.

Dan thought another contributing factor might be the hiring freeze imposed by the MTS administrators earlier in the year. Eleven mechanics had retired since the freeze was initiated and these positions were currently unfilled. Maintenance foremen were now using lower category staff to perform some of the tasks traditionally done by mechanics.

Problem area	Garage				
	East	West	North	South	Central
Brakes	13	10	22	3	14
Air pressure	7	5	12	4	8
Cooling system	6	5	16	5	19
Climate control	16	10	13	9	11
Electrical	21	16	27	14	20
Engine	11	5	20	12	19
Suspension/steering	6	8	8	3	5
Transmission	10	6	6	6	18
Body/doors	6	3	22	8	25
Misc.	6	2	18	4	15
Totals	102	70	164	68	154

Note: 4,773 miles between service roadcalls; Misc. = belts, lifts, fuel pumps, etc.

Exhibit 1   November 1993 Roadcall Report

	1992	1993
January	5254	5374
February	6533	5966
March	5531	6332
April	5750	6531
May	4904	5595
June	4188	4225
July	5589	4255
August	6469	4172
September	5147	4769
October	5314	4678
November	4246	4773
December	3614	

Exhibit 2   Monthly Roadcall Experience Average Miles Between Roadcalls.

Bus Roadcalls.

The roadcall statistic for MTS was a major way of evaluating how well the maintenance function was performing within the transit agency. The greater the number of miles between breakdowns, the better the maintenance performance. A roadcall was particularly troublesome for MTS, since it involved a major commitment of driving a bus out to pick up the stranded passengers and hauling the failed bus back to the garage for repair. This normally meant two extra vehicles on the road, the replacement bus with driver and the wrecker with a mechanic.

After transferring passengers, the wrecker hauled the crippled bus to the nearest garage, where six to eight hours were often required to identify and correct the problem. Certain breakdowns, transmissions and engines, were very time consuming to fix. About 10 percent of engine and transmission roadcalls involved a swap of the unit. While one to two days was usually spent on a transmission exchange, performed at a garage, an engine swap took up to three days and was done at the Overhaul Base.

Beside the time, cost, and maintenance commitment to replace the broken bus on the street, Dan was greatly concerned about the negative image of this breakdown as viewed by the customer. MTS had expended a great deal of effort through advertisements and promotions over the last three years to improve rider interest in transit service. Breakdowns on the road frustrated passengers, since it made them late for appointments and meeting specific schedules. While buses were equipped with two-way radios so drivers could quickly communicate a breakdown to the garage, depending upon the availability of equipment, traffic, and personnel, it might be up to half an hour before a replacement bus could get to the scene of the breakdown and have passengers on the move again.

MTS Background.

Formed in 1971 by the county's purchase of the old private bus company, MTS provides bus transit service to the greater Lake County region. The MTS service area includes 18 municipalities, 1,063 square miles, and a population of 2.1

million individuals. It is chartered by the state to provide transportation services in this region, with operating revenue and capital equipment support coming from different funding sources. Exhibit 3 provides a financial summary for fiscal year 1992.

As in most bus transit agencies, ridership is not uniformly distributed throughout the week or course of the day. Weekdays are much heavier than weekends, with five to six times more passengers on an average weekday versus a Sunday. Within a typical weekday, two significant workload peaks exist for the agency. In the morning, the first buses move out onto the streets at 5:00 A.M. and reach a peak of over 850 buses at about 7:30 A.M., covering the 119 routes. After the morning rush, things taper off to a normal workload level of about 400 buses on the road, with a second peak (evening rush hour) starting at 4:00 P.M. and running to about 6:00 P.M. Buses start returning to the garages at 6 P.M., with a slow reduction in the number of buses on the road until 1 A.M. No bus service is provided from 1:00 A.M. to 5:00 A.M. On weekends passenger traffic is much smaller and less cyclical, with a range of buses in service at any time from a high of 422 to a low of 280.

Both full-time and part-time drivers are employed by MTS. Full-time drivers are primarily used during the weekday, with a higher proportion of part-time drivers operating buses on the weekend. Because of the morning and afternoon rush periods, many drivers are assigned a split shift. A split shift has a driver working three to four hours, off three to six hours, and returning for the last work stretch later in the day. While the average wage for a driver is $16.50 per hour, only full-time employees receive any significant fringe benefits, currently funded at 31 percent.

Sources of operating funds	
Passenger fares	$ 39,815,643
Local assistance	63,880,732
State assistance	0
Federal assistance	7,300,495
Other revenues	4,357,022
Total	$115,353,892
Operating expenses	
Salaries/wages/benefits	$ 90,061,378
Material & supplies	11,633,028
Purchased transportation	439,126
Other expenses	7,028,248
Total	$109,161,780
Sources of capital funds expended	
Local assistance	$ 6,965,873
Federal assistance	4,500,538
Total	$ 11,466,611
Uses of capital funds	
Bus purchases	$ 11,466,611

Exhibit 3 Financial Information July 1992–June 1993.

For fiscal year 1992, the following demographic and performance statistics were collected on MTS's bus service:

- 66.22 million customer trips
- 222,300 customers carried on an average weekday
- 104,218 customers carried on an average Saturday
- 55,162 customers carried on an average Sunday
- 120,000 peak hour (morning and evening) ridership on average weekday
- 101,500 miles traveled during average weekday
- 2,218 total employees
    1,200 full-time drivers
    230 part-time drivers
    280 administrative staff
    228 clerical staff
    380 mechanics/helpers/cleaners

MTS has over a thousand buses in its fleet to cover the 119 service routes in the county. While the bus fleet is 100 percent diesel powered, it has a significant mix of different manufacturers, models, and ages (see Exhibit 4 for current break-down of the bus fleet). Both U.S. and foreign manufacturers have provided equipment to MTS over the last 20 years.

While MTS has over a thousand buses, the two peak periods in a day require only about 850 units to be on the street at any one time. This excess fleet capacity reflects the recommended guideline from the Federal Transit Administration (FTA) of 20 percent to 25 percent, issued in the early 1970s. Because of the oil embargo and the possibility of fuel shortages, the federal government recom-mended that transit agencies maintain excess fleet capacity. If a fuel shortage did result, the public would still be able to use mass transit service on a routine basis. Another FTA guideline suggests that buses older than 12 years should be retired from a fleet because of poor reliability and excessive maintenance cost.

MTS has both standard and reticulated buses in its fleet. The longer, 60-foot reticulated buses are hinged in the middle and are primarily used over express routes that run from the city center out to suburbs, along highly populated corridors. Smaller buses are used for low passenger loads across town, and short haul routes. Route cycle times vary from as short as 15 minutes for some downtown circle paths to 1.5 hours for city to suburb routes.

The buses themselves represent a rather significant capital investment for MTS. A standard 40-foot bus runs between $210,000 and $220,000, while a reticulated bus costs between $300,000 and $320,000. Bus prices have increased significantly over the past few years due to escalating manufacturing costs and regulations. For example, handicapped access capability requires new designs for doors and lifts, increasing the bus price. Currently, 18 percent of MTS's fleet is handicapped accessible, and all new equipment in the future will have handicapped-accessible systems.

Model year	Manufacturer	Seats	Number Active	Period Miles	Average Lifetime Miles
1976	AMG	49	11	197,000	547,000
1978	AMG	67	15	241,000	472,000
1982	Carpenter	23	14	163,000	214,000
1983	Bluebird	26	14	190,000	136,000
1983	MAN	67	55	1,111,000	184,000
1984	MAN	67	17	135,000	165,000
1984	MAN	44	70	1,921,000	154,000
1985	MAN	44	64	1,925,000	240,000
1986	GMC	51	82	1,327,000	234,000
1986	Bluebird	28	21	262,000	125,000
1986	Scania	42	22	579,000	156,000
1987	FLXIBLE	50	43	638,000	147,000
1987	FLXIBLE	40	25	293,000	99,000
1987	MAN	44	93	3,015,000	121,000
1988	MAN	45	81	2,468,000	170,000
1989	Gillig	45	126	4,599,000	135,000
1990	Gillig	45	130	4,896,000	103,000
1990	Gillig	43	78	3,547,000	74,000
1991	Flyer	64	25	254,000	65,000
1992	Gillig	43	37	1,130,000	30,500
Totals			1023	28,891,000	
Annual miles per active bus			28,241		
Total miles on fleet			155,051,500		
Average age (years)			5.88		
Average life miles			151,565		
Number of road calls			5221		
Miles between road calls			5534		

Note:
Number Active = Number of available buses by year and by model.
Period Miles = Total miles driven during year.
Average Lifetime Miles = Average miles per bus.

Exhibit 4   Bus Fleet Profile July 1992-June 1993

In the fall of 1993, MTS's management was planning to upgrade the fleet over the next three years, using a new ordering practice. New bus specifications and a request for bids were sent to bus manufacturers covering a three-year period. Bus producers were asked to provide a total price for supplying sixty buses per year for the next three-years. This three-year requirement was new for MTS, since past contracts covered only one year.

As a public agency, MTS was required to award bus purchase contracts on a lowest price basis. Since buses were purchased every year, different manufacturers would often submit the lowest bid each year. This resulted in a mixed fleet for MTS and a greater maintenance effort. The new three-year approach was an attempt to go with one manufacturer for a longer time period and have a more homogeneous fleet.

Maintenance Shops and Facilities.

The Maintenance department of MTS, with an annual budget of $31 million, performs all support functions through six major facilities: five operating garages and one central maintenance facility (Overhaul Base). Each of the five operating garages houses maintenance, servicing, and indoor storage for MTS's fleet. Exhibit 5 presents a summary of these facilities, with Exhibit 6 presenting the staffing assignment.

The East, South, and Central garages are newly constructed and designed for maintenance and operations facilities. The West garage is a former warehouse purchased by MTS and converted to a bus garage. It has some shortcomings that are typical of a facility not designed for bus support, including indoor storage capacity and interior layout limitations. The North garage is an old streetcar barn built in the early 1900s and was most recently remodeled in 1982.

As shown in Exhibit 5, the overall indoor bus storage capacity of the operating garages is below the overall fleet size, necessitating outdoor overnight storage. The lack of capacity is most pronounced at North, where over 40 buses are stored outdoors each night. Indoor overnight storage is very important in winter months because of the difficulty of starting diesel-powered buses in extremely cold weather.

The design and layouts of the East, South, and Central facilities provide for a smooth flow of buses throughout the three complexes, even during the busy period when buses return to the garage after completing their late afternoon/ evening routes. At each of these facilities, buses enter the facility and remain indoors during the entire servicing cycle.

A smooth flow is not the case at the West and North garages. At these facilities, buses must be driven out of doors from one part of the facility to

	East	West	North	South	Central
Year built	1990	1982	1982	1981	1984
Indoor capacity (parking)	152	155	230	165	244
Buses assigned	155	169	260	175	264
Peak period buses	132	140	212	140	217
Work bays	12	12	20	14	18
Hoists/lifts/pits	8	9	14	9	15
Fuel lanes	2	2	3	2	3
Bus washers	1	1	2	1	2

Notes: MTS currently uses 2 to 3 portable hoists in each garage to elevate a bus anywhere in a garage for under carriage work. These portable units provide greater flexibility than the lifts and pits that are a permanent part of the maintenance bays.

A fuel lane contains two pumps for simultaneous refueling of two buses after route service.

Exhibit 5 MTS Garages.

Function and position	East	West	North	South	Central	Overhaul	Total
Bus maintenance							
Mechanics	20	22	33	20	29	101	225
Skilled helpers	7	8	10	8	15	18	66
Helpers	2		5	1	3	—	11
Cleaners	7	7	10	7	10	—	41
Subtotal	36	37	58	36	57	119	343
Non-revenue support							
Building maintenance	2	2	2	2	2	6	16
Service vehicle mechanics	—	—	—	—	—	4	4
Radio technicians	—	—	—	—	—	6	6
Shelter maintenance	—	—	—	—	—	11	11
Stores	2	2	2	2	2	17	27
Subtotal	4	4	4	4	4	44	64
Maintenance management							
Managers	1	1	1	1	1	10	15
Foreman	4	5	4	5	4	9	31
Clerks	1	1	1	1	1	4	9
Subtotal	6	7	6	7	6	23	55
Grand total	46	48	68	47	67	186	462

Note: MTS hourly employees are in the second year of a three-year contract, negotiated by their union. Wages range from $18.75 per hour for mechanics to $13.40 for cleaners. Fringe benefits are estimated to be 31 percent for full-time employees. Staff get two, three, or four weeks vacation based upon length of service, plus five sick days and ten holidays.

Exhibit 6 Maintenance Staffing.

another during the servicing cycle. The bus flow is particularly bad at North, where buses often wait on the street for several minutes before they can be driven into the facility.

West's servicing workers must drive the buses outside of the building to the servicing sections of the facility, and then re-enter the facility at the service lanes where the buses are fueled, washed, and fluids added. After leaving the bus washer, the buses then cross paths with the buses just arriving at the facility after revenue service, resulting in some accidents.

At North there is insufficient room for buses to queue up within the facility or even outside on the driveway at the end of the day's service. This lack of on-site queuing space results in some buses waiting on North Avenue each night to enter the facility, with the drivers getting overtime pay for waiting, and the buses obstructing traffic on the street. Because of the crowded conditions at the North garage, an employee is assigned throughout the day to direct bus movements throughout the facility.

With the exception of North, the MTS facilities are located near the areas that they serve. North primarily houses buses that serve the northern and eastern suburbs. The facility is located about four miles northwest of downtown.

North's buses operate over routes that begin service in the eastern and northern suburbs, which results in a large amount of deadhead (i.e., empty bus) miles due to the facility location.

Most of the MTS administration offices are at the Central Administrative Complex located adjacent to the Central operating garage. The administrative facility is a five-story office building constructed in 1984.

The Overhaul Base.

The Overhaul Base is the major maintenance facility that consists of the overhaul and rebuild shops, the central stores warehouse, administrative offices for several maintenance managers, and the offices for the MTS purchasing department. It was constructed in 1981 and was designed to accommodate its current use. The Base has an extensive and up-to-date set of tools and shop equipment appropriate for repair, rebuild, and rehabilitation of buses. The Base also serves as the home for the passenger shelter maintenance crew, which cares for the 624 bus stop shelters located through out the county.

The Overhaul Base provides system wide maintenance and repair activities for:

- body repair and painting
- engine and transmissions rebuilding
- small components and electrical systems
- brake and drum turning
- radio maintenance
- shop tools and equipment maintenance and repair
- non-revenue equipment maintenance
- upholstery

The Base is divided into the Overhaul Shop, Body Shop, and Brake Shop. The Overhaul Shop has 40 mechanics and repairs/rebuilds engines and transmissions, electrical systems, injectors, radiators, turbo-chargers, and other bus components. Within the Body Shop, 37 mechanics repair body sections, doors, glass, upholstery, and fuel tanks. The Brake Shop is staffed by 24 mechanics and repairs brake systems, steering mechanisms, and suspensions. Between the three shops, the Base has an extensive manufacturing capacity that includes capability of forging, machining, welding, testing, wiring, sheet metal fabrication, molding, painting, carpentry, metal turning and milling, grinding, and dipping and cleaning.

The practice at the MTS Overhaul facility is to perform a complete assessment of the condition of buses that are brought to the Overhaul Base for any reason. Mechanical repairs and repairs of all minor body and paint damage are made to the buses before they are returned to their home garages. At peak times, there are 30 to 40 buses in queue or process at the Base.

Inspections and Preventive Maintenance.

MTS carries out five different types of inspections, performed at the five maintenance garages. The first type is a pre-run inspection. Pre-run inspections are carried out by the operator/driver before the bus leaves the garage. This inspection consists of checking seats, body, mirrors, lights, door operation and windshield wipers. If a defect is detected that cannot be immediately repaired or if a safety related defect is found, the bus is held back from service. Driver inspection of the coach is a written MTS policy.

The second type of inspection is a post-run inspection. This inspection is carried out only if an operator calls in a roadcall or fills out a driver defect card. A mechanic, with the skill level depending on the reported problem, inspects the bus to determine the source of the problem. The foreman then schedules the repair of any defect found.

The third type of inspection is a mechanic's scheduled inspection and forms the basis of MTS's preventive maintenance (PM) program. Minor inspections are scheduled every 3000 miles (requiring 4 to 6 hours), while a major inspection is completed at 6000-mile intervals (requiring 8 to 10 hours). For example, during the first quarter of 1993, the following number of 3,000-mile and 6000-mile inspections were performed.

	3000 MILE	6000 MILE
July	345	310
August	367	317
September	325	338

In addition to 3000- and 6000-mile inspection intervals, depending on the particular vehicle, additional inspection activities are added at 12,000, 18,000-, 24,000-, and 36,000-mile intervals. Any potential problems or impending system failures observed during the inspection are reported to the foreman, who then assigns a mechanic to correct the situation.

A form is used by all mechanics when performing preventive maintenance inspections. Different forms are used depending on type of bus being inspected and the mileage interval of each inspection.

The remaining inspections are semi-general and general inspections. Semi-general inspections are carried out at 36,000-mile intervals and include the same systems as the minor inspection with the addition of testing engines, transmissions, differentials, and the replacement of several valves. The general inspection is done when a bus reaches 200,000 to 250,000 miles and involves a major overhaul of the engine and transmission, as well as the replacement of several components, body repairs, new upholstery, and complete painting. This mid-life rehabilitation program, which takes two weeks to complete at the Overhaul Base, focuses upon returning the bus to an almost new condition.

The general preventive maintenance work, which is scheduled by the foreman, fits within other maintenance work. Preventive maintenance at MTS is postponed only when buses are needed to meet schedules (as replacements for breakdowns) and the safety of the passengers is not jeopardized.

In addition to the above inspections, MTS also performs some monitoring and analysis work on its fleet. For example, four ounces of old engine oil is sent to a laboratory for analysis each time an oil change is completed. This analysis detects trace metals, water, and antifreeze. Increases in specific trace metals over a period of time help to indicate maintenance problems before they become major.

Depending upon the manufacturer, the maintenance interval for certain bus subsystems vary to some degree. However, MTS has standardized some of the more common tasks. Engine oil changes are scheduled every 6,000 miles, with transmission fluid changes occurring at 24,000 mile intervals. Engine and transmission filters are also replaced during the change process. Replacing brakes occurs every 36,000 miles. An oil or transmission fluid change takes about two hours to complete, while brakes require about eight hours per axle. Either mechanics, skilled helpers, or some combination of mechanics and skilled helpers perform the maintenance, depending upon staff availability.

The major inspections generally take a total of about sixteen hours, performed by either one person or two people for eight hours each. The inspection process not only involves the evaluation of the bus's subsystems, but also includes much of the repair work found during the inspection. While inspections and repairs are the important tasks for mechanics, they also spend time completing bus log books, attending training programs, maintaining their tools, etc. These functions consume between 25 percent and 30 percent of their time during a typical week.

Inspected buses are generally repaired during the inspection so that the bus will be immediately available for service. However, in some cases buses inspected during the day shift are not repaired immediately, but are made available for service for the afternoon peak. They are then repaired during the evening shift.

Vehicle Servicing.

All buses are serviced at the end of each day's revenue operations. Servicing consists of removing the fare box vaults from the bus, refueling the bus, adding other consumables, and washing and sweeping the bus so that it is ready for operations the next day.

After the completion of all daily runs, drivers return the buses to their designated garages for vehicle servicing. Drivers first drop off their defect card reporting any mechanical problems with the bus, then they stop to have the farebox vault exchanged and turn in their "paddle," which describes the route and schedule for the service that the bus has been on during the day. They then proceed to a storage area where the driver parks the bus.

The next step in the servicing procedure involves moving the bus from the parking spot to the service lane. At the first servicing stage, fuel is added and other fluids are checked and replenished if necessary. The worker records such essential information as bus number, mileage from the hub-odometer, amount of fuel added, and amount of other fluids added. At all garages, the recording process is computerized with a key card system that helps monitor mileage performance.

The current MTS diesel fleet averages 3.4 miles per gallon (MPG) and a minor deterioration in mileage performance can be very costly. Compared to the industry, MTS is in the middle. For a benchmark, listed below are a few agencies in different parts of the United States:

AGENCY	MPG
Boston—MBTA	3.6
Los Angeles—SCRTD	3.1
New York—CTA	2.9
Seattle Metro	3.9

When fueling is complete, the buses move through the adjacent drive-through automatic bus washer and then to parking locations. While the buses are parked overnight, a worker sweeps the inside of each bus. A more detailed interior cleaning of each bus is performed every four to five weeks, where the interior floors are washed with a hose.

The larger MTS facilities (North and Central) have two bus washers and three fueling lanes while the smaller garages have one bus washer and two fuel lanes. The industry standard is one fuel and bus wash lane per each 100 buses, with 10 to 20 minutes as the average time to refuel, top off fluids, wash, and move a bus.

Work Scheduling and Processing.

Work is scheduled on a daily basis by the shop or garage foreman at each facility. Inspections are scheduled the day before, with breakdown and defect repairs scheduled as necessary. With the exception of special maintenance campaigns, there is very little, if any, weekly scheduling of work at the garages. Day and night shift foremen schedule work for their shift only, unless the day foreman requests that the night foreman finish a job that was not completed during the previous shift.

Work at each garage is processed in the following way:

1. Work is initiated by the driver either via a defect card or via a routine inspection. When a defect is detected, the foreman is notified.
2. The foreman assigns the job to a mechanic on the basis of skill level required. All assignments are done by the foreman.

3. The mechanic checks the part or system reported broken, determines what should be done, and repairs it. If the job was initiated by a defect card or roadcall, he then writes up what was done on the form and returns the card to the foreman.
4. If necessary, the mechanic will road test the bus to check the repair.
5. If the job was initiated by a defect card or roadcall, the repair is signed off by the mechanic who performed the job. The back copy of the defect card is returned to the driver operating the defect.

Work at Overhaul Base is processed in the following way:

1. Buses are sent to the Overhaul Base when the garage foreman fills out a Condition Report of Vehicle card. This card identifies the garage the bus is from, the date the bus was sent to the shop, and the work needed or problem with the bus.
2. The foreman assigns the job to a mechanic on the basis of the skill level required.
3. The mechanic then checks the part or system reported broken, determines what should be done, and repairs it.
4. If necessary, the mechanic will road test the bus to check the repair.

Mechanics keep track of their own job times. The mechanics at both the garages and the Base select the parts necessary for the job from the central floor storage area at each facility. If a part is out of stock or a special part is needed, the mechanic fills out a requisition form. If this occurs at a garage, the part or supply item is brought from the Central Store at the Overhaul Base. If the outage occurs at the Base, the mechanic gives the requisition to a stock chaser, who fills the order and forwards it to purchasing.

At the Base, special tools (drills, etc.) that are required for a job are requisitioned by the mechanic from the tool room. No additional approval is needed to obtain tools. When the requested tools have been gathered, the mechanic picks them up from the tool room and proceeds with the job. A limited number of special tools are kept at each garage. These tools are distributed as needed by the garage foreman and have been always available when needed.

Each mechanic owns his own hand tools. A yearly allowance is paid by the agency to purchase or replace worn or broken tools. A problem with this arrangement has recently arisen because of several European bus models that were purchased. These buses require metric tools while some mechanics at MTS have only English unit tool sets. This often limits the availability of mechanics to fix these buses.

Stores Division.

This unit of MTS's Maintenance department is responsible for maintaining the inventory at the five garages and the central warehouse at the Overhaul Base. This central warehouse, which includes a storeroom function for the Overhaul

Base, is the key component of the entire inventory control function. All parts are received and stored at this facility and are then dispersed to each operating garage.

When parts are received at the central stores, their arrival is entered into both the computerized inventory system and a manual record keeping system. The new computerized system was implemented in early 1993 on an IBM AS/400 system, with the manual system running in parallel until all major implementation problems are corrected. There are two clerks responsible for the receipt of parts and supplies. Once parts are received, they are either placed in the central stores inventory or distributed immediately to one of the garages. Normally, each garage prepares a daily list of parts required to sustain the local inventory or to complete a specific maintenance task, and the parts are delivered each day from the warehouse.

The central stores manager is responsible for reviewing spare part inventory positions and requested components from the garages and Overhaul facility. Based upon needed material, requisition orders are sent to the purchasing department for execution. For many commonly used parts, replenishment occurs within one to two weeks. However, other parts may take two to three months between requisition and receipt. Some of this delay is due to purchasing's search for the lowest priced supplier, as well as the general unavailability of some components. For example, components for MAN buses require a long lead time since MAN is located in Germany. Also, bus manufacturers traditionally maintain very small parts inventory for their products. To highlight this issue, the case writer reviewed the recent November outstanding order report for central stores and noted that for the 122 part numbers on the list, 37 had been ordered before September and that 7 part numbers had been ordered before June.

The entire inventory at the central warehouse is staffed by nine storekeepers and material handlers. One of the responsibilities of the central stores' staff is the daily cycle count, which is a check of a sample of part numbers of inventoried items. MTS currently stores $7.5 million in spare parts inventory, distributed across 21,000 part numbers.

Twice a day, a supply truck distributes parts to the garages from the central stores. If necessary, a particular part can be delivered on an emergency basis. A quick turn-around can be accomplished due to the location of the central facility, which is within a 20 minute drive from all of the operating garages.

There are two storeroom clerks assigned to each operating garage and to the Overhaul Base parts room. These clerks are responsible for the complete inventory system during the first and second work shifts, which span from 6:45 A.M. to 9:45 P.M. During the unmanned periods, a garage foreman accesses the parts room and obtains a needed part, recording the part transaction on a log sheet.

The inventory "turn rate" (total parts expenditures in one year divided by current inventory value) was about .50 for fiscal 1992, with parts inventory of about $7.5 million at the end of fiscal 1992 and $3.6 million in spare parts expense for fiscal 1992. The current inventory investment does not include the rebuilt backup engines, transmissions, and some other major components MTS maintains to provide quick swaps when breakdowns occur or overhauls are required. For example, MTS averages one backup engine for each model/year combination and one transmission for each garage/model/year combination.

Other Maintenance Work.

The MTS has an intensive program to maintain its 624 passenger waiting shelters located throughout the county. This task requires a complement of 11 mechanics and a manager. Each mechanic has a van that contains the necessary tools and equipment to maintain all shelters, including removal of snow. Each mechanic is assigned a route of 55 to 60 shelters.

Bus Appearance.

Dan Blocher recognized that the bus's appearance was very important in projecting a good image, encouraging customers to repeat their use of bus service if pleased with the transit facilities and equipment. A recent spot check of buses by garage, summarized in Exhibit 7, gives an indication of the fleet's physical appearance.

Study Guide Questions.

1. Evaluate the current maintenance effort at MTS. Is it adequate to support the bus fleet?
2. What is your evaluation of MTS's new three-year bus purchasing plan? Would you recommend moving ahead with it?
3. Is the high spare parts inventory a problem? What would you recommend to Dan Blocher?

	Exterior condition				Interior condition		
Garage	Body rust	Dent/ scrapes	Dirty backs	Misc.	Torn seats	Broken glass	Graffiti
East	3%	20%	33%	0%	0%	0%	3%
West	7	20	60	0	6	0	0
North	14	40	22	26	22	4	16
South	16	21	38	0	17	10	0
Central	9	21	16	19	10	0	8

Exhibit 7 Bus Appearance Summary by Garage. Percent Buses with Indicated Problems.

USA SERVICES:
LOAN DISBURSEMENT SERVICES[1]

It had not been a good week for Cheryl Pearson. First, she was marooned in Sacramento by bad weather during a business trip. Then, she was calling her voice mail and repeatedly hearing the litany of client complaints, one after another. And, now, after actually seeing the data that one of her managers had developed at her instigation (Exhibit 1), this report showed that some client correspondence was still in the system two months after it had been entered, and this when the standards for turnaround were in no case longer than five working days. No wonder the clients were upset.

Something had to be done to establish more control of the process, but what? The tracking system pilot that had been established to improve management of this process was a month old. None of the workforce liked it, and it looked like this version of the tracking system was going down in flames just as its two predecessor versions had done.

Should she work hard to save the pilot, perhaps an expensive proposition? Or, should she abandon it? But what to put in its place? Keeping the status quo just did not seem acceptable.

USA GROUP and
Loan Disbursement Services.

USA GROUP Inc., located in Fishers, Indiana, just northeast of Indianapolis, was the nation's largest guarantor and administrator of student loans. Started in 1960 as United Student Aid Funds Inc. (hence USA GROUP), the company served as an agent for banks and colleges and offered a variety of student financial lending services.

At a basic level, the company "guaranteed" loans by checking that student applications (or those of their parents) for a variety of federally-sponsored education loan programs were in compliance with regulations and that the student was eligible for them and providing the "collateral" for the lenders making the loans. The company could add more value for its lenders by administering their loans and actually disbursing the checks to pay for tuition. And, it could service the loans, following up on loan repayments once students had left school.

The Loan Disbursement Services (LDS) department of USA Services Inc., one of several USA GROUP companies, was responsible for the disbursement of checks for over 200 banks granting loans to students from across the country. Cheryl Pearson was its director. The department had experienced significant business growth. It currently employed 76 people and was divided into the following areas:

[1] This case was written by Professor Roger W. Schmenner of the Indiana University School of Business.

DATE   March 11, 1994

SUBJECT   **LDS Backlog Update**

Cheryl, per your voice mail on March 8, listed below are the functions identified that are greater than two weeks outstanding in the Client Services, Client Balancing, Affinity and WhizFund Operations.

Task	Number outstanding	Oldest date	Action to be taken
Client Services			
Stop pay reissues	3	1/27/94	
Cancels	50	2/28/94	
Increases	1	2/18/94	
Decreases	16	2/28/94	
Grad date changes	2	2/28/94	
School code changes	N/A		
Disbursement date changes	N/A		
SSN correction	1	2/28/94	
Loan period change	7	2/28/94	
Cost-aid	36	1/5/94	
Reguarantee	9	1/18/94	
Reinstatements	9	1/27/94	
Late disbursement	1	1/10/94	
Reissues	19	2/1/94	

(Continued)

Exhibit 1   Status of Outstanding Client Correspondence

Task	Number outstanding	Oldest date	Action to be taken
Excessive loan adjustments	1	2/1/94	
Miscellaneous research	86	10/93	
Citibank tape exchange analysis	100	1/17/94	
Posting refunds to EAGLE	70	12/22/93	
Client Balancing			
Late disbursement report			Report wasn't run for a while. Report has been run 2/28 & 3/7, but has not been worked yet. Will be worked ASAP.
Cancel logs	203	2/15/94	2/15 cancel logs sent to accounting on 3/10. 2/28 log 1 missing documentation and is not balanced; all others have been submitted for approval. 2/15 cancel logs have gone to accounting. 2/28's are being approved and will be sent to accounting by the end of the week.
Fee billing statements	50	1/31/94	Waiting for registers.
Past dues	134	2/28/94	Working on, processing, & researching.
ELSC research	41	9/93	Researching
Late disbursement	28	3/3 3/7	Completed. Keying info on CRIT 3/10.
Fees not paid	51	1/31/94	Processing

Exhibit 1 (*continued*)

LDS Disbursement Approval This team was responsible for reviewing loan applications and matching data to the notice of guarantee to approve the disbursement of the loan.

LDS Operations The Operations staff was responsible for handling all paper check disbursements, including the management and distribution of loan checks and lender/servicer loan documentation packets.

LDS WhizFund and Affinity Programs The WhizFund and Affinity team managed all electronic fund transfers between LDS and participating schools as well as alternative loan disbursements through special USA Funds "Affinity" programs.

LDS Client Services This service team was responsible for receiving and processing changes for loans disbursed by LDS and for performing all special functions required to ensure high quality loan disbursement.

LDS Client Balancing The Client Balancing staff was responsible for handling ongoing balancing operations, such as reconciliations and fee billing.

Correspondence Processing.

Within LDS Client Services was an area known as Correspondence Processing. During an average month, the Loan Disbursement Services department received 15,000 pieces of correspondence. This correspondence was of three major types:

- Letters or faxes from clients, either schools or lenders. This correspondence might employ some standard forms that USA Services provided to clients or it might be on the clients' own stationery.
- LDS service requests received by USA Services' customer assistance representatives (who received the requests from borrowers, lenders, and/or schools). These reports were known as "blue sheets," as they always came on distinctive blue paper.
- Interoffice mail from other units of USA Services.

In addition, clients called the account representative assigned to them directly. The account representatives would fill out a "call sheet" to document the call and process the call sheet.

The purpose of all this correspondence was to order some change in a student loan with which the lender and/or the school was associated. There was a list of 36 different types of correspondence that could enter the area (see Exhibit 2), but most of that correspondence could be broken down into four major categories:

1. Cancellations of the loan.
2. Stop payments on the check, followed either by a reissuance of a check for a different loan amount or by a cancellation.
3. Reissuance of a check.
4. A large catch-all category of changes to the terms of the loan or the information on the identity of the loan. These changes included such things as changes in the amounts of the loan, length of the loan, check disbursement dates, social security number corrections, school code changes, and the like. These changes typically had to be data-entered into the USA Services computer for a nightly batch run.

1/10/94 Standard Report

Correspondence type	Correspondence type description	Expected turnaround
1	Cancellation	1
2	NRB cancel	1
3	Stop pay/reissue	3
4	Stop pay/cancel	2
5	Reissue check	2
6	Disbursement date change	3
7	Cost—aid change	3
8	Loan period change	3
9	Grade date change	3
10	Grade level change	3
11	First pmt date change	3
12	SSN change	3
13	NRB decrease	1
14	Disbursed decrease	5
15	NRB increase	4
16	Disbursed increase	5
17	Paid-in-full	1
18	Applicant delete	3
19	Guarantee date change	3
20	Application ID change	3
21	School code change	4
22	Reguarantee	5
23	Reprocess	5
24	Late disbursement	5
25	Leave of absence	5
26	Check copies—here	1
27	Check copies—RAMM	3
28	Check copies—INB	5
29	ELSC suspense	1
30	Guarantee fee only	1
31	Miscellaneous checks	2
32	Miscellaneous	5
33	Interest rate change	3
34	Reinstatement	3
35	Refund	2
36	Expected family contribution	3

Exhibit 2   Types of Correspondence

There were standards set on how long each of the 36 different kinds of changes called for by client correspondence should take (see Exhibit 2 for the expected turnarounds), but these standards had been established years ago and did not reflect current business requirements. The ability to meet these standards depended greatly on the volume of correspondence striking the department. During peak months, typically September/October and December/January, the correspondence could be over 20,000 pieces per month, while correspondence in July might only be 12,000 pieces per month.

The correspondence entering the department was handled first by one of two correspondence processors who were responsible for counting the correspondence and distributing it to the account representatives, currently five in number, but soon to be increased to eight in anticipation of the next peak season. For years the account representatives had been matched to lenders, so that lenders could call a single person and have their questions resolved by someone familiar with them and the way they operated. This, in turn, meant that the mail had to be sorted by lender.

Although some lenders had accounts scattered across the country, most lenders' loans were concentrated in the particular regions of the country in which they did most of their business. Specific lenders tended to serve specific schools. A student's social security number, lender, and school were all tied together in USA Services' computer system, so it was an easy matter to go from one to the other.

Once the correspondence processors sorted and counted the correspondence for the account representatives, they did not see it again. After the account representatives had completed the changes requested, they forwarded the correspondence to one of three file clerks. The file clerks followed the convention of filing the correspondence by lender, within lenders, and by social security number, in case reference had to be made later.

The processing task involved a number of steps. Account representatives had to read the correspondence carefully to determine exactly what was being requested. Requests frequently required multiple operations, and these often had to be done in a specific order. All of the account representatives had a computer terminal at their desks through which they could access EAGLE™, USA Services' computer system. Through EAGLE™ they could find out different things about the loan. Some of the required changes could be made directly "on-line," but others had to wait for the nightly batch run of EAGLE™. To manage the pending work, the account representatives filed the correspondence into a series of 12 trays in an overhead bin. Account Representatives were given the freedom to file work to best meet their needs. Therefore, different account representatives filed their work in different ways.

The time it took the account representatives to work through the correspondence given them depended on several factors:

- The mix of items to process. Some changes were more complex and time consuming to make than others. The changes that could be made "on-line" with EAGLE™ were naturally much faster than the changes that had to be run overnight. If, for some reason, the overnight batch run on EAGLE™ was not successful, then another day, at least, would be spent before the change could be completed.

- The volume of work on the account representative's desk. Obviously, if the account representative had received large volumes of correspondence recently, getting through that volume would take more time and thus lengthen the turnaround time for the request. Each of the account representatives was assigned a set of lenders (usually between 30 and 40) that were unique to him or her. Because of the mix of lenders, conceivably, one account representative could be overloaded with work, while another enjoyed a manageable load. Typically, due to volume fluctuations that affect all representatives, if one account representative was swamped, odds were that all of the account representatives were swamped.

- Phone traffic. The account representatives also constantly received service requests via the telephone. Lenders would frequently call their account representative to ask a particular question, request a change, or inquire about the status of specific loan disbursements. The more calls and the longer they took to respond to, naturally, the less time available to work through the correspondence volume on their desk.

Controlling Correspondence Operations.

The current controls in place for the correspondence operations were rudimentary:

1. The incoming mail was counted for each account representative by the correspondence processors. There were, however, other ways by which an account representative could receive an item on which to work. For example, interoffice correspondence was not routed through the correspondence processors but placed directly in an account representative's in-box.

2. The account representatives themselves kept tallies each day on what they had received and what they had completed (See Exhibit 3 for a tally sheet summary for a day's work by all five account representatives.) It took an account representative about half an hour to fill out a tally sheet completely and correctly. Doing so meant going through each bin of correspondence, sorting it if it was not sorted correctly, and counting it.

   Mounting volumes often caused the account representatives to be less than religiously diligent with the tally sheets. Estimates were often made. What was left outstanding today might not have been counted completely and, thus, not fully reconciled with the amount of work carried forward from yesterday and the amount of work received today. Similar estimates were often made about the phone calls received or placed during the day. The account representatives suggested that the tally sheets were 80 percent accurate.

3. The account representatives' tally sheets and the correspondence processors' counts were combined each week into a summary report. The quality of the weekly summary report was uneven, given that it depended on estimates and tally sheets.

NAME: _Tally_

DATE: _3-10-94_

Telephone Call Volume

	Incoming	Outgoing
Lender		
School		
Borrower		
Interoffice		
Customer Assistance		
TOTALS	_116_	_69_

Correspondence Volume

NRB Decreases/Cancels	Stop Payment/Cancels	Stop Payment/Cancels
Carried forward _18_	Carried forward _4_	Carried forward _17_
Received today _59_	Received today _1_	Received today _3_
Completed today _14_	Completed today ___	Completed today ___
Outstanding _3_	Outstanding _5_	Outstanding _20_
Oldest data ___	Oldest data ___	Oldest data ___
		Submitted ___

Batching Updates	Late Disbursements	Graduation Date Report
Carried forward _142_	Carried forward _1_	Carried forward _1_
Received today _54_	Received today ___	Received today ___
Completed today _15_	Completed today ___	Completed today ___
Outstanding _121_	Outstanding _1_	Outstanding _1_
Oldest data ___	Oldest data ___	Oldest data ___
Submitted ___		Submitted ___

Reinstatements	Reguarantee/Reprocess	Loan Decreases
Carried forward _5_	Carried forward _3_	Carried forward _18_
Received today ___	Received today ___	Received today _1_
Completed today ___	Completed today ___	Completed today _2_
Outstanding _5_	Outstanding _3_	Outstanding _17_
Oldest data ___	Oldest data ___	Oldest data ___
Submitted ___		Submitted ___

Miscellaneous	Reissue Checks	Totals
Carried forward ___	Carried forward _14_	Total Correspondence Received _118_
Received today ___	Received today ___	Total Correspondence Completed _151_
Completed today ___	Completed today ___	Total Correspondence Outstanding _256_
Outstanding ___	Future reissues _30_	
Oldest data ___	Outstanding _14_	Miscellaneous totals _41_
Submitted ___	Oldest date ___	

Exhibit 3 LDS Client Services Daily Status Report

The department did not know precisely how much correspondence it received of different sorts, nor did it know exactly how many items the account representatives completed during any period of time. There was no mechanism to verify that a particular piece of correspondence had made it to the department and if the computer system did not show the requested change, there was no mechanism to track its location. Thus, when a client called to request status information or to complain of something not yet accomplished, the department's supervisors could not easily track it down. They could, of course, start with the knowledge that the client's request should have been processed by a particular account representative. That account representative then could examine all the work stored at his or her desk. Often this search would reveal the request, and discussion with the account representative would usually reveal why the request was taking so long to run through the system. However, there were no guarantees that such a search would resolve the client's request.

The present 12-trays-in-the-overhead-bin system had been in place for about two years. Prior to that the account representatives used a system with a tray for every day of the week. The account representatives were instructed to work on the oldest day first, with the expectation that when the week was over, all of the work from the oldest day would have been completed. However, with increases in volume and with problems clearing some client requests in a week's time, the old tray system got clogged and account representatives many times lost control of what they should work on. This prompted the new system that sorted correspondence by type, without regard for its "age" in the system.

The Controls Desired.

There were a number of reasons why the Loan Disbursement Services management team wanted more controls in place. Some pertained to resolving client inquiries, while others pertained to the measurements and management of workload, service, and throughput.

- Knowing which client correspondence had not been processed within the standard turnaround times. If Loan Disbursement Services knew what was aging, it could be more proactive and not wait to react to a client call or complaint. This meant knowing when correspondence was received, where it was in the process, and when it had been completed.

- Knowing what current turnaround times actually were, so that such information could be communicated to the clients by USA Services field representatives and by the phone-based customer assistance representatives who also handled client inquiries. This would help educate clients about service levels and reduce processing update inquiries. This meant knowing how much work was outstanding with the account representatives and how long requests were in the system.

- Knowing current processing capacities so that accurate staffing decisions could be made.

- Knowing how much work individual account representatives had done during the year would make performance reviews easier to develop. Many managers did not trust the service level sampling that was current procedure.

The Tracking System Pilot.

In an effort to gain more control over the correspondence processing area, Cheryl Pearson had authorized the development of a PC-based tracking system for all the correspondence entering the department. Currently, the tracking system was operating as a pilot involving just one of the account representatives, John Doe. It was accepted that the tracking system and its usage was in its infancy. A somewhat similar tracking system had worked well at Education Loan Servicing Center, Inc. (ELSC), one of the other USA GROUP companies.

The tracking system worked as follows:

1. After receiving and sorting correspondence for each account representative, the correspondence processor sat down with John Doe's incoming correspondence and called up a program on a stand-alone PC.

2. For each piece of correspondence, the processor would enter the date received, the student's social security number, John's name as the account representative, a 6-digit lender code, and the type of correspondence it was (which one of the 36 types listed in Exhibit 2).

   If the lender code was not already on the correspondence, the processor had to use the EAGLE™ system to determine the lender number from the social security number of the student. On average, the determination of the various codes to enter plus the entry of the information onto the PC took between 45 seconds and 1 minute for each piece of correspondence.

3. Once all the pieces of correspondence were entered, a report was generated from the information keyed into the tracking system (a portion of which can be seen in Exhibit 4).The report and the correspondence were then given to John.

4. Once John received the packet of materials, he verified, with a check mark, each piece of correspondence on the report. Sometimes, due to the newness of the process and the correspondence processors, some pieces of correspondence were not really for him and had to be routed elsewhere within USA Services, and the report would have to be corrected to indicate such change.

5. John then worked through the correspondence, noting his completion of the request on both the correspondence itself and the report sheet.

6. When he had worked through all the correspondence, but usually before all of it had been successfully completed (that is, before all of the problem cases had been resolved), John returned the report and as much of the correspondence as possible to the correspondence processor.

7. The correspondence processor then keyed the completion date into the PC program and routed the completed correspondence to the file clerks.

Date Received	SSN	Check Mark	Correspondence Number	Correspondence Description	Lender ID	Lender Name	Follow-up Date	Comments
3/09/94			9	Graduation date change	11111	Bank A		
3/09/94			10	Grade level change	22222	Bank B		
3/09/94			12	SSN change	33333	Bank C		
3/09/94			13	NRB decrease	44444	Bank D		
3/09/94			13	NRB decrease	22222	Bank B		
3/09/94			14	Disbursed decreased	33333	Bank C		
3/09/94			32	Miscellaneous	55555	Bank E		Research
3/09/94			32	Miscellaneous	55555	Bank E		Research
3/09/94			32	Miscellaneous	55555	Bank E		Research
3/09/94			32	Miscellaneous	66666	Bank F		Research
3/09/94			32	Miscellaneous	77777	Bank G		Research
3/09/94			32	Miscellaneous	88888	Bank H		
3/09/94			32	Miscellaneous	77777	Bank G		Research
3/09/94			32	Miscellaneous	88888	Bank H		Research
3/09/94			32	Miscellaneous	22222	Bank B		
3/09/94			32	Miscellaneous	99999	Bank I		Research

Exhibit 4 Daily Received Correspondence Report

Problems with the Pilot.

The pilot met resistance from both John Doe and from the correspondence processors. For John, the tracking system meant a good deal more work. Due to the newness of the process, on average, tracking took him between 60 and 75 minutes per day. He kept the same number of lenders as clients, so he was obliged to work overtime and Saturdays to keep up. Although he understood the reason for the tracking system, he still did not like it.

The correspondence processors found it difficult to examine each piece to determine which of the 36 codes applied. They also had to jump between the PC and EAGLE™ computer systems to find the lender code, if it was missing. They felt it took too much time as well.

In addition, there were some problems in how the tracking system operated. The pieces of correspondence in any packet were almost certain to have different expected turnaround times. Thus, John could never return a report and a fully completed packet; some items always had to be retained for additional work. Reconciling reports and leftover pieces of correspondence then became a problem. John had resorted to running off copies of the report so that stray items could be identified.

Some items of work escaped the tracking system altogether. Sometimes work showed up in John's in-box from elsewhere at USA Services without going through the correspondence processors, and thus, without being entered into the tracking system. For this reason, even carefully done tally sheets would not match what the tracking system showed that John had completed.

This was the third pilot of a tracking system to be used in the correspondence processing area. Both previous attempts had failed within the past year, largely for lack of support from the account representatives who saw it as extra work with no benefit to them. The reaction to this third pilot was apparently much the same.

On the Horizon.

It was Cheryl's dream, shared by her management team, that the problems of control would go away with some expected investments over the next several years:

> The EAGLE™ computer system was being revamped in the next two years. Gone would be the overnight batching and computer processing that caused so many delays and prevented the real time modifications of many accounts.
>
> Documents could be imaged when they were received so that Loan Disbursement Services could avoid the handling of so much paper. This was already done in the application processing area of USA Services. Adapting imaging to LDS would require process changes, systems development work, and an investment of approximately $100,000 in new equipment that the company was not prepared to make at this time.
>
> Common forms and bar coding of key information would also help keep the process under control. This, too, would require investment and some care in rolling the changes out to the lenders and schools that would be encouraged to use them.

For the time being, however, these innovations were "on the horizon," not something that Loan Disbursement Services could count on in the short term.

Cheryl's Dilemma.

Cheryl recognized that the pilot tracking system was not efficiently meeting the original objectives and was not being embraced by the workforce. Nevertheless, she also recognized that the current system was deficient and would continue to be so, especially if volumes kept increasing as they had been over the past several years. Although Loan Disbursement Services had not lost any clients due to these problems, those clients were more and more disheartened with LDS's correspondence processing performance.

Certain members of the LDS department wanted to try some further refinements that might make the tracking system work more smoothly. One idea was to develop some common, color-coded forms for the area that would be easy to identify and would ease the job of classifying the correspondence type for the correspondence processors. A separate mail code for the Correspondence Processing area would also help to route the correct mail from clients to the area. They also wanted to introduce a new, trained worker to the system, one who could check on the validity of the correspondence coming to the area so that only the proper correspondence for the area would be entered into the tracking system and could be done so quickly.

Cheryl Pearson felt she needed to take some action. The pilot needed either to be scrapped or infused with some new features and with more commitment. But, if it were to be scrapped, then what could replace it? She could not wait two years for systems enhancements to relieve her of the area's control problems. Something had to be done now.

Exercises

1. Flowers' Gourmet Food Store has come into vogue; sales are up by 20 percent over last year. On an increasing number of occasions, however, the wait for checkout has been uncomfortably long. The store is served by only two cash registers, which are located near the exit. The store's management realizes that an additional cash register or two must be installed, but where? One option, of course, is to install the register(s) near the other two, although this would necessitate some rearrangement of the exit area. Another option, requiring less rearrangement, would be to put a cash register in a particularly busy department or two (such as deli, wine bins, butcher shop). Many customers come in for one or two items only and could use these cash registers.
   a. How should Flowers' Gourmet make such a decision?
   b. What data should be collected?
   c. What factors would tip the decision toward one option or the other?
   d. Would a simulation model be helpful for such a decision, and if so, what should its structure be?

2. Several hundred different kinds of paperwork passed through the back office of this "service factory." Two of them, however, account for 30 percent of the total output. Both of these "products" follow the same general sequence of operations: sorting, telephoning, processing, and copying. The following percentages of production time are spent by the two parts on each set of operations: 20 percent sorting, 40 percent telephone inquiry, 10 percent processing, and 30 percent copying.

   The inventory of machines in the department is as follows:

OPERATION	NUMBER IN DEPARTMENT	SYMBOL TO USE IN LAYOUT
Sorting	7	□
Telephone inquiry	8	○
Processing	3	△
Copying	4	◊

The utilization has been fairly even at about 75 percent for each type of operation. Using the symbols (1 symbol = 1 machine), design a layout for the department. Explain your reasoning.

3. The Thunder Bank was a regional processor of VISA and Mastercard transactions for merchants. For transactions over a certain dollar limit, merchants were required to phone in for an authorization before the sale could be completed. The Thunder Bank handled an average of 2000 authorization calls per hour during most of the year and 4000 calls per hour during the Christmas buying season. The receptionists at the bank could handle 45 calls per hour, on average. The bank wanted to maintain a service standard of 60 seconds average wait per call.
   a. How many receptionists do you estimate the bank needs to employ during the nonpeak period of the year in order to meet its service standard? What assumptions have you made to come up with this estimate?
   b. How many receptionists does it need for the Christmas season?

4. Suppose that the Thunder Bank purchased the credit card business of another bank that had a substantial volume of transactions (1000 per hour average during the off-peak season and 200 calls per hour on average during the Christmas peak). How would the additional volume of calls affect the authorization process? Would you expect the number of receptionists to have to increase in the same proportion as the increase in calls (50 percent more), less than proportionately, or more than proportionately? Why?

5. Refer back to Problem 3. Suppose that the service standard was relaxed to a 75-second average wait per call? How would that change the number of receptionists needed for both the nonpeak times and the Christmas season? What would happen if the service standard were tightened to a 45-second average wait?

6. Refer back to Situation 4-1. Suppose that the office can handle 22 an hour. Recalculate the queuing performance formulas for this change.

7. Refer back to Situation 4-1. Suppose that the office handles 22 an hour but that 20 per hour enter the line. Recalculate the queuing performance formulas for this change.

8. Sal's Pizza operates a delivery service that promises delivery within 40 minutes of a call-in order or the customer gets $2 off the price. Sal's operation can make a pizza every 3 minutes, on average. Pizzas take 12 minutes to bake, leaving Sal's delivery team 25 minutes to deliver the hot pizza. The travel area around the pizza shop was 10 minutes maximum. Assuming that calls for pizza came in at the rate of one every 5 minutes, and that both pizza demand and supply are Poisson distributed, what do you think of Sal's policy? Support your answer as best you can.

9. Using the order sequence provided in Situation 4-2, how would the simulation of the Burger Queen restaurant's operations change if one meat pattie of each size were kept in steamer inventory? If two meat patties of each size were kept in steamer inventory? How must you monitor and replenish the steamer inventory to get the best results possible?

10. Suppose that in Situation 4-2 we cannot assume that sandwich assembly is simultaneous and that board capacity is always great enough not to cause delays. Suppose that there were only four workers assembling sandwiches. How would that affect transaction times in the simulation? Suppose that there were five workers. What would change?

11. The Burger King restaurant description in Tour B describes a shift in the way the company managed its queuing phenomenon. Describe this shift in the language introduced in this book. Why would the company favor such a switch?

12. Ticketrend was a national chain of ticket vendors for sporting events, concerts, exhibitions, and the like. Offices operated out of malls and department stores and sold tickets both to walk-in customers and to those who mailed or telephoned in orders. Management was interested in controlling the quantity of errors made in the ticketing process. A number of different errors were possible, including incorrect dates for the event, wrong class of ticket, incorrect number of tickets, sent to wrong address, bill incorrect, and so on. No one type of error was significantly more prevalent than the others. Management was intent on reducing all types to 1 percent or less of the volume.

    From 20 samples of 200 ticket orders each, taken at random, the following number of defects were determined:

SAMPLE	NUMBER OF DEFECTS	SAMPLE	NUMBER OF DEFECTS
1	6	11	2
2	2	12	0
3	4	13	4
4	1	14	7
5	11	15	5
6	3	16	12
7	7	17	3
8	9	18	8
9	13	19	2
10	8	20	5

    a. What type of control chart is appropriate for determining the process capability of the operation? Why?

    b. Construct a control chart using these data. What observations can you make about the process?

13. H. H. Kettle's Furniture and Appliance Store on the north side of Metropolis was interested in improving its ordering process. From time to time, customers complained about errors in their orders, particularly wrong pieces ordered. The store wanted to keep order errors to less than 2 percent of the total number of orders, and they assigned Janet Lynne to the project. Janet looked at a number of orders, in samples of 50, and classed each order as either "OK" or "Has a problem." The results of this inspection are as follows:

SAMPLE NUMBER	ORDERS OK	PROBLEM ORDERS
1	48	2
2	50	0
3	49	1
4	47	3
5	50	0
6	48	2
7	50	0

SAMPLE NUMBER	ORDERS OK	PROBLEM ORDERS
8	46	4
9	49	1
10	48	2
11	50	0
12	50	0
13	49	1
14	48	2
15	49	1

a. What type of control chart is appropriate for determining the process capability of the ordering operation? Why?

b. Construct a control chart using these data. What observations can you make about the process?

14. Calculate the forecast of sales (broken down by month) for year 3, given the following information on textbook sales:

YEAR 2	SALES/MONTH	PERCENT OF TOTAL
January	$ 71,025	7.3
February	63,429	6.5
March	82,630	8.5
April	51,345	5.3
May	74,350	7.7
June	82,964	8.6
July	94,899	9.8
August	108,465	11.2
September	97,048	10.0
October	63,748	6.6
November	83,971	8.7
December	95,437	9.8
	969,311	100.0

Calculate the forecast first using the following simple rule, which uses these three assumptions:

Year 3's total sales will grow at the same rate at which this year's sales grew.

The monthly breakdown of sales for year 3 will match this year's breakdown.

Year 2's sales were 17.3 percent greater than year 1's sales.

15. Using the same data, predict monthly sales for year 3 using the moving average technique.

16. Assume that you found a trend in the data. What would be your next step in dealing with the data?

17. Using several of the techniques of forecasting described in the text (moving average, exponential smoothing, decomposition) and the data in the table below, make a forecast for the next year. Do not hesitate to play with the data. How do these various techniques differ in the forecasts they make? What explains the differences?

ACTUAL AND FORECASTED MONTHLY SALES (IN MILLIONS OF DOLLARS) FOR A CERTAIN RETAIL PRODUCT (PROBLEM 17)

Month	Year 1		Year 2		Year 3		Year 4	
	Actual	Forecast	Actual	Forecast	Actual	Forecast	Actual	Forecast
January	$ 3,934	$ 3.9	$ 2,639	$ 3.4	$ 4,016	$ 3.1	$ 3,633	$ 3.4
February	3,162	3.3	2,899	2.9	3,957	3.2	4,292	3.6
March	4,286	3.9	3,370	3.2	4,510	3.7	4,154	3.8
April	4,676	4.5	3,740	4.0	4,276	4.3	4,121	4.4
May	5,010	5.3	2,927	3.1	4,986	4.5	4,647	4.8
June	4,874	5.1	3,986	3.9	4,677	5.0	4,753	5.0
July	4,633	4.6	4,217	4.3	3,523	4.4	3,965	4.5
August	1,659	1.8	1,738	1.6	1,821	1.7	1,723	1.8
September	5,951	6.0	5,221	5.3	5,222	5.7	5,048	5.8
October	6,981	6.8	6,424	6.6	6,832	6.9	6,922	6.9
November	9,851	10.0	9,842	10.0	10,803	10.2	9,858	10.1
December	12,670	13.1	13,076	12.9	13,916	13.4	11,331	13.0

18. How good were the forecasts in Problem 17? How would you measure the quality of those forecasts? Was one year's forecast better than the others?

19. The Digital Watch Company had demand for the year of 200,000 units. It found that its average order cost on its supplier was $30 per order and its carrying cost is $4.00 per unit per year. What is its economic order quantity?

20. Digital has found that it can order watchbands from an outside vendor on the following price schedule:

ORDER QUANTITY	PRICE
500 or less	$5.00
501 or more	$4.50

With demand information as in Problem 19 and average inventory carrying cost for a watchband of $0.75 per unit per year, what is Digital's economic order quantity?

21. The CutCorrect Company clerk manages a retail inventory of consumer goods that are ordered from a local wholesaler. The clerk has recently read about the EOQ and wonders if it would produce a different result than their current policies. An example product has virtually constant demand of 40 units per week. It costs $20 wholesale and order costs are estimated to be $10 per order. The accountant said that the cost of carrying inventory (including cost of capital tied up, storage, and an obsolescence charge) was 23 percent of item cost. Would the use of the EOQ be different from the current policy of ordering in lots of 100 units?

22. Joel Huber had recently joined the corporate staff of the fast-food division of Midwest Brands. The company operated about 300 restaurants in the Midwest. Rather than standardize these restaurants, management had allowed about 30 different sizes and layouts to develop over the years. Joel's immediate concern was with a restaurant where the local management wanted to add 40 seats without expanding the kitchen.

The dining area currently seated 112, and the restaurant was doing a booming business during lunch and dinner peak hours. Management at this division had been rather lax. Few systematic data were kept on the operation and use of the restaurants, and there were no guidelines on the steps to take in expanding a restaurant's seating capacity. It was Joel's job to study this request for expansion, using some systematic analysis. How should his decision be structured, and what data should he collect to analyze the problem properly?

23. A large domestic airline employs one reservation clerk in a local office during the day. The reservation clerk has suggested that another clerk be hired so that customers calling for reservations will not have to wait an inordinate amount of time. Management has decided that the average customer should not have to wait more than two minutes. In order to study the desirability of adding another reservation clerk, a study was done to determine the distribution of arrival times and service times. Calls arrived in a Poisson manner on average of 30 per hour. The time it took to make a reservation was exponentially distributed with a mean of 1.5 minutes. Given the company's policy of an average waiting time of less than two minutes, what should the manager of the local office do with regard to hiring an additional reservation clerk?

24. Two lawyers are in partnership. Each lawyer has a secretary. Jobs arrive for each secretary in a Poisson manner at a rate of three per hour, on the average. It takes each secretary an average of 15 minutes to accomplish each individual job. This service time is exponentially distributed.
    a. Assuming that each secretary does only the work of one lawyer, what is the expected waiting time for each job?
    b. What would be the effect of pooling the secretaries?

25. Emergency calls coming to a central ambulance dispatcher result in some unnecessary ambulance responses; in other words, sometimes ambulances are dispatched when not needed. It is the dispatcher's responsibility to ascertain the presence of a real need for the emergency care. Each day, 50 emergency dispatches are used to determine whether or not the dispatcher is doing an adequate job in screening emergency calls. Use the following data to construct a p chart for the process described above:

SAMPLE NUMBER	SAMPLE SIZE	NUMBER OF FALSE ALARMS
1	50	5
2	50	6
3	50	7
4	50	4
5	50	7
6	50	6
7	50	5
8	50	3
9	50	2
10	50	3

26. The Toll Road Authority wants to know how many toll booths to design into its Main Road exit. Naturally, an objective is to minimize cost, but there is also a stipulation

that the expected line length during peak hours should not exceed five cars. From data taken from other toll-road exits, it has been determined that interarrival times and service times are exponentially distributed. The peak arrival rate is expected to be ten cars per minute. The average service time is 15 seconds. How many toll booths should be designed into the system?

27. The owner of a large laundromat is considering the opening of a second store. The location she has in mind can accommodate 20 washers and 10 dryers. At peak times, she has found time between arrivals to be exponentially distributed with a mean of 10 minutes. The number of washers used by one customer is random and distributed according to the table below.

NUMBER OF WASHERS	RELATIVE FREQUENCY
1	.20
2	.35
3	.20
4	.15
5	.05
6	.03
7	.01
8	.01
	$\overline{1.00}$

Dryers can accommodate two loads of washing. Both washers and dryers take 30 minutes. The owner has found that in order for her to make a profit, the washers must be operated at 40 percent capacity during peak hours. Simulate manually for two hours. Should the new laundromat be installed at the proposed location? Assume that there are five customers waiting when the doors are opened for business.

28. In an attempt to control the process of a medical laboratory, the following sampling plan has been instituted for a particular urine test in which human life is not involved. The results of tests are classified as either positive or negative, and it is known that the national average of positive results is 10 percent. Five samples of 100 tests each yielded the following results:

SAMPLE NUMBER	SAMPLE SIZE	NUMBER DEFECTIVE
1	100	.11
2	100	.09
3	100	.12
4	100	.13
5	100	.07

Construct a *p*-chart and determine whether the urine test process is under control or not.

References

AAKER, DAVID A., "How Will the Japanese Compete in Retail Services," *California Management Review* 33, no. 1 (Fall 1990):54–67.

ALBRECHT, KARL, *At America's Service: How Corporations Can Revolutionize the Way They Treat Their Customers.* Homewood, IL: Dow Jones-Irwin, 1988.

ALBRECHT, KARL, and RON ZEMKE, *Service America! Doing Business in the New Economy.* Homewood, IL: Dow Jones-Irwin, 1985.

ASHTON, J. E., and F. X. COOK, JR., "Time to Reform Job Shop Manufacturing," *Harvard Business Review* 67, no. 2 (March–April 1989):106–11.

BANKS, ROBERT L., and STEVEN C. WHEELWRIGHT, "Operations vs. Strategy: Trading Tomorrow for Today," *Harvard Business Review* 57, no. 3 (May–June 1979):112–20.

BERRY, LEONARD L., VALERIE A. ZEITHAML, and A. PARASURAMAN, "Five Imperatives for Improving Service Quality," *Sloan Management Review* 31, no. 4 (Summer 1990):29–38.

BITRAN, GABRIEL R., and JOHANNES HOECH, "The Humanization of Service: Respect at the Moment of Truth," *Sloan Management Review* 31, no. 2 (Winter 1990):89–96.

BOWEN, DAVID E., RICHARD B. CHASE, and THOMAS G. CUMMINGS, AND ASSOCIATES, *Service Management Effectiveness: Balancing Strategy, Organization and Human Resources, Operations and Marketing,* San Francisco: Jossey-Bass Publishers, 1990.

BOWER, J. L., *Managing the Resource Allocation Process.* Homewood, IL: Richard D. Irwin, 1972.

BROWN, STEVEN W., EVERT GUMMESSON, BO EDVARDSSEON, and BENGTOVE GUSTAVSSON, EDS., *Service Quality: Multidisciplinary and Multinational Perspectives.* Lexington, MA: Lexington Books, 1991.

CHASE, RICHARD B., "The Customer Contact Approach to Services," *Operations Research* 29 (1981):698–706.

CHASE, RICHARD B., "Where Does the Customer Fit in a Service Operation?" *Harvard Business Review* 56, no. 6 (November–December 1978):13, 42.

COLLIER, DAVID A., *Service Management: Operating Decisions.* Englewood Cliffs, NJ: Prentice-Hall, 1987.

COLLIER, DAVID A., *Service Management: The Automation of Services.* Reston, VA: Reston, 1985.

CROSBY, PHILLIP B., *Quality is Free.* New York: McGraw-Hill, 1979.

CROSS, JAMES C. and BRUCE J. WALKER, "Service Marketing and Franchising: A Practical Business Marriage," *Business Horizons,* (November–December 1987): 50–58.

CZEPIEL, JOHN A., MICHAEL R. SOLOMON, and CAROL F. SURPRENANT, EDS., *The Service Encounter: Managing Employee/Customer Interaction in Service Businesses.* Lexington, MA: Lexington Books, 1985.

DAVIDOW, WILLIAM H., and BRO UTTAL, "Service Companies: Focus or Falter," *Harvard Business Review* 67, no. 4 (July–August 1989):77–85.

DIPRIMIO, ANTHONY, *Quality Assurance in Service Organizations.* Radnor, PA: Chilton Book Co., 1987.

ENDERWICK, PETER, "The International Competitiveness of Japanese Service Industries: A Cause for Concern?" *California Management Review* 32, no. 4 (Summer 1990):22–37.

FITZSIMMONS, JAMES A. and MONA J. FITZSIMMONS, *Service Management for Competitive Advantage.* New York: McGraw-Hill, 1994.

FITZSIMMONS, JAMES A. and ROBERT S. SULLIVAN, Service Operations Management. New York: McGraw-Hill, 1982.

GRONROOS, CHRISTIAN, "New Competition in the Service Economy: The Five Rules of Service," *International Journal of Operations & Production Management (UK)* 8, no. 3 (1899):9–19.

GRONROOS, CHRISTIAN, *Service Management and Marketing: Managing the Moments of Truth in Service Competition,* Lexington, MA: Lexington Books, 1990.

GUILE, BRUCE R., and JAMES BRIAN QUINN, EDS., *Technology in Services: Policies for Growth, Trade, and Employment,* Washington, DC: National Academy Press, 1988.

HACKETT, GREGORY P., "Investment in Technology: The Service Sector Sinkhole?" *Sloan Management Review* 31, no. 2 (Winter 1990):97–103.

HART, CHRISTOPHER W. L., "The Power of Unconditional Service Guarantees," *Harvard Business Review,* (July-August 1988):54–62.

HART, CHRISTOPHER W. L., JAMES L. HESKETT, and W. EARL SASSER, JR., "Surviving a Customer's Rage," *Successful Meetings* 40, no. 5 (April 1991):68–79.

HART, CHRISTOPHER W. L., JAMES L. HESKETT, and W. EARL SASSER, JR., "The Profitable Art of Service Recovery," *Harvard Business Review* 68, no. 4 (July–August 1990):148–156.

HAYES, ROBERT H., and WILLIAM J. ABERNATHY, "Managing our Way to Economic Decline," *Harvard Business Review* 58, no. 4 (July–August 1980):67–77.

HAYWOOD-FARMER, JOHN, "A Conceptual Model of Service Quality," *International Journal of Operations & Production Management (UK)* 8, no. 4 (1988):19–29.

HERRON, D. P., "Managing Physical Distribution for Profit," *Harvard Business Review* 57, no. 3 (May–June 1979):121–32.

HESKETT, JAMES L., "Lessons in the Service Sector," *Harvard Business Review* 65, no. 2 (March–April 1987):118–126.

HESKETT, JAMES L., *Managing in the Service Economy.* Boston, MA: Harvard Business School Press, 1986.

HESKETT, JAMES L., W. EARL SASSER, JR., and CHRISTOPHER W. L. HART, *Service Breakthroughs.* New York: The Free Press, 1990.

HOROVITZ, JACQUES, *Winning Ways: Achieving Zero-Defect Service.* Cambridge, MA: Productivity Press, 1990.

JAPAN HUMAN RELATIONS ASSOCIATION, ED., *The Service Industry Idea Book: Employee Involvement in Retail and Office Improvement.* Cambridge, MA: Productivity Press, 1990.

JURAN, JOSEPH M., and FRANK M. GRYNA, JR., *Quality Planning and Analysis,* 2nd ed. New York: McGraw-Hill, 1980.

JURAN, JOSEPH M., ED., *Quality Control Handbook,* 4th ed. New York: McGraw-Hill, 1988.

KANTER, JERRY, STEVEN SCHIFFMAN, and J. FAYE HORN, "Let the Customer Do It," *Computerworld* 24, no. 35 (August 27, 1990):75–78.

KANTER, ROSABETH M., "Service Quality: You Get What You Pay For," *Harvard Business Review* 69, no. 5 (September–October 1991):8–9.

LEVITT, THEODORE, "The Industrialization of Service," *Harvard Business Review* 48, no. 5 (September–October 1970):63–74.

LEWIS, BARBARA R., "Customer Care in Service Organisations," *International Journal of Operations & Production Management (UK)* 8, no. 3 (1988):67–75.

LOVELOCK, CHRISTOPHER, *Managing Services: Marketing, Operations and Human Resources.* Englewood Cliffs, NJ: Prentice-Hall, 1988 and 1992.

LOVELOCK, CHRISTOPHER, and ROBERT YOUNG, "Look to Consumers to Increase Production," *Harvard Business Review* 57, no. 3 (May–June 1979):168–79.

MAISTER, DAVID H., "Balancing the Professional Service Firm," *Sloan Management Review* (Fall 1982):15–29.

MAISTER, DAVID H., and CHRISTOPHER LOVELOCK, "Managing Facilitator Services," *Sloan Management Review* (Summer 1982):19–31.

MAISTER, DAVID H., "The Psychology of Waiting Lines," in John A. Czepiel, Michael R. Solomon, and Carol F. Surprenant, *The Service Encounter.* Lexington, MA: D.C. Heath and Company, 1985.

MAISTER, DAVID H., "The One-Firm Firm: What Makes It Successful," *Sloan Management Review* (Fall 1985):3–13.

MCLAUGHLIN, CURTIS P., RONALD T. PANNESI, and NARINDAR KATHURIA, "The Different Operations Strategy Planning Process for Service Operations," *International Journal of Operations & Production Management* 11, no. 3 (1991):63–76.

MERSHA, TIGINEH, "Enhancing the Customer Contact Model," *Journal of Operations Management* 9, no. 3 (August 1990):391–405.

MILLS, PETER K., *Managing Service Industries: Organizational Practices in a Post-Industrial Economy.* Cambridge, MA: Ballinger, 1986.

MURDICK, ROBERT G., BARRY RENDER, and ROBERTA RUSSELL, *Service Operations Management.* Boston: Allyn and Bacon, 1990.

PARASURAMAN, A., LEONARD L. BERRY, and VALARIE A. ZEITHAML, "Understanding Customer Expectations of Service," *Sloan Management Review* 32, no. 3 (Spring 1991):39–48.

QUINN, JAMES BRIAN, JORDAN J. BARUCH, and PENNY C. PAQUETTE, "Exploiting the Manufacturing–Services Interface," *Sloan Management Review* 29, no. 4 (Summer 1988):45–56.

QUINN, JAMES BRIAN, THOMAS L. DOORLEY, and PENNY C. PAQUETTE, "Beyond Products: Services-Based Strategy," *Harvard Business Review* 68, no. 2 (March–April 1990):58–68.

QUINN, JAMES BRIAN, THOMAS L. DOORLEY, and PENNY C. PAQUETTE, "Technology in Services: Rethinking Strategic Focus," *Sloan Management Review* 31, no. 2 (Winter 1990):79–88.

QUINN, JAMES BRIAN, AND CHRISTOPHER E. GAGNON, "Will Services Follow Manufacturing into Decline?" *Harvard Business Review* 64, no. 6 (November–December 1986):95–103.

QUINN, JAMES BRIAN, AND PENNY C. PAQUETTE, "Technology in Services: Creating Organizational Revolutions," *Sloan Management Review* 31, no. 2 (Winter 1990):67–78.

ROACH, STEPHEN S., "Services Under Siege—The Restructuring Imperative," *Harvard Business Review* 69, no. 5 (September–October 1991):82–91.

SASSER, W. E., "Match Supply and Demand in Service Industries," *Harvard Business Review* (November–December 1976):133–140.

SASSER, W. EARL, R. PAUL OLSEN, and D. DARYL WYCKOFF, *Management of Service Operations.* Boston: Allyn and Bacon, 1978.

SCHLESINGER, LEONARD A., and JAMES L. HESKETT, "Breaking the Cycle of Failure in Services," *Sloan Management Review* 32, no. 3 (Spring 1991):17–28.

SCHLESINGER, LEONARD A., and JAMES L. HESKETT, "The Service-Driven Service Company," *Harvard Business Review* 69, no. 5 (September–October 1991):71–81.

SCHMENNER, R. W., "Before You Build a Big Factory," *Harvard Business Review* 54, no. 4 (July–August 1976):100–104.

SCHMENNER, ROGER W., "How Can Service Businesses Survive and Prosper," *Sloan Management Review* (Spring 1986):21–32.

SCHMENNER, R. W., *Making Business Location Decisions.* Englewood Cliffs, NJ: Prentice-Hall, 1982.

SHAW, JOHN C., *The Service Focus: Developing Winning Game Plans for Service Companies.* Homewood, IL: Dow Jones-Irwin, 1990.

SHERMAN, H. DAVID, "Improving the Productivity of Service Businesses," *Sloan Management Review* 25, no. 3 (Spring 1984):11–23.

SHERMAN, H. DAVID, *Service Organization Productivity Management.* Hamilton, Ont.: Society of Management Accountants of Canada (SCMS), 1988.

SHIFFLER, RONALD E., and RAY W. COYE, "Monitoring Employee Performance in Service Operations," *International Journal of Operations & Production Management (UK)* 8, no. 2 (1988):5–13.

SHOSTACK, G. LYNN, "Designing Services That Deliver," *Harvard Business Review* 62, no. 1 (January–February 1984):133–39.

SPIRER, HERBERT F., "The Basic Principles of Project Management," *Operations Management Review* 1, no. 1 (Fall 1982):7–8ff.

TEAL, THOMAS, "Service Comes First: An Interview with USAA's Robert F. McDermott," *Harvard Business Review* 69, no. 5 (September–October 1991):116–127.

THOMAS, DAN, "Strategy Is Different in Service Businesses," *Harvard Business Review* 56, no. 4 (July–August 1978):158–65.

VOSS, C., C. ARMISTEAD, B. JOHNSTON, and B. MORRIS, *Operations Management in Service Industries and the Public Sector.* London: Wiley & Sons, 1985.

ZEITHAML, VALARIE A., A. PARASURAMAN, and LEONARD L. BERRY, *Delivering Quality Services, Balancing Customer Perceptions and Expectations.* New York: Free Press, 1990.

Index